THE WORLD OF WAREHOUSING

previously published as

Warehouse Management and Inventory Control

3rd edition

P.M. Price, Ph.D.

N.J. Harrison, M.Ed.

Printed in the United States of America
First Printing: April 2023
Paperback
Third edition

ISBN 978-1-934231-11-1

Table of Contents

Chapter 1

Warehouses and the Supply Chain

Before reading this book, you are already a warehouse expert. You manage a warehouse and visit it at least once every day. Its exterior may be white, black, stainless steel, or even a lovely retro shade of mint green. You store goods in a temperature-controlled setting in this warehouse and later distribute them to their end consumers.

Have you guessed what this warehouse is that you so skillfully manage every day? I'll give you a final clue: It's actually located in your home and unless you're a millionaire, a celebrity, or a top chef, it typically takes up no larger than a 3' by 3' by 6' space in your kitchen. Have you guessed it yet? This warehouse is your refrigerator!

In your refrigerator, you may have a gallon of milk, a box of strawberries, two dozen eggs, five bags of frozen vegetables, and many other perishable goods that it would take more than a day to consume. Without a refrigerator, you would have to purchase perishable foods in small quantities on a daily basis unless you wanted to keep your home cooled to a chilly 32° to 50°F, which even those of us above the 60 degree latitude line might find uncomfortable. Having a refrigerator allows you to buy milk, cheese, meat, and vegetables in large quantities because you can store them for future use without the fear of next-day spoilage. Your refrigerator also allows you to buy these items in bulk, such as buying 18 eggs instead of the six you will need for your weekend breakfast plans. Because you can buy in bulk, you get better shopping discounts, have plenty of extra food on hand in case unexpected guests arrive, and save time by not going to the grocery store every day. Imagine settling down to watch the Super Bowl, the World Cup, or the Westminster Dog Show and having to go to the local grocery store each time you want a cold can of your favorite beverage!

Our personal, temperature-controlled, kitchen warehouses, otherwise known as refrigerators, operate on the same principles as large, commercial warehouses. We purchase goods in greater quantities than we immediately need, we inspect them, we store them, we issue them when we are going to use them, and, every so often, we have a look to see if we need to replace our old or used inventory. Just like a refrigerator, a warehouse plays a major role in receiving, inspecting, storing, and issuing inventory.

In this chapter, we introduce the concept of a *warehouse*: what warehouses are and why we need them; the functions of a warehouse; the role a warehouse can play in the internal logistics and external supply chain management of a company; and how logistics and supply chain management are related to warehouse management. Throughout this chapter and later chapters, we will also explore the world of warehousing and inventory in a variety of settings, including the manufacturing, retail, and service settings. Whether it's a warehouse, a distribution center, fulfillment center, or a retail store, the principles of warehouse management and inventory control are the same!

1.1 WHAT IS A WAREHOUSE?

We already mentioned that a warehouse plays a major role in receiving, inspecting, storing, and issuing inventory. In non-logistics vernacular, this means that a warehouse takes in, holds, and gives out stuff. And when we take a look at the stuff around us, it likely passed through multiple warehouses across multiple states or countries on its way to us.

Most goods, which make up almost all this stuff around us, have either *producers* or *manufacturers*. **Producers** are those companies who gather and supply natural products at their most basic form, such as fruits and vegetables or metal and timber. Similar to producers are **manufacturers**, who build, mix, or assemble products, such as cars, computers, and loaves of bread. Both producers and manufacturers need to store and issue the products they produce and manufacture, which means they need warehouses.

Many goods also pass through the hands of suppliers and retailers. **Suppliers**, also known as **vendors**, are companies that provide things that other companies need. For example, a computer manufacturer might make the most highly complex and intricately detailed computers, but it's not likely to also manufacture the cardboard and styrofoam packaging their computers are sold in. The computer manufacturer needs a packaging supplier. Similarly, the computer manufacturer might be so busy building millions of computers that it doesn't have the time or expertise to sell them. Instead, it uses **retailers**, which are businesses that sell goods to consumers, such as end users like you and me. The retailers that sell computers could include electronics stores, big box discount stores, and online sellers. Both suppliers and retailers need to be able to receive, store, and issue out goods, which means they need warehouses, too!

For a more formal definition, a **warehouse** is a facility or an area within a facility in which an organization receives, inspects, stores, picks, packs, and issues any of a variety of materials needed for the organization's operations or its customers' orders. Warehouses range in size and structure, from the back storeroom of your favorite local restaurant to the mammoth complex of warehouses of amazon.com. A warehouse may be an enormous building the size of twenty football fields or just a back corner of a neighborhood shop. We'll learn about the many different kinds of warehouses in Chapter 2.

But what is stored in these facilities called *warehouses*? Just about anything and everything! Getting a little bit more technical, however, when we talk about the contents of a warehouse, we typically mean its **inventory**. *Inventory* is the composition of raw, in-process, finished materials, and other inputs needed for the creation of a company's goods or services. Basically, all the stuff in a warehouse, except for the equipment used to store or move goods, is its inventory! For example, the following list includes typical inventory items found in the warehouse of a medium-sized manufacturing operation: *raw materials*; *component parts*; *packaging*; *spare parts*; *tools and equipment*; *work in progress*; *finished inventory*; and *maintenance materials*. We'll explore more about these types of inventory in Chapter 3.

The range, value, and complexity of items held by any particular warehouse will depend upon the size and complexity of the operations involved. For example, picture the difference between the inventory of a lumberyard and the inventory of a luxury automobile manufacturer's warehouse. Because warehouses and their corresponding operations and inventory can vary greatly, warehouse managers and staff need to have an extensive knowledge of a large number of material types and operations. Throughout later chapters in this book, we will examine examples of different types of inventory in the warehouses of manufacturing, retail, and service operations.

POP QUIZ!

WHICH OF THE FOLLOWING LOCATIONS ARE WAREHOUSES?

RETAILER'S REGIONAL DISTRIBUTION CENTER

FISH PROCESSOR'S STOREROOM

CRUISE SHIP'S COLD STORAGE

YOU GOT IT! THEY'RE ALL WAREHOUSES.

THE LESSONS TO BE LEARNED FROM THIS BOOK CAN APPLY TO ALL OF THESE SETTINGS.

1.2 A FIRST LOOK AT WAREHOUSING

We mentioned earlier that most goods we encounter likely passed through multiple warehouses on their way to us. But why do companies go to all the time and expense of building and using warehouses? To keep the customers happy! As customers, when we want something, we want it immediately in the exact color, size, and quantity we desire. When we can't find what we need from one store or supplier, we immediately move on to other stores and suppliers. Companies need us (the customers) to survive and don't want to lose our business, so they want to make sure they have enough goods on hand to meet our desires, or enough *supply* to meet our *demand*. Terms common in the field of economics, **supply** is how much of an item a company has available or wants to sell and **demand** is how much consumers desire this item and want to buy it. Companies try to keep a balance between supply and demand, but sometimes one can exceed the other. For example, supply can exceed demand when a company has too much of a product, such as holiday-specific candy the day after the holiday, which can cause store to offer deep discounts on Halloween candy corn, Hanukkah chocolate coins, or Easter marshmallow peeps. Demand can also exceed supply, such as when an early snow falls and all the snow shovels and ice scrapers seem to sell out at all the local home improvement and hardware stores. To ensure that supply can meet demand, companies have to be able to store and quickly access goods that customers will want when they are desired.

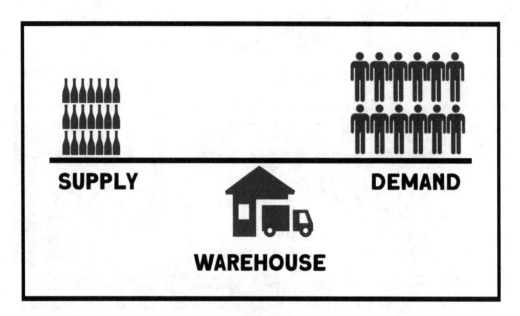

FIGURE 1.1 - WAREHOUSES HELP COMPANIES KEEP THE BALANCE BETWEEN SUPPLY AND DEMAND

Warehouses fill the need of keeping enough goods nearby so that they can be accessed easily when customers need them. In fact, warehouses are so important that warehousing has become a core business function for most organizations. This act of storing goods in any facility or areas of a facility, regardless of size, is called ***warehousing***.

As a business function within a company, *warehousing* involves eight key activities, which we will cover in greater detail throughout later chapters of this book:

1. Goods are received from suppliers and inspected;

2. Goods are put away so they can be found when needed;

3. Goods are maintained and kept safe;

4. Goods are picked from their place in storage when needed;

5. Goods are consolidated and packed for outbound distribution to leave the warehouse for their next destination in the supply chain;

6. Shipments are scheduled and goods are shipped to customers;

7. Inventory is controlled as it moves inbound, internally, outbound, and in transit; and

8. Records are kept and the flow and inventory of goods within the company is documented.

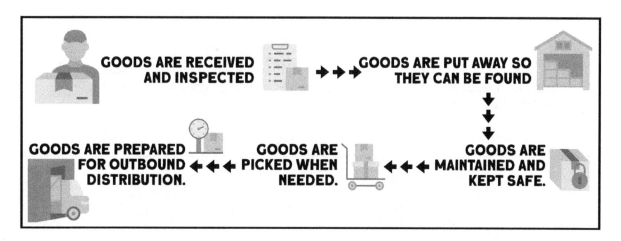

FIGURE 1.2 - FIVE OF THE EIGHT KEY ACTIVITIES IN WAREHOUSING

These eight warehousing activities do not happen seamlessly or in isolation. Companies must manage these activities surrounding the flow of goods through their warehouses. **Warehouse management** is the planning, directing, and controlling of warehouse activities to achieve *efficiency* (don't let it cost too much) and *effectiveness* (get the goods where they need to be and don't let them get damaged). Figure 1.2 shows five of the eight key activities of warehousing in which goods are handled and *directed* by managers within the warehouse under this umbrella of *warehouse management*. The *planning* and *controlling* of warehouse management occurs in activities 6, 7, and 8 from our list above, in which shipments are planned, the inventory flow is controlled, and records are maintained for both daily control and future planning.

These eight activities of warehousing may look somewhat different for different companies or industries, but the principles remain the same. For example, within a warehouse for a manufacturing or production company, a few additional activities occur surrounding the production of new finished goods. For the first five key activities of warehousing listed above, below is a modified version for the flow of goods for a manufacturing or production company. Note that this list expands from five to seven activities.

1. Raw materials and semifinished goods are received from suppliers and inspected;

2. Raw materials and semifinished goods are put away so they can be found when needed by manufacturing;

3. Raw materials and semifinished goods are maintained and kept safe;

4. Raw materials and semifinished goods are picked from their place in storage when needed by manufacturing;

5. Newly finished goods come in from manufacturing, typically into a different warehouse or section of the warehouse, and are inspected;

6. Finished goods are picked according to customer orders and corporate distribution plans;

7. Finished goods are prepared for outbound distribution to leave the warehouse for their next destination in the supply chain, such as to a customer or a regional distribution center.

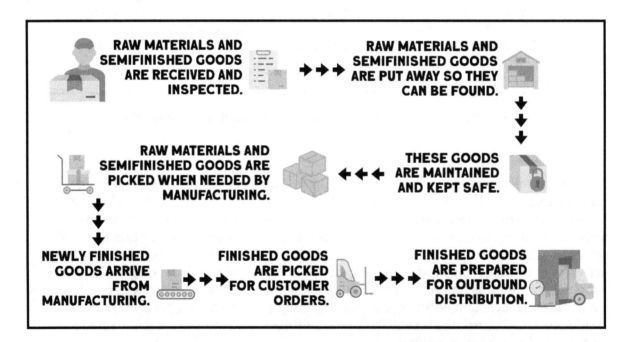

FIGURE 1.3 - ACTIVITIES WITHIN A MANUFACTURER'S WAREHOUSE

Warehouses and warehouse management have become increasingly important as customer demand has increased in complexity. In the past few years, consumers have become accustomed to instant gratification. This expectation makes customer demand a complex problem to tackle because demand does not always remain *static*, which means lacking movement or change, with the same customers wanting the same quantity of goods at the same locations all the time. Instead, customer demand is often an uncertain and **dynamic demand**, constantly changing based on any number of reasons from weather patterns to customer whims and fashion trends. Warehouse management must ensure that goods are held in places that can be readily accessed to fulfill this dynamic demand while balancing demand with the cost implication of storing too many goods or having too few.

Depending upon the size and structure of a company, its warehousing function may be housed in one department, such as the *Warehousing Department* or the *Logistics Department*, or it may be spread across many departments with names like the *Receiving Department*, the *Packaging Department*, and the *Inventory Control Department*. In addition, although the physical receipt, inspection, storage, and issuing of goods have historically been linked with the term *warehousing*, they are now increasingly becoming linked under the broader heading of *logistics*, which we will define later in this chapter.

Now that we have a basic understanding of warehouses and warehouse management, let's take a brief look at the role of a warehouse and what a warehouse does for an organization. In later chapters of this text, we will explore these functions in greater depth and examine how they relate to different kinds of warehouses and companies. Although warehouses have many functions, twelve of them are:

1. **CUSTOMER SERVICE.** First and foremost, the primary reason to have a warehouse is all about customer service and making sure that an organization has the the right quantity and quality of goods a customer wants when and where the customer needs them.

2. **ECONOMY.** A warehouse manager must ensure that all operations within the warehouse are performed as effectively and economically as possible. Warehouses can be quite expensive to operate, so an important function is maintaining inventory levels that minimize or optimize overall costs of operations.

3. **INVENTORY RECEIPT.** Warehouse managers and staff must receive and handle all of the items delivered to the warehouse. They must check all incoming inventory documentation, from electronic delivery notes and to printed packing notes, and inform those in the purchasing department about all goods received.

4. **INSPECTION.** Warehouse managers must work with the Quality Control Department to inspect and check all deliveries made to the warehouse. The factors checked include correct quantity, requested quality, and possible damage. In many cases, suppliers will not accept responsibility for damaged or missing quantities of goods unless they are reported within a specified number of days of delivery. Therefore, it is critical that warehouse managers conduct inspections and report their results to the purchasing department within required timeframes.

5. **INVENTORY STORAGE.** Another core function within a warehouse is that managers and their staff must unload, unpack, and store all of the goods received. This storage process also entails establishing the correct storage conditions of goods in connection with suppliers' instructions. Sometimes unique storage conditions are required, such

as when goods must be kept frozen, refrigerated, dry, or warm. It is the warehouse manager's responsibility to ensure that goods do not suffer damage or deterioration as a result of improper storage conditions.

6. **INVENTORY IDENTIFICATION AND LOCATION.** Warehouse managers must also formulate and update a system of warehouse coding so that goods stored within a warehouse may be put away and located quickly and efficiently. Furthermore, a good warehouse manager ensures that, when an item is not available, suitable replacements to be recommended can easily be found within the warehouse coding system.

7. **SAFETY AND SECURITY.** Another important function of a warehouse is to ensure that security is maintained at all times within all warehouse buildings and external inventory yards, which involves protection from theft, damage, fire, and spillage. It also includes ensuring that all doors, windows, and external fences are secure.

8. **PHYSICAL INVENTORY CONTROL AND CHECKING.** In this warehouse function, a warehouse manager is responsible for organizing, supervising, and collating all physical inventory checks carried out by an organization. These checks may be made on a continuous schedule or at set periods of time, such as the end of the fiscal year.

9. **INVENTORY RECORDS.** An important behind-the-scenes function of a warehouse is ensuring that adequate and up-to-date inventory records are maintained for every item held in inventory, whether on-site or in an external contract warehouse. These records provide information required to control and maintain the inventory levels the organization has established, such as recording inventory levels, order levels, code numbers, and suppliers' reference information.

10. **PICKING, PACKING, ISSUE, AND DISPATCH.** It is also the duty of warehouse management and staff to ensure that the goods and services required for an organization's operation are *picked*, or selected from the storage area, and *issued*, or given to the requestor, as required and when required, while maintaining authorization procedures and strict control of all inventory issues. Before issued, most items will need to be packaged for subsequent dispatch and transportation. Inferior packaging could lead to costly physical materials and customer loyalty losses.

11. **PRODUCT FLOW.** The issuance and dispatch of goods must have a smooth flow and be as efficient as possible because it is often the efficiency and effectiveness of inventory issuance that determines the image and status of the warehouse function throughout the entire organization. In the case of manufacturing, goods must get to the factory exactly when needed so that manufacturing processes can continue without having to stop and wait for inventory. In the case of retail operations, goods must get from the warehouse to the shopping store floor exactly when needed by the customer. Imagine a delay that causes a warehouse not to send out St. Patrick's Day decorations to a local retail chain until March 18th!

12. **MATERIALS HANDLING.** Finally, perhaps the most fundamental function of a warehouse is the quick and safe handling of all materials. This core task of moving goods to, within, from, and between factories and warehouses can be achieved manually, mechanically, or with automated equipment.

In later chapters, we will look at all of these functions in greater depth. We will also explore practical implications for warehouse managers and examine current examples of best, and sometimes worst, practices from a variety of industries.

1.3 WAREHOUSING AND OTHER DEPARTMENTS

So far, we have focused on the importance of **external customers**, those from outside of the company, and how warehousing benefits them from having the right quantity of goods where and when they want them. Warehousing and its many functions also provide vital services to an organization's **internal customers**, those inside the company or organization receiving goods or services. For example, how efficiently and effectively a warehouse is run impacts the overall efficiency and effectiveness of the entire company. This makes the relationships between a warehouse and the other major functions or departments of a company very important. No warehouse is an island. It needs participation and information from other major departments to ensure that a company's warehousing practices are efficient, and effective and that they meet corporate needs and goals.

Below are brief descriptions of the relationship between the warehousing department and other departments and functions within a company.

Warehousing and Manufacturing. In a manufacturing organization, the manufacturing function is one of the most important users of a warehouse. Warehouse managers must ensure that all materials needed for continued manufacturing operations are available in the right quantity, with the right quality, at the right time, and at the right place. If any of these rights become a wrong, the manufacturing function may have to cease production, which may result in extra cost, angry customers, an irate manufacturing department and company president, and a very embarrassed and berated warehouse manager. Therefore, it is critical that warehouse and manufacturing managers work together to keep open lines of communication about each function's needs and timeframes.

Warehousing and Physical Distribution. Physical distribution involves the movement of finished goods from manufacturing plants to warehouses and then on to external customers. The physical distribution function must get finished goods to depots, regional distribution centers, fulfillment centers, and other warehouses throughout the organization's national and international distribution network. The warehousing function must ensure that adequate inventory is available for picking, packaging, and loading onto the mode of transport chosen by the physical distribution function. Open and continuous communication is also important in this relationship. For example, physical distribution managers must supply warehouse managers with up-to-date information about the needs and wants of the distribution system, making every effort to give adequate notice of loading quantities, destinations, types, and marshaling points to ensure efficient service from the warehouse system.

Warehousing and Maintenance. An organization's maintenance function is responsible for ensuring that the manufacturing plant, its machinery, and other machinery used by the organization are kept in working order and performing to designed efficiency standards. The warehousing function plays a critical supporting role, ensuring that all required maintenance spare parts, tools, and equipment are held in inventory or are easily available from a supplier's inventory. For example, a warehouse must hold emergency spare parts in case of unscheduled machine breakdowns. Again, open communication is critical because the maintenance department will often work to a set schedule of engineering maintenance activities covering two or three months. The warehouse manager then plans according to this maintenance schedule, making sure that specialized maintenance materials are available in advance to avoid the dreaded scenario of disassembled machines sitting out of commission for weeks while awaiting spare parts.

Warehousing and Quality Control and Inspection. Organizations set standards for the materials they use and produce. The quality control function or department inspects goods and ensures that these standards are followed. Warehousing plays a role by holding all delivered goods aside until they are checked by Quality Control and making sure that the items labeled for rejection are not allowed to become part of the organization's working inventory. When rejected items are used, costly problems may arise, damaging an organization's budget and reputation.

Warehousing and Purchasing. Historically, the link between warehousing and purchasing has been very close. In many organizations, these two functions are united under the heading of *integrated materials management*. Where two separate operations do exist, a smooth relationship between them is vital. As a separate function, purchasing is responsible for buying all of the goods and services needed by the organization.

The purchasing function relies on the warehousing function for a wide variety of support activities. For example, purchasing managers depend on warehouse managers to keep them constantly informed about physical inventory levels and conditions. When inventory loss, damage, or deterioration occurs, warehouse managers inform purchasing managers so that problem inventory may be replaced immediately, ensuring a balanced and economic flow of goods and services to the end users. Today, much of this is done through automated warehouse management and inventory control systems.

The purchasing function in many organizations is physically separated from the warehouse area or manufacturing floor, often located in different buildings, states, or even countries. Therefore, the purchasing function relies on warehousing to provide real time, up-to-date, accurate information about the performance of goods and services it is providing, based on manufacturing and user feedback. Such inventory performance information can be critical in ensuring maximum efficiency of the purchasing operation and its evaluation of the materials purchased.

Because they typically receive goods directly from suppliers, those in the warehousing function must resist the temptation to become directly involved with suppliers unless they are directed to do so by those in the purchasing function. Such a situation can cause problems when warehouse management makes decisions about delivery, quality, progress, and goods selection without the full background information that purchasing managers will have. Organizations that employ an integrated logistics management approach tend to suffer less from this type of problem, but more on this in later chapters.

Warehousing and Marketing. The marketing department relies on the warehousing department to ensure that finished inventory is available to be sold to customers when required, which is especially important for sales promotions and other marketing events. Warehousing is sometimes also responsible for the control of spare parts and accessories used in connection with an organization's finished products, which are supplied to users by an after-sales service function. Finally, warehouse managers must be aware of future sales forecasts in order to plan for possible increases or decreases of inventory and corresponding warehouse space and staff.

Warehousing and Accounting and Finance. Accounting and finance functions rely on the warehousing department for information about the quantities of inventory held and items damaged that need to be written off the organization's assets list. The accounting function also asks warehousing to confirm the receipt of goods as invoiced, especially in the case of doubt or query. The warehousing function also provides a continuous supply of data on inventory use in operations, which is especially useful for accounting in cost allocation to particular batches or jobs as carried out by operations. In addition, warehousing supplies information on physical stocktaking which helps accounting and finance prepare annual financial statements for an organization.

1.4 WAREHOUSING AND THE SUPPLY CHAIN

Warehouse management resides within the realm of *logistics* at the individual company level and within the realm of *supply chain management* at the cross-company strategic level. But what on earth do we mean by logistics and supply chain management?

Logistics is the name of the business discipline and the function within an organization that handles the flow of goods and information into, within, and out from that organization. Similar yet distinctly different, ***supply chain management*** is the business discipline and function within an organization that focuses on the flow of goods, information, and related finance across multiple organizations, often as goods move and transform from a raw materials or unfinished stage to a finished product received by an end user. Although these terms technically have different meanings, they are often used interchangeably by organizations in the real world to signify anything at all that has to do with the movement of goods. As goods and their supporting information and documentation all flow into and depart from an organization, they follow a path known as a ***supply chain***. If the perspective of the supply chain is from the internal workings of one organization, the supply chain has a *logistics focus*. If its perspective is broader and spread across multiple organizations, the supply chain has a *supply chain management focus*.

FIGURE 1.4 - A SIMPLE SUPPLY CHAIN

Figure 1.4 shows a simple supply chain, in which a supplier provides goods to a manufacturer, who in turn supplies manufactured finished goods to a retailer, who, at the end of it all, provides these finished goods to customers or end users. For example, a local apple orchard may have a glass container supplier for the cider and apple butter that it produces. When the orchard orders and receives the glass containers from its suppliers, it stores them in its warehouse until they are needed when cider and apple butter are produced in their manufacturing facility. Finished containers of cider and apple butter are then stored in the orchard's finished goods warehouse until they are delivered to a regional distribution center and then to local grocery stores and other retail locations across the state, where they are sold to end users like you and me.

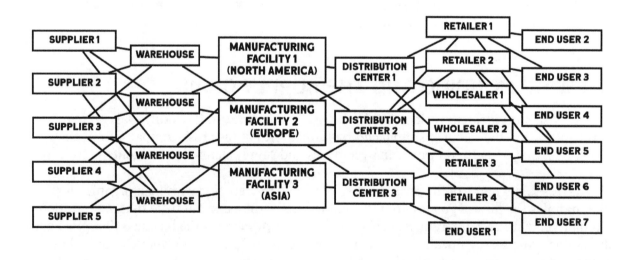

FIGURE 1.5 - A COMPLEX SUPPLY CHAIN

Most supply chains today are not that simple. Actual supply chains may look less like the simple supply chain of Figure 1.4 and more like the complex supply chain in Figure 1.5, which spans many organizations in multiple locations around the world. For example, unlike the local apple orchard's simple supply chain, a popular breakfast cereal manufacturer might have many suppliers, manufacturing facilities, and retail sellers across the world, resulting in a complex global supply chain. For example, the cereal manufacturer may have separate suppliers for wheat, oats, vegetable oil, milk, preservatives, and cardboard packaging, with items going to the warehouses of the cereal company's different manufacturing facilities across the country and across the world. After the cereal is manufactured at each of the company's multiple manufacturing facilities, it is shipped to different regional distribution centers and then on to the multiple grocery stores within their region. As we will see later in this chapter, all of the locations indicated in the boxes in Figure 1.5 may have their own warehouses associated with them, even if the box is not labelled *warehouse*. For example, Retailer 4 might be a specific grocery store in Akron, Ohio. This grocery store is likely to have a small warehouse area in the back of the store to receive the cereal when it comes in and hold the extra boxes that don't currently fit on the grocery store shelves.

Warehouse management plays a significantly strategic role in the realm of logistics and supply chain management. In Price and Harrison's model of logistics management from *Looking at Logistics, 3rd Edition*, as shown in Figure 1.6, warehouse management plays a key role in inbound processes, internal processes, and outbound processes in logistics

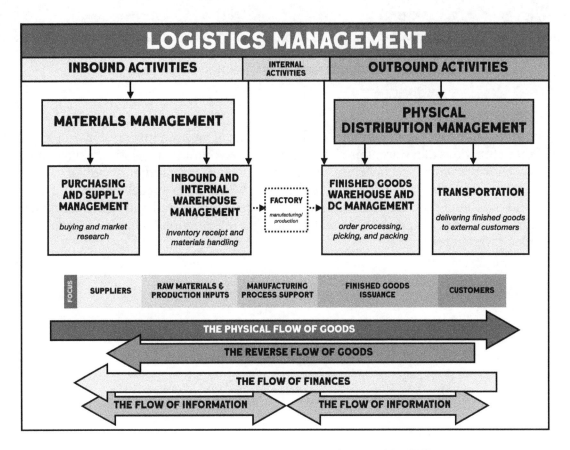

FIGURE 1.6 - MODEL OF LOGISTICS MANAGEMENT

management. Internal warehouse management is a part of *materials management* and spans across logistics management processes that are both ***inbound***, or into the company, and ***internal***, or within the company. Warehouse management is also the critical component of the ***outbound***, or out from the company, process of *external distribution* from warehouses, distribution centers, and fulfillment centers. No matter where you look within the world of logistics management, you are likely to find a warehouse!

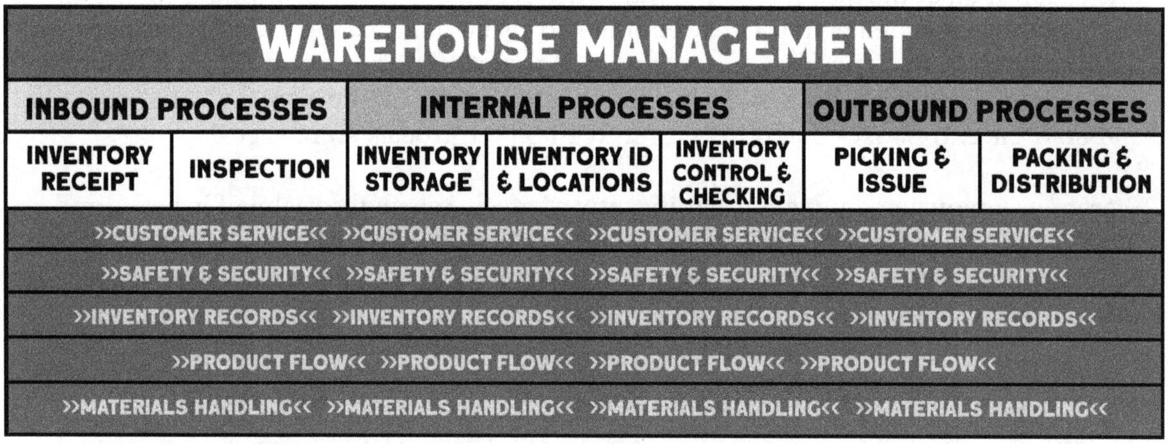

WAREHOUSE MANAGEMENT						
INBOUND PROCESSES		INTERNAL PROCESSES			OUTBOUND PROCESSES	
INVENTORY RECEIPT	INSPECTION	INVENTORY STORAGE	INVENTORY ID & LOCATIONS	INVENTORY CONTROL & CHECKING	PICKING & ISSUE	PACKING & DISTRIBUTION
>>CUSTOMER SERVICE<<		>>CUSTOMER SERVICE<<		>>CUSTOMER SERVICE<<		>>CUSTOMER SERVICE<<
>>SAFETY & SECURITY<<		>>SAFETY & SECURITY<<		>>SAFETY & SECURITY<<		>>SAFETY & SECURITY<<
>>INVENTORY RECORDS<<		>>INVENTORY RECORDS<<		>>INVENTORY RECORDS<<		>>INVENTORY RECORDS<<
>>PRODUCT FLOW<<		>>PRODUCT FLOW<<		>>PRODUCT FLOW<<		>>PRODUCT FLOW<<
>>MATERIALS HANDLING<<		>>MATERIALS HANDLING<<		>>MATERIALS HANDLING<<		>>MATERIALS HANDLING<<

FIGURE 1.7 - THE FUNCTIONS OF WAREHOUSE MANAGEMENT

Earlier in this chapter, we explored many of the functions of a warehouse. In Figure 1.7, many of these functions of a warehouse have been mapped out into a logistics management framework, showing which functions are associated with each *inbound, internal,* or *outbound* processes. Subsequent chapters of this book will first cover each of these inbound, internal, and outbound processes in warehouse management in detail and will then follow with explorations of safety and security, technology and information technology, and the human side of warehousing.

CHAPTER 1 REVIEW QUESTIONS

1. What is a *warehouse*? Provide three examples of warehouses in your town.

2. How are the concepts of *supply* and *demand* related to warehousing?

3. Which is more related to warehouse management - *static* demand or *dynamic* demand? Explain your answer.

4. What is the *inspection* function of warehousing? Why is it important?

5. What are the *security and safety* functions of warehousing? Why are they important?

6. What is the *inventory records* function of warehousing? What kind of information is kept and in what form is it recorded?

7. What is the difference between an *internal customer* and an *external customer*?

8. What is the relationship between warehousing and *manufacturing*?

9. What is *physical distribution*? What is its relationship to warehousing?

10. How are warehouses related to *supply chains* and *supply chain management*?

CHAPTER 1 CASE STUDY

WAREHOUSE MANAGEMENT IN ACTION

The chapters to follow will include examples of the inbound, internal, and outbound functions of warehouse management from three businesses: a retail chain, a manufacturer, and a service provider.

The retail chain we will examine is an Alaska gift and souvenir chain of retail stores called Once in a Blue Moose, a family owned and family run business headquartered in Anchorage. Perhaps the best known and most highly regarded gift shop chain in Alaska, Once in a Blue Moose has received awards and accolades based on customer nominations. For example, it received the 2018 Unique Experience award in the Americas category from *Travel and Hospitality* magazine and is a regular recipient of the KTUU Channel 2 Viewer's Choice Award for Best Gift Shop. Once in a Blue Moose has been a feature in downtown Anchorage since 1969 and is family run, with a history of company leaders spanning multiple generations. Once in a Blue Moose has five retail locations across Anchorage and two retail locations in each Seward and Talkeetna, Alaska. It also has an online storefront and ships goods to customers around the world. Once in a Blue Moose has a positive impact on the local economy, too, by working with local vendors and encouraging artisans to stop by to show and sell their creations. As a result, the company purchases products made both overseas and locally. Of its 732 vendors, an impressive 284 of them are located in Alaska. The company's headquarters and central warehouse are located in the same building in midtown Anchorage. As the company has grown, its owners have come up with innovative

AT ONCE IN A BLUE MOOSE, SPECIAL FLOOR TILE DESIGNS SERVE AS AN IMMEDIATE VISUAL LOCATION CODE FOR DIFFERENT TYPES OF INCOMING INVENTORY.

ALTHOUGH DIFFICULT TO TELL IN A BLACK AND WHITE PHOTO, COLOR CODING IS ALSO USED IN THE MOVABLE STORAGE RACKS FOR INCOMING INVENTORY TO INDICATE INFORMATION ABOUT THE INVENTORY AND ITS STAGE IN THE INVENTORY RECEIPT PROCESS.

solutions for warehouse management and inventory control, especially in its creation of a tailor-made inventory management system. They even created a YouTube video featuring an original song they wrote about it. As a local retail chain without the warehousing and inventory management resources available to larger chains, Once in a Blue Moose has come up with efficient and effective solutions for managing and moving its inventory, such as its use of coding and clever use of low cost materials handling solutions.

The manufacturer we will examine is an internationally renowned winery called Tabalí, located in the Limari Valley of Northern Chile. The winery owns three vineyards from which all of its wines are sourced. The first plantings for the vineyards began in 1993 and the beautiful, open-air winery was built in 2004. The Tabalí winery processes 1300 tons of wine per year and many of its wines have received multiple national and international awards, with fifteen of them scoring 90+ points. Tabalí ships large quantities of its fragile bottles of wine around the world and must provide exceptional care and customer service throughout its inbound, internal, and outbound warehouse management processes to ensure that its bottles of wine get to their end consumers in perfect condition. Careful packaging and meticulous materials handling, while still maintaining a good speed of service, are the company's keys to exceptional customer service, with a perfectly balanced and consistent tasting wine hitting the customers' palates every time wherever they may be.

IN THE NORTHERN DESERT OF CHILE, TABALÍ CREATES EXCEPTIONAL WINES AND MUST ENSURE THAT ITS CUSTOMERS RECEIVE THE SAME EXCEPTIONAL WINES.

THE WINERY DOES AN OUTSTANDING JOB PAYING SPECIAL ATTENTION TO INTERNAL CUSTOMER SERVICE IN THEIR OUTBOUND PROCESSES OF WAREHOUSE MANAGEMENT.

Finally, the service provider we will examine is an Alaskan telecommunications service provider called Alaska Communications. The company began as a telecommunications utility and has been in operation for more than 100 years. It now provides broadband and managed IT services for businesses and private customers. Alaska Communications employs almost 600 people across Alaska and has a central warehouse in Anchorage. The company is an Alaskan leader in warehouse management and supply chain management with its forward thinking. Alaska Communications has long been one of the state's shining examples of vendor managed inventory, with vendors taking ownership for managing their items inside the company's warehouse. The company also significantly streamlined its supply chain operations, warehouse management, and inventory control through an extensive lean initiative, which completely changed the company's way of thinking about processes and waste.

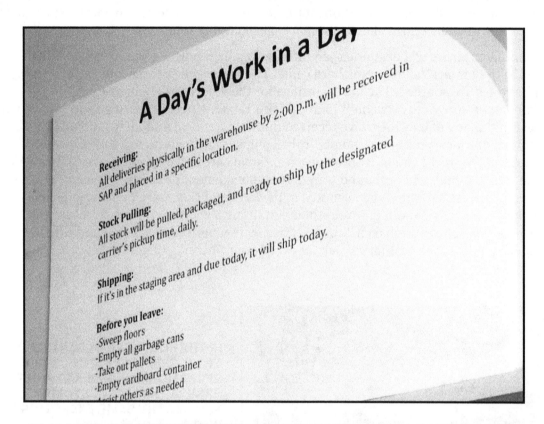

AT ALASKA COMMUNICATIONS, THE COMPANY– WIDE LEAN INITIATIVE TO STREAMLINE AND STANDARDIZE PROCESSES IS REINFORCED ON POSTERS THROUGHOUT THE COMPANY'S WAREHOUSE.

INSTRUCTIONS:

1. For the three companies described, which of the twelve functions of a warehouse might each of the company's warehouses engage in? Please explain your answer.

2. What might the supply chains for each of the three companies look like?

3. Do you think they will have simple or complex supply chains? Please explain your answer.

Chapter 2
The What and Where of Warehouses

From Chapter 1, we learned that a *warehouse* is a facility or an area within a facility where a company or other organization receives, inspects, stores, picks, packs, and issues materials needed for the organization's internal operations or its external customers' orders. As we will learn later in Chapter 3, these materials that we find in a warehouse are called **goods**, which can be defined as tangible items that are owned and can be moved. Throughout this chapter, we will take a closer look at warehouses themselves, examining the wide variety of types of warehouses and why the layout and location of a warehouse is important.

2.1 WAREHOUSE SIZE

Sizes of warehouses vary greatly, from the back storeroom of your favorite local restaurant to enormous warehouse buildings larger than multiple football fields. Some warehouses are even millions of square feet large. An Amazon Fulfillment Center in Tennessee is a colossal 3.6 million square feet. A Target warehouse in Savannah, Georgia that handles imported goods is almost two million square feet. In Europe, the Conforama home furnishing distribution facility in Paris, France is also almost two million square feet and the Inex Sipoo retail goods distribution center in Finland is 2.4 million square feet.

But does every company need a warehouse over 2 million square feet? When considering warehouse space, a company needs enough space for its current warehousing functions while considering its growth and future warehousing needs. At the same time, the company must consider the cost of the space and how well the space is utilized. To make warehouses more efficient and cost effective, companies examine **warehouse space utilization**, which is an assessment of how efficiently the warehouse square footage and vertical space is being used. Companies use experts and a variety of apps and information systems to improve their warehouse space utilization for both current and planned warehouses.

When considering a new warehouse, the size of a company's warehouse building can be influenced by any of the following factors:

- **the size, amount, and variety of goods to be stored.** It is common sense to understand that larger items and larger quantities of items will need larger warehouses. For example, a warehouse that stores 10,000 refrigerators will need to be much larger than the size of a warehouse that stores 10,000 packs of buttons. What might be less obvious is that a warehouse that stores a variety of goods will need to be larger than a warehouse that stores only one version of one item, even if there are the same number of goods of exactly the same size in both warehouses. When there is only one type of item in a warehouse, such as pallets of standard size boxes of a new product called Boring Oat Rings Cereal, the items can be stacked high, wide, and deep without gaps because there only needs to be one access point for pickers to pick orders of the cereal. Wide aisles in the warehouse are less necessary. Now imagine the same cereal company increasing its range to include 25 types and varieties of cereal, including Super Sugary Oat Rings, Caramel Drizzle Oat Squares, Oatless Oat Flavored Rings, and Chocolate Oat Chomps. There would then need to be more empty warehouse space for those storing and retrieving these various cereal types so they could easily find and access the locations of the pallets of each of these 25 types of cereal.

- **the usable height of the warehouse.** Although a warehouse may be 40 feet high, not all of the space near the ceiling may be usable for storage or stacking systems. Organizations need to consider the building's *clear height*, which is the measurement from the warehouse floor to the next warehouse construction or architectural element as you move upward, such as steel beams, lighting fixtures, or smoke detectors. The clear height rather than the actual height measurement from the floor to the ceiling is used to determine how much space can actually be utilized in a warehouse. For example, a warehouse may measure 40 feet from floor to ceiling, but there may be lighting fixtures that suspend five feet down from the ceiling, making the *clear height* and actual usable height of warehouse space 35 feet.

FIGURE 2.1 - WAREHOUSE HEIGHT VERSUS CLEAR HEIGHT

- **how high pallets of products can be stacked.** Items in warehouses are often received, stored, and shipped on pallets, which you will learn more about in Chapter 6. Some products are more awkwardly shaped or more fragile. The number of pallets of these items that can be safely stacked one on top of another without fear of breakage or toppling might be lower than items that are less awkwardly shaped and less fragile. For example, you might see pallet loads of bricks stacked on a home improvement store warehouse floor two to four pallet-loads high. Looking in the same warehouse, refrigerators are typically stored only one pallet-load high because the refrigerators are taller, more fragile, and more expensive than the bricks. If refrigerators need to be stored one on top of another, racking systems are used, which take up more warehouse space. This all means that warehouses that can safely store goods in pallet loads stacked one on top of another need less warehouse space. Conversely, warehouses that cannot stack pallet loads of items one on top of another will need more warehouse floor space because much more vertical space is lost. Even if racking systems are used, the racks and the space between the top of the item and the next rack shelf are all extra space needed.

FIGURE 2.2 - DOUBLE-STACKED PALLETS OF BOTTLES OF WATER (LEFT) AND SINGLE STACKED PALLETS ON A RACKING SYSTEM (RIGHT)

- **how quickly inventory must be picked.** Some companies may need to pick items to be delivered immediately, such as Amazon or Walmart with their same-day deliveries. In these cases, more space is needed in the warehouse so inventory pickers and their equipment, such as forklifts, hand trucks, or robots, can quickly and easily maneuver and zoom to the items to be picked for a customer's order. When companies have more time to pick an order, such as orders than don't have to be delivered for one week, less warehouse space is needed because items can be stored in ways that maximize space but are more difficult to access, such as items stored in the upper half of a warehouse or items stored in racking systems with multiple racks that have to be moved to access the item.

- **what equipment is needed to pick orders.** Some items and storage methods may need larger or more cumbersome equipment to pick orders, while others may be on conveyor systems with the person picking the order moving very little. When larger equipment is needed, such as forklifts or automated retrieval vehicles, empty warehouse space is needed on every aisle to maneuver and turn around. In these situations, more warehouse space overall is needed.

- **anticipated growth of an organization's operations.** When considering warehouse size, a company must look at not only their current needs, but also their needs for the next ten to fifteen years. If a company plans to grow their operations to sell more product or offer more product lines or offer a different product that takes up more warehouse space, they must consider the corresponding additional space that will be needed in the future so they do not make the expensive mistake of having to move to a new warehouse every three to five years.

- **non-storage areas needed.** In addition to storage space, an organization may need non-storage space in a warehouse for offices, bathrooms, and utility areas for heating and cooling systems. To get the actual storage square footage of a warehouse, subtract the measurements of all non-storage areas from the total square footage of the building.

Now that we have looked at a few considerations for the size of individual companies' warehouses, let's look at some national trends in warehouse size. There have been a couple of interesting trends over the past decade regarding the increasing *and decreasing* size of warehouses overall across the United States. The U.S. Energy Information Administration (EIA) studies the energy consumption of commercial buildings on a regular basis. Interestingly, these studies have revealed interesting things about how the number and size of warehouse buildings have changed in recent history. Data from studies in each 2012 and 2018 reveal that the number of warehouse and storage buildings in the United States grew from approximately 790,000 in 2012 to approximately 1,004,000 in 2018. Also, in 2012, 14% of all commercial buildings in the US were warehouses, but by 2018, that percentage had grown to 17%. These EIA studies also revealed that the average size of warehouse buildings grew from 16,400 square feet in 2012 to 17,300 in 2018, representing a growth of almost 6% in six years.

FIGURE 2.3 - ROBOTIC WAREHOUSE FACILITY IN ARIZONA WITH A FOOTPRINT OF 855,000 SQUARE FEET, FOUR LEVELS, AND AN OVERALL SIZE OF 2.3 MILLION SQUARE FEET

Although these studies show that warehouses are growing larger, they are also growing smaller. This paradox of warehouses growing both larger and smaller has to do with lack of available large warehouse space near customers to achieve next day and same day deliveries. As the average number and size of warehouses are growing, there is a growing shortage of warehouse space across the United States and in other countries around the world. E-commerce has grown by more than 100% in the past decade and the need for large warehouses and fulfillment centers has grown. There is often no available land left to build new warehouses near many customer locations while much existing warehouse space is too old, too small, or not high enough to handle current warehousing technology and needs. In many densely populated urban areas, this lack of warehouse space has forced companies to use whatever space is available as small warehouses. In New York City, a company called Bond offers storage space to companies in its *nano warehouses*, which are small warehouse spaces throughout the city located in former retail space.

Famous for its massive warehouses around the world, Amazon initiated a push in 2020 and 2021 to add 1500 small warehouses in suburban US neighborhoods. Although not small by many standards, these smaller suburban Amazon warehouses were approximately 200,000 square feet, or one quarter of the size of a typical Amazon Fulfillment Center. Their goal was to help place more frequently purchased items closer to customers, allowing Amazon to achieve next-day and same-day deliveries in more locations for more goods.

Another alternative for traditional retail companies who need additional warehouse space for their e-commerce operations is to use their stores for both retail sales and warehouse storage. For example, rather than construct large warehouse distribution centers, Walmart has moved to a mini-warehouse model in which it uses many of its existing retail stores also as warehouses for online sales. With this model, shoppers peruse the store aisles and buy their milk and cereal alongside Walmart inventory pickers who pick orders for online customers. With the growth of warehouses both big and small, successful companies are those that are flexible in their approach to warehouse space, using the most effective and efficient space available to meet the needs of the company and its customers.

2.2 WAREHOUSE OWNERSHIP

In addition to variations in warehouse size, warehouses can also have different forms of ownership. Warehouses that vary according to *ownership*, or who owns the actual warehouse facility, can fall under the following classifications:

- *private warehouse:* This is a warehouse facility that is owned by a company to store its goods. Manufacturers, wholesalers, distributors, and retailers can own private warehouses. Although they are quite costly and involve a significant commitment, private warehouses allow companies complete control over their warehouse space. The giant Amazon fulfillment centers worldwide, distribution centers for grocery store chains, and a small warehouse building on the same lot behind a local pet store are all examples of private warehouses.

- **_private contract warehouse:_** Like a private warehouse, a private contract warehouse is a facility operated by one company to store its goods. Similarly, manufacturers, wholesalers, distributors, and retailers all use private contract warehouses. The difference is that private contract warehouse buildings are not owned by the company storing the goods but are instead leased from the building's owner. These private contract warehouses are typically empty shells when they are leased. The company renting them usually has a long-term lease and is responsible for supplying all warehouse racking and equipment, paying all utility bills, and supplying all warehouse workers.

FIGURE 2.4 - EXAMPLE OF A 793,000 SF PRIVATE CONTRACT WAREHOUSE FOR LEASE

- **_public warehouse:_** This is a facility that stores goods from multiple companies and is owned and operated by another company, such as a third-party storage or logistics service provider. Although public warehouses don't allow companies as much control over space as private or private contract warehouses do, they offer the advantage of lower costs and flexibility, because companies use and pay for only as much of a warehouse is needed at a given time. Storage at a public warehouse is usually on a first-come, first-served basis and pallets are rolled in and placed where there is space available. A small local self-storage facility used by pharmaceutical sales representatives to store marketing materials and a large regional third-party refrigerated warehouse used by small grocery and convenience stores would both be examples of public warehouses.

- **_contract warehouse:_** This facility is very similar to a public warehouse because it stores goods from multiple companies and is owned and operated by another company, such as a logistics service provider. The distinction is that there are more fully outlined terms in the contract between the company storing the goods and the warehouse. For example, most contracts with contract warehouses are for a specific amount of dedicated storage for a longer period of time. Instead of the first-come, first-served month-based contracts of public warehouses, contract warehouses have longer year-based contracts for a dedicated location and amount of space, even if that space may sometimes be empty because the company contracting the space may not always have need for it. Contract warehouses can also offer services such as order fulfillment, inventory picking, and packing. Be aware that some companies may use the terms *public warehouse* and *contract warehouse* interchangeably or with different definitions depending on unique company terminology, the industry involved, or the country in which the warehouses are located.

One way to understand the key differences between these types of warehouses is to compare them to structures people live in. A *private warehouse* is like owning your own home. You may have it custom-built or you may buy an existing structure and modify it to your needs. Either way, you own it and can do what you like with it. You are also responsible for setting up the inside of the home, hiring any labor needed, and paying for all taxes, utilities, and insurance associated with ownership. With a private warehouse, the company owns the building and it is typically empty. The company can do whatever they want to modify the building as long as they are following local laws and ordinances. The company provides their own shelving, equipment, and warehouse labor and they pay all utilities, tax, and insurance costs.

A *private contract warehouse* is like renting a house or apartment for your home. It is an empty shell when you rent it. With a rental home, you can do what you like with it, as long as you don't make any drastic modifications that the owners will have to fix when you leave. You are similarly responsible for setting up the inside of the rented home to suit your purposes, hiring any labor needed, and paying for all utilities and related rental taxes and insurance, which are typically less than if you owned the home. With a private contract warehouse, it is empty when a company rents it. They set up the shelving and provide their own equipment. They provide all warehouse labor and pay all associated utilities, taxes, and insurance costs.

A *public warehouse* is like renting a hotel room and a *contract warehouse* is like renting an apartment in an extended-stay or executive-stay hotel. In both situations, you do not own and cannot modify the facility you live in. You stay in the same facility with others, and the hotel provides needed supplies, such as furniture and towels; utilities, such as electricity and cable tv; and labor, such as housekeepers and security guards. The difference between the two involves the length and location of your stay. With a standard hotel room, you can stay for a short amount of time and stay only as long as needed. If you return to the hotel, you can get a room if it is available, but you are not likely to get exactly the same room you had before. With an extended-stay hotel, you have a contract to stay in a specific apartment or suite for a longer, specific length of time. If you go away for the weekend, you will return to the exact same room and no one will have occupied it in your absence. With public and contract warehouses, the company using them pays to use storage space, but their payment also covers the warehouse racking, equipment, utilities, warehouse labor, and more. With a public warehouse, a company pays to store goods only as long as needed and the storage location provided is based on what is available at the time the goods are stored. With a contract warehouse, a company pays to have access to a specific storage location of a specific size for a specific longer length of time, even if they might not use 100% of the storage space all of the time.

No one of these four types of warehouse ownership types is better than another. Instead, companies needing to store goods must assess their needs, storage costs, and facilities availability when selecting which ownership type is most beneficial. While private, private contract, public, and contract warehouse are more common, two additional types of warehouse ownership classification you may encounter are:

- ***cooperative warehouse:*** This is a warehouse facility that is owned and operated by an industry-based cooperative organization. The primary goal of a cooperative and its warehouse is to help cooperative members. Typically, cooperatives are more focused on benefitting their members and less focused on making a profit. One example of a cooperative that you may have noticed when shopping in your grocery store's dairy aisle is Cabot Creamery, a cooperative of 800+ family owned farms and dairies across New England and New York that has existed for more than 100 years. Cabot Creamery owns multiple warehouses that store the combined products of cooperative members, such as a warehouse facility in Middlebury, Vermont that can store 2 million pounds of cheese!

FIGURE 2.5 - CABOT CREAMERY COOPERATIVE IN VERMONT

- ***government warehouse:*** This is a warehouse facility owned and controlled by the government. Government warehouses can be used by the government or private companies to store goods. For example, the US Department of Homeland Security owns warehouses to store its government owned ammunitions and disaster relief supplies. Private companies may also use government warehouses, as in the case of some *bonded warehouses* that will be covered later in this chapter. When this occurs, there is considerably more paperwork involved than when using a private contract or public warehouse.

Of the six types of warehouses we have covered in this section that vary by ownership, only one is owned directly by the company storing the goods: the *private warehouse*. The other five types of warehouses, *private contract, public, contract, cooperative,* and *government warehouses*, are owned by other companies, organizations, or government entities. Before any materials can be stored in these warehouses, a contract or agreement is formulated between the company wishing to store goods in the warehouse and the warehouse owner. It is absolutely vital that a company's legal team and warehouse managers examine the warehouse rental or service contract carefully before it is signed. Some of the factors closely examined in these contracts and agreements include:

- **Cost.** The actual cost of storage must be clearly determined and an agreement regarding the nature of the costs should be outlined. For example, does the cost given include the whole storage space, regardless of usage, or only the space used?

- **Termination.** It's important to examine the notice of termination, clearly outlining what is required of each party when the contract term ends and what is required to terminate the contract.

- **Inventory Checking.** The contract should also outline the responsibility and access for physical inventory checking. Some warehouses may conduct all inventory checks themselves while others will provide access to the company storing goods so it can conduct inventory checks.

- **Damage and Insurance.** Contracts should clearly outline which party should provide which type of insurance and who is responsible for which type of damage to goods.

- **Storage Conditions.** The exact environmental conditions under which the inventory must be handled and stored should be clearly outlined and agreed. For example, perishable or hazardous goods have specific temperature or environment conditions that must be met. Imagine storing ice cream in a temperature controlled warehouse, but the warehouse owners decided to save money on electricity bills by turning off the warehouse cooling systems in the evening. The ice cream company storing goods there might end up with a melted mess if storage conditions aren't made part of the storage contract.

- **Inventory Control and Records.** The contract should also outline the responsibility for physical inventory control and record-keeping. Similar to inventory checking, some warehouses may handle all inventory control themselves and supply records to the company about its goods stored while others may be hands-off and expect the company to control and keep records about its own goods.

- **What's Included.** Contracts should also out line any extras that are included in the terms of service, such as provision of labor and materials handling equipment.

2.3 WAREHOUSE LOCATION

When a company is considering a variety of warehouse options based on ownership structure, the *location* of each potential facility is also considered. An organization determines its optimal warehouse location based on a variety of factors, including:

- **Proximity to other locations within the supply chain.** Ideally, a warehouse should be located near the company's operations or its suppliers and customers. Even though all of the other factors might make Buckeye, Arizona the optimal location for a company's warehouse, it wouldn't make sense to operate a warehouse there if all of the company's manufacturing operations and customers are located over 2000 miles away in Pennsylvania and Ohio.

**FIGURE 2.6 - WAREHOUSE BUILDINGS IN ARIZONA
LOCATED NEXT TO MAJOR ROADWAY (LEFT)**

- **Proximity to major transportation routes.** Warehouses both receive goods and send them out for distribution. The goods get to the warehouse and leave the warehouse using transportation routes. These transportation routes could include highways, railroad lines, cargo airports, and ship ports. Companies can save time and money by locating warehouses near the transportation routes used to get goods into and out from the warehouse. Sometimes this may involve being close to more than one form of transportation, such as along both a major highway and a rail network. Even when ideally situated along transportation routes, companies also have to consider the traffic flow and congestion along those routes to see if they adversely will impact transportation times.

- **Availability of local workforce.** For an organization to have a working warehouse, it needs to have people available to work in it. Just being near population centers does not necessarily mean that there is an available workforce for the warehouse. In areas with very low unemployment or in areas with a very highly skilled and highly paid workforce, a company may have difficulties in finding employees to occupy the entry-level positions that the warehouse may need.

- **Availability of land or warehouse buildings.** Sometimes a company may find the perfect location for a warehouse based on its supply chain, local transportation routes, and the available workforce. However, there might not be any warehouses available to rent or even any available land to build a warehouse on. Companies will often have to begin their search for a potential warehouse with only those facilities that are currently available to them.

- **Local economic and infrastructure factors.** Companies must look at the local economy and infrastructure when consider warehouse locations. The local economy can have an impact on local warehouse rental rates, local and state tax structures for businesses, and how safe an area may be and how responsive its police and fire forces are in case of emergency. Companies may also need to consider the reliability of the local utilities infrastructure and how often the provision of power or water may be disrupted by local weather events. The local telecommunications infrastructure is also becoming an increasingly important factor as warehouses become reliant on location systems and cloud based software to run its operations. For example, a warehouse that has only satellite internet available at its location may not be suitable for a company reliant on cloud based inventory systems because of the slower speeds and frequent disruptions of satellite internet.

- **Transportations costs.** Finally, when a company has a variety of warehouse location options based on the factors listed above, it may need to use mathematical calculations to find the location that offered the lowest overall transportation costs between the links in its supply chain. One method used to determine a location that offers the lowest transportation costs when adding a new warehouse to an existing network of warehouses is the Center of Gravity Method. The existing warehouses are plotted on a map-based grid and their location and volume of outbound goods are plugged in to a formula to get the grid location that represents the optimal location for a new warehouse. Most warehouse managers are not likely to ever have to calculate this value themselves or if they do, they would typically plug values into an online system. However, it is useful to know that it is an option for determining an optimal warehouse location to reduce transportation costs.

2.4 WAREHOUSE FACILITIES BY TYPE

In addition to varying by size and ownership type, warehouse facilities also vary according to *type* and *function*. Three categories of contrasting warehouse facilities that vary by *type*, such as specific design features or descriptions, are:

- **Single-Story versus Multi-Story Buildings.**

  As the name suggests, ***single-story warehouse buildings*** are built on one level without stairs or full upper floors. Single story warehouse buildings are the more popular option in most locations because of the many advantages they offer, including lower construction and operating costs and a smoother flow of materials in and out of the building without having to take goods up and down elevators.

  In more populated areas where land is scarce and land costs are high, companies want to get as much warehouse square footage as possible onto a limited amount of land, which leads them to consider ***multi-story warehouse buildings***, a warehouse facility built on two or more levels. Even though improvements in warehouse building designs that allow trucks to get directly to bays in multiple levels of a building to improve product flow, these multi-story warehouse are still more expensive to construct that single-story buildings. However, in these situations, companies are finding that it is less expensive to build truck ramps and bays or install elevators and complex conveyor systems in a multi-story facility than it is to buy enough land to construct a single-story facility. Whether a company decides to build a single-story or multi-story warehouse building is dependent on many factors and we'll cover more about these and the construction and design on single-story and multi-story warehouse buildings later in Chapter 4, "Putaway and Storage."

  Popular in congested areas of Asia and Europe, multi-story warehouses are rapidly gaining popularity in the United States, especially for online retailers' interest in *the last mile*. In the world of warehousing and logistics, ***the last mile*** refers to the final link in the supply chain that gets products from the last warehouse facility, distribution center, or fulfillment center to the end customer. Customers have come to expect same-day delivery, especially in e-commerce transactions. To achieve this, companies must locate their distribution centers and other final warehouse facilities as close to the customer as possible, ideally within only a few miles. This important *last mile* between company and customer has led to warehouses now being located as close to consumers as possible and many of these warehouses are multi-story warehouse buildings. In some urban areas, large department stores have been closing as either large retail chains go bankrupt or they move more of their operations online as people turn increasingly to online shopping for much of their clothing and household goods. As a result, there has been a recent trend in real estate development for investors to buy up vacant retail space in inner cities, such as former department stores and vacant shopping malls, and turn these vacant multi-story building into last mile warehouse space to rent out to retail companies that wish to have their goods close to urban consumers so that they can also enjoy same-day deliveries from online shopping like suburban shoppers already do.

Finally, when considering single-story and multi-story warehouse buildings, there is also a type of newer warehouse that seems to be a hybrid of both single-story and multi-story buildings. Automated storage and retrieval systems also now allow for multi-story-height ***rack-supported warehouse buildings***, which are storage facilities built entirely on the structure of storage racks that are many stories high, but the building itself is still a one-story structure, as shown in Figure 2.7 below. The walls and ceiling are supported by the storage racks. Multiple floors or even aisles for warehouse workers to pick goods are not needed. Instead, automated warehouse equipment moves along the racking systems to both pick and put away goods.

FIGURE 2.7 - RACK-SUPPORTED WAREHOUSE BUILDING UNDER CONSTRUCTION

- **Purpose-Built versus Converted Buildings.**

When considering new warehouse space, a company must consider whether they want to use a new building or refit an existing structure. A ***purpose-built warehouse building*** is a warehouse that has been designed and constructed according to an organization's specific needs and operational requirements. Purpose-built warehouse buildings are typically associated with large companies that have the resources to design and construct these specialized buildings that cater to the needs of the company and the items to be stored. A company storing a large amount of heavy palletized materials would require a large, open-plan warehouse building, while another company holding numerous small, manufactured items my need a multi-story warehouse building with several open and closed shelves.

Designing and constructing a purpose-built warehouse building offers three primary advantages. First, warehouse managers have the opportunity to ensure that the warehouse has the most efficient layout design for materials handling and storage. Second, the latest techniques, innovations, and warehouse developments can be incorporated into the warehouse's basic design requirements. For example, the use of some automated materials handling systems requires laying down guide tracks, which can best be installed during the building construction phase. Finally, purpose-built warehouse buildings provide a company with exactly what its needs dictate, leaving no wasted space and instead leaving room for expansion based on the company's projections of future requirements. Purpose-built warehouse buildings can also be constructed to ensure that the foundation and flooring can handle the current and future weight needs of the organization. As shown in Figure 2.8, a grid of **rebar**, or reinforced steel bars, is being put in place before the concrete flooring is poured to allow for the heavy weight of warehouse machinery, racking, and storage items.

FIGURE 2.8 - REBAR GRID BEFORE CONCRETE WAREHOUSE FLOOR IS POURED

While purpose-built warehouse buildings may sound ideal, they do bring some disadvantages, primarily in terms of: *expense* and *misjudgment*. Designing and constructing a purpose-built warehouse building consumes a great deal of time and money. Similar to purchasing a home, it is typically more expensive to buy newly constructed house than to buy an older, previously constructed house. Whether it is a for a house or a purpose-built warehouse building, the price of new construction is dependent upon the current market rate of design costs, construction materials, and labor costs.

Also, companies have to be careful to avoid misjudgments during the design phase concerning the real needs of the organization. Even the smallest misjudgment may result in a great waste of resources. For example, a bathroom products wholesaler decided to construct a new purpose-built warehouse. The company was in a rush to complete the project due to an immediate need for warehouse space. In their haste, company executives signed off on the architectural plans and began construction without reviewing the plans with the company's warehouse and logistics managers. When the warehouse construction was complete, the warehouse managers were horrified to find that they could stack their larger inventory items into two tiers of pallets loads, but that they were just 1" short of being able to stack a third tier of goods. Had the company paid greater attention to its needs and its inventory during the warehouse design phase, the warehouse storage capacity could have been increased by a full fifty percent had the building been made just one inch taller!

Unlike a purpose-built warehouse building, which is designed and constructed according to specific needs, a **converted warehouse building** is a building which was originally designed for one purpose but then converted to be used for warehousing purposes for a specific company and items to be stored. When companies develop and expand, their needs for storage space and handling facilities also expand. Such companies sometimes convert existing buildings of all kinds into warehouse facilities. These buildings can range from old factories to large residential houses, depending upon the size of the operation and the properties available.

Converted warehouse buildings have the advantage of being relatively inexpensive to acquire, either by outright purchase or by lease from the owner. With a lease, less capital is invested and the company has the option to move its inventory to another location in the future should its demands change. With careful planning and layout, converted warehouse buildings can produce very useful and cost-effective storage facilities. Earlier in this chapter, we mentioned a company called Bond, which is creating nano warehouses in New York City to allow online retailers to store their goods closer to consumers for quicker delivery times. Bond and other similar last-mile warehouse service companies in densely populated areas often use converted warehouse buildings, converting former restaurants, townhouses, stores, shopping centers, apartment buildings, office buildings, and movie theaters into warehouses.

Before converting a building into a warehouse facility, a company and its warehouse management team must consider the possible disadvantages of a converted warehouse building. For example, environmental conditions needed to store materials may not be correct in the existing building, making it necessary to install expensive equipment during the conversion process. This is especially true for frozen foods or materials requiring damp-free storage. The converted area also may not be suitable for the materials handling and storage systems needed by the organization. For example, many buildings available for conversion do not have the doors and loading bay access needed for warehouses. Also, older buildings sometimes do not have the level floors required by many electric trucks. Finally, when using a converted warehouse building, further expansion may be restricted by factors outside the control of the organization, such as local government planning permission.

• Inside versus Outside Storage.

When considering the storage space required, companies must consider whether goods are best suited to be stored *inside* in a warehouse building or outside in an external inventory yard. An **external inventory yard** is an open, outside warehousing area used for storing various weather-resistant goods and raw materials. **Weather-resistant goods** are those that will not deteriorate or perish when exposed to the elements over long periods of time. Depending upon the organization and the nature of its inventory, it may have an external inventory yard, a warehouse building, or both.

FIGURE 2.9 - AERIAL VIEW OF PICKUP TRUCKS IN AN EXTERNAL INVENTORY YARD

Also known as an **outdoor storage area** or a **yard**, an external inventory yard is typically exposed to the elements, so it provides excellent storage for materials that are destined to spend their working lives in open or exposed conditions. These types of materials often stored in an external inventory yard include:

• **stoneware**, such as concrete slabs and bricks;

• **heavy iron and steel casting**, such as drains, piping, bridge units, and lamp posts;

• **heavy duty electrical cable**, such as the type used to carry high voltage electricity in underground conditions;

- **outdoor machinery**, such as tractors, tractor-trailer trucks, drilling equipment, cranes, and cars, as shown in Figure 2.9;

- **scrap and waste materials**, such as filings, turnings, obsolescent inventory, chemical waste, and byproducts;

- **coal, coke, and other fuels**, typically stored in drums and which might be too dangerous to be stored inside because of toxic fumes or the risk of fire; and

- **garden materials and supplies**, such as topsoil, plant seedlings, and fertilizer.

Compared to a warehouse building, an external inventory yard offers low construction cost, low operating cost, and a large storage capacity. Construction costs for an external inventory yard are far less expensive because only a sound base, secure fencing, and strong gates are required, unlike a warehouse building, which requires a foundation, walls, roofing, ventilation, and heating or cooling.

FIGURE 2.10 - OUTDOOR STORAGE AREA ON THE FRONT SIDEWALK OF A BIG BOX HOME IMPROVEMENT STORE WITH PALLET LOADS OF PAVERS AND BRICKS

Organizations may also use external inventory yards for temporary storage of goods within shipping containers. Because they have the protection of a shipping container, even temperature-controlled refrigerated containers, these goods stored outside are not limited to weather-resistant ones. Although items stored in shipping containers outdoors may be less accessible than goods stored in a warehouse, this type of storage can be useful when warehouses are full or if the container holds seasonal goods that have arrived too early for distribution, such as Christmas decorations for a chain of retail stores that have arrived in September.

2.5 WAREHOUSE FACILITIES BY FUNCTION

In addition to varying by size, ownership, and type, warehouse facilities also vary according to *function,* or the intended purpose of the warehouse. While the primary purpose of all warehouses is to receive, inspect, store, pick, pack, and issue goods, many warehouses have an additional purpose, like keeping goods at a specific temperature, saving distribution costs, or adhering to international laws. Below are a few different warehouse facilities that vary according to five different functions.

FUNCTION #1: Keep Goods Safe

- *Climate Controlled Warehouse.* This is a warehouse facility that carefully controls the facility's inside temperature and humidity according to the needs of the goods being stored. When we think of climate-controlled warehouses, we might first think of food, particularly the refrigeration and freezer needs of many grocery store items. However, many non-food companies also need climate-controlled warehouses to avoid damage to their goods. For example, the warehouses for Martin Guitars in Pennsylvania and Mexico must be kept precisely within the ranges of 68-75 degrees Fahrenheit and 40-46 percent humidity to avoid cracks and warping of the wood guitars.

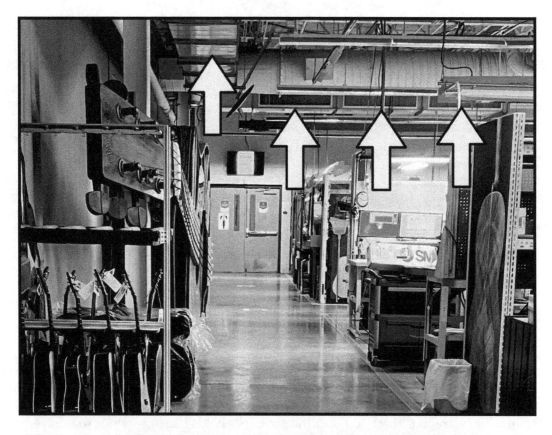

FIGURE 2.11 - EXTENSIVE CLIMATE CONTROL SYSTEM IN THE WAREHOUSE OF THE MARTIN GUITAR MANUFACTURING FACILITY IN NAZARETH, PENNSYLVANIA

- **Hazardous Materials Warehouse.** Also called a **hazmat warehouse** or a **dangerous goods warehouse**, a hazardous materials warehouse is a warehouse facility that stores goods requiring extra handling and storage safety precautions. These hazardous materials stored could include poisonous materials, flammable gasses, and corrosive liquids. Hazardous materials warehouses have specific storage requirements for goods and protective equipment requirements for the warehouse personnel handling the hazardous goods. After a robot punctured a can of bear repellant spray in one of its warehouses and sent 24 workers to the hospital, Amazon.com built a series of special hazmat warehouses for the dangerous goods sold on its website.

FUNCTION #2: Keep Goods Moving and Shorten Storage Times

- **Distribution Center.** Also known by its abbreviation, **DC**, a distribution center is a warehouse facility that receives large quantities of goods to be stored for shorter periods of time and then be sent on to multiple locations. Its function is to create a more efficient distribution network through faster and more cost effective movement of goods from supplier to customer. Companies often use information systems and automated equipment to control and automate operations at distribution centers to facilitate this quick movement of goods into and out of the facility. Distribution centers are typically located where there is access to lower labor and utilities costs and where there are a variety of transportation systems to facilitate the fast movement of goods.

- **Regional Distribution Center.** Distribution centers are often strategically located along highway and railroad networks to help facilitate the rapid movement of goods into and within one geographic region. Because of this geographic focus, distribution centers are often called *regional distribution centers* or **RDCs**. For example, grocery store chains across the world have their own regional distribution centers strategically located on highways and in between the stores they service to provide the quickest average transportation times. At these RDCs, they receive groceries from suppliers across the country and then distribute them to all of their retail grocery stores within the designated region, such as within the state or within a 200-mile radius. The terms *distribution center* and *regional distribution center* are often used interchangeably. Regardless of the terminology used, these facilities are commonly found in more complex supply chains for larger regional, national, and global companies.

- **Fulfillment Center.** Also known as a **customer fulfillment center**, **CFC**, **warehouse fulfillment center**, and an **order fulfillment center**, a fulfillment center is a warehouse facility that stores products manufactured by a variety of companies and from which a completely different company fills customers' orders, usually from online sales. The company filling the order is a third-party logistics service provider and it owns and operates the fulfillment center. Like distribution centers, fulfillment centers focus on the fast movement of goods into and out from the facility. One significant difference is that distribution centers typically distribute goods to retail stores while fulfillment centers send goods directly to end users based on online orders. The most widely known fulfillment centers are those of amazon.com. At the time of this writing, amazon.com operates 425 fulfillment centers across the United States and many more across the globe. In the late 2010s, fulfillment center began to spread across a wide range of industries focusing on online sales to end users, including grocery stores. Known for its automated customer fulfillment centers, the British online supermarket Ocado partnered with The Kroger Company in the US in 2018 to bring automated customer fulfillment centers for online grocery shopping in multiple regions of the United States.

FUNCTION #3: Keep Goods Moving and Eliminate Storage

- *Cross-Docking Facility.* Also called a **cross dock**, a **cross-docking warehouse**, and a **cross-docking distribution center**, a cross-dock facility is a specialized distribution center that doesn't store goods because it moves them so quickly from a wide range of suppliers' incoming trucks to multiple outbound trucks headed for different locations. Goods from a variety of suppliers or locations are received at one end of the facility, immediately sorted, and then immediately placed into trucks or containers at the other end of the facility for shipping. During the cross-docking process, goods are usually moved and sorted on their original pallet-loads for quicker movement of goods. When a truckload of goods arrive, the entire cross-docking process of sorting and moving goods from the single inbound truck to a variety of outbound ones usually takes less than 24 hours and can sometimes take less than a single hour. This rapid movement of goods eliminates the need for storage because items from incoming shipments are transferred directly onto outgoing shipments. It is already known who the customers will be for each item in an incoming shipment long before they reach the cross-docking facility. For example, the home improvement retailer, Home Depot, operates 18 enormous, mechanized cross-docking facilities called Rapid Deployment Centers that take in goods from suppliers and rapidly place them into outgoing trucks to its stores across the country with much of the process automated based on specific information about where each incoming item needs to go.

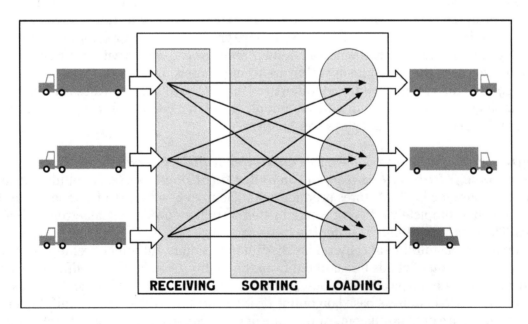

FIGURE 2.12 - HOW CROSS-DOCKING WORKS

- *Flow-Through Facility.* Very similar to a cross-docking facility, a flow-through facility also receives goods from a variety of suppliers or locations and places them into a variety of outbound trucks for shipping with little to no warehouse storage time needed. The primary difference is that in a cross-docking facility, goods are kept palletized or in larger units for quicker movement. In a flow-through facility, inbound pallet loads are broken down and sorted into new outbound pallet loads, resulting in a longer process. While goods may spend only an hour or less in a cross-docking facility, they may spend 24 hours or more in a flow-through facility. Please note that terminology may differ from company to company. For example, some organizations do not make a distinction between a cross-docking facility and a flow-through facility and instead refer to both as cross-docking facilities.

- *Transloading Facility.* Similar to a cross-docking facility, goods in a transloading facility are moved quickly from an inbound vehicle to an outbound vehicle and typically not stored. In a cross-docking facility, however, goods are typically moved across vehicles using that same mode of transportation, such as from truck to truck. In a transloading facility, goods are moved from one mode of transportation to another, such as from within a shipping container at an ocean port into a container on a truck or train. In the *transloading* process, goods are taken from the original inbound container and moved into a variety of outbound containers that involve a different mode of transportation.

FIGURE 2.13 - SEAFOOD TRANSLOADING FACILITY IN USHUAIA, ARGENTINA WHERE BOXES OF FISH FROM ARE MOVED FROM A PROCESSING VESSEL, PALLETIZED, AND TRANSFERRED TO CONTAINERS FOR ROAD AND RAIL TRANSPORTATION ACROSS SOUTH AMERICA

Transloading should not be confused with ***intermodal transportation***, in which the entire shipping container is moved from one mode of transportation to another.

FUNCTION #4: Reduce Costs

- ***Consolidated Warehouse.*** Also called a ***consolidation warehouse***, a consolidated warehouse is a facility for multiple suppliers located in one geographic area. It is used collectively to store and combine shipments of outbound goods from multiple companies to the same customers for larger, more cost-effective shipments. These facilities can help suppliers save money on shipping costs and provide the flexibility of sending smaller, more frequent shipments because their shipments are combined with those of other suppliers. Alba Wine and Spirits Warehousing and Distribution LLC owns and operates a consolidated warehouse in New Jersey. Local wine and spirits producers store their beverages here in a secure, temperature-controlled setting, and Alba also provides order picking service and daily deliveries to the beverage companies' customers in New Jersey, New York, and Connecticut.

- ***Bonded Warehouse.*** Also called a ***customs bonded warehouse***, this is a warehouse facility that stores imported goods until the import duty has been paid. They are found in areas where goods first enter a country, often near international airports and cargo ports. When goods arrive from another country, the company receiving the goods must immediately pay excise taxes and customs duties when the goods cross the international border. However, if a company secures a warehouse bond for potential taxes and duties of future incoming goods, it may temporarily store these foreign goods in a bonded warehouse. A ***warehouse bond*** is a contract between the warehouse operator, the government of the country in which the warehouse is located, and a financial underwriter. The purpose of the bond is to provide financial protection for all parties in the agreement. When its goods are stored in a bonded warehouse, a company may then legally defer taxes or duties until the goods are removed from the warehouse. In addition to being stored, goods can also be sorted, repacked, assembled, or even manufactured in the bonded warehouse. The company that has imported the goods does not have to pay any excise taxes or customs duties until the goods leave the facility. When moving goods internationally, most organizations consider the option of a bonded warehouse to save money because of this deferred payment of import duties and taxes, allowing companies time to find customers for these incoming goods before incurring the financial risk of paying duties and taxes for goods that they may not be able to sell right away.

FUNCTION #5: Automate and Get Smart

- ***Automated Warehouse.*** This is a warehouse facility that automates some or all of the movement, storage, and picking of goods so that machines handle more tasks and fewer rely on manual labor. When all of its operations are automated, it is sometimes called a ***fully automated warehouse***. The software systems and technology required to set up automated warehouses are costly. However, automated warehouses have more reliable order picking accuracy and may be less expensive to operate in the long term than warehouses without automation.

FIGURE 2.14 - SMALL GOODS MOVING ACROSS AUTOMATED WAREHOUSE IN BINS ON CONVEYORS, WHERE HUMAN WORKERS PICK ORDERS AND PUT GOODS INTO ALLOCATED BINS AND AN AUTOMATED CONVEYOR SYSTEM TAKES EACH SET OF GOODS TO SEPARATE AREAS OF THE WAREHOUSE FOR CONSOLIDATION AND PACKING

- *Smart Warehouse.* A smart warehouse is a fully automated warehouse that uses real-time data through artificial intelligence systems and automation technology to achieve optimum efficiency in moving and storing goods. UPS has made a big push to include smart warehouses in their distribution systems through their Warehouse Execution System (WES) that connects their global warehouse network and coordinates with each warehouse's Autonomous Mobile Robots (AMR).

A single warehouse facility might have multiple additional functions and be described using many of the terms covered in this section. For example, you might encounter a *hazardous materials fully automated warehouse*, where hazardous goods are handled by robots and automated machinery instead of human workers, or a *climate-controlled bonded warehouse* for specialty food arriving from overseas. Some organizations may also use the terminology differently and interchangeably, such as different organizations using the terms *distribution center* and *fulfillment center* to refer to the same type of warehouse facility. As with all supply chain terminology, it is best to know how your organization, your customers, and your suppliers each use warehouse terminology for their organizations.

2.6 WAREHOUSE LAYOUT AND FLOW

In Section 1.2 of Chapter 1, we looked at the twelve functions of a warehouse. Let's now consider where some of these functions might take place within one facility or set of warehouse facilities.

To meet a company's needs for inventory receipt, storage, picking, packaging, issue, and dispatch, a company's warehouse typically includes the following areas:

- **Loading bay.** This is the area of a warehouse with external doors where goods are either (1) received into the warehouse from an inbound transportation vehicle, such as a truck or rail car, or (2) moved out from the warehouse onto an outbound vehicle or container. Also called **receiving docks**, **goods-in bays**, **loading docks**, **unloading docks**, or **unloading bays**, loading bays may be flush against the outside wall of the warehouse building or they may be partially to fully enclosed for protection against the elements. *Inbound loading bays* and *outbound loading bays* may be located side-by-side in a warehouse or at opposite ends of the warehouse, depending on the warehouse's needs and the designed flow of goods. To let those on both inside and outside the warehouse know which bay to use, loading bays are typically numbered when there is more than one. They also often have external **indicator lights** resembling stop lights to let drivers know when it is safe to pull into or out from the loading bay.

FIGURE 2.15 - UNCOVERED LOADING BAY IN CANADA (TOP), ENCLOSED LOADING BAY IN A GARAGE IN AUSTRALIA (LEFT), AND CANOPIED LOADING BAY IN SPAIN (RIGHT)

- **Receiving area.** After goods are unloaded from a vehicle through the loading bay, they are temporarily held in this area while the incoming order of goods is checked, inspected by the company's Quality Control department, and then coded and labeled for subsequent storage. This area is also called a **reception area**.

- **Storage area.** After they are inspected and labeled, goods are held in a storage area until an order is received and they are picked. Goods may be held in a storage area for varying amounts of time, from minutes to months. A storage area can include: **floor storage**, where large, bulky items or high volumes of items secured on pallets can be kept; **pallet racks**, where unitized pallets of items are stored; **shelves and bins**, where smaller individual items are kept; and other types of **specialized storage**, such as carousels, refrigerated storage areas, or hazardous materials storage areas.

FIGURE 2.16 - STORAGE AREA OR ORDER PICKING AREA?
IN ALL THREE PHOTOS, IT IS DIFFICULT TO TELL IF THE WAREHOUSE WORKERS ARE PUTTING AWAY GOODS OR PICKING THEM BECAUSE THE ORDER PICKING AREAS AND STORAGE AREAS ARE THE SAME AREAS OF THESE WAREHOUSES!

- **Order picking area.** After an order has been received, goods are selected from this area. In many cases, the *order picking area* and *storage area* may be exactly the same areas of the warehouse, but they may also be opposite aisles flanking the same rows of goods with goods coming in from one side of a shelf and going out from the other side of the shelf. In the case of an automated warehouse, storage and order picking areas may be in separate sections of the warehouse with goods automatically moving from one section to the other as needed.

- *Packing and unitization area.* Goods are packed and placed into unit loads in this area. Outbound orders that have been picked are typically consolidated into containers or onto pallets. This area is also called the *packing and consolidation area*.

- *Staging area.* This is where packed or unitized goods are labeled for issuance to the next destination in the supply chain and held until transportation arrives. It is also called a *dispatch area*. In some warehouses, the *packing and unitization area* and the *staging area* are combined in one location.

When designing a warehouse layout, organizations select the location of each of the sections listed above to achieve a logical, sequential flow of goods. A warehouse's layout should *minimize the manual, mechanical, or automated work needed* to put away and retrieve goods and *maximize warehouse floorspace* for quick and safe movement for all warehouse operations. Depending on the warehouse building, its interior configuration, and the company's warehousing needs, the inbound and outbound loading bays may be located at the same end or, as shown in Figure 2.17, at opposite ends of the warehouse building.

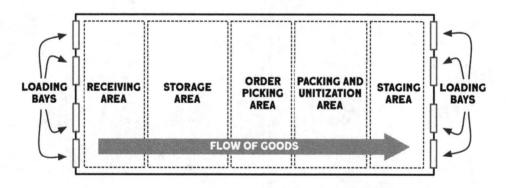

FIGURE 2.17 - WAREHOUSE LAYOUT AND FLOW

One of the primary design and construction factors that affect the efficiency of the entire warehouse operation is the layout. When designing a warehouse layout, the following additional ten factors must be considered to achieve efficient operations overall:

1. **Item Specifications and Handling Requirements.** The range of items to be stored within one warehouse is likely to be quite diverse. Items of similar size and handling requirements tend to be stored together. For example, car tires, light bulbs, and ice cream might all be in the same warehouse but are unlikely to be stored in the same locations.

2. **Frequency of Issue.** Different items and categories of items held in a warehouse are usually *issued* (pulled out of storage and given to its requester) at different rates of frequency. If frequency of issue is not considered when planning a warehouse layout, the problem of **honeycombing** can arise, in which slow-moving inventory items are scattered in different places throughout the warehouse, taking up valuable space in an uneven and random manner. Materials that are constantly being delivered and issued should typically be placed closer to ends of aisles and warehouse entrances and exits. This method of placement reduces the handling times of these high usage materials and minimizes traveling time for inventory pickers. The same logic applies to medium and low usage rate materials, with less frequently delivered and issued inventory located progressively further away from the ends of aisles and warehouse entrances and exits. When considering the importance of *frequency of use*, it is connected less to **volume**, or how much of the item is put away and retrieved, but is related much more to **hits**, or the number of times an item is requested and the number of trips needed to retrieve or put away the item.

3. **Space Optimization.** To avoid current and future issues of crowding and congestion, warehouse layout designers must consider how to use the space available. To optimize valuable warehouse floor space, layout designers consider: (1) the use of *mezzanines and racking*; (2) *ceiling height*, not only for the product, but for stacked pallets of products; and (3) *aisle width*. One thing to keep in mind about ceiling height is that goods stored at spaces over 30 feet high might not be able to be retrieved using lift trucks and will instead need automated storage and retrieval systems. In addition, many warehouses have traditionally set aisles at fourteen feet wide, but narrower, twelve-foot aisles can be considered because aisles should only be as wide as necessary without taking up unnecessary floor space.

4. **Loading Bays.** Depending upon how frequently inventory is issued and received, the size and number of loading bays required will vary across organizations and their warehouses. Smaller warehouses may have only one inbound loading bay and one outbound loading bay located side by side. Larger, more complex warehouses have multiple loading bays, often with each handling different types of incoming and outgoing inventory and assigned corresponding specialized materials handling equipment.

5. **Equipment Maneuvering Space Needed.** In all warehouse layout design, one factor that must be considered is the amount of space needed to safely and effectively move and maneuver materials handling equipment. Sufficient space is needed for maneuvering equipment when loaded to maximum capacity while maintaining safe walkways for warehouse pedestrians.

6. **Office Accommodation.** Inclusion of effectively placed office accommodation is a critical but easily overlooked component on any warehouse's layout. The office is the management and information center for the entire warehouse and materials handling operation and thus demands a central location from which almost all operations can be viewed. Warehouse offices are sometimes built on mezzanines, allowing

underutilized vertical space to be used and providing a bird's-eye view of warehouse operations.

7. **Gangways and Access.** In order to keep all who enter and work in the warehouse safe from injury, location and types of gangways and pedestrian access must be considered in warehouse layout, especially as they relate to materials handling equipment and procedures. Government regulations, such the U.S. Occupational Safety and Health Administration (OSHA) standards in the Code of Federal Regulations (CFR), require that there are permanent, often require clear, lighted, and marked walkways so that pedestrians can find the warehouse exit in case of an emergency.

8. **Electric Charging Points.** If battery powered lift trucks and other rechargeable materials handling equipment will be used, warehouse layout designers must consider strategic placement of maintenance and charging points so that the equipment can be charged and accessed easily and safely. These areas should typically be in well ventilated, dry, dust-free locations that are not near flammable goods.

9. **Structural Limitations and Immovable Obstacles.** Although they may keep you from achieving your dream layout, structural limitations and immovable obstacles are a reality of both newly constructed and converted warehouse buildings. Such obstacles that must be considered in warehouse layout design include support pillars and warehouse floor weight-bearing limitations.

10. **Current and Future Automation Needs.** Many warehouses are moving toward automation. Much of this automation equipment and warehouse management systems equipment will have specific space and environmental conditions requirements, such as the clear vertical space needed for automated storage and retrieval systems or if there is enough floorspace for both robot areas and pedestrian walkways. Even if a company has not yet automated its warehouse, it must consider future automation possibilities when planning for warehouse layout.

CHAPTER 2 REVIEW QUESTIONS

1. What is the difference between *warehouse height* and *clear height*? Why is this difference important?

2. Why are you more likely to find a *nano warehouse* in the middle of Tokyo than in the middle of a rural farming community in Nebraska?

3. I have just launched a small business that makes mobile standing desks called Desk-A-Go-Go. I make the desks in my garage and currently only have a few customers. I want to make a wide range of desks of different sizes before I start marketing to new potential customers, but I have no room in my garage to store the desks. Which type of warehouse ownership classification might be the best for my business right now? Why?

4. In which situation might a company opt for a *single-story warehouse building*? In which situation might the same company opt for a *multi-story building*?

5. What is *the last mile*? Why is it important when considering warehouse location?

6. List five different types of items that could be stored in an *external inventory yard*. List five different types of items that should not be stored in an external inventory yard.

7. Which three types of warehouse facilities help a company keep goods moving and shorten storage times? Provide a brief explanation of each type.

8. What is the difference between a *transloading facility* and a *cross-docking facility*?

9. In your own words, describe each of the six areas of a warehouse in a single sentence.

10. If an item in a warehouse is one that is frequently picked, where should it be located within the warehouse? Please explain your answer.

CHAPTER 2 CASE EXERCISE

WHERE TO PUT A WAREHOUSE

Earlier in Chapter 2, we learned that companies decide *where* to put their warehouses based on the advantages that a location offers, such as proximity to a major highway or an available workforce. When a company has an existing network of warehouses and needs to add a new warehouse to handle its volume of goods, the company can select a location in that will offer the lowest transportation costs. In this situation, a mathematical method of analysis called the ***center of gravity method*** is used to find a location that offers the lowest overall transportation costs between the links in its supply chain. In this case, it is used to find a warehouse location by taking into account the locations of the current network of warehouses and the volume of goods being handled by each of those warehouses.

Now it's time for you to be the expert! You work for a company called New England Edible Eggs that distributes edible eggs from a wide range of birds, reptiles, and fish to specialty grocery stores, food manufacturers, and restaurants. New England Edible Eggs currently has four warehouses that handle 20,000 crates of eggs per day, but it needs to set up a fifth warehouse for more efficient operations at this volume and to be closer to customers so the delicate eggs can be delivered as quickly and as safely as possible. All four current warehouse locations are shown in the map below.

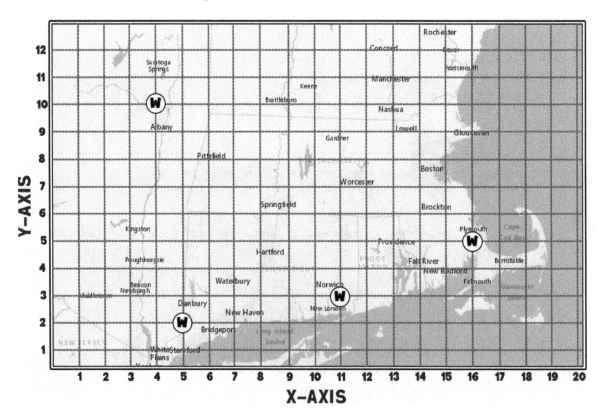

As shown in the table below, each warehouse location corresponds to a grid value on the x-axis and y-axis on the map. Also listed is the volume of crates of eggs that each warehouse distributes on a daily basis.

WAREHOUSE (NEAREST CITY)	X–AXIS COORDINATE	Y–AXIS COORDINATE	VOLUME – OUTGOING CRATES (DAILY)
ALBANY	4	10	8000
DANBURY	5	2	3000
NORWICH	11	3	6000
PLYMOUTH	16	5	3000

To calculate the optimal location for a fifth warehouse to reduce transportation costs and work within the existing network of warehouse and the volume of items they handle, you can use a simple center of gravity location analysis based on the following formulae:

$$Cx = \sum (Wix * Vi) / \sum Vi$$

$$Cy = \sum (Wiy * Vi) / \sum Vi$$

You are solving for the map coordinates of your new ideal warehouse location. **Cx** is the x-axis coordinate on your map and **Cy** is the y-axis coordinate on your map for the ideal new warehouse location based on the location and volume of the outgoing handled by the existing warehouses. **Wix** is the x-axis coordinate for each existing warehouse and **Wiy** is the y-axis coordinate for each existing warehouse. **Vi** is the volume of outgoing product for each warehouse.

Using the values from the table above, you can now calculate Cx to find the x-axis coordinate for your new warehouse location!

$$Cx = \sum (Wix * Vi) / \sum Vi$$

$$= ((4 \times 8000) + (5 \times 3000) + (11 \times 6000) + (16 \times 3000)) / (8000 + 3000 + 6000 + 3000)$$

$$= (32{,}000 + 15{,}000 + 66{,}000 + 48{,}000) / (20{,}000)$$

$$= 161{,}000 / 20{,}000 = 8.05$$

Rounding to the nearest whole number, you have found that Cx, or the x-axis coordinate for your new warehouse location, is **8**.

You can now use the y-axis values from the table above to calculate Cy to find the y-axis coordinate for your new warehouse location.

$$Cy = \sum (Wiy * Vi) / \sum Vi$$

$$= ((10 \times 8000) + (2 \times 3000) + (3 \times 6000) + (5 \times 3000)) / (8000 + 3000 + 6000 + 3000)$$

$$= (80{,}000 + 6{,}000 + 18{,}000 + 15{,}000) / (20{,}000) = 119{,}000 / 20{,}000 = 5.95$$

Rounding to the nearest whole number, you have found that **Cy**, or the y-axis coordinate for your new warehouse location, is **6**. With the map coordinates of **(8,6)**, you have determined that your new warehouse location should be just southwest of Springfield!

The center of gravity location analysis doesn't provide all of the location solutions a company will need. Companies will also have to see if there are major transportations networks, such as highways or rail lines, near their desired location. They will also have to see if there are buildings or land available in the area to set up a new warehouse. Although it doesn't provide the entire solution, the center of gravity analysis can be a useful tool for helping companies hone in on a potential warehouse location that can reduce transportation costs.

INSTRUCTIONS:

1. Looking at the map provided below, what kinds of areas would a company completely eliminate if a calculation determined that a warehouse should be there?

2. You now work for Walter's Wonderful Wildlife Woolies, a seller and distributer of woolen socks for humans, dogs, and barnyard animals. Walter's has three warehouse facilities in the northeastern area of the United States. However, the volume of sales has increased and another warehouse facility is needed in the area. The volumes of outgoing inventory for its three current warehouse facilities are: Saratoga Springs - 70,000 pallets; Newburgh - 100,000 pallets, and Rochester - 30,000 pallets. Using this data and the coordinates from the map below, create a table of coordinates and volume by city like the one shown earlier in the case exercise.

3. Using the data from your table and the Cx and Cy formulae for the center of gravity analysis, find the coordinates and closest city for a new warehouse.

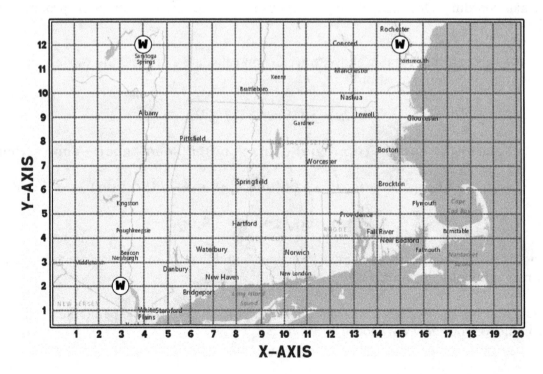

Chapter 3

Introducing Inventory

We began with the concept of *warehousing* in Chapter 1 and *warehouses* in Chapter 2. Now it's time to move through the inbound, internal, and outbound processes of warehouse management, from inventory receipt to packing and distribution. This chapter focuses on the *inventory* that is managed throughout these processes and the initial exciting world of the *inbound processes* of warehouse management, when inventory makes its first introduction to the warehouse.

3.1 WHAT'S IN A WAREHOUSE?

So what is in a warehouse? Just about anything and everything! When we talk about the contents of a warehouse, we typically mean its *inventory*, which is essentially all the stuff in a warehouse needed to create a company's goods or services except for the equipment used to store or move goods. For a more formal definition, **inventory** is the collection of goods, materials, and physical resources held by a company or organization, typically in warehouse facilities, distribution centers, fulfillment centers, or external inventory yards. Inventory found in a warehouse includes items from any of the following five categories:

1. ***raw materials.*** Also called ***commodities***, raw materials are unprocessed or minimally processed goods used to make other goods. Examples of raw materials include raw timber for a furniture manufacturer, oranges for an orange juice producer, and grain for a flour manufacturer.

2. ***semifinished goods***. Also known as ***intermediate goods***, semifinished goods are goods produced to be used in the manufacture or production of other goods, such as lumber, sheet metal, flour, and orange juice concentrate. These goods are no longer raw materials but are not quite yet fully assembled, produced, or manufactured. A subcategory of semifinished goods is ***work-in-process***, which includes partially finished goods. Examples of work-in-process goods are lumber cut, shaped, and sanded to be used in bookshelf production; crates of programmed computer chips to be placed in automobiles being assembled; and barrels of non-carbonated syrup base for soft drink bottling.

Sometimes it is economically advantageous for companies to transport and hold work-in-process until these goods are closer to the customer for final assembly or production. In our soft drink example, it is more economically advantageous for a company to ship the work-in-process syrup base of a carbonated drink to a bottling plant overseas than to ship finished bottles and cans of the drink. Shipping cost would be doubled or tripled when shipping the finished soda because it would weigh more and take up more space than the proprietary syrup used to produce the soda. In addition, some companies transport and hold work-in-process to postpone finishing final production of goods so they can be customized for specific regional needs or individual customer preferences.

3. ***finished goods.*** These goods are the fully assembled, produced, or manufactured items to be sold or delivered to a customer. Examples of finished goods include boxes of Quaker chocolate chip granola bars, Huffy bikes rolling off the assembly line, and 3/8" screws used in toy assembly with a toy manufacturer as the final customer. As the final example shows us, the *customer* of a finished goods is not always a person who is an end user. The finished goods' customer can also be another company that will be using these goods for their own operations or manufacturing process. Even another department within the same finished goods company can be the customer of those finished goods.

4. ***MRO supplies.*** Also known as ***maintenance, repair, and operating supplies***, MRO supplies are goods essential to the operation of an organization but not used to become part of its finished products. Examples of MRO supplies include cleaning liquids, machine parts and oils, manufacturing equipment replacement hardware, paper for company offices, light bulbs for a warehouse, and stretch wrap for packing goods.

5. ***Capital goods.*** The physical, durable assets used in the production, manufacture, or movement of other goods or in the support of a company's operations or services are called capital goods. These are manufactured items that are expected to last for a long time or for many uses. Examples of capital goods include machinery, equipment, buildings, and vehicles.

FIGURE 3.1 - FIVE CATEGORIES OF INVENTORY FOUND IN A WAREHOUSE

The five categories of inventory listed above can be found in a warehouse. One category of inventory not found in a warehouse is **distribution channel inventory**, which refers to any items and components located in the distribution system. These are likely to also fall into any of the five previous categories of inventory, but the important distinction is that they are not in static storage but are in movement in the distribution system, often on the way to or from a warehouse.

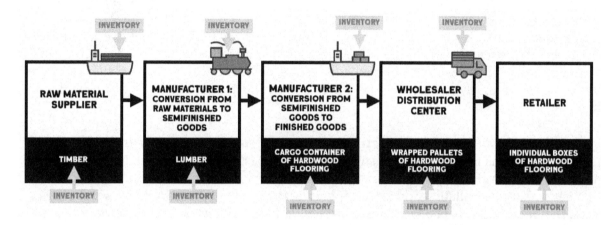

FIGURE 3.2 - INVENTORY IN THE SUPPLY CHAIN

As shown in Figure 3.2, inventory can be found throughout a product's entire supply chain, from the suppliers of raw materials to the finished goods being delivered to a final customer. The range, value, and complexity of items held by any particular warehouse will depend upon the size and complexity of the operations involved. For example, picture the difference between the inventory of a lumberyard and the inventory of a luxury automobile manufacturer's warehouse. Warehouses and their corresponding operations and inventory can vary greatly, so warehouse managers and staff need to have an extensive knowledge of a large number of material types and operations. However, no matter what type of inventory or warehouse is involved, one common term that you must know in the world of warehousing is **SKU**, or **stock keeping unit**, which refers to a distinct type of item held in inventory. In a coffee retailer's warehouse, for example, each size and type of container of coffee will have a unique SKU, which means that the SKU for the one pound bag of the decaf Sumatra-blend coffee is different from the SKU for the two pound bag of the decaf Sumatra-blend coffee.

Inventory and inventory holding are critical to an organization's ability to produce quality goods and deliver them to customers in a timely manner. For example, if a carbonated soft drink bottling plant did not hold an inventory of bottle caps, the drink would lose its defining fizz with bottles sitting idly, waiting for caps to be produced as they are needed. Therefore, let's charge forth and learn more about *inventory*!

3.2 INVENTORY TERMINOLOGY AND MANAGEMENT

Understanding the primary types of inventory can also help us understand the importance of holding inventory. The two primary types of inventory are: *cycle inventory* and *safety inventory*.

Cycle inventory, also called **cycle stock**, **cycle stock inventory**, or **working inventory**, is the inventory that is most often "in action." Goods in cycle inventory are continuously issued and replenished. Their holding times are typically brief and temporary. In the warehouses and distribution centers of a large one-stop retailer like Walmart, cycle inventory might include loaves of bread, toothpaste, and the latest in t-shirt fashions. These items are continuously sent to Walmart stores because customers are buying them and they must be replenished.

Safety inventory, also called **safety stock**, **safety stock inventory**, or **buffer stock**, is inventory that is held and used as supply and demand dictate. These are the extra quantities of items held to protect an organization from losses that might be incurred from fluctuating supply availability or customer and market demands. Again in the warehouses and distribution centers of a large one-stop retailer like Walmart, safety inventory might include umbrellas, which would be sold in stores even on the sunniest days but might get a sudden surge in demand due to unexpected rainstorms. Another example of safety inventory could be an expensive new toy, which is so new that its demand patterns are not yet known. The retailer would want to keep safety inventory of this new toy in case it becomes an overnight sensation and begins to fly off the shelves. If the retailer didn't have safety inventory of this item, it could miss out on potential profits from lost sales opportunities.

Although *cycle inventory* and *safety inventory* are categorized as different types of inventory, they can be the same goods held in the same location. For example, the umbrellas that were an example of safety inventory because of weather-based surges in demand are also an example of cycle inventory. The store would have a steady, predictable demand for umbrellas and would need to replenish these umbrellas on store shelves regularly. Cycle and safety inventory quantities are determined, contained, and tracked within warehousing or inventory management information systems.

A few additional terms commonly associated with types of inventory are:

- ***anticipation inventory.*** Also called **anticipation stock**, this is a form of safety inventory in which raw materials, semifinished goods, or finished goods are held in anticipation of a particular event that will occur, such as an upcoming holiday or a supplier phasing out a product line. Examples of anticipation inventory might be candy and costumes before Halloween and beer and salty snack foods before the Super Bowl or World Cup Finals.

- ***hedge inventory.*** Also called **hedging stock**, this is another form of safety inventory in which raw materials, semifinished goods, or finished goods are held in anticipation of an event that may or may not occur, such as a forecasted weather pattern, a potential increase in gasoline prices, a potential plant shutdown for a nearby supplier, or a potential transportation worker strike. For example, most large home improvement and grocery stores carry a hedge inventory of snow shovels when television meteorologists forecast large winter storm fronts approaching.

- **allocated inventory.** This type of inventory is assigned to and held for specific customers based on their orders or regular purchase patterns. For example, in some areas of large home improvement stores, you may see flat carts and pallets piled high with stretch-wrapped items, labeled with codes allocated to specific business customers, such as building contractors or plumbing businesses.

- **decoupling inventory.** This is another form of safety inventory in which work-in-process goods are held at work stations within a manufacturing or assembling facility. These work-in-process goods are held to prevent operations from slowing down or halting entirely when delays occur, such as expected delays caused by shift changes and employee training or unexpected delays caused by machine failure or worker injury.

FIGURE 3.3 - EXAMPLE OF DECOUPLING INVENTORY:
ASSEMBLED BICYCLE WHEELS IN BACKGROUND AT BICYCLE ASSEMBLY FACILITY

- **pipeline inventory.** Also called **transportation inventory**, this is a form of cycle inventory that includes the raw materials, semifinished goods, or finished goods that are in transit or "in the pipeline." This is the same inventory we referred to earlier as *distribution channel inventory*, but the terminology *pipeline inventory* is the one often used in inventory efficiency studies of finished goods, focusing on the amounts of time inventory spends in transit throughout different segments of its transportation pipeline.

Much of the inventory terminology above deals with having enough inventory to keep companies from having to go through the costly process of shutting down operations because they don't have enough inventory on hand. Inventory is also managed to help companies reduce their inventory holding costs. When practicing **inventory management**, an organization tracks its inventory levels and determines the amount of inventory of raw materials, semifinished goods, finished goods, and supplies that should be held in storage to keep the organization operating most efficiently and effectively as it faces fluctuating supply availability, changing customer demands, and an array of anticipated and unanticipated events. Throughout a supply chain, inventory management is typically conducted using a variety of technological hardware for gathering counting and tracking data and software systems for managing and analyzing this inventory data.

Inventory management can provide a company many benefits, including benefits which act in conflict with one another. Benefits of inventory management include:

- **Increased Customer Service.** When organizations don't practice inventory management, they often maintain a stock of excess inventory to try ensure that customers get the goods they want without having a long wait while additional quantities are ordered or produced. This doesn't always work and companies may either not have enough of an item customers want or they may have too much of an item, costing the company more money in purchasing too much of an item and in having to store all these extra items. When implementing inventory management, however, companies can use demand forecasting to reduce inventory levels held while maintaining the same timeliness of delivery to customers. They can determine how much of an items is needed and when it will be needed. In addition, companies can pass savings on to their customers with guaranteed deliveries, meaning that their customers don't have to hold their own excess safety inventory.

- **Increased Efficiency.** Organizations can use inventory management to help them achieve greater efficiency in production and purchasing operations. For example, inventory management can help organizations determine the most efficient production run sizes, or *how many products to manufacture*, based on customer demand forecasts and cost efficiencies to be achieved from longer runs of the same product. Similarly, inventory management can help organizations determine the most efficient purchasing volumes, or *how many supplies to order*, based on forecasted amounts of supplies actually needed and discounts offered by suppliers for purchasing bulk volumes.

- **Reduced Cost.** As previously mentioned, organizations can use inventory management to help reduce operating costs. Holding excess inventory across its supply chain creates negative cash flow and drains a company of potential profits. Companies use effective inventory management systems every day to mitigate these potentially disastrous effects by enabling companies to only hold the amount of inventory that they need.

Inventory management plays a balancing act between the needs of those in an organization's operations and marketing departments and those in its finance department. The inventory goals of those in operations and marketing are to hold enough inventory or even more than enough inventory to maintain a constant production and inventory flow to meet customers' demands and to keep sufficient safety inventory levels to cover anticipated events and unforeseen demands. Conversely, the inventory goal of those in the finance department is to minimize inventory levels as much as possible to minimize holding costs. *Inventory management* and *inventory control systems* balance these conflicting needs to achieve optimum inventory efficiency levels. (We'll learn more about inventory control systems in Chapter 7.)

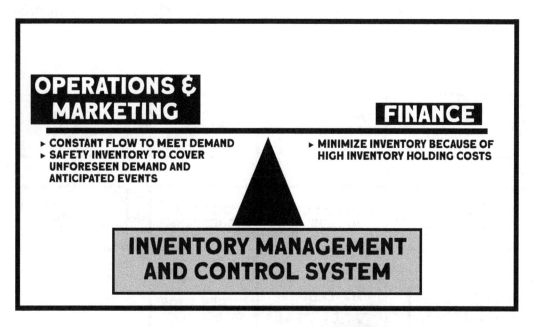

FIGURE 3.4 - BALANCING ACT BETWEEN THE NEEDS OF OPERATIONS/MARKETING AND FINANCE

When goods start rolling in through the doors of your warehouse, you need to examine how you will control this incoming inventory. Within a warehouse, the ***inventory receipt team*** is responsible for receiving all materials and items supplied to the organization, both from internal transfers within the organization and from external sources, such as deliveries from suppliers. Whether the incoming goods are from an internal or external source, the inventory receipt team has many specific tasks it must complete, including:

- **engaging in the inventory receipt process**

- **planning for incoming inventory and unloading inventory when goods arrive**

- **handling all accompanying inventory documentation**

- **inspecting inventory as part of the inventory receipt process**

- **coding incoming inventory**

3.3 THE INVENTORY RECEIPT PROCESS

The inventory receipt team of an organization typically follows a standard and logical sequence of events, known as the **inventory receipt process**, the **inventory receipt cycle**, or the **inventory receipt cycle process**. Each stage of the inventory receipt process is important for efficient and cost effective inventory management. Each stage must also be carefully controlled and supervised by the warehouse. Eleven uniquely important stages of this process are:

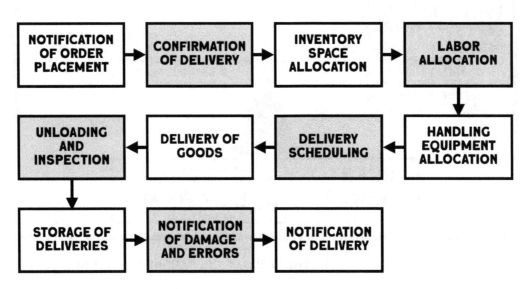

FIGURE 3.5 - THE INVENTORY RECEIPT PROCESS

1. **Notification of Order Placement.** In this stage of the inventory receipt process, the purchasing department notifies the warehouse that goods have been ordered and that a provisional delivery date and method of delivery have been set. Warehouse managers can then make provisional plans within the inventory receipt portion of the company's inventory management software or warehouse management software. Even when things are done automatically within computer systems, it is important for warehouse managers to check and verify the details of orders, especially larger orders. Imagine the chaos of a container load of eggs arriving at a Florida warehouse on a hot August day with no available loading dock to receive them or nowhere to put them because of a delayed repair on a malfunctioning warehouse loading bay door.

2. **Confirmation of Delivery.** In this second stage of the inventory receipt process, the warehouse confirms the upcoming delivery date, time, and contents with the distributor, who may be either internal or external to the organization. This allows the warehouse manager to make definite arrangements for the delivery within the warehouse, especially if any last minute changes have been made.

3. **Inventory Space Allocation.** After the delivery has been confirmed, the warehouse manager then ensures that sufficient space has been allocated within the warehouse for this new delivery, which may include inventory rearrangement. Space allocation is vital if double handling and extra warehouse labor time are to be avoided.

4. **Labor Allocation.** In almost every situation, inventory unloading requires some degree of manual or mechanical handling. In some cases, a large number of staff may be needed. The warehouse manager makes plans to ensure that the necessary amount of staff will be available at the time of delivery.

5. **Materials Handling Equipment Allocation.** The warehouse manager also needs to plan for the materials handling equipment to be used during inventory unloading and storage. Certain types of materials and packaging will require specialized materials handling equipment to unload and store them properly. For example, palletized goods require forklift trucks. The warehouse manager must ensure that this equipment is allocated and ready and that trained and licensed equipment operators are available.

6. **Delivery Scheduling.** Upon confirmation of delivery and simultaneously with stages 3, 4, and 5 above, scheduling the delivery of the goods into the warehouse's operating calendar is the sixth step of the inventory receipt process. Proper scheduling enables deliveries to be handled using the full resources of the warehouse operation. The ideal schedule provides a steady stream of well-timed deliveries throughout the warehouse's working day to maximize the use of both available warehouse loading bays, staff, and handling equipment.

7. **Delivery of Goods**. At this stage of the inventory receipt cycle, the goods finally arrive at the warehouse. Someone from the inventory receipt team checks the delivery note against the inventory supplied. If the warehouse is not able to check a load, perhaps if it is undermanned or experiencing too many simultaneous deliveries, the delivery document must be signed and the word *unchecked* must be written so that any claim for shortage or damage will not be complicated by a delivery note signature alone, which typically indicates that the delivery was received and checked as acceptable.

8. **Unloading and Inspection.** This eighth stage of the inventory receipt process is unloading and inspecting the inventory delivered. This eighth step is so important that multiple portions of subsequent sections of this book are devoted to it, including Section 3.6 in this chapter.

9. **Storage of Deliveries.** After the goods have been delivered, unloaded, and inspected, they must then be stored. Some incoming goods may be stored in the same form as they are delivered, such as a palletized load of 2-gallon bottles of laundry detergent that will be moved by a forklift and stored on a warehouse shelf as-is. Other deliveries may have to be broken down into smaller units and then stored on the shelves, bins, racks, or whatever storage equipment is available and most appropriate. As will be explained further in this chapter in Section 3.7, before goods are put away, they are often assigned internal codes and given a barcode or QR code sticker to help with internal inventory management. Goods are then ready to be placed in their correct storage location so that

the entire inventory issuance and checking system is not adversely affected. This stage is covered in greater detail in Chapter 4, "Storage and Putaway."

10. **Notification of Damages, Shortages, or Errors.** As goods are received and stored, warehouse personnel sometimes uncover damage, shortages, or errors. When this happens, warehouse management must send a notification of the damage, shortage, or error to the purchasing, production planning, quality control, and inventory control or records departments.

11. **Notification of Delivery.** In addition to notification of damages, shortages, and errors, the warehouse must notify interested internal departments that the goods have been delivered and accepted as inventory. These interested departments, including the purchasing, production planning, quality control, and inventory records departments, can check their records and make adjustments as necessary to note the increase in inventory.

The eleven stages of the inventory receipt cycle process outlined above are standard for most warehouse situations. Depending on the nature of the organization, its products, the goods being delivered, and the warehouse itself, there is a range of other elements, which may also influence the inventory receipt process., such as *special deliveries*, *special handling*, *communications* between the Warehouse and Purchasing departments, and *internal transfers*.

In some instances, different arrangements may need to be made for certain types of ***special deliveries*** and materials. An example of such an arrangement might be to accommodate a delivery outside of normal working hours, such as nighttime deliveries for unusually large items to avoid roadway and warehouse traffic and congestion. In addition, some materials, such as hazardous explosives and chemicals, may require ***special handling*** upon receipt into the warehouse. These instances require careful planning by warehouse managers to ensure that all preparations and safety measures are taken to reduce the risk of accident or damage.

During the inventory receipt cycle process, sound and meaningful ***communication*** between the warehouse and the purchasing department is vital. Purchasing must keep the warehouse fully informed of all developments concerning inventory delivery. Changes in delivery schedules occur often due to factors beyond the control of the supplier or buyer. Unless the warehouse is advised of these changes, much preparation and work will go to waste and the warehouse will continue to work to a schedule that has no real meaning, making management of the whole operation very difficult. It is equally vital for the warehouse to inform the purchasing department immediately of any faults, shortages, or errors made by the supplier so that the purchasing department can contact the supplier immediately to arrange for a new delivery. If the warehouse does not contact them, those in the purchasing department may incorrectly assume that all went well with the delivery and thus take no action. Even when automated systems may handle this communication between departments, it is important to understand the culture of your organization and know when human-to-human communication is needed.

While the importance of open and continuous communication between the warehouse and purchasing departments is undeniable, different organizations have different ways of achieving this desired communication. For example, the Goose Creek Consolidated independent School District in Texas decided to combine both the warehouse and purchasing functions under the heading of Purchasing & Warehouse Operations, with all warehouse communications going through the Director, as shown in a portion of the school district's organization chart in Figure 3.6.

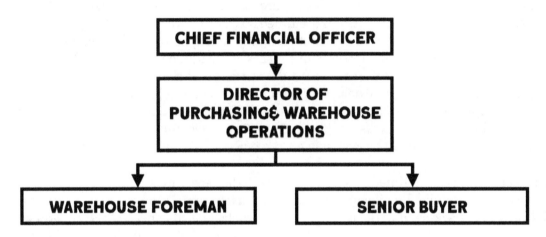

FIGURE 3.6 - WHAT THEY DID IN TEXAS

The final item in our list of elements that influence the inventory receipt process is the **internal transfer**, which is the process of moving inventory from one location to another within the organization. Each location, such as a depot or warehouse, may have its own inventory record and inventory control system, making properly documented control of inventory transfer a necessity. One important part of internal transfers is the **internal transfer note**, the standard document used to transfer inventory and check all internal deliveries. The internal transfer note is very similar to the supplier's delivery note, as described in Section 3.5 of this chapter.

3.4 PLANNING FOR AND UNLOADING INVENTORY

One of the key activities of warehouse management is getting goods into and out from the warehouse facility. Getting goods into a warehouse facility is called **inventory receipt** and getting goods out from a warehouse facility is called *distribution*, which we will cover in greater detail in Chapter 9, "Distribution."

Inventory receipt involves activities as simple as receiving and signing for a single package from a delivery person to activities as complex as unloading endless streams of trucks and railroad cars into a cross-docking distribution center for subsequent sorting and delivery while continually checking the accompanying documentation to make sure that the tens of thousands of items being received are the ones that were actually ordered. The more goods a company receives, the more likely it is to have a ***shipping and receiving department***, a department in an organization dedicated solely to making sure the inventory receipt process is followed efficiently and effectively. This department manages the flow of goods into and out from warehouse facilities, keeps track of who owns the goods at which stage of the process, and keeps accurate inventory control records of the goods.

The receiving and shipping department also holds a tight control over the schedule of incoming receipts. They must work with the purchasing department to make sure that the flows of goods into warehouse facilities are timed so that the warehouse docks aren't cluttered with too many trucks and truck drivers idly sitting in line racking up unnecessary cost in labor hours. In addition, if trucks or railcars are held too long at a warehouse facility, the organization may incur ***detention and demurrage charges***, which are extra fees charged by the shipper for these delays. Warehouses also have a limited amount of materials handling equipment to move goods from the trucks or trains into the warehouse or onto other trucks in the case of a cross-docking facility. Deliveries must be timed to make sure that handling equipment will be available for the type and amount of incoming inventory.

Even when deliveries are timed and scheduled well, the receiving and shipping department must also plan for individual incoming delivery vehicles. Some trucks may need assistance and direction in backing in to the assigned dock. Trucks may also need ***dock levelers***, which the trucks drive onto to ensure that the floor of the truck's trailer is level with the warehouse floor. Imagine having to drive a forklift or wheel a hand truck into a truck that is eight inches below the surface of the warehouse floor! Warehouse receiving personnel should also check to make sure that truck drivers place ***chocks***, wooden or metal barriers, against the truck's tires to prevent it from moving while it is parked in the warehouse dock. Finally, warehouse receipt personnel must do an initial inspection of goods in the truck or train car to make sure there is not major damage, deterioration, contamination, or insect infestations before unloading it into the warehouse. Imagine a warehouse worker forgetting this step as damp and roach-infested bags of sugar are unloaded into a doughnut factory!

When a truck or rail car arrives at the warehouse loading dock, goods must be unloaded from the container or truck and placed into inventory in the warehouse facility. Depending on the needs of the company receiving the goods, either the people delivering the goods unload them or the company receiving the goods has their own crew to handle all unloading. For example, if heavy goods are received that need forklifts to get them out of the truck, the company receiving them may want their own forklift-trained drivers to handle all unloading. In especially busy facilities, such as larger distribution centers and cross-docking facilities, drivers delivering goods may drop off the trailers and detach them from their trucks so that they can be on their way to work on other deliveries. This leaves the company receiving the goods to unload them when they are ready.

When companies receive goods into a warehouse facility, they are not always placed immediately into the far reaches of the warehouse shelves. Instead, goods are first unloaded into a ***staging area***, which is often located close to the bays where goods are received. Items remain here until they are inspected and checked formally by the quality control department, which we'll learn more about in Section 3.6 of this chapter.

3.5 INVENTORY DOCUMENTATION

One vital element of the inventory receipt process is **documentation**. Organizations engaged in any aspect of warehouse management develop a comprehensive set of documents to facilitate the control of the inventory receipt process. Each of these documents has a specific and important role to play. Although documents will vary as individual organizations develop them to meet their own unique needs and companies may have digital or paper-based documents, the logic behind inventory receipt documentation remains constant. Examples of categories of inventory receipt documents include: *Bill of Lading, Need to Reorder Notification, Purchase Order Copies, Advice Note of Intended Delivery, Delivery Note, 3rd Party Carrier's Consignment Note, Internal Packing Note*, and *Receiver Report*. These documents may have different names in different countries and even in different companies within the same country, but the concepts are the same. As we explore each of these document categories below, you will see that documentation may occur in a variety of forms, from cloud-based digital forms to paper hard copy varieties. Despite the fact that the documentation of larger companies is almost entirely digital, many small- to medium-sized companies still rely heavily on a mix of digital and paper-based documentation.

> **Bill of Lading.** Also referred to as **BOL** or **B/L**, a bill of lading is a document issued by a shipper. The shipper may either be the supplier of the goods or a third party logistics service provider. The document acknowledges that specific, listed goods have been received as cargo for conveyance to a specific, listed place for delivery to an identified consignee. This is one of the most important documents in the inventory receipt process because it serves as proof of acceptance and controls the acceptance, transport, and delivery of goods. The Bill of Lading contains a wealth of information about the shipment, including: *shipment date and weight, order number, city of shipment origin, whether or not the shipment charges have been prepaid, the shipper's identification information, the destination name and address, a BOL tracking number*, and *special handling and payment instructions*.

> **Need to Reorder Notification.** This notification is typically created by an organization's inventory control or inventory records department. It is sent to the purchasing department, who uses the information on the *need to reorder notification* to place orders with the appropriate suppliers. The warehouse is also typically sent a copy of this notification so that it is aware of the impending inventory delivery, even though it may be a long time for some orders to actually arrive at the warehouse.

> **Purchase Order Copies.** A **purchase order**, also called a **PO**, is a signed, legally binding document outlining a purchase agreement between a buyer and a supplier. Copies of the purchase order are also sent to the warehouse receiving area with information including: *the code number and description of goods, quantity ordered, method of delivery, required delivery date, the purchase order number, date of order placement, the supplier's name and address*, and *special instructions for inventory receipt and quality control inspections*. The price of items is not typically included in the purchase order copies sent to the warehouse.

U.S. GOVERNMENT BILL OF LADING
INTERNATIONAL AND DOMESTIC OVERSEAS SHIPMENTS

B/L NUMBER

TRANSPORTATION COMPANY TENDERED TO | SCAC | DATE B/L PREPARED

DESTINATION NAME AND ADDRESS | SPLC *(Dest.)* | ORIGIN NAME AND ADDRESS

SPLC *(Orig.)*

CONSIGNEE *(Name and full address of installation)* | GBLOC *(Cons.)* | SHIPPER NAME AND ADDRESS

APPROPRIATION CHARGEABLE | BILL CHARGES TO *(Dept./agency, bureau/office mailing address and ZIP code)* | AGENCY LOC CODE

VIA *(Route shipment when advantageous to the Government)*

MARKS AND ANNOTATIONS

PACKAGES		HM	DESCRIPTION OF ARTICLES *(Use carrier's classification or tariff description if possible; otherwise use a clear nontechnical description.)*	19. WEIGHTS* *(Pounds only)*	FOR USE OF BILLING CARRIER ONLY		
NO.	KIND				Services	Rate	Charges
			CLASSIFICATION ITEM NO.		TOTAL CHARGES		

TARIFF/SPECIAL RATE AUTHORITY | CARRIER WAY/FREIGHT BILL NO. AND DATE

STOP THIS SHIPMENT AT

FOR

FURNISH INFORMATION ON CAR/TRUCKLOAD/CONTAINER SHIPMENTS

SEAL NUMBERS	LENGTH/CUBE		MARKED CAPACITY		DATE FURNISHED
	ORDERED	FURNISHED	ORDERED	FURNISHED	
APPLIED BY:					

CARRIER'S PICKUP DATE *(Year, month, and day)*

MODE | ESTIMATE | NO. OF CLS/TLS | TYPE RATE | PSC | REASON

This U.S. Government shipment is subject to terms and conditions of 41 CFR 102-117 and CFR 102-118.

CERTIFICATE OF CARRIER BILLING -- CONSIGNEE MUST NOT PAY ANY CHARGES

DELIVERED ON *(Year, month, and day)*

FOR USE OF ISSUING OFFICE

ISSUING OFFICE *(Name and complete address)* | GBLOC | ISSUING OFFICER

CONTRACT/PURCHASE ORDER NO. OR OTHER AUTHORITY | DATED

FOB POINT NAMED IN CONTRACT

*Show also cubic measurements for shipments via air, truck or water carrier in cases where required.

AUTHORIZED FOR LOCAL REPRODUCTION

STANDARD FORM 1103 (REV. 9/2003)
Prescribed by GSA/FMR 102-118

FIGURE 3.7 - BLANK BILL OF LADING FORM USED BY THE U.S. GOVERNMENT

***Advice Note of Intended Delivery*.** The supplier, who is contracted by the purchasing department to supply the inventory ordered, issues the *advice note of intended delivery*. This note is issued when the goods are dispatched from the supplier. It provides the following information: *confirmation that the order will be delivered, a provisional delivery date and time, the method of delivery to be used by the supplier, the quantity of goods that will be supplied*, and *the code number and description of the inventory concerned.*

Delivery Note. Also called the ***delivery slip***, the *delivery note* is usually supplied with goods as they are delivered, listing what the supplier has actually delivered to the warehouse. When goods arrive at the warehouse, the delivery note must be carefully checked by a member of the inventory receipt team to ensure that the quantity and description of items listed are accurate and match with the items delivered. The delivery note is an important inventory receipt document, largely because of the information it contains, which includes inventory: *quantity*, *type*, *color*, *code*, *delivery date*, and *cost*.

Company Logo Here

+88 12 345 6789
yourbrand@gmail.com
www.yourbrand.com

Praesent viera street no. 27
West Nulla city,
Leaflove 5100

DELIVERY NO :
2612002028

Delivery Order

ISSUE DATE :
December 28, 2020

DELIVER TO :
Ariella Moldekin
+88 12 345 6789 100
email_here@gmail.com

DELIVERY ADDRES :
Vomnes derovit street no. 18
North Sequi city,
Leaflove 5100

CUSTOMER P.O. :
A-8202002162

NO	DESCRIPTION	QUANTITY
1	Item description here	10
2	Item description here	15
3	Item description here	10
4	Item description here	15
5	Item description here	10
6	Item description here	15

NOTE :

SELLER   DRIVER   BUYER

FIGURE 3.8 - BLANK DELIVERY NOTE FORM
WHAT INFORMATION COULD BE ADDED TO THIS DELIVERY NOTE?

Third Party Carrier's Consignment Note. Also called the ***consignment slip***, a *third party carrier's consignment note* is used when the supplier has *outsourced* or contracted out the actual physical delivery of inventory to a third party carrier. The third party company provides its own form and delivery note so that delivery control can be maintained and claims for non-delivery may be processed properly. In most cases, the goods delivered will have both a supplier's delivery note and a carrier's consignment note.

Packing Slip. Also provided by the supplier at the time of delivery, a *packing slip* is used for a more detailed check of the inventory delivered after the shipment has been broken down for storage. Unlike the *delivery note*, which describes the contents of the entire shipment, the packing slip lists what is actually within each individual unit delivered, such as each box, parcel, pallet load, or drum. It includes specific data about quantities, types, sizes, colors, and specifications of the inventory within the individual delivery unit.

FIGURE 3.9 - BLANK TEMPLATE FOR A COMPANY'S PACKING SLIP

Receiver Report. This report is generated by the company receiving the goods and a new report is created for each shipment received. It typically lists the items received, the time and location received, and notes if there are discrepancies between the suppliers' and shippers' documentation and the actual goods received, including incorrect quantities received or initial visible damage that occurred to items in shipment.

3.6 INSPECTING INVENTORY

As goods arrive into the warehouse, it is important that those receiving the goods inspect the incoming items. **Inventory inspection** begins with those responsible for receiving goods into the warehouse, such as the shipping and receiving department. This department checks the order to make sure the goods received match the goods listed in the accompanying paperwork, such as the delivery note or the internal packing note. When someone from this department signs off on the delivery, the ownership of the goods transfers from the *sender*, such as the seller or third party logistics service provider, to the *receiver*, such as the buyer.

The person in the warehouse handling and initially inspecting the goods checks the accuracy of the shipment and make sure the quantity and quality of the items matches the documentation. Warehouses must have procedures in place for when there are discrepancies or if damage has occurred during the shipping process and some incoming goods need to be rejected. Warehouse must also have procedures in place for how to address special inspections and handling requirements for specific goods, such as hazardous materials or those with specific climate control requirements.

In many situations, the truck driver delivering the goods cannot leave until the goods have been checked and signed for by the receiver. The more streamlined the inventory inspection and receipt process is, the more efficient and cost-effective the process is for all involved. A company may plan for contingencies by allowing partially damaged shipments to be accepted if the following rules are followed:

1. *Check all incoming goods for quantity and accuracy.*

2. *Check all incoming goods for immediate signs of visible damage.*

3. *If there are any discrepancies with #1 or #2 above, take photographs of the items involved, especially damaged items. Make sure to take photos of the items while they are still in the shipper's truck or container.*

4. *Write down all of these discrepancies on the Bill of Lading and any additional documentation that the driver or deliverer asks you to sign. Such discrepancies could include differences in pallet counts or specific damage to goods. Initial all areas where you have written additional information and ask the driver to initial these areas, too.*

5. *Sign the required documentation and make sure to get a copy of the signed documentation from the driver. If the quality of your copy is poor, make sure to take a photograph of the original copy held by the driver.*

In addition to this initial eyeball inspection of goods as soon as they are received, there is also a more thorough inspection of goods received as they are unpacked. Depending upon the size of the company and the nature of the goods received, warehouse staff or specially trained employees from the company's **quality control department** may perform this inspection. Sometimes both may be involved, with the warehouse responsible for ensuring that physical quantities are correct and the quality control department responsible for checking the quality of the incoming inventory.

When the quality of goods are checked, this inspection is typically made against predetermined levels of acceptability using one of two basic inspection methods: the **100% method**, in which all items are tested, or the **sampling method**, in which only a sample of each batch delivered is tested. If the sampling method is used, the warehouse might supply samples of each delivery to the quality control department so that regular quality checks and tests can be made for each delivery, thus maintaining consistency in supply quality. If inspected items are rejected upon delivery, the warehouse and quality control department must notify all relevant departments immediately. The warehouse typically holds this rejected inventory aside in a dedicated area to ensure that these faulty materials are not used, which might subsequently cause faulty manufacturing output or customer dissatisfaction. Similarly, the warehouse must store accepted incoming goods in a manner that ensures that they will not be damaged while in storage.

FIGURE 3.10 - THE SAMPLING METHOD IN A BAKERY
QUALITY CONTROL IN A BAKERY USING THE SAMPLING METHOD TO TEST THE BAKE AND FRESHNESS OF RANDOMLY SELECTED LOAVES OF BREAD

The reputation and survival of an organization depend upon its ability to satisfy its customers' needs. Poor product and service quality can lead to a loss of credibility and increased cost due to scrapped inventory, rework, and late deliveries, all causing the need to repeat tasks that were not completed correctly the first time. One measure developed to address this pivotal issue of quality is **TQC**, or **total quality control**. Developed in Japan in the 1970s as a means of preventing waste by not producing defective products, TQC focuses on the goal of achieving first-class quality. This approach integrates the relationship between the supplier, buyer, and ultimate customer to prevent poor quality.

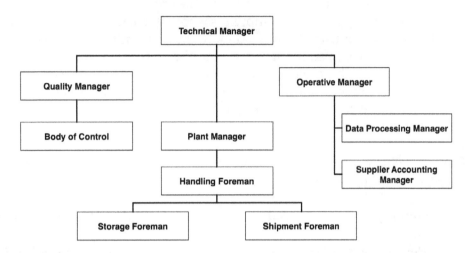

FIGURE 3.11 - ORGANIZATION CHART FROM AN ITALIAN STEELWORKS COMPANY OUTLINING A SEPARATE QUALITY CONTROL DEPARTMENT

From the Japanese idea of TQC, quality control has become a standard practice in organizations throughout the world. **Quality control** is today known as the process of setting standards of acceptability for goods purchased and produced by an organization and then accepting or rejecting goods based on these standards. In setting quality control standards, **specifications** are outlined, which are detailed descriptions that include information about an item's: *size; dimensions; performance; characteristics*, such as color, texture, and form; *quality; chemical analysis;* and *functions*. Once an item's specifications have been drawn up, all goods of this type received by the warehouse will have to meet the requirements of the specifications. If they are found to be below the standards set within the specifications, they will not be accepted into the warehouse and will instead be classified as **rejected inventory**. Once an item has been rejected, a procedure like the one below is typically followed carefully:

- *The rejected goods are double checked to ensure that the real cause for rejection exists. A senior member of the warehouse staff is typically involved with this step.*

- *The quality control department is then notified so that it can inspect the items to confirm the rejection order.*

- *The purchasing department is then informed of the rejection so that it can immediately contact the supplier to arrange for collection and replacement of the faulty items.*

- *The production or planning department is then informed so that it will be aware of the shortage of inventory caused by the rejection. This step is a vital one because inventory shortages can affect the organization's production output.*

In order to carry out this quality control function, many organizations have their own **quality control department**, whose sole function is to monitor the standards and quality of the goods used and manufactured or produced by the organization. In an ideal world, organizations would only buy items from suppliers whose items were all consistently of acceptable quality, thus never needing inspection. In the real world, however, even the best suppliers can make mistakes. In addition, many organizations do not have the market power needed to demand consistently perfect quality from their suppliers. This leaves the average organization with the need for a quality control department, which inspects incoming inventory to prevent faulty items from making their way into the production process or into the hands of end users.

Once it is formed, a quality control department sets its aims and objectives. Examples of the aims and objectives for a standard quality control department would include:

- *Set and monitor standards of quality for all items handled by the organization.*

- *Eliminate the possibility of faulty production from becoming distributed and sold to the consumer, which might damage the organization's reputation.*

- *Act as a liaison between all departments involved with setting standards to ensure that all standards set are acceptable and workable for all those concerned.*

- *Ensure that the quality and performance of all items delivered from suppliers and internal sources into the warehouse are acceptable.*

For a quality control department to function effectively, the organization must first establish a system of standards based on its own needs and objectives. These standards, which vary in stringency from organization to organization, are influenced by a range of factors, including: *company policy, complexity of the items*, and a*greement between departments*.

Most organizations set a global company policy regarding their reputation and the quality of their products. A company facing strong competition, especially when quality is a factor of this competition, will need very stringent quality control standards so that it won't fall behind its rivals. In addition, the degree and nature of quality control inspections depend largely upon the type, nature, and complexity of the goods involved. Effective inspection of highly specialized and technically advanced materials will require highly skilled and knowledgeable quality control inspectors.

Finally, when an organization's quality control standards are being set, an effective and productive working environment is created when all of the organization's departments involved agree on and accept these standards. This desired acceptance of standards is best achieved when a representative from each department participates in initially setting the standards. If the approach used to set quality control standards is indeed one of joint consultation among departments, the departments involved can include the:

- **Production Department.** Because the production department, also known as the **manufacturing department**, must work with the materials purchased during the production process, it is most interested in establishing standards that guarantee a high quality of input. With higher quality input materials, productive output improves because machine output improves and delays arising from rejected materials are reduced.

- **Marketing Department.** Because the marketing department has to sell the organization's products in the marketplace, it is most interested in establishing quality control standards, which will result in high quality output in terms of finish, performance, design, and packaging.

- **Design Department.** Designers must be involved in setting quality control standards because they are responsible for meeting the quality and performance requirements set by the company and the customers.

- **Quality Control Department.** While it seems obvious that the quality control department would be involved in setting quality control standards, it is important to note that quality inspectors and monitors themselves should be involved in setting the standards because it will be their responsibility to enforce them.

- **Warehouse Management.** In many cases, the warehouse is the first line of defense against faulty materials being introduced into the organization. The warehouse has traditionally been responsible for the initial inspection of all materials delivered to the warehouse, whether they are received from external suppliers or from internal production. Warehouse managers are now responsible for initial inspections and for liaising with the quality control department for quality control standards inspections and monitoring.

- **Purchasing Department.** Although their role in setting quality control standards is not an obvious one, the purchasing department must be involved throughout the entire standards-setting process so that they are fully aware of the needs of the organization in terms of the quality and price of the materials it will purchase. The purchasing department will also be able to provide information on the availability of the requirements needed for the specification proposed and its impact on the overall cost of production, which will ultimately play a large part in determining the sales price.

- **Customers.** Although not an official department of an organization, the customers are indirectly involved in setting quality control standards. For example, if goods produced by the company are inferior to other brands, the customers might not buy them.

While it is important for departments to work together to set quality control standards, there are no guarantees that all of the departments within an organization will always agree. Conflicting interests are not uncommon at this stage and may include: *a production department unwilling to be tied to strict standards of output that might result in subsequent delays; a marketing department demanding high quality yet unwilling to accept the increased prices this will bring; or a purchasing department that understands the need for high quality materials but is itself conflicted because it knows it must keep costs down.*

3.7 INVENTORY CODING

The organizations that handle the majority of the world's goods are complex. The range and types of items held in inventory by these organizations are correspondingly complex. In order to manage a complex range of inventory, an organization needs an inventory classification system so that individual inventory items can be stored, identified, and issued quickly and efficiently. Common names of items such as *table* or *pump*, which work well in the everyday world, present difficulties in the world of inventory management.

Common name terms are very limited and often not very descriptive. For example, the word *table* reveals some information about the look and function of the item, but it reveals nothing about its size, color, or composition. An item may also have more than one common name, which can lead to confusion. This is especially true for global organizations, in which different languages and even variations of the same language may be used across its global operations. For example, what is called a *tractor-trailer truck* or *eighteen-wheeler* in the United States is called an *articulated lorry* in England. Finally, many items used in manufacturing are too technical for plain language labels that are sufficiently descriptive.

Because of problems encountered with common names, most organizations have developed extensive codes to identify all of the items held in their inventory. These **codes** are usually a homogeneous, concise system of letters, numbers, and symbols used across the entire organization, which convey a wealth of necessary information about each item. Even those of us not currently in the inventory management field already use codes in our everyday lives, from *UAA* for the University of Alaska Anchorage to our library's Library of Congress Numbering System to the label of *MP3* for the audio files we listen to on our computers or phones, which actually means *Moving Picture Experts Group Audio Layer 3*. Could you imagine having to say all of those words every time you wanted to talk about a music file?

In addition to the advantage of replacing a complex item's tongue twister name with only a few numbers or letters, inventory codes a offer a wealth of advantages, such as:

- **Advantage #1: Increased Efficiency.** With an inventory coding system, a long and complex requisition no longer needs to be completed. Using only a simple series of numbers or letters, an exact item required can quickly be communicated to warehouse staff, thus saving considerable time and effort. Remember how long it used to take your local grocery store cashier to ring up unusual produce selections, such as papayas, mangoes, and cassavas? First they would have to figure out what the item was and then they would have to look up the price because the prices of infrequently purchased items would not always be the easiest to memorize quickly. Meanwhile, you would begin to regret your yen for papayas! Today, however, papaya shopping is hassle-free because most grocery stores code their produce and place a bar coded sticker on each fruit or vegetable, resulting in streamlined efficiency at the cash register.

- **Advantage #2: Improved Accuracy.** When a warehouse receives a correct code for an item required, it may then easily select and issue the item without the fear of issuing the wrong item. This aspect of inventory coding is particularly advantageous when multiple items appear visually similar and their differences are not immediately discernible, such as screws with a 3/4-inch thread versus those with a 7/8-inch thread. A simple code can classify and isolate such differences for immediate and accurate identification.

- **Advantage #3: Error Reduction.** Because of the exact nature of an inventory coding system and its logical approach, it is actually quite difficult to make an error in item identification, unlike the process of using long and complex written inventory requests, which is traditionally an open invitation for mistakes.

- **Advantage #4: Inventory Location and Marking Benefits.** Because of the logical nature of inventory coding, it lends itself well to inventory location planning and marking within a warehouse. In many cases, different types of materials are stored within different sections of a warehouse. A well-devised inventory coding system can be integrated with the actual physical placement of inventory so that an item's code and placement work together in a logical, easily understood system. This combination of inventory placement and the coding system can then be used for marking-up storage areas quickly and efficiently.

- **Advantage #5: Purchasing Department Benefits.** Not only do warehouse staff members benefit from an inventory coding system, but the purchasing department does, too. One of the basic responsibilities of warehouse management is to keep the purchasing department informed about inventory levels and goods required for purchase. When the warehouse and purchasing departments use an inventory coding system together, there is greater and more efficient understanding between the two departments. By using a simple yet informative code, requisition requests are shorter and less time-consuming.

- **Advantage #6: Assistance to Suppliers.** In some cases, a copy of the inventory coding system can be sent to an organization's major suppliers, who would then be able to easily interpret purchase requests completed using the code. This extra use of an inventory coding system would save both time and effort at all stages of an organization's purchasing cycle, and thus reduce the administrative costs of ordering.

- **Advantage #7: Information Technology Benefits.** For a computer system to operate efficiently and effectively, it must be able to locate and identify the files associated with the items held in its inventory so that inventory transactions can all be processed as quickly and as accurately as possible. A logical inventory coding system makes this possible. Because of the logical way in which computers operate, they are able to immediately identify items in question and all of accompanying documentation by code numbers.

Different organizations have their own needs and resources, all of which influence the different coding systems they each develop. The coding systems they choose to employ may be as simple or as complex as the organizations need them to be. There are, however, different basic types of coding systems. An organization may choose to employ one of them, all of them, or any combination in between. A few of these basic coding systems are:

- ***Item-based coding***, in which an inventory item is classified and coded with a mix of letters, numbers, and symbols according to its nature and make-up. For example, an item-based code could first reveal that the item is a pipe and then might reveal its length, diameter, thickness, and composition, such as copper or plastic. Because it can hold a great deal of information about an individual item and be universally applied with infinite variations, item-based coding is the most widely employed coding system in inventory management.

- **End-use coding**, in which an item is coded according to its final operational or product use. End-use coding is very similar to item-based coding, but its emphasis and primary classification scheme is based on the final use of the item and not the item itself. For example, in an assembly line operation, items are end-use coded according to a production line. Items heading to a Ford automobile assembly line will be coded first according to their designated production line, whether the item will be used in assembling a Fusion or an Explorer, with secondary sections of the code perhaps revealing information about the item itself, such as details about the engine.

- **Color coding**, which is an identification system based upon using different colors as the primary means of coding and identifying items held in inventory. While it can be a very effective means of immediate identification, color coding has the disadvantage of being limited in its range. A box of crayons may have 164 colors, but at a distance, how discernible is *brick red* from *burnt sienna*? There are a finite and relatively small number of immediately discernible colors, such as red, blue, yellow, black, white, green, orange, and purple. Once these colors have been used, color coding alone is no longer effective in creating new code categories. Therefore, color coding is used primarily in lumber warehouses or in connection with other coding systems.

- **Supplier coding**, in which the organization adopts and uses the codes of the item's supplier. This system can be an easy one to implement and use when an organization has only one supplier, but it can become very confusing when multiple suppliers are involved because each will typically have their own unique coding systems.

- **Location coding**, in which inventory is assigned a code that is based on the item's location, such as warehouse, row, bay, and shelf. Often a location code will be used in conjunction with one of the other coding systems, such as item-based coding.

Before a new coding system is introduced into any inventory management system, an organization must consider a range of issues. First, it must consider the *range and type of inventory* to be coded. The more complex and variegated the items held in inventory, the more complex and flexible the coding system will have to be. It is critical for a newly constructed inventory code to be both logical and flexible enough to accommodate inventory change and growth. Second, it must consider the *staff and resources available* to introduce and update the inventory code. A very complex system will need a great deal of time and skill for its introduction and warehouse personnel will require specialized training to ensure its success. Finally, in introducing a new coding system, an organization must consider whether or not the system will be *digital or manual* in its operation. Information technology systems play an integral role in most inventory management systems, especially those of large, widespread organizations. In such systems, numerical coding systems are preferred and even essential for efficient digital data storage and retrieval systems. Be aware, however, that smaller organizations with small volumes and variety of inventory may still be reliant on manual coding systems with little to no information technology involved.

Once an organization has determined its need for an inventory coding system, it must now construct the coding system. Let's take a code-building journey as we code an item according to a new item-based coding system! Our coding system is numerically based for digital inventory management. Let's code the glamorous and exciting item of ¼ inch copper rods. Our final code will contain six fields, each with a distinct number revealing a different bit of information about our item. So that the numbers within our fields don't become confused, they are separated by decimal points. For example, a code within our system might look like: 3.2.10.6.5.24. Let's get coding!

CREATING AN INVENTORY CODE FOR ¼ INCH COPPER RODS

FIELD 1: To begin coding our illustrious ¼ inch copper rod, we determine which number will be assigned to its first field. In our coding system, our first field reveals the following information about the basic nature of the item:

1 = raw material, 2 = component part, 3 = finished product, 4 = electrical

Our item, the ¼ inch copper rod, is a raw material. We begin by assigning 1 to the first field of our code: **1.**

FIELD 2: Now that our code's first field shows that our item is a raw material, we will use the coding system's second field to classify our item's type of raw material, using the following system:

1 = metal, 2 = plastic, 3 = wood

Our item, the ¼ inch copper rod, is base metal, so we assign 1 to the second field of our code: **1.1**

FIELD 3: Having classified our item's type of raw material, we next assign a number to the third field of our code, which is used to identify type of metal, using the following system:

1 = lead, 2 = steel, 3 = copper, 4 = aluminum

Our ¼ inch copper rod is obviously copper, so we assign 3 to the third field of our code: **1.1.3**

FIELD 4: The fourth field in our coding system will now classify the basic three-dimensional form of our raw material, metal, copper item. We use the following system to code the fourth field:

1 = nuggets, 2 = bars, 3 = flatsheets, 4 = rods

Again, our ¼ inch copper rod is obviously a rod, so we assign 4 to the fourth field of our code: **1.1.3.4**

FIELD 5: Having established the form in which our item is stored, the fifth field in our coding system now provides more refined information about the item's rod shape and its two-dimensional cross-section shape:

1 = square, 2 = hexagonal, 3 = round/circular, 4 = oval

Our ¼ inch copper rod is round, so we assign 3 to the fifth field of our code: **1.1.3.4.3**

FIELD 6: The sixth field within our coding system provides the final bit of information about our copper rod, its diameter, using the following numeric system:

1 = 1 inch, 2 = ½ inch, 3 = ¼ inch

Because our copper rod is ¼ inch in diameter, we assign 3 to the sixth field of our code: **1.1.3.4.3.3**

Interpreted, **1.1.3.4.3.3** *in our imaginary inventory coding system means:*

raw material (1), metal (1), copper (3), rod (4), round (3), and ¼ inch diameter (3)

When organizations create their own inventory coding systems, they may use a series of six fields of numbers separated by decimal points, as we have in the example above, but they may also use any number of fields containing numbers, letters, or a combination of both, separated by any other symbol, such as a dash, slash, asterisk, or whatever else may strike the code designer's fancy. The overall design, however, must be logical, relevant, and easy to use by the organization and all those involved in its inventory management.

Once an organization has devised and introduced an inventory coding system, information related to the new system must be stored and made accessible to those who will need to know and understand the new system. Usually a glossary or catalogue within a book or computer file is created to contain information on the logic behind the coding and full descriptions for each of the fields of numbers or letters within the code. These explanations of the coding system must be clear and thorough because they serve as a guide to many users, including those in the production, inventory control, warehouse, and purchasing departments. The explanation of a coding system is also used by suppliers and others involved in accounts and invoice-checking because the inventory code is also typically used on invoices and delivery documents. Because many rely on these coding glossaries or catalogues, they must be updated frequently and regularly. They must also include coding criteria for all current and planned future items within the organization's inventory.

An inventory coding system is judged by its immediate results, typically how efficiently and successfully the item sought is identified. When striving to achieve the most efficient and easy-to-use inventory coding system, an organization typically abides by the following rules of inventory coding:

- **Rule #1:** Be able to cover every item held in inventory. An inventory coding system that does not include a means for coding even the most obscure and rarely used items can quickly experience control problems.

- **Rule #2**: Make it flexible! New products are created. Design, packaging, and performance changes occur in existing products. All product creations and alterations must be assigned new, logically consistent codes. A truly efficient inventory coding system must be flexible and able to expand to accommodate increases in inventory type, range, and scope.

- **Rule #3:** Use consistent and logical formatting. Once the basic logic of an inventory coding system is established, such as 1 = raw materials, use it throughout. Don't make the mistake of creating several different coding systems for different parts of the warehouse.

- **Rule #4:** Meet your organization's needs. For example, Ford Motors would use a far more complex inventory coding system than the warehouse of a local auto parts store.

- **Rule #5:** Include other departments. In addition to the inventory management and warehouse departments, other departments must also use the newly developed coding system, such as the purchasing, production, distribution, marketing and engineering departments. To enhance cross-departmental communications and develop an efficient, fully workable inventory coding system, other departments must understand the logic of the system and its common classifications and headings.

CHAPTER 3 REVIEW QUESTIONS

1. What are the five categories of inventory? Please provide two examples for each category that are not listed in the textbook.

2. What is *decoupling inventory* and why might it be important for an organization that manufactures goods?

3. During the *inventory receipt process*, what is typically allocated before the goods actually arrive? Why?

4. What are *chocks* and why are they important for inventory receipt? What are *dock levelers* and why are they important for inventory receipt?

5. For an organization receiving goods, how might an *Advice Note of Intended Delivery* from the supplier help assist the inventory receipt cycle process?

6. Your company has received a shipping container full of 5000 Tiny Toddler Cheepo-Sheepo plastic toys. Which inspection method might your company be more likely to use: *the 100% method* or *the sampling method*? Why?

7. Why should customers be considered when setting *quality control standards*?

8. In your own words, describe three of the advantages of *inventory coding*.

9. When might an organization use *color coding*? When might it be best not to use color coding?

10. When might an organization use *supplier coding*?

CHAPTER 3 CASE EXERCISE

FABULOUS FLOATING FERRIES

The story you are about to read is true. The names and places have been changed to protect the innocent. And not-so-innocent.

A European ferry company called Fabulous Floating Ferries currently runs a car ferry between New Winterfell and Narniaville. The ferry crossing time is eight hours. The ferry leaves New Winterfell at 8am each day and arrives at Narniaville at 4pm, resulting in an eight hour crossing time. The same ferry then leaves Narniaville at 8pm and arrives back at New Winterfell at 4am the next day. As with all Fabulous Floating Ferries ships, the New Winterfell-Narniaville ferry has a full restaurant, buffet bar, lounge, and various snack machines throughout the ship. The ferry's supplies are all ordered from local suppliers and loaded at the port of New Winterfell. It is loaded with enough supplies to cover both the trip to Narniaville and the subsequent return journey back to New Winterfell.

The system for resupplying the New Winterfell-Narniaville ferry has been the same for years. On the return journey from Narniaville, the ferry's onboard supply officer contacts a purchasing officer at the Fabulous Floating Ferries headquarters onshore and orders what is needed for the next trip from New Winterfell to Narniaville and back. Many of the same supplies are ordered consistently during each trip, but they must be ordered in small quantities because there is very little room for storage on the ship.

The onshore purchasing officer for Fabulous Floating Ferries then contacts the local suppliers, usually around 10 to 12 suppliers, and orders the ship's requirements for delivery. This takes place while the ship is loading and unloading the cars and people that are traveling at New Winterfell, which is between the ship's docking time of 4am and its departure time of 8am. Early every morning, there is a line of suppliers waiting on the dock for the ship to arrive. The ship's storage area is below deck and can be accessed only by a single elevator and a very narrow circular stairway. In the winter months, when fewer people are traveling, this resupplying system works pretty well. In the summertime, however, the volume of cars and people traveling is much higher, which results in a constant state of quayside chaos as all the suppliers try to get their goods unloaded and their documentation signed. For years, this has resulted in far too many late ferry departures from New Winterfell.

The supply officer onboard the New Winterfell-Narniaville ferry is growing weary of this recurring problem and has often complained to the higher-ups at Fabulous Floating Ferries about the lack of time to properly receive and inspect the goods in New Winterfell. Often, because of this tight resupplying schedule, items ordered were not sent or the quantities were short or goods were damaged. The finance department at Fabulous Floating Ferries is also concerned about the price the company is paying for these goods. The process of ordering goods every day and in such small quantities means that they always pay full price and never receive a bulk discount from any of their vendors.

INSTRUCTIONS:

After reading the case of Fabulous Floating Ferries, please answer the following questions.

If Fabulous Floating Ferries were to purchase or rent an affordable warehouse within five minutes of the ferry's New Winterfell docking site:

1. *What types of goods might be stored in the warehouse?*

2. *What inventory management benefits might Fabulous Floating Ferries experience? Please explain your answer.*

3. *How might the inventory receipt process change from the existing process? Would this change be beneficial or detrimental to Fabulous Floating Ferries? Please explain your answer.*

BONUS EXERCISE: INVENTORY CODING!

Look at the example of "Creating an Inventory Code for 1/4 inch Copper Rods" on page 73 of Section 3.7 of this chapter. Using the fields and coding system provided, create inventory codes for the raw materials listed in the questions below. Make sure to use the following format: 1.1.1.1.1.1

QUESTIONS:

1. *What would the inventory code be for 1 inch oval lead nuggets?*

2. *What would the inventory code be for 1/2 inch hexagonal aluminum rods?*

3. *What would the inventory code be for 1/4 inch circular sheets of copper?*

Chapter 4

Putaway and Storage

4.1 INTRODUCING PUTAWAY

In Chapter 3, we tackled the topic of incoming inventory in warehouse management and the inventory receipt cycle. After goods come in and are inspected, they must go somewhere. In a standard warehouse, the goods might be put away onto warehouse shelves. At a cross-docking distribution center, goods might be taken from one incoming truck and placed onto ten different outgoing trucks. After goods have been received and inspected and corresponding paperwork has been completed and signed, the internal process of placing goods in their appropriate location is called *putaway*.

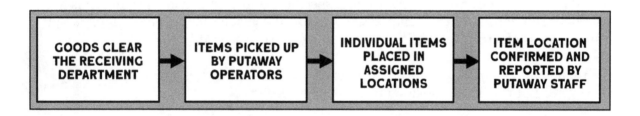

FIGURE 4.1 - THE PUTAWAY PROCESS

Depending on the size of the warehouse operation and the nature of the goods, the warehouse staff handling putaway may be the same people who handle inventory receipt or it may be handled by an entirely department or set of people. If someone else takes over, they now take responsibility for and ownership over getting the goods to the right place, usually as quickly as possible. An important goal of putaway is to minimize *dock-to-stock time*, which is the amount of time it takes to transition unloaded and inspected goods in the receiving area to their next destination, such as onto warehouse shelves or immediately onto outbound trucks. Goods need to be cleared from the receiving area quickly to make room for new incoming goods. Incoming goods also need to be put into their warehouse or cross-docking locations as quickly as possible so they can be available for distribution to their internal or external users. Imagine a retail warehouse receiving a last minute shipment of sold-out Halloween costumes of this year's favorite celebrity just two days before Halloween! If those costumes don't get put away and made available for distribution to end users immediately, it's pretty likely the warehouse will be stuck with pallets of reality star costumes that will be yesterday's news next Halloween.

After the receiving department signs off on the delivery of incoming goods, the company receiving them now has legal ownership of the goods. Those handling the putaway process should understand that they are handling the company's potential profits when they put the goods away. To ensure that goods are handled correctly so that they won't be damaged, putaway operators check with the receiving department to see if there are any special handling instructions for the goods being put away. For example, some goods may be especially fragile or need temperature-controlled storage and handling conditions. In addition, there may be special handling instructions to keep putaway operators safe while handling the items, including the need for protective clothing, gloves, masks, or lifting belts.

4.2 LOCATION AND THE PUTAWAY PROCESS

As shown in Figure 4.1, during the putaway process, goods must not only be put away quickly, but those putting the goods away must also confirm and report each item's new location. When put away in a warehouse, goods are placed in a specific **location**, which could be a designated area of the warehouse floor for larger items or a designated rack, shelf, or storage bin for smaller items. In addition, during the putaway process, goods may be placed in either a *slot* or in a *reserve area*. A specific area designated for specific items to be placed for subsequent order picking is called a **slot**. When determining an inventory's slot, also known as **slotting** or **profiling**, three things are considered:

1. *what is being stored:* the product, its physical characteristics, any special storage needs it may have, and how often it will be needed

2. *the storage location:* its shape, its structure, exactly how much of the item it can hold, exactly where it can be found in the warehouse, and the warehouse inventory code used to identify its location

3. *maintenance requirements:* what type of maintenance will be needed to keep the slot in regular working order and keeping track of how often items are taken from slots to see if they need to be moved to areas of items picked less frequently or more frequently

If goods do not need to be picked immediately, they may instead be placed in a **reserve area** where they are stored until they are needed to be placed for picking. For example, if Kudzoo's Contemporary Kitchens received more hot pink granite countertop material than it might need in a year because the purchasing department got a smoking hot deal on them, it might place 300 square feet of the hot pink granite in a specific hot pink granite slot in the warehouse. It might then place the remaining 30,000 square feet of the hot pink granite from the incoming order in a reserve area further back in the warehouse, to be placed in the warehouse slot for picking on future dates as needed. Reserve areas are typically located in the less accessible areas of a warehouse facility, such as in areas furthest back from the warehouse entrances, exits, and main aisles or furthest up in the warehouse's shelves or racking system. When a company has multiple buildings for a single warehouse facility, a building that has fewer or no external loading docks may be set aside as the reserve area.

FIGURE 4.2 - SLOTS AND RESERVE AREAS IN A WAREHOUSE

When goods are being put away in a location, they may also be coming from an *internal* or an *external* location. For example, when the hot pink granite is taken from the Groovy Granite delivery truck and placed into the Kudzoo's Contemporary Kitchens warehouse in our previous example, it is coming from an **external location**, which is any location or entity outside of the company receiving the materials. A few weeks later, when the hot pink granite has been picked from its slot in the warehouse and needs to be replaced, or **replenished** in warehouse management terminology, it is taken from the warehouse's reserve area, which is an **internal location**. Other internal locations could include any location from within the company needing the goods, such as within another warehouse or distribution center that belongs to the same organization.

When the putaway process involves taking goods from one internal location and placing them into another internal location, replenishment is often the reason. **Replenishment** is the process of moving goods from a reserve area to a **forward pick location**, which is another term to describe the slot into which goods are placed in a warehouse for subsequent order picking. Items are replenished and placed in their forward pick locations when product levels are running low. Depending on the size of the warehouse and the scope of its operations, the exact quantity level at which items are replenished may be determined by the judgment of the putaway operators or by warehouse management software and inventory control systems. When replenishment happens, it is documented by the putaway operator so that the warehouse's inventory systems accurately reflect the new location of the inventory. In most warehouses, replenishment is documented using a combination of software, such as a warehouse management system, and hardware operated by warehouse staff, such as a barcode readers or voice-directed headsets.

But why on earth do warehouses bother to move goods internally from a reserve area to a forward pick location? Wouldn't it be simpler to put goods in one spot until they are needed, without all this internal to-and-fro? While using a single location for goods may appear to be simple, it is not cost effective for many goods and organizations. In the world of warehouse management, time is money. The more time it takes to pick an order and the further warehouse workers must travel into the depths of the warehouse on a regular basis, the more it costs an organization in labor and equipment costs. As you may remember from Chapter 2, a more efficient warehouse layout design is achieved when goods are stored according to their *frequency of use*, or how often it is used and must be accessed. Materials are often grouped in three logical sections: *high usage rate*, *medium usage rate*, and *low usage rate*. In most cases, materials that are constantly picked and issued out should be placed near entrances and exits or near the ends of aisles along the main warehouse thoroughfares. This method of placement reduces the handling times of these high usage materials and minimizes traveling time for order pickers. The same logic is applied to the medium and low usage rate materials, placing the less frequently delivered and issued inventory progressively further away from the warehouse's points of entry and exit and further from the ends of the warehouse aisles.

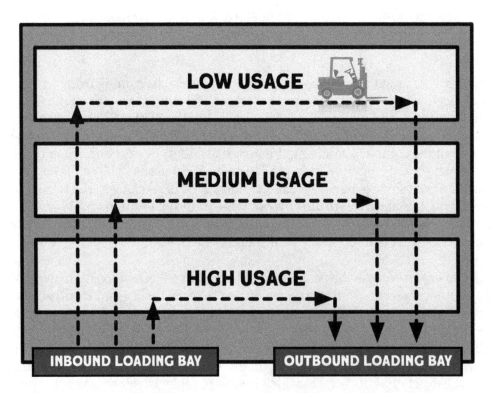

FIGURE 4.3 - INVENTORY LOCATION BY FREQUENCY OF USE

Similarly, there is a ***golden zone of inventory location*** on vertical warehouse shelves which is determined by frequency of usage. Those items which are placed into and taken out of inventory most frequently are placed so that they are in slots that are easiest for warehouse workers to reach. This golden zone is generally in the area between the shoulders and the knees of the average warehouse worker. Items that have medium and low usage rates are placed in higher or lower locations on the shelves, so that warehouse workers don't have to bend down, stretch up, or use ladders, stools, or forklift trucks as frequently. Lighter items that a warehouse worker could lift are also placed in the *golden zone* between shoulder- and knee-height. Heavier, palletized goods are placed higher, with more frequently used palletized goods placed closer to the floor and less frequently picked goods placed closer to the ceiling.

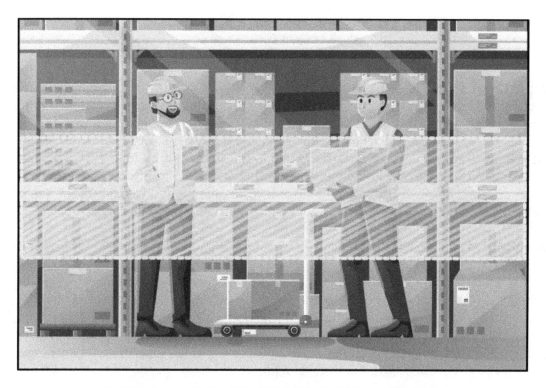

FIGURE 4.4 - THE GOLDEN ZONE OF INVENTORY LOCATION

For an everyday example of the golden zone, visit a large grocery store near you. Peruse any aisle and consider whether or not the items on the middle shelves are the ones that most people buy, with items on higher and lower shelves the less frequently purchased ones. Effective retailers want to make shopping an easy experience for as many customers as possible, so those items that the majority of people buy more frequently are likely to be located in the golden zone of the middle shelves.

For exceptionally large warehousing operations that pick and ship hundreds of thousands of items per day, such as the Amazon Fulfillment Centers around the world, inventory is put away when it comes in through a process called ***random stow***. In this process, after the warehouse receives a shipment of inventory, warehouse employees put them away in the first available locations they can find. For example, an Amazon employee putting away 85 two pound bags of Java Jolt coffee might put them away in 85 different locations. There is not a "coffee section" with all Java Jolt coffees on one shelf. Instead, a bag of coffee might be put away on the same shelf as a twelve pack of toilet paper, a book about gardening, a Teenage Mutant Ninja Turtles shower curtain, and a ten pound specialty bag of green M&Ms. When putting away the Java Jolt coffee in each of 85 different locations, handheld barcode scanners are used to record the item and its location. Then, when Amazon receives a customer order for a bag of Java Jolt coffee, the employee picking the order will use handheld inventory picking technology to find the closest bag of coffee by area, shelf, row, and bin. For Amazon's colossal warehouses, random stow saves putaway and picking time and optimizes storage space.

4.3 THE "WHERE" OF WAREHOUSE STORAGE

So far in Chapter 4, we introduced the putaway process that occurs in a warehouse facility and examined how location factors in to this process. Now that we've covered how goods are put away, let's explore *storage*, the next step for our incoming goods. In the world of warehousing, **storage** is the act of holding goods for a future use or for future outbound distribution. Storage occurs over any period of time with no minimum or maximum amount of time. It also occurs in all warehouses and warehousing facilities except those that engage in cross-docking, in which goods are directly moved from inbound transportation vehicles to outbound distribution vehicles and are not held by the company in storage.

Remember that way back in chapter 1, we defined a *warehouse* as a facility or an area within a facility in which an organization receives, inspects, stores, picks, packs, and issues any of a variety of materials needed for the organization's operations or its customers' orders. In Chapter 2, we introduced types of warehouses, their ownership structures, and layout considerations. These warehouse facilities in which storage takes place may either be inside buildings or outside in inventory yards. Let's now take a deeper look at warehouse facilities, building design, ownership structures, external inventory yards, and inventory coding and the way they each connect with the storage of goods.

Well-designed warehouse buildings are an important element of any successful supply chain. Their design can either help or hinder the efficiency of materials storage and movement. How warehouse buildings are designed, their size, and their scope will all differ based on the: *size and complexity* of the operation involved, *resources and capital available* for building or conversion, *location of existing operations*, and *future plans and expectations* of the organization.

While the functions of a warehouse building may vary with the needs of individual organizations, some of the more common functions of warehouse buildings that are connected to *storage* include:

- *Storage for all materials within a company, including semifinished inventory, finished inventory, and raw materials*

- *A large central storage area within a manufacturing plant, which acts as the distribution and collection point for all inventory*

- *Central storage for materials for one or more companies, which acts as a regional collection, consolidation, and distribution point*

- *A location for administrative and management resources for the warehousing function, including offices, issue counters, and delivery bays*

- *A central location for Quality Control and Inspection operations that are performed within the confines of the warehouse building*

- *Storage for materials handling equipment used within the warehouse, including stations for electrical charging of equipment*

- *Pricing and hand-shelving customers' orders*

Remember from Chapter 2, we discussed two basic types of warehouse building design: the *single-story warehouse building* and the *multi-story warehouse building*. The most widely used is the ***single-story warehouse building***, which is built on one level without full upper floors. Many single-story warehouse buildings actually do have a smaller type of second story through the use of ***mezzanines***, smaller upper stories in a warehouse building with low ceilings built above functioning warehouse areas. Mezzanines are built to provide office space or additional storage and are typically only a fraction of the square footage of the main lower floor.

FIGURE 4.5 - MEZZANINE AT HOUSEHOLD GOODS RETAILER WAREHOUSE
THIS MEZZANINE IS USED FOR BOTH STORAGE (RIGHT) AND AN OFFICE (LEFT).

Single-story warehouse buildings have several advantages, including:

- **Cost.** They are relatively cheap to construct and maintain because of their simple design and lack of upper floors. Multi-story building are more expensive to construct because of the costly foundation support needed for the extra weight of upper floors.

- **Flow.** With a well-designed warehouse building, the logistics of materials handling and the natural flow of materials through the warehouse can occur at maximum efficiency by keeping everything at one level.

- **Convenience.** Ventilation and other basic services such as electricity, water, and gas, are easier to install and operate.

- **Weight.** When using only a ground floor, greater weights may be stored without the problems associated with the upper-floor weight limitations of multi-story buildings.

Single-story warehouse buildings sound perfect, so why don't we see only single-story buildings in our wonderful world of warehousing? In a word: space. Many organizations operate within a confined geographic area and do not have the availability or resources to purchase large plots of land for single-story warehouse construction. As we covered back in Chapter 2, in areas of high population density, where land and resources are scarce and expensive, or in situations where an organization is based on a multi-story site, with different floors housing different sections of the organization, the ***multi-story warehouse building*** becomes the design of choice.

In addition to handling space restrictions, multi-story warehouse buildings also have the following advantages:

- **Flexibility.** The multi-floor environment allows for greater flexibility in alternative use of storage space for offices and production facilities should the need arise.

- **Safety and Security.** Separating areas of inventory by floor lends itself more to security and fire safety. For example, a fire outbreak can be contained on one floor without damaging the rest of the inventory located on other floors.

Multi-story buildings are well suited to handling small, light units of high value, such as electronic components. For these organizations, the advantage of having an optimal warehouse building location outweighs the advantage of having warehouse operations all on one floor. The primary disadvantage multi-story warehouse buildings bring is *cost*, including both the high capital outlay in construction and the subsequent costs of maintaining the building.

When considering new warehouse space, an organization must consider whether they want to *construct a new building, refit an existing structure*, or *rent warehouse space*. As we covered back in Chapter 2, a ***purpose-built warehouse building*** is a one that has been designed and constructed based on what an organization needs according to the types and quantity of products it will take in, store, and distribute. As previously covered, designing and constructing a purpose-built warehouses has some definite advantages, such as allowing a company to create the most efficient design and layout for their needs, allowing for the latest warehousing innovations to be incorporated into the design, and letting the company maximize every inch of space while allowing for the company's future growth. However, purpose-built warehouses can be very expensive to construct and when a mistake is made in the design, the company may have to live with that mistake for many years because of the financial investment made in the design.

FIGURE 4.6 - BEST BUY DISTRIBUTION CENTER UNDER CONSTRUCTION IN ARIZONA

In situations when an organization decides to refit an existing structure as a warehouse, the result is a ***converted warehouse building***, which we defined in Chapter 2 as a building originally designed for another purpose but modified to be used as a warehouse facility. Converted warehouse buildings can be less significantly expensive than purpose-built warehouse buildings and this lesser expense can sometimes allow a company to change warehouse locations quicker because fewer of the company's resources have been invested into the building. Converted warehouse buildings do offer disadvantages, however, because the buildings were not originally designed as warehouses, especially to store specific goods that might have very specific environmental conditions for storage, such as specific temperature or humidity levels. Additional construction for loading bays may be needed and there may be more complicated government planning permission involved.

In some situations, an organization may not want to become involved in either construction or conversion projects. It may instead decide to rent a facility to meet its storage needs. Motives for ***renting warehouse space*** include:

- **Inventory level variations.** When inventory levels fluctuate, storage space may only be needed for a short period of time, making it less cost-effective to build or convert warehouse space. Such inventory level variations are most common in organizations with seasonal products, such as swimming pool supplies, snow blowers, or Halloween candy.

- **Lack of resources.** When an organization cannot afford to buy or convert warehouse space, it can still continue its warehousing function by renting storage space.

- **Temporary changes in demand.** When a company experiences a drop in sales, its inventory typically increases because it is stuck holding the inventory it hasn't sold. Rather than build or convert another warehouse to house this excess inventory, rented warehouse space can offer the company the most cost-effective solution to its temporary storage needs.

- **Local government planning issues.** When in the process of planning, constructing, or converting warehouse space, organizations often face challenges in gaining required local government planning permissions needed. While ironing out these issues, organizations often turn to temporary rented storage facilities to ensure that warehousing operations begin or continue as scheduled.

- **Future demands.** When an organization is unclear of the future demand of its product, it may decide to rent warehouse space until future demand can be determined, at which time it may then build or convert warehouse space.

FIGURE 4.7 - ALMOST 800,000 SQUARE FEET OF WAREHOUSE SPACE FOR RENT

Before committing to renting a particular warehouse space, organizations consider a range of factors including: the location of the warehouse in relation to the organization, the transportation links and traveling time between the warehouse and the other links in the logistics chain, the cost of storage, and whether the conditions of storage are suitable for the materials involved. When a company is considering renting, constructing, or converting a warehouse facility, the new facility's location is a tool the company can use to reduce transportation costs and speed up delivery times, as we saw with the use of the *center of gravity method* in the Case Exercise in Chapter 2.

4.4 WAREHOUSE BUILDING CONSTRUCTION AND LAYOUT

You can never have too many chefs in the kitchen when starting a warehouse construction or conversion project. Architects, engineers, and company CEOs alone do not constitute an effective warehouse design team. Any decision related to the design and construction of a new warehouse or converted warehouse space should also be made with the advice and guidance of the warehouse manager and the managers of the organization's additional logistics activities. While *capital* and *land* available form two key factors in warehouse design and construction, warehouse and other logistics activities managers provide invaluable information for design and construction, including information on:

- **Volume of inventory involved.** Warehouse designers must know how much inventory is to be moved and stored according to both present inventory and future demands.

- **Nature of inventory involved.** In most cases, a wide variety of inventory is to be stored. Special sub-warehouse and storage sections may be required where specific environment conditions can be maintained.

- **Value of the inventory and the security systems.** Goods stored in warehouses have varying levels of value, which correspond to varying levels of security systems needs to protect these goods. These security systems may include security doors, alarms, motion sensors, CCTV (closed circuit television), remote monitoring, and locked doors with biometric entry .

- **Materials handling systems already used by the organization.** When an organization already uses specific types of materials handling equipment and systems within its other warehouses, a new warehouse may be designed to be compatible with these existing sets of equipment and systems. For example, an organization using diesel-powered trucks for outside handling may not be able to operate these trucks within a closed warehouse building.

- **Primary method of transport used by the organization and its suppliers.** These methods of transport must be considered because they will have a direct effect upon the design and construction of new and converted warehouse buildings.

- **Environmental conditions needed for inventory storage.** These conditions include the type of ventilation and climate conditions required according to the goods being stored, along with the heating and lighting systems needed to maintain these conditions.

- **Ancillary services.** Within the warehouse, accommodation will need to be made for ancillary services, thus reducing the overall storage capacity of the space. Ancillary services include: warehouse offices for inventory records, inventory control, and general administration; computer terminals; washroom and restroom facilities; and employee canteen facilities.

- **Loading docks required.** Loading dock requirements in terms of number, location, and size will depend on the volume and frequency of inbound deliveries, the transport method used by suppliers, the method of packing and unitization of inbound goods, the rate of issue from inventory, the method of outbound transportation used, and the volume and frequency of delivery to customers.

When contemplating any warehouse construction or conversion project, there are many costs to be considered. Each of these costs must be carefully examined to ensure that the project is economically feasible and that the organization will be financially able to operate the warehouse once construction is completed. Typical costs that warehouse construction projects face are often those related to: *construction and labor*; *materials handling and storage equipment required*; and *rates levied upon the new building by local authorities*.

Once warehouse construction is completed, an organization faces an array on ongoing costs, including those related to: *maintenance and depreciation*; *energy needed for operation*, such as gas, electricity, and fuel; *operational labor, administration, and management needed*; *transportation*, including delivery to customers; *cleaning*, which involves cleaning floors, janitorial service for offices, and pest control; and *security* which includes hiring outside security, alarms, specialized locks, firefighting equipment, and insurance cover premiums.

4.5 STORAGE IN EXTERNAL INVENTORY YARDS

So far in Chapter 4, we have been addressing storage and putaway within the context of warehouse buildings. However, remember from back in Chapter 2 that there is also a type of outside warehouse space called an external inventory yard. We defined an ***external inventory yard*** as an open, outside warehousing area used for storing various weather-resistant goods and raw materials. These inventory yards are often set aside from the rest of the organization's warehouse installations and are connected by a link road. In some cases, inventory yards may be located miles from the primary warehouse building and instead be part of the organization's distribution system, acting as a constant source of inventory to business and individual customers in the area. Small unit warehouses and retail organizations may have inventory yards as an extension of their main buildings. For example, to handle their large quantities of extra gardening inventory every summer, many Walmart, Target, Lowes, Home Depot, and Fred Meyer stores fence off part of their parking lots.

When an organization is deciding where to locate its external inventory yard, specialist advice is typically sought from warehouse managers. Five factors that influence location decisions for an inventory yard include:

1. **Cost of land.** The cost of land in the immediate area or surrounding districts directly affects whether or not the external inventory yard is set up close to the organization's present warehouse buildings or retail locations. In the case of high local land prices, it may have to be located at some distance away.

2. **Space available.** If space is not available near the organization itself, the external inventory yard may again have to be located some distance away.

3. **Transportation connections.** Depending upon the requirements of the organization, its product, its suppliers, and its distributors, the inventory yard may need to be located near a major transportation link or transportation route, such as near a major highway or along a railroad route.

4. **Size needed.** In most cases, the larger the inventory yard needed, the more likely it will be set up outside an inner-city area because land is too scarce in densely populated areas.

5. **Materials stored.** The type and character of materials to be stored also influences inventory yard location. For example, highly dangerous materials would have to be stored away from population centers and the rest of the organization's installations in case of accident.

Similar to a warehouse location, a company may determine its external inventory yard location in an effort to reduce transportation costs and time. Factors such as those listed above can be placed into formulae and computer models to determine optimal external inventory yard locations.

Compared to warehouse buildings, external inventory yards offer low construction and running costs. Inventory yard construction costs are far less expensive because only a sound base, secure fencing, and strong gates are required, unlike complex warehouse buildings, which require foundations, walls, roofing, ventilation, and heating. There are four basic methods of external inventory yard construction based on flooring type: *open ground*, *gravel surface*, *asphalt surface*, and *concrete surface*. The construction method used is determined by both the cost of construction and the material to be stored.

Open ground is the cheapest form of inventory yard because it needs no outlay for a base. This type of inventory yard consists of standard ground with no additional surface construction and often includes a surrounding fence. It provides basic security, requires no maintenance, and it can easily be removed and set up in another location when desired. Because it is difficult to manage and locate inventory in open ground yards, they are often limited to storing scrap or obsolete materials. Using open ground inventory yards also restricts pallet loads because materials handling equipment tends to sink on unsupported surfaces, especially when faced with heavy loads or rainy weather conditions.

Gravel surface inventory yards are popular with many organizations, especially when storing low value inventory in large quantities when limited resources are available. These yards support more weight than open ground inventory yards, remain relatively inexpensive to install, and can be relocated easily. Gravel surface inventory yards still tend to become waterlogged in adverse weather conditions and do not support heavily laden equipment and pallets.

Asphalt surface inventory yards are, by far, the most popular of the inventory yard surface types. The asphalt surface is very strong and will support most heavy loads in all weather conditions. Because asphalt surface inventory yards offer excellent storage, can easily be laid out and marked for location systems, and can be easily maintained and repaired, many organizations make them their permanent inventory yard of choice. Asphalt surface construction is more expensive than open ground or gravel surface construction, however, and is subject to damage in very hot weather, with heavy loads creating indentations and holes in the surface.

Concrete surface inventory yards are the strongest and most stable of the four inventory yard surface construction types. They are able to handle the heaviest loads, remain operable all year round regardless of weather conditions, and can easily be laid out and marked for efficient location and selection. Concrete surface inventory yards, however, are relatively expensive to construct and even more expensive to relocate, typically limiting their use to organizations with materials that have very heavy storage loads, such as heavy cables or construction equipment, which need corresponding heavy materials handling equipment.

FIGURE 4.8 - FLOORING TYPES FOR EXTERNAL INVENTORY YARDS:

OPEN GROUND LUMBER STORAGE AREA IN BOSTON, MASSACHUSETTS; REFRIGERATED CONTAINER STORAGE AREA FOR FISH PROCESSOR IN NUUK, GREENLAND; ASPHALT SURFACE EXTERNAL INVENTORY YARD FOR FLOUR FACTORY IN REYKJAVIK, ICELAND; AND CONCRETE SURFACE EXTERNAL INVENTORY YARD FOR CONCRETE SLAB COMPANY IN LERWICK, SCOTLAND

As previously mentioned, external inventory yards have a few advantages over warehouse buildings as a means of storage. Compared to warehouse buildings, they are relatively inexpensive to set up and surface. They also offer an ideal set-up for storing non-perishable, unusually bulky, and heavy materials at a very low cost per unit stored. External inventory yards also allow for the use of heavy, diesel-powered inventory handling equipment without the problems of ventilation associated with using such equipment in an enclosed warehouse building. Finally, external inventory yards consume less energy in lighting and heating and have lower maintenance costs in repairs and replacements of fittings when compared to typical warehouse buildings.

Despite all of these advantages, external inventory yards often have a variety of constraints or faults. Most of these disadvantages can be avoided in the early stages of inventory yard design, however, with proper planning and expert advice. Such design and planning faults include:

- **Incorrect surface.** Organizations may sometimes choose an external inventory yard surface that does not match the materials being stored and handled, especially when they select the cheapest rather than the most appropriate material available. Such organizations create a false sense of savings, however, because they must later pay to have the lesser surface pulled up and replaced with the more appropriate surface needed to cope with their heavy loads in adverse conditions.

- **Waterlogged surfaces.** When drainage designs and facilities fail, waterlogged surfaces result. Materials handling is then more difficult and more dangerous, especially in the winter when surface water can turn to ice. In addition, even the most highly resistant surface materials can deteriorate when left in constant contact with water.

- **Inadequate lighting systems.** In the hours of poor daytime light or nighttime darkness, adequate lighting with floodlights and spotlights is essential. Such lighting makes accurate materials selection possible and reduces the accident rate, especially in inventory yards in which materials are handled 24 hours per day and 365 days per year. It also decreases the risk of theft because there is no cover of darkness.

- **Inadequate security.** When fencing and alarm systems are inadequate or nonexistent, external inventory yards may experience frequent visits from a variety of unauthorized personnel.

- **Poor location and marking system.** Inventory yards are often used as a dumping area for all types of materials. In such situations, goods are typically stored anywhere, without any thought given to utilization of space or the frequency of materials usage. This leads to greater materials handling costs and reduced available storage space.

- **Inefficient and neglected control centers.** *Inventory yard control centers* (described later in this section) should be centers for documentation, control, and location plans. When there is a lack of supervisory control, these centers are often neglected, leading to loss of control over storage and inventory selection.

- **Inadequate transportation links.** Many organizations make the mistake of providing resources for an excellent inventory yard while failing to ensure that links to the main transportation systems, such as rail or highway systems, are adequate. As a result, these inventory yards can become isolated from the rest of the organization's storage system in adverse weather conditions and transportation costs remain high throughout the life of the inventory yard.

For an external inventory yard to operate efficiently and effectively, a logical, workable yard layout must be designed and implemented. Exactly as we discussed when examining warehouse layout design, external inventory yards must also consider *frequency of usage* of the inventory stored, with the most highly used items put away and stored closest to the entrances, exits, and ends of aisles of the inventory yard. Other factors to consider in inventory yard layout include: *entrances and exits*, *control centers*, and *location systems*.

When considering inventory yard layout design, **entrances and exits** must be placed so that a one-way traffic flow system can be implemented. Such one-way systems are essential for reducing inventory yard delays and traffic accidents, especially because fork lifts and other heavy machinery equipment are involved. In many large external inventory yards, the entrance and exit gates are side by side with the control center or gatehouse situated between them, enabling materials to be easily recorded on delivery and issue. Furthermore, in a well-designed inventory yard, the entrance and exit gates are secure, lockable, and wide enough and high enough to allow the largest vehicle used in the yard to pass through.

The **control center**, also called a **gatehouse**, is another important element of inventory yard layout design. The control center must be located in a position of central control because it functions as an observation center for the main areas of activity within the external inventory yard. The control center must also have the resources needed to control and record the movement of inventory into and out from the yard.

Finally, to ensure that inventory can be stored in and selected from the external inventory yard as quickly and efficiently as possible, a logical and workable **inventory location system** is required. With a well-designed location system, the inventory yard controller is able to locate any item in the yard at any time and direct materials handling resources appropriately. In such a system, a master copy of the yard location plan is kept in the control center, often on a large board-type visual aid that can easily be used as an immediate reference. In the external inventory yards of larger companies, there are often computerized inventory location systems, with those in the control center or gatehouse able to pinpoint exact locations of inventory within massive inventory yards with only a few quick keystrokes.

In addition to considering layout design, industrial external inventory yard designers and planners also consider the basic equipment needed for efficient operations. The type and amount of equipment required will depend upon the size of the yard and the materials being handled. Five types of equipment essential for most external inventory yards are:

- **Mechanical handling devices.** Mechanical handling devices, such as forklifts or pallet trucks, are used primarily in the external inventory yard for bulk inventory storage and picking.

- **Manual handling equipment.** When small loads or orders must be moved or when mechanical devices fail, external inventory yards use manual handling equipment, such as pump lifts and hand trucks.

- **Security equipment.** No matter how large or small, all external inventory yards should have security equipment. This equipment may range from key, locks, and chains to complex, multi-zone alarm systems.

- **Firefighting equipment.** Another necessity for all external inventory yards is firefighting equipment, such as fire extinguishers, fire blankets, and hose reels. The organization should also have fire instructions with details on how to deal with the kinds of fires their inventory might produce, such as chemical or petroleum fires.

- **Racking equipment.** Except in the case of very large, bulky, or oddly shaped inventory, racking equipment is another common find in external inventory yards. Such equipment allows items on pallets or other standardized platforms to be stored vertically, thus maximizing the inventory yard's storage capacity.

FIGURE 4.9 - CONTROL CENTER AT A CANNED VEGETABLE PROCESSOR AND DISTRIBUTION CENTER IN NEWPORT, TENNESSEE; SECURITY EQUIPMENT IN THE FORM OF HIGH FENCING, ARMED AND LOCKED GATES, AND LIGHTING AT AN EXTERNAL INVENTORY YARD FOR A HOME IMPROVEMENT STORE IN ANCHORAGE, ALASKA; AND RACKING EQUIPMENT AT CONSTRUCTION SUPPLY STORAGE AREA IN VANCOUVER, CANADA

Because they often hold the organization's finished product, external inventory yards play a vital role in the physical distribution system. By **distribution**, we mean the process of getting the organization's product from the place of production to the point of consumption. In the physical distribution system, external inventory yards can be used as a "topping-up" center, where goods are stored in bulk from the place of production and distributed to customers in the local area. In addition, small external inventory yards with an emergency inventory of goods can be located up and down the distribution network to be used in the event of sudden high demand or emergencies, such as adverse weather conditions that make movement over long distances impossible. Finally, external inventory yards can be used as **marshaling areas** where goods are collected from various parts of the production system, sorted into customers' requirements, and dispatched to various centers of demand.

In order to play a full part in the physical distribution process, external inventory yards must be fully integrated with warehouses and depots throughout the distribution system. Coding systems, location codes, warehouse procedures, and materials handling equipment must be uniform to ensure that the inventory yard, despite its open construction, will be managed the same way as the warehouses and other links in the system.

Finally, external inventory yards must be carefully and professionally managed to provide their organizations with full the potential storage capacity at the minimum cost per unit. A vast amount of capacity is wasted in many external inventory yards due to poor management, with organizations using the yard as a dumping ground, leaving it to its own devices, and not integrating it into the organization's larger warehouse management system. To avoid waste and ensure full use of resources, the following factors should be considered when managing an external inventory yard:

- **Placement.** Overall placement of pallets, bins, and drums must be neat and logical to avoid accidents and wasted space.

- **Staff.** The staff who are involved in running and supervising the external inventory yard must not be isolated from the rest of the warehouse staff. Such isolation leads to slack control and low morale. Both training and staff rotation are useful means of avoiding warehouse isolation.

- **Management.** Management involvement and resources must be provided to ensure adequate control of inventory and operations and to ensure full integration into the logistics management system as a whole.

- **Equipment.** Up-to-date and well-maintained equipment is vital for an external inventory yard to operate efficiently.

- **Location system.** As previously mentioned, a sound and logical inventory location system is vital to the efficient operation of any external inventory yard.

- **Security.** Security systems provided to protect an organization's main warehouse and other installations must also be extended to cover the external inventory yard.

- **Delivery and issuance supervision.** Diligent supervision of inventory delivery and issuance is vital if storage control is to be established and dumping of materials is to be prevented. This is possible only with an enforced policy of constant manning of the inventory yard and control center.

4.6 INVENTORY LOCATION CODES FOR STORAGE

Warehouses vary greatly in size, layout, and types of specialized equipment used within them. Some warehouses can be as large as several football fields, while others may be no larger than the refrigerated section of your local gas station convenience store. While their sizes and the items they store may differ, warehouses all have one thing in common: they must have an inventory location coding system, which we introduced back in Section 3.7. An **inventory location coding system**, whether it is complex and digital or basic and manual, is a coding system that lets those working in the receiving area of the warehouse know where to store goods. It also lets those completing order picking and issuing tasks know where to find goods after they have been stored.

In an inventory location coding system, an item is given a code that indicates where the item is to be stored and found. This code has been given a variety of names and two of the. more common names are the **warehouse inventory location code** and the **warehouse inventory address code**. No matter what name a company uses, the objectives of this code remain the same: to provide an *efficient and effective means of putting goods away* within the warehouse and to provide an *easy means of finding them* again.

There are two principle approaches to allocating space to incoming inventory: *fixed* and *random*. In the **fixed approach** to allocating space for incoming inventory, each item in inventory has a pre-assigned location. These pre-planned location assignments may be based on item quantity, weight, or frequency of use. The advantage of a fixed location system is that it allows warehouse staff to become familiar with the location of an item. Such location familiarity can save considerable time when goods are stored or picked for issue. One drawback of a fixed location system, however, is that more space is required to facilitate the greatest possible item quantity. For example, Cycles-R-Us might store 60 days inventory of an item such as the Road Rage Racing Tricycle, also called the Triple-R Trike. After 30 days, half of the space allocated for the Triple-R Trike is empty and not being used but must remain unoccupied until the Cycles-R-Us warehouse receives its next shipment of the popular tricycle.

FIGURE 4.10 - FIXED APPROACH A TELECOMMUNICATIONS COMPANY WAREHOUSE (LEFT) WHERE TECHNICIANS PICK THEIR OWN ORDERS AND NEED TO KNOW WHERE CERTAIN ITEMS ARE AT ALL TIMES. RANDOM APPROACH AT A WAREHOUSE-STYLE RETAIL STORE (RIGHT) WITH INCOMING PALLETS OF GOODS PLACED IN FIRST AVAILABLE SPACES.

Unlike the fixed approach, in the ***random approach*** to allocating space for incoming inventory, goods are stored in the first available space in the warehouse. This system makes greater use of space, but for it to work effectively, there must be a highly effective set of warehouse inventory location codes and a corresponding digital inventory location coding system. At the enormous Amazon fulfillment centers around the world, goods are put away based on the random approach to space allocation. Inventory management is based on highly specific scannable codes and goods are stored in places to maximize space and facilitate the speedy flow of goods. With this random approach, you find goods that are not at all similar or related in the same storage bins or in adjacent slots, such as boxes of bicycle parts and Irish lace handkerchiefs next to each other in the same storage slot.

While warehouses may differ in their use of fixed or random space allocation systems, they share the need for an inventory location coding system, unless they are a small "Mom and Pop" operation who enjoy the thrill of the hunt when "Pop" invariably forgets where he placed the light bulbs. The complexity of an inventory location coding system, however, will depend upon the size of its warehousing network and the volume, variety, and complexity of items to be stored.

When an organization begins to construct a new inventory location coding system, it typically works from the outside and moves inward. It starts at the level of geographic location of the warehouse with a network of company warehouses, moving eventually to a specific location on a specified shelf. Let's again take a code-building journey, this time as we assign a warehouse inventory location code to an item according to an organization's inventory location system. Let the coding begin!

The warehouse inventory location code format for our company, We-Do-Food, is based on six fields. Although inventory location codes can be a mix of letters, numbers, and symbols, the We-Do-Food inventory location codes are entirely numeric and are written within six sequential boxes:

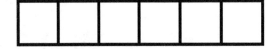

The first field of the We-Do-Food warehouse inventory location code tells us in which warehouse our item, papayas, is located. The We-Do-Food Company has five warehouses throughout Alaska and the codes for each warehouse by geographic location are:

Eagle River: 1   Anchorage: 2   Fairbanks: 3   Juneau: 4   Soldotna: 5

Our papayas happen to be located in the Soldotna warehouse, which means that we can fill in the first field of our warehouse inventory location code:

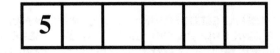

The second field of the We-Do-Food warehouse inventory location code tells us in which sector of a warehouse our item is located. We-Do-Foods uses only single-story warehouses, but companies with multi-story warehouses might use this field to indicate which floor within the warehouse an item is located. The sectors of the We-Do-Foods Soldotna warehouse are:

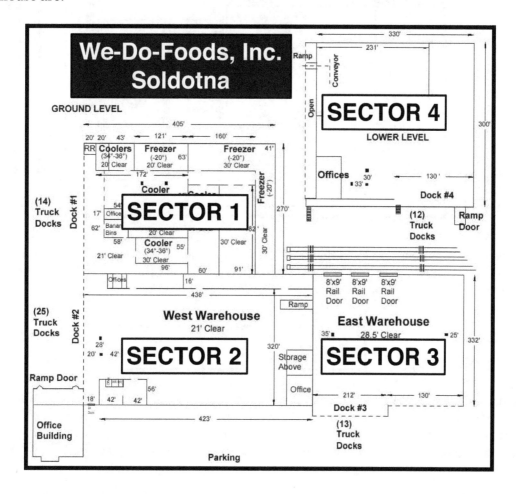

Because our delicate papayas must be refrigerated, they are located in the coolers within Sector 1 of the Soldotna warehouse, which means that we can fill in the second field of our warehouse inventory location code:

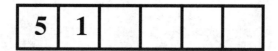

The third field of the We-Do-Food warehouse inventory location code tells us the aisle or row of the specified warehouse section in which our item is located. For Sector 1 of the Soldotna We-Do- Foods warehouse, the aisle or row numbers are:

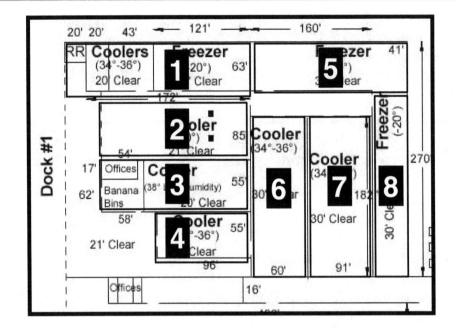

Our refrigerated papayas are located within the cooler in Aisle 7 of Sector 1 of the Soldotna We-Do-Foods warehouse, which means that we may now fill in the third field of our papaya warehouse inventory location code:

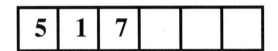

The fourth field of the We-Do-Food warehouse inventory location code tells us in which bay of the specified aisle or row our item is located. Within warehousing, a **bay** is a compartment of a building or section used for a specific purpose. In the We-Do-Foods warehouse, the bays are the vertically divided cooler subsections of each row or aisle. For Aisle 7 of Sector 1 of the Soldotna, the cooler bays are numbered as follows:

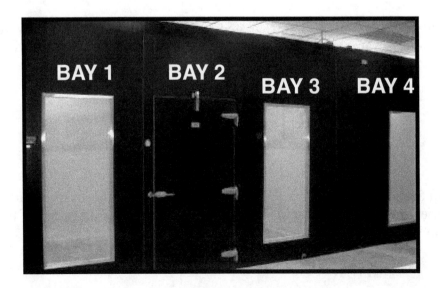

Our We-Do-Foods papayas are located within Bay 2 of Aisle 7 of Sector 1 of the Soldotna warehouse, making the papaya warehouse inventory location code now read:

The fifth field of the We-Do-Food warehouse inventory location code tells us on which shelf within Bay 2 our delicious papayas are located. The shelves in Bay 2 are labeled as:

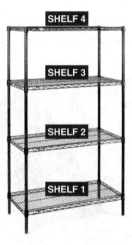

Our papayas are located on the third shelf, which means that our warehouse inventory location code now reads:

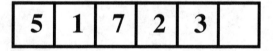

The sixth and final field of the We-Do-Foods papaya warehouse inventory location code reveals the section on the third shelf in which the papayas are located. The sections on Shelf 3 are divided as follows:

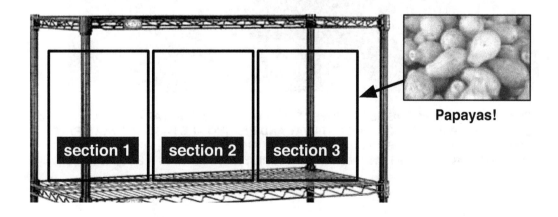

Papayas!

Lo and behold, our delectable papayas appear to be in Section 3 on Shelf 3 of Bay 2 within Aisle 7 of Sector 1 of the Soldotna We-Do-Foods warehouse. Therefore, our completed warehouse inventory location code reads:

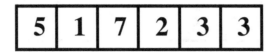

Inventory location codes for different companies will be different because they are based on the needs of that company, its products, and the layout of its warehouses and external inventory yards. No matter what company or what warehouse, developing an inventory location coding system, *and making sure all warehouse staff understand the system*, is essential to quick and accurate putaway and inventory picking when storing goods.

FIGURE 4.11 - EFFECTIVE USE OF INVENTORY LOCATION CODES AT A SMALL BUSINESS HELP TO MAKE SURE PUTAWAY AND PICKING ARE FAST AND ACCURATE. THEY ALSO HELP TO KEEP WAREHOUSES TIDY AND ORGANIZED, LIKE THIS ONE OWNED BY ALASKA GIFT AND MEMORABILIA RETAILER, ONCE IN A BLUE MOOSE.

CHAPTER 4 REVIEW QUESTIONS

1. In your own words, what is *dock-to-stock time*? Why is it important?

2. What is *slotting*? When and how is it used?

3. If an item in a warehouse is one that is frequently picked, where should it be located within the warehouse? Where should it be located on a shelving system and in what situations might it not be located in this area of the shelving system?

4. In the world of warehousing, what is a *mezzanine*? Provide an example of a company's warehouse that might have a mezzanine and describe what the mezzanine might be used for.

5. When might a company want to rent warehouse space? Describe a potential situation not from the chapter in which a specific company might consider a renting a warehouse building or warehouse space in a specific location instead of using a purpose-built or converted warehouse building.

6. What is an *external inventory yard*? For what types of goods is it used?

7. Under what circumstances might a company choose to use *open ground flooring* in their inventory yard? Under what circumstances might a company choose to use a *concrete surface* inventory yard?

8. Why might a one-way flow of traffic be important to an external inventory yard?

9. What is an *inventory location system*? How might one be used in an external inventory yard setting?

10. What is the difference between a *fixed approach* and a *random approach* to allocating space for incoming inventory? What are the primary advantages of each approach?

CHAPTER 4 CASE EXERCISE

EXTERNAL INVENTORY YARD CONSTRUCTION...
YOU DECIDE!

You're the expert! You must figure out which type of external inventory yard construction to use for six different situations. Remember, the four different types of external inventory yard construction are:

open ground, **gravel surface**, **asphalt surface**, and **concrete surface**

Read the following six scenarios and decide which type of external inventory yard construction would be the most effective and cost effective. For each scenario, write which of the four construction types you have selected and explain why that is the best choice.

1. A Christmas tree company needs a place to store its freshly cut trees before bundling them and taking them to individual lots across the northeastern United States.

2. A bridge building company in Florida needs to create a permanent inventory yard for its finished bridge parts, including 2-story-high concrete pillars and 15-foot wide coils of steel cable.

3. A sailboat manufacturer needs a place to store its meticulously handcrafted finished inventory: 250 sailboats of different sizes, each on small 2-wheeled trailers.

4. A log home building supplier in rainy Seattle needs a temporary location to store freshly cut and debarked logs for five nearby new homes. The lot must be able to handle some vehicular traffic.

5. Sand and Gravel America, Inc. needs a permanent inventory yard that will be a receiving and distribution center for palletized loads of cultured stone, which is lightweight stone used on house exteriors. The stone comes in 125 varieties and sizes.

6. Sub-Sub-Z, Inc., the premier refrigerator manufacturer in central Asia, has had to recall its MegaFreeze refrigerator because it was found to spontaneously combust when placed next to a microwave. The company needs a temporary place to store its recalled MegaFreeze refrigerators before they are dismantled and hauled away for destruction.

Chapter 5
Materials Handling

You are now on your way to becoming a superstar of warehouse management! You now know about warehouse buildings and external inventory yards. What more could you possible need to know? Imagine that you are the regional warehouse manager of We-Do-Food, a grocery retail company catering to the cost conscious customer. You have the perfectly designed warehouse. You have a perfect place for everything and everything is in its place. It's a stupendous warehouse for a static world! What more could you possibly need?

Apples, frozen crab legs, and potato chips are coming in. Trucks are waiting at the dock for sodas, cheese, and our beloved papayas to go out. Meanwhile, more delivery trucks arrive. The inevitable has come: goods must move in and other goods must move out. Our perfectly designed static warehouse has entered the reality of our dynamic world. We must now physically handle the goods coming in as we enter the big, wide world of *materials handling*.

FIGURE 5.1 - THE MATERIALS OF MATERIALS HANDLING

**RAW MATERIALS *(LEFT: LUMBER TRANSPORTED VIA BARGE IN VENICE, ITALY)*,
SEMI-FINISHED GOODS *(CENTER: RAW MILK FROM THE SWISS ALPS READY FOR
TRANSPORT TO A PASTEURIZATION FACILITY IN LUCERNE, SWITZERLAND)*, AND
FINISHED GOODS *(RIGHT: WASHING MACHINES IN A RETAIL
WAREHOUSE IN ANCHORAGE, ALASKA)***

5.1 A FIRST LOOK AT MATERIALS HANDLING

We know we need to move things into, within, and out of our warehouse, but where do we begin? Let's begin with **materials handling**, the discipline that focuses on safe and efficient short-distance movement and storage of goods within a supply chain. The materials being handled can be raw materials, semi-finished goods, or finished goods and their movement occurs as they are handled anywhere *within one location* along the supply chain, such as within one cargo port or within one warehouse building. When goods are moved longer distances between different locations in a supply chain, such as from an ocean cargo port to an inland regional distribution center 100 miles away, the discipline that focuses on this longer movement of goods is called **transportation**, which we will explore later in Chapter 9.

FIGURE 5.2 - MATERIALS HANDLING (SHORT-DISTANCE MOVEMENT OF GOODS) AND TRANSPORTATION (LONGER-DISTANCE MOVEMENT OF GOODS)

It is important to note that some organizations use the terms *material handling* and *materials handling* interchangeably, while other organizations may prefer one term over the other. A recent trend in North American publications is the use of *materials handling* as a noun to represent the discipline focusing on the movement and storage of goods and *material handling* as a related adjective in terms such as "material handling equipment" or "material handling systems." Regardless of whether you prefer *material* or *materials* with your *handling*, it's best to know the terminology of your company, its customers, and suppliers and adjust your language accordingly.

When a company is focused on materials handling, it typically hopes to optimize its use of at least one of the following:

- **Space.** How goods are handled when moved and stored has a direct impact on warehouse space needed. Warehouses must plan for the amount of floor space needed for the materials handling equipment to be used. For example, if materials are to be stored and retrieved using a large forklift, more aisle space will be allocated than if materials are to be stored and retrieved using a small hand truck. Conversely, if the objective of an organization is to work within existing warehouse space limitations, materials handling equipment and methods chosen will be those that fit and work within the existing space constraints. For example, in a downtown city warehouse with no room for expansion, a company may decide to use small hand trucks or narrow aisle forklifts instead of standard forklifts for storage and retrieval palletized goods.

- **Labor.** When more labor hours are needed in a warehouse, employees work longer hours or more warehouse employees are used. Either way, more money must be allocated to pay for these increased labor hours. Therefore, organizations look to materials handling to reduce labor cost by designing and utilizing materials handling systems which allow people to work more effectively and require fewer labor hours to accomplish the same movement and storage tasks.

- **Service.** A company's materials handling can enhance its levels of customer service. For example, if the We-Do-Food regional grocery warehouse revamped its materials handling system, it would get fresh produce onto delivery trucks 50% quicker in the middle of a sub-zero Alaskan February, allowing less freezing damage to set in, resulting in a fresher papaya for the grocery store customer.
The way in which a company handles its goods during their movement and storage can dramatically increase or decrease warehousing costs. While an organization may incur significant set-up costs for a well-designed materials handling system, it can reap substantial cost-saving benefits for many years to come. Thus, when considering the array of materials handling systems covered throughout the remainder of this chapter, companies are ever mindful of the system set-up costs, their long-term cost saving benefits, and the positive impact that could result for internal and external customer satisfaction.

As a discipline, materials handling has continued to gain increasing momentum across the world into the 21st century. The largest international professional association for materials handling, MHI, reports that, in the United States alone, the annual expenditure on the materials handling industry had grown from $34.5 billion in 1990 to $64 billion in 2000 to a whopping $173 billion in 2018. Organizations invest money and time into materials handling because of the significant benefits it can bring, which include:

- **Enhanced output and distribution.** Materials handling addresses the movement and storage of materials within physical indoor or outdoor facilities in the supply chain. For example, for a manufacturing company, materials handling focuses on the receipt of goods into storage, the internal movement to the production process, the movement back to internal storage, and the final movement to the outbound distribution system to external customers. When organizations focus on this movement and attempt to make materials flow quickly, efficiently, and seamlessly, output becomes more efficient and distribution experiences fewer delays and product shortages. For example, the United States Federal Bureau of Investigations (FBI) constructed a 256,000 square-foot climate-controlled, robotic warehouse facility for its physicals records. These records used to be located across 56 of its field offices and other locations around the world. The FBI is estimated to be 40 years away from digitizing all its records, so when original records were needed for new investigations, court cases, or Freedom of Information and Privacy Acts requests from the public, it formerly took a long time to track down and receive records. With all of the FBI records now housed under one roof in the new robotic facility in Virginia, records can be stored and retrieved in a fraction of the time it used to take, making for quicker and smoother operations.

FIGURE 5.3 - ROBOTS AND STORAGE GRID IN THE FBI RECORDS WAREHOUSE

- **Reduced operating cost.** A poorly operated or designed materials handling system is not only dangerous to people and products, but it can also increase logistics cost dramatically. When materials are handled unnecessarily or inefficiently, materials handling equipment, plant, time, and labor costs all increase. Conversely, when materials are moved and stored quickly and more efficiently, the cost per unit moved reduces. Imagine the cost savings from previous example of the FBI's robotic warehouse facility. Instead of tracking down and shipping records to and from any of the 56 FBI locations where they were formerly stored, FBI employees now work in one area of one facility to either program a putaway or retrieval of a record bin. The conveyors and the racking system robots do the rest of the work, either putting away or retrieving any of the 360,000 bins in a gigantic steel cube-grid. Although the cost to construct this system was $135 million, the operating costs for records storage and retrieval is now dramatically reduced, with very few labor hours needed for per unit movements.

FIGURE 5.4 - PUTAWAY AND RETRIEVAL AREA OF THE FBI RECORDS WAREHOUSE

- **Employee health and safety.** The quality of a company's materials handling system, including the equipment used and the training received by equipment operators, can have an enormous impact on the health and safety of employees within its warehouse, production, and distribution facilities. A faulty system or a poorly trained driver can lead to serious or even fatal accidents. For example, as reported in the February 2023 *Journal of Food Safety Research* in a research article entitled "Severe Injuries from Product Movement in the U.S. Supply Chain" by Judd Michael and Serap Gorucu, injuries and deaths increased significantly in 2020 over previous years for materials handling workers in the U.S. food supply chain. With the onset of the COVID-19 pandemic, the nature of our food preparation and consumption changed because we spent most of our time at home and working from home. This meant that food had to be packaged, prepared, stored, and moved in new and different ways to adapt to these changes, which had an enormous ripple effect and learning curve for those working in the materials handling industry. Adjusting to new changes that had to be put into place immediately likely contributed to increased work-related injuries and death.

- **Reduced damage.** Poor or careless materials handling can result in damage and premature stock deterioration, not to mention the associated exorbitant increases in cost. Careful and consistent materials handling can reduce the risk of such costly damage. For example, in warehouses with metal racking systems and forklifts, some organizations find that the forks on the forklifts can damage both stored goods and the pole bases of the metal racking systems, especially when forklift operators are inexperienced, if the aisles are too narrow, or if the operation is under a tight time deadline. Organizations can reduce damage to their racks by investing in materials handling devises such as 24" bull-nosed, bright orange steel column guards to protect the base of the columns of the steel racks. They can also dramatically increase damage to stored goods from forklift by investing in automated guided vehicle (AGV) lift trucks, which have laser guidance systems to ensure that the vehicle's forks do not hit goods, racks, or anything else in its path.

5.2 MATERIALS HANDLING SYSTEMS

In order to reap the potential benefits of materials handling, organizations look to the design and efficiency of their materials handling systems. A ***materials handling system*** is the network of equipment, methodologies, procedures, standards, and rules used by an organization for the movement, storage, control, retrieval, and protection of goods. A materials handling system may be as simple as a small refrigerated storeroom at the back of a restaurant into which food is delivered by a small hand truck, stored on shelves, and retrieved by hand by restaurant kitchen staff or it may be as complicated as the computerized system of containers, trains, cranes, and forklifts found at many sea ports.

When selecting or designing a materials handling system, an organization will typically seek input from corporate strategic planners and logistics managers, specifically those leading the warehousing, production, and physical distribution departments. This cross-departmental team will then consider a variety of factors when selecting, planning, and designing a materials handling system, such as:

- **Materials Center Locations.** *Materials centers* are where an organization's goods and other are located. These materials centers include warehouse facilities, external inventory yards, production facilities, and distribution areas. For most organizations, materials centers are separated from each other by barriers, such as roads, railroad tracks, or pure distance. The presence of such physical barriers often creates a need for a combination of various forms of materials handling systems and devices, such as a forklift to gravity conveyor to tow truck to pallet truck system.

- **Nature of Materials Handled.** Different materials, especially those with different weight, size, and shape characteristics, will require different materials handling methods. This may sound like common sense, but we can't tell you how many new business owners we've met who are both shocked and dismayed to learn that, despite the salesman's assurances, their one forklift doesn't lift everything! Palletized items will need some form of forklifts and smaller items may need to be moved in bins on any form of conveyance, while very dense and heavy materials, such as steel, tend to be handled best by very large and powerful trucks or cranes.

- **Capital Resources.** When an organization has meager funds allotted for a materials handling system, they will often end up with a materials handling system with meager capabilities. No matter how much is available in capital resources, the materials handling planning and design team has as one of its primary goals to find the most effective and most suitable system and equipment available for the organization's budget.

- **Future Needs.** Very few organizations will remain exactly the same size throughout the useable lifespan of their materials handling system. Materials handling systems planners must consider the future growth or contraction of logistics and warehousing needs by creating a flexible system which can be easily adjusted to meet the changing needs of the organization. Imagine that a We-Do-Food warehouse purchases $1 million in special handling equipment, which will handle only large volumes of oranges and grapefruit. The following year, a severe drought occurs in Florida and California, resulting in We-Do-Food receiving 70% fewer oranges and grapefruit, which, in turn, results in the special handling equipment sitting idle and the portion of warehouse space it takes up being unused 70% of the time.

- **Total Cost.** It may seem obvious that a materials handling system planning and design team would consider the total cost of a potential new systems, but less obvious, however, is what makes up the total cost. Not only must the planning and design team consider the actual cost of the pieces of equipment they will purchase, but they must also consider system's operating costs, such as fuel, power, maintenance, labor, spare parts, and depreciation costs.

- **Equipment Compatibility.** Unless a company is building an entirely new warehouse and materials handling facility from the ground up, the materials handling system planning and design team will have to consider the nature of the existing equipment and facilities. For example, a warehouse with primarily small shelf storage and narrow aisles would be unsuitable for forklift trucks or palletized materials.

- **Devices Available.** There are many materials handling system devices and equipment available on the market. Before a hasty decision based on which equipment looks the best, which system is used successfully by a competitor, or which salesperson seemed the friendliest, the materials handling system design and planning team must consider the wide range of devices and equipment available, while remaining mindful of their company's unique needs and any cross-device or cross-system compatibility issues.

- **Packaging Used.** The forms of packaging used by both the organization and its suppliers and distributors often play a defining role in the types of materials handling equipment ultimately used. Later sections of this text highlight different forms of packaging and the handling methods required for each.

5.3 MANAGEMENT FOR EFFICIENCY

Before looking at types of materials handling systems in depth, we must first dig a bit deeper into the principles of materials handling. As was mentioned at the beginning of this chapter, *materials handling* is the discipline that focuses on safe and efficient short-distance movement and storage of goods within a supply chain. Three of the guiding principles of materials handling are:

- *Manage for efficiency.*

- *Avoid the curse of double handling!*

- *Look at your flow.*

One of the most significant benefits that can be reaped from materials handling is increased efficiency, which is connected to the first of our three guiding principles of materials handling. Materials handling efficiency requires careful and professional management by senior logistics professionals. Many organizations have adopted the practice of appointing a senior member of the logistics management team as ***materials handling manager***, a logistics or supply chain manager with the overall responsibility and authority for all materials handling. Assigning someone to this important role offers many efficiency advantages, including:

- *Centralization of materials handling authority with a logistics manager, who has a broader view of the organization's total requirements, may result in better utilization of materials handling resources. Assigning the materials handling manager role to someone on the logistics management team assures that the role will be filled by someone with a big picture view of the organization and its supply chain needs.*

- *A skilled and specialized logistics professional will be able to recommend and utilize the best and most efficient systems in line with their professional knowledge and experience.*

- *Central control of materials handling within logistics management will help reduce the bottlenecks and holdups that plague many organizations. When the person filling the materials handling manager role is part of the logistics management team, they understand the organization's supply chain and have a better appreciation for what happens before and after goods are at their location.*

The materials handling manager can also follow set procedures to continue to dramatically increase efficiency, including:

- **Using only the correct equipment** for each task and never allowing materials handling devices to be misused, which can result in accidents and stock damage.

- **Properly training and testing all materials handling operators** in the use of relevant materials handling equipment. Many larger producers of materials handling equipment provide on-location training as part of their purchase and service packages.

- **Ensuring that the materials handling system selected truly meets the needs** of the organization. For example, a small company with a simple materials flow will require only a simple system. Managers must resist the temptation to use overly elaborate systems, no matter how attractive all the shiny and sparkly the expensive state-of-the-art features may be.

- **Ensuring that all other departments concerned are fully aware** of the problems and limitations of the materials handling system used. This will reduce system bottlenecks by reducing unreasonable demands placed on the system.

5.4 THE CURSE OF DOUBLE HANDLING

Remember that our second guiding principle of materials handling was: *Avoid the curse of double handling!* While management practices and procedures can be used to enhance materials handling efficiency, *double handling* can be one of its greatest hindrances and must be addressed to achieve a truly efficient materials handling system. In the world of warehousing, **double handling** is the term used to describe the practice of handling materials more times than necessary, primarily due to inefficiencies within the entire logistics management system.

When materials are delivered to a warehouse facility, they should make only a limited number of journeys, such as: from the delivery vehicle to the place of storage; selection from the place of storage; or from the storage or selection area to delivery vehicle or production location. In many organizations, however, this simple flow is not maintained and materials are handled too many times. As a result, the costs of handling, especially in fuel, warehouse space, and labor increase, accompanied by an increased risk of accidents and damage to goods. We once knew of a top automobile spare parts store in Ireland that received goods into its warehouse area loading bay, then transferred the goods to a "to-be-shelved" area, then moved them to a temporary shelving area which divided the incoming automobile parts into model number categories, then moved the goods to the primary storage and shelving area, and finally, moved the goods into the retail store. In this case, goods were not only double handled, but *triple* and *quadruple* handled as well! When this excess handling was eliminated, labor costs fell dramatically, warehouse shelving space was freed up, and materials damage decreased by an impressive 300%.

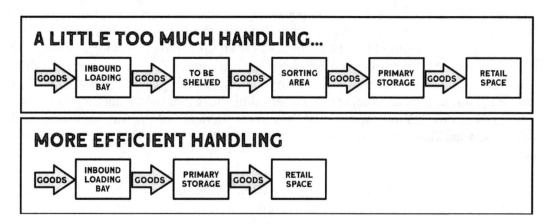

FIGURE 5.5 - EFFICIENT MATERIALS HANDLING

Double handling can occur in organizations and facilities of all sizes. The causes of this costly problem of double handling include:

- **Lack of Inventory Location Systems.** In Chapter 4, we examined how an inventory location systems lets those in the warehouse know where to store goods and where to find them again when picking orders. We even constructed our own location code for

We-Do-Foods warehouses. No imagine if those grocery warehouses did not have an inventory location systems and warehouse workers had to put away incoming grocery items before they would be picked for distribution to grocery stores. Without an inventory location system, all of the items in the warehouse would likely be handled far more times than they should be from workers moving them and even opening boxes every time they were in search of other items. It might take hours to find our beloved papayas and only after multiple non-papaya fruits had been handled in the search.

- **Inefficient Materials Handling Systems.** Most organizations already have systems for materials handling in place, but their systems may not be efficient enough to meet their needs. Remember our example of the new FBI robotic warehouse facility from Section 5.1, "A First Look at Materials Handling?" Before the new central warehouse was constructed to manage records, the FBI did have system to handle the management of its physical records, but it was not a very efficient one. People requesting records had to find which of the 56 FBI locations around the world had the records. Then they had to contact them to request them. After the FBI employee who had the records would then pass then to a courier who handled them and may have even had to put them on a truck or plane with others handling them to get them to the location where they needed to be. With the records now centralized and handled primarily by robots and automated systems, the risk of double handling has been exponentially decreased.

- **Poor Communications.** Good communications between the departments involved in materials handling is essential. For example, materials should be supplied to retail or production departments only when there is space for them and someone is ready to handle them for the purpose requested. Retail or factory floor space can become clogged with materials when there is poor communication between those in materials handling and those in retail or production. Imagine our Road Rage Racing Tricycle manufacturer requesting three boxes of tires for an upcoming specialty assembly job but without communicating the exact date they were needed. Now imagine that the warehouse delivered the tires to the factory floor immediately and did not know that the tires were not needed for another two weeks. For those two weeks, factory workers might have move around the boxes of tires to get them out of the way for whatever the day's task was. This would be a lot of excessive handling before the tires were actually needed!

- **Incorrect Materials Handling Device Use.** When the wrong device is used for the job, the job may need to be duplicated, resulting in double handling. For example, a small capacity truck will need to make several journeys to unload a vehicle with very heavy units, while a large device could perform the task in one movement. Think also of a large warehouse-style store, such as Costco, Sam's Club, or BJ's, which uses forklift trucks to move large quantities of a product straight from the delivery truck to the store aisle, instead of using smaller hand-trucks to move lesser quantities of the product. Definitely a labor-saving and cost-saving avoidance of double handling, as long as you avoid the speeding forklifts!

- **Lack of Space.** The most common cause of double handling is lack of space. This often happens when an organization has grown over time and its warehousing and materials handling space has not grown accordingly. When there is a lack of space and a need to unload delivery vehicles as quickly as possible, materials tend to be placed temporarily in the nearest available space, resulting in a sure-fire-recipe for double handling!

One strategy used by most contemporary companies to minimize the scourge of double handling is digital control of materials handling. For most companies, the materials that are handled are valuable and important to the operation as a whole. As such, many companies have developed complex digital and cloud-based materials handling systems. For example, central control boards displaying the position of every materials handling device can feed data into a warehouse management system program, which can then analyze the current situation and direct the most efficient use of materials handling resources.

In some warehouse facilities, like the FBI facility in Virginia, materials handling can become entirely or almost entirely automated with the aid of information systems, scanners, conveyors, and robots. Automated systems eliminate the excess human error which can result in double handling. Organizations may also choose to have their materials handling equipment radio-controlled, especially in situations where operations are spread over a wide area and a great deal of outdoor handling is performed. This enables central control to be in constant touch with every lift truck, allowing them to minimize double handling by overseeing and controlling the flow of the entire operation from a central point.

5.5 EXPLORING MATERIALS FLOW

Our third and final guiding principle of materials management focused on *flow*. In order to ensure that materials are handled with maximum efficiency and that all unnecessary double handling is eliminated, materials handling experts examine the flow of materials within the organization. For example, one item is selected and its movement is examined and documented from the time an organization received it to the time the item is either used by or leaves from the organization. Materials handling practitioners and analysts use ***flow process charts*** to document and examine this flow of goods. Materials flow process charts document both current and proposed methods or stages of materials flow.

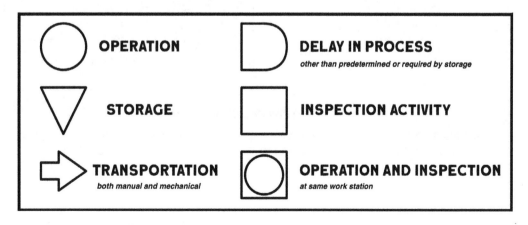

OPERATION

DELAY IN PROCESS
other than predetermined or required by storage

STORAGE

INSPECTION ACTIVITY

TRANSPORTATION
both manual and mechanical

OPERATION AND INSPECTION
at same work station

FIGURE 5.6 - STANDARD FLOW PROCESS CHART SYMBOLS

In flow process charts, standard symbols are used to represent action within the flow of goods. For example, a circle represents an operation, an upside-down triangle represents storage, a block arrow represents transportation, the letter *D* represents an unnecessary delay in process, and a square represents an inspection activity. Symbols may also be superimposed when actions occur simultaneously at the same place, such as a circle inside a square for when an operation and inspection occur at the same workstation.

Flow process charts may also take many forms, depending on the needs of the organization. For examining and documenting materials flow in relation to physical space and the location of goods, a flow process chart can be superimposed on an actual facility layout map, documenting a spatial materials flow. More often, however, materials flow is documented on a tabulated flow process chart, which highlights the actual number of times a material is handled within an organization. These charts are often used for efficiency analysis with the goals of reducing the number of times a material is handled.

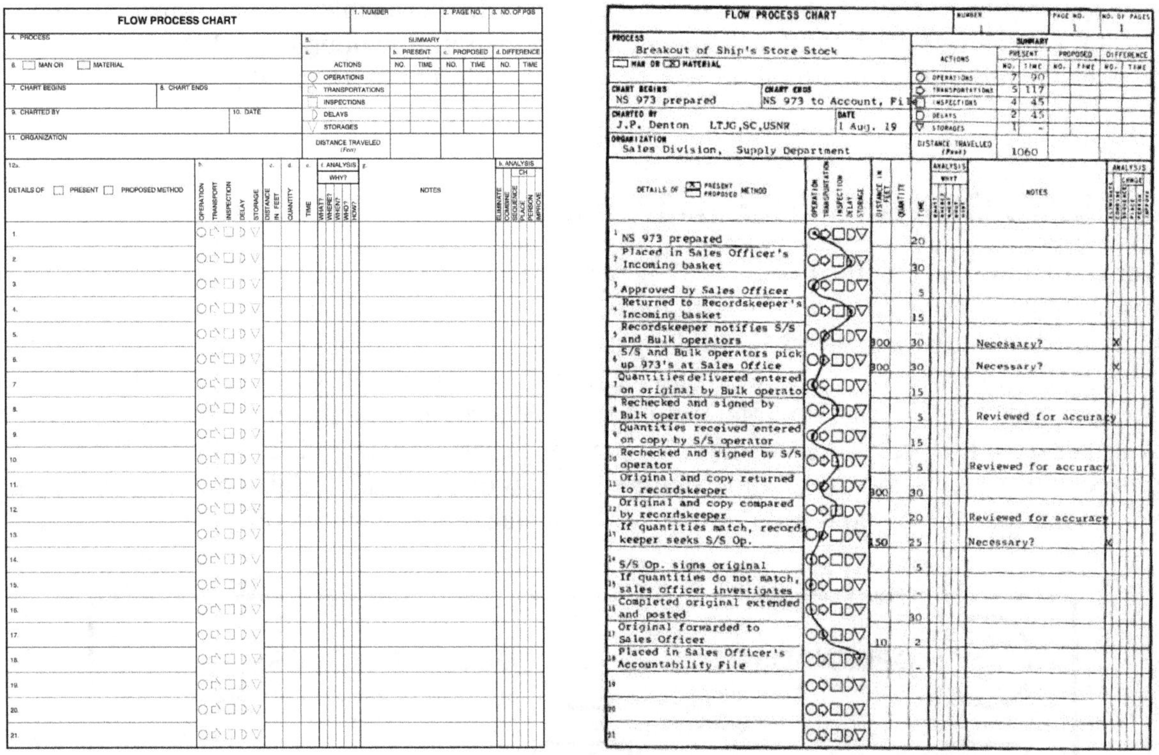

FIGURE 5.7 - FLOW PROCESS CHARTS

A BLANK FLOW PROCESS CHART USED BY THE U.S. DEPARTMENT OF DEFENSE (LEFT) AND A COMPLETED CHART (RIGHT) USED TO ANALYZE MATERIALS FLOW

5.6 MATERIALS HANDLING EQUIPMENT

Now that you understand some of its primary principles, think you're ready to make a move away from the wonderful world of materials handling? Not so fast! It's now time to delve into the nitty-gritty of materials handling equipment! Any device used to move or store a material during any segment of its logistics chain falls under the broad spectrum of **materials handling equipment**. Materials handling equipment can be **static**, which means that it is *stationary* and stays in one place while it is moving or storing materials. Examples of static materials handling equipment include shelves and pallet racks that store goods in a warehouse facility or conveyor systems, which move goods in a facility while the conveyor systems stay in place. Materials handling equipment can also be **dynamic**, which means that it is *movable* and the equipment itself changes its location while moving or storing materials. Examples of dynamic materials handling equipment include rack systems in warehouses that store goods while the racks move to desired locations when goods are being put away or picked. Examples also include equipment that itself moves while moving goods, such as forklift trucks and robotic pallet movers.

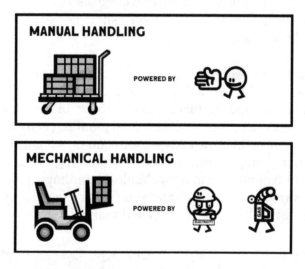

FIGURE 5.8 - MANUAL VERSUS MECHANICAL HANDLING

Materials handling equipment can also be **manual**, which means that it is hand operated, or **mechanical**, which means that it is powered by an energy source. **Manual handling** occurs when materials are handled by hand or by hand-operated devices. For example, moving goods from one end of a warehouse to another by carrying it in your arms, pushing it on a hand truck, or pulling it using a hand-operated pallet jack are all forms of manual handling. Although many of us love to shop for highly mechanized gadgets with lots of whistles and bells, materials handling system designers and planners must always first seriously consider manual handling as an option for materials handling systems. Manual handling equipment such as hand trucks and manual pallet jacks are typically less expensive to purchase, easier and less expensive to maintain and repair, easier to use in confined spaces, and more efficient in relation to the loads that can be handled, especially when equipment with hydraulic jacks are used.

Despite these advantages, manual handling is not the best choice. For example, a ten-person hot tub or a crate of concrete birdbaths may be too large, too heavy, or too cumbersome to be handled manually. In these cases, we instead need ***mechanical handling***, which occurs when materials are handled using machinery or powered devices. Using mechanical handling equipment can be extremely advantageous for many situations because they are able to handle extremely heavy loads, typically far in excess of a person's carrying capacity, and are able to move these materials quickly. For example, the average person could lift up to 100 or even 150 pounds of goods. If they used a hand truck or dolly, they could increase their load to up to 1000 pounds or more with some hand trucks. If they used a manual pallet jack, they could increase their load to somewhere between 2000 and 6000 for most equipment. If they decided to instead use mechanical handling equipment, such as a high-capacity forklift, their lifting capacity would increase to 40,000 pounds or more, with the heaviest forklifts able to lift loads of almost 200,000 pounds. Mechanical handling equipment can also be used 24 hours per day, with many forklift trucks in constant use as their drivers rotate work shifts. Mechanical handling equipment is also designed to cope with many dangerous and difficult situations safely, such as lifting goods to dangerous heights. For example, you might be able to carry a large load of cotton balls across a warehouse, but could you lift them to be stored on a shelf 36 feet above you? Sounds like you'll need mechanical handling equipment!

As wonderful as mechanical handling equipment is, it also has some distinct disadvantages, such as higher purchase costs, higher maintenance and operating costs, training and specialized employment costs, and the increased possibility of machine failure, which can significantly delay an entire operation. While manual handling equipment and mechanical handling equipment each have their own advantages and disadvantages, both should be considered when designing and planning a materials handling system. Most warehouse facilities use a combination of manual and mechanical handling equipment. Go to any medium to large sized warehouse near you and you're more than likely to find both forklifts and hand trucks, representing both mechanical and manual handling equipment.

FIGURE 5.9 - DISTRIBUTION CENTER MANUAL HANDLING *(HAND TRUCKS IN FOREGROUND)* AND MECHANICAL HANDLING *(FORKLIFT IN BACKGROUND)*

Aside from its obvious role in moving and storing goods, why else might today's materials handler want to use materials handling equipment? In three words: *cost*, *quality*, and *service*.Effective use of materials handling equipment can help an organization **reduce its materials handling or warehousing costs**. For example, forklifts allow an organization to store palletized materials far higher than human arms can reach. Using vertical storage space effectively in a warehouse means that less horizontal floor space is needed, which means that the warehouse has more space to store goods, making the overall holding cost per unit lower. Materials handling equipment also helps to ensure that a **high quality standards** can be attained and maintained for goods and operations. For example, in an ice cream factory, conveyors zipping from production floor to refrigerated trucks can ensure that precious tubs of its frozen goodness can stay frozen with no hot little human hands melting the tubs of Rocky Road ice cream. Finally, effective use of materials handling equipment can **increase service levels** to an organization's internal and external customers. For example, although unheard of fifty years ago, grocery store customers in cold and snowy Alaska now have the same selection of tropical produce available in sunny California, thanks to containers and dockside cranes that allow tropical fruits to be delivered quickly in sub-zero winter temperatures before freezing or spoiling. This allows the Alaskan shopper to enjoy papayas all year long!

Now that you know materials handling equipment can be static or dynamic and manual or mechanical, let's explore the major categories of materials handling equipment, which include:

- *transport equipment*. This category of equipment is used to move goods from one location to another. Transport equipment is typically dynamic and can be either manual or mechanical. Examples include industrial trucks and forklifts. Cranes and conveyors are other examples of transport equipment and may be either static or dynamic, as we will examine later in this chapter.

- *storage equipment*. This category of equipment is used to hold materials while it is kept in warehouse facilities for temporary to long-term storage timeframes. Examples include static shelves, racks, and bind and dynamic racks and shelving that move to make space for people or equipment as goods are put away or picked.

- *bulk handling equipment.* This category of materials handling equipment is used to move or store loose, unpackaged materials in bulk forms, such as loose coal, gravel, sugar, oil, or milk. Bulk handling equipment includes a mix of transport and storage equipment but specifically for large quantities of loose materials. Examples of bulk handling equipment include bulk conveyor systems, bucket elevators, storage silos, and liquid handling systems.

- *positioning equipment*. Used to reposition goods in place so that they are in the correct location and alignment for subsequent handling, this category of equipment is more product-specific than the other categories listed. we'll leave coverage of positioning equipment to more detailed, industry-specific materials handling publications.

- **unit load formation equipment**. This category of equipment is used to restrain goods and form them into a single unit load for subsequent transport and storage. We'll explore this category in much greater detail in Chapter 6, "The Unit Load."

- **engineered systems**. Also called **automated systems**, this category of materials handling equipment are typically at a stationary location, such as a single warehouse facility. Their purpose is to move and store goods through either assisting human operators or through functioning without human operators. Examples of equipment in engineered systems include automated guided vehicles, robot order pickers, and automated storage and retrieval systems. We will explore engineered systems in greater detail in Chapter 11 "Information Technology and Systems."

- **identification and communication equipment**. This category of equipment is used to identify goods to assist with inventory control and materials flow, although they do not typically come into direct physical contact with or actively handle goods. Some are used by humans while others are used without direct human operators. Examples of identification and communication equipment include barcode scanners, RFID readers, and voice assisted technology. We will explore this category of equipment in greater detail in Chapter 11 "Information Technology and Systems."

In the sections to follow in this chapter, we will examine the first three of these seven equipment categories. As previously mentioned, with the exception of positioning equipment, we will explore the remaining categories later in this book in Chapter 6 and Chapter 11.

5.7 TRANSPORT EQUIPMENT

Transport equipment is a category of materials handling equipment used to move goods from one place to another, typically within a specific facility or location. Remember from the beginning of this chapter that *materials handling* focuses on the short-distance movement and storage of goods within a supply chain. Therefore, our definition of *transport equipment* within the context of materials handling equipment does not include transportation vehicles that move goods from one facility to another, such as trains, planes, tractor-trailer trucks, and ships. Within the world of materials handling equipment, there are three primary types of transport equipment: *industrial trucks*, *cranes*, and *conveyors*.

When many of us think of materials handling equipment, especially those of us who spend a little too much time in Costco or Home Depot, our minds first wander to industrial trucks. **Industrial trucks** include hand trucks, forklift trucks, automated guided vehicles, and any other transport device with movement and maneuvering as its primary functions and carrying, stacking, loading, and unloading as additional functions. Industrial trucks typically operate by picking up loads from underneath, such as a forklift placing its forks underneath a palletized load before lifting and moving it. Industrial trucks can also maneuver goods of different sizes and types over variable paths at varying speeds. They can go almost anywhere, carrying almost anything, at almost any speed! These superheroes of the materials handling world do have their limitations, however. They can function effectively only on flat, level surfaces, such as asphalt or concrete. Because they need maneuvering room, they also don't handle well in confined or congested areas.

FIGURE 5.10 - NON-PALLETIZED TRUCKS.

A WALKIE PLATFORM TRUCK IN PIKE'S PLACE MARKET IN SEATTLE, WASHINGTON (LEFT);
A RIDER PLATFORM TRUCK IN A RETAIL DISTRIBUTION CENTER IN ANCHORAGE, ALASKA (CENTER);
AND A UPS RIDER PLATFORM TRUCK ON THE ISLE OF CAPRI, ITALY (RIGHT).

While there is a wide range of industrial truck types, they all fall into one of the following three categories: *non-palletized trucks*, *palletized trucks*, and *automated guided vehicles*. **Non-palletized trucks** are built to maneuver and carry items and unit loads other than those secured to a pallet. Because of their adaptability in the types of items and loads they can handle, non-palletized trucks typically cannot stack their loads or lift them more than a few inches. Manual non-palletized trucks include hand trucks and dollies. Mechanical non-palletized trucks include platform trucks, in both their **walkie** version, in which the operator walks to push and steer, and their **rider** version, in which the operator rides and steers.

 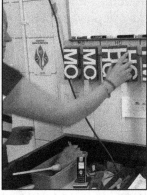

FIGURE 5.11 - NON-PALLETIZED TRUCK SOLUTION AT ONCE IN A BLUE MOOSE.

FOR THIS SMALL BUSINESS, SHOPPING CARTS AND BASKETS SECURED WITH ZIP TIES ARE THE MOST
EFFECTIVE SOLUTION FOR PUTAWAY AND ORDER PICKING. TAGS REPRESENTING EACH OF
THE COMPANY'S RETAIL LOCATIONS ARE SECURED TO THE CARTS USING VELCRO.

Palletized trucks, as their name suggests, are built to maneuver and carry palletized unit loads. In Chapter 6, we'll cover pallets and palletization in greater detail. Simple manual palletized trucks, such as *pallet jacks*, can be manually pushed or pulled by its operator, while simple mechanical palletized trucks, such as *pallet trucks*, can be ridden on by an operator. These simple pallet jacks and pallet trucks lift loads only a few inches high so goods don't drag on the ground while being moved.

FIGURE 5.12 - MANUAL PALLET JACKS IN LUCERN, SWITZERLAND (LEFT) AND ALASKA (RIGHT)

With other palletized trucks, however, palletized unit loads can be lifted several feet high and stacked. These, too, may be pushed by a walking operator, as with manual or powered *walkie stackers*, or ridden on and steered by an operator, as with *forklift trucks.* Powered palletized trucks are powered either by electricity through a rechargeable battery or by gas, using any range of liquid petroleum gas, compressed natural gas, gasoline, or diesel, depending on the equipment and where it will be used. Electric palletized trucks are used inside and gas-powered ones are used outdoors.

Forklift trucks come in a variety of styles based on the function they are intended to perform, including:

- *counterbalanced forklift trucks*, which have forks at the front and are weighted at the rear for heavier loads. They are used for standard maneuvering, carrying, lifting, and stacking palletized loads up to 13 feet.

- **narrow aisle forklift trucks**, also called **very narrow aisle trucks**, which are specially constructed for narrow aisle maneuvering and can operate in aisles as narrow as six feet wide.

- **reach fork truck**, which can have a greater reach than most forklifts with their extended length forks that can maneuver in racks that may be two pallet-loads deep. Some reach fork trucks may also be narrow aisle forklift trucks.

- **turret trucks** and **swing mast trucks**, which are designed to lift and stack palletized loads in narrow aisles up to 40 feet high, far above what is humanly possible without such equipment.

- **pallet jacks** and **pallet trucks**, which are designed to lift palletized goods only high enough to clear the floor so that it can be moved across the warehouse without dragging on the floor.

After reading about palletized trucks, you may be interested in hopping on the nearest forklift to try it out. If you are so inclined for that type of exciting warehouse adventure, STOP! The U.S. Department of Labor Occupational Safety and Health Administration (OSHA) requires operators of lift trucks and other types of materials handling equipment to be formally trained in the equipment they plan to operate.

FIGURE 5.13 - NARROW AISLE FORKLIFT (TOP LEFT), POWERED PALLET JACK (TOP CENTER), COUNTERBALANCED FORKLIFT (BOTTOM LEFT), AND TURRET TRUCK (BOTTOM RIGHT)

Automated guided vehicles, also known as *AGVs*, are purpose-built to handle either palletized or non-palletized loads of varying weights over fixed or variable paths. Unlike the previously discussed industrial trucks, AGVs do not require a hands-on operator. Because they are very expensive to purchase and require little to no direct labor, AGVs are typically used in environmentally sensitive environments, such as sterile medical equipment storage, or hazardous environments, such as sub-zero refrigeration warehouses.

FIGURE 5.14 - AUTOMATED GUIDED VEHICLE (AGV)

Now that we have provided an introduction to industrial trucks, the second category of transport equipment within the world of materials handling is cranes! *Cranes* are characterized by their ability to move individual items or unit loads of varying weights over a variable horizontal and vertical path within a fixed area. Their movement is less adaptable than that of the industrial trucks previously discussed, but they can often carry heavier loads, such as stacked containers. The primary function of a crane is to lift and carry a load or to place a load into a specific position. Cranes typically lift loads from above and can be used indoors or outdoors. They are also useful in dangerous or congested areas because they utilize vertical airspace instead of congested ground space. The four most common types of cranes are:

- *jib crane*, which uses a 360-degree pivoting arm extended out from a vertical support structure or a wall, in which case it pivots 180 degrees.

- *bridge crane*, which enables items to be moved to any location within an entire facility. Tracks are mounted on opposite walls of a facility with a perpendicular moving beam placed on these tracks and a moving hoist placed on the beam.

- *gantry cranes*, which are similar to bridge cranes but have floor-based support tracks rather than wall-based ones. They are typically used outside where there are no walls or inside when less facility floor space is needed for crane operations.

- *stacker cranes*, which are also similar to bridge cranes but have a fork-based or container-based apparatus suspended from its tracks instead of a beam with a hoist. Stacker cranes are primarily used for container and pallet load applications, especially when storage and retrieval needs exceed 40 feet. These are the cranes you typically see in a large sea port moving cargo containers.

FIGURE 5.15 - JIB CRANE (UPPER LEFT), BRIDGE CRANE (UPPER RIGHT), GANTRY CRANE (LOWER LEFT), AND STACKER CRANE (LOWER RIGHT)

Our third and final category of transport equipment is... conveyors! **Conveyors** move individual items and unit loads across a fixed path. An item is placed onto or attached to a conveyor at a fixed point and, with no human accompaniment, the item is transported to a different fixed point. The primary function of conveyors is to move goods. Unlike industrial trucks and cranes, which may have maneuvering, lifting, and positioning as additional functions, conveyors focus almost entirely on movement. Unlike industrial trucks and cranes, conveyors work continuously without stopping and need items or loads of relatively uniform weight and size for them to function effectively. While the same crane could be used to lift an elephant and a snow pea, placing an elephant on a conveyor you use everyday to move snow peas might cause a bit of damage. Like the other forms of transport equipment, conveyors may be purpose-built for indoor or outdoor use.

Although there are many types of conveyors built for a wide range of materials and transport needs, most fall into one of three major categories:

- *gravity conveyors*, which are based on a downward slope and use chutes, wheels, or rollers onto which items are placed. Following the rules of gravity, the items slide or roll downward to their ultimate destination. Gravity conveyors are not powered and are the most inexpensive type of conveyor system, but a decline is essential for them to work. Because of their lack of control over individual items, they are not recommended for fragile or breakable goods.

- *powered conveyors*, which are operated on electrical power. They are typically based on a system of rollers, belts, or chains. The next time you're collecting your luggage after a sun-soaked vacation, check out your airport's luggage conveyor belt to see if it operates using rollers, belts, or chains or a combination of any of the three! Some powered conveyors include vertical lift components, allowing items to be carried to higher or lower floors of a facility. They may also include an automated sorting component, which use sensors to identify items or loads and sort them onto one of multiple divergent paths.

- *overhead conveyors*, which are gravity or powered conveyors that operate using ceiling-mounted tracks, chains, or monorails. Items or unit loads are suspended onto these conveyors from overhead, making this type of conveyor extremely useful when floor space is unavailable.

FIGURE 5.16 - GRAVITY CONVEYOR (LEFT) AND POWERED CONVEYOR (RIGHT)

5.8 STORAGE EQUIPMENT

Along with transport equipment, ***storage equipment*** is another important category of materials handling equipment. The primary purpose of storage equipment is to store or hold items or unit loads for a specific period of time, ranging from temporary, 2-hour storage of papayas in the We-Do-Foods distribution center to indefinite storage of hazardous chemical waste at a remote government facility. Storage equipment is often very straightforward and not nearly as complex or as expensive as other types of materials handling equipment. In the next chapter, you will be introduced with one of the most common forms of storage equipment: *pallet racking*. Additional types of storage equipment for non-palletized goods come in a range of static and dynamic forms.

With ***static storage equipment***, the items or loads being stored remain stationary. The most common forms include standard shelves and drawers. ***Static shelving*** is typically 12" to 36" deep and products may be placed directly onto the shelves or into bins placed on the shelves. Another popular form of static storage is the ***mezzanine***, a storage system that can add a second layer of storage or office space to a warehouse. Because they are not a permanent part of a warehouse facility's structure, mezzanines are somewhat adaptable and can be moved or readjusted to suit an organization's needs.

With ***dynamic storage equipment***, the goods stored move within the storage equipment's framework, typically to assist with putaway and order picking. Parts of the dynamic storage equipment move in varying degrees to assist with the movement of goods and this movement can be either gravity-based or powered. One example of gravity-based dynamic storage equipment is a ***flow rack***, which looks like static shelving, but goods are loaded onto the racks from the back and flow or move forward as goods are taken from the front. These racks are angled downward from the back to the front and goods flow forward by letting gravity do all the work!

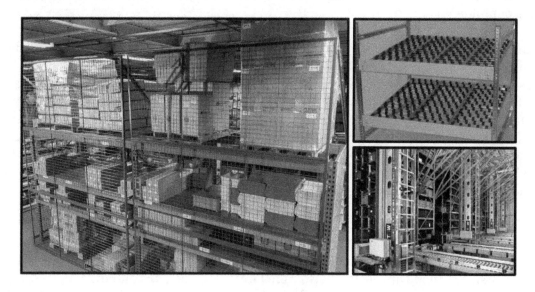

FIGURE 5.17 - STATIC SHELVING (LEFT), FLOW RACK (TOP RIGHT), AND ASRS (BOTTOM RIGHT)

Two examples of powered dynamic storage equipment are storage carousels and automated storage and retrieval systems. **Storage carousels** are made up of a set of bins or shelves that revolve either vertically or horizontally. Because they bring bins to the end of the aisle for an operator to pick or place items, storage carousels maximize floor space by allowing for extremely narrow aisles. Storage carousels also allow for high pick rates, allowing warehouse workers to pick orders quickly because they don't have to move all over the warehouse. The items come to them instead. **Automated storage and retrieval systems**, also known as **ASRS**, are systems of rows of racks with each row able to move vertically and horizontally to get goods to the person picking an order in the warehouse. ASRS maximizes floor space by allowing for narrow aisles that are 100 feet tall or higher. This type of storage is also fully automated throughout the retrieval, picking, and placement process. As a result, ASRS is more efficient, controlled, secure, and expensive than carousels and other forms of storage equipment. Later in Chapter 11, we'll examine ASRS again, especially how it connects with information technology systems and identification and communication equipment.

5.9 BULK HANDLING EQUIPMENT

Bulk handling equipment is a category of materials handling equipment used to move or store loose, unpackaged materials in bulk solid or liquid forms. The kinds of materials that are handled using bulk handling equipment include loose coal, gravel, wheat, sugar, oil, or milk. Be aware that some companies refer to bulk handling equipment as the equipment that only handles dry goods, while other companies refer to this category of equipment as handling dry or liquid bulk goods. Neither classification is incorrect but it is important that you understand the definition used by your company, its customers, and its suppliers.

Bulk handling equipment includes a mix of transport and storage equipment but it is equipment designed specifically for large quantities of loose materials. Examples of bulk handling equipment include:

- **bulk conveyors**, which are examples of the gravity and powered conveyors described previously in Section 5.7. We call this equipment a *bulk* conveyor when it has been designed specifically to move loads of loose and potentially heavy materials. They can be found inside or outside and are sometimes on wheels so they can be moved and maneuvered depending upon the location of the bulk materials to be moved. Bulk conveyors often have a **conveyor belt**, which is a closed loop of heavy duty material that moves along a system of pulleys, sometimes as simple as two pulleys with one at each end. At the baggage claim area at an airport or at a large grocery store where you unload your cart for a cashier, you may see conveyor belts at work.

- **screw conveyor**, which is a form of bulk conveyor that is shaped like a closed or open-topped tube with a large screw-shaped auger inside. As the auger moves, bulk loose dry or semi-dry goods can be moved along the screw conveyor vertically, horizontally, or along any incline. Also called **helix conveyors** and **auger conveyors**, screw conveyors are used to move grain, wood chips, ice, ash, meat, and food waste.

- *bucket elevator,* which is a system of buckets along a vertical conveyor belt with the goal of scooping up loose bulk materials and moving them continuously to a desired vertical locations where they are deposited. A *grain elevator* is a type of storage facility that uses bucket elevators to continuously move loose grain up to a location in the upper part of the building where the grain is funneled and dropped into silos.

FIGURE 5.18 - CONVEYOR BELT WITH HOPS (LEFT), SCREW CONVEYOR WITH SLEDGE WASTE (TOP RIGHT), AND BUCKET ELEVATOR WITH GRAPES (BOTTOM RIGHT)

- *stackers and reclaimers*, which are large machines that are used to move loose, bulk material and either dump it into a pile or pick it up from a pile to move it to another location. The equipment is called a *stacker* when its purpose is to dump the loose material into a large pile. It is called a *reclaimer* when it picks up loose materials from the pile to move it elsewhere. In some machines, both of these functions are combined so the equipment can either stack or reclaim. In this case, the equipment is called called a *combined stacker reclaimer* or a *stacker-reclaimer*. Stackers and reclaimers are commonly used for gravel, ores, coal, and grains.

- *hopper*, which is a type of storage equipment that looks like a large funnel. Loose bulk materials are placed into a hopper temporarily until the materials are to be moved. A door at the bottom of the funnel device opens and loose bulk materials flow out, typically into a container or along a conveyor system. Hoppers can be used for any free-flowing bulk materials, including both solids and liquids.

- **_storage silo_**, which is also a type of storage equipment but is considerably larger than a hopper and is typically used for longer storage timeframes. Silos are most often tall and cylindrical and can store both solid and liquid bulk materials.

FIGURE 5.19 - STACKER-RECLAIMER AT A SALT REFINERY (TOP LEFT), HOPPER WITH COFFEE BEANS (TOP RIGHT), AND GRAIN STORAGE SILOS (BOTTOM)

CHAPTER 5 REVIEW QUESTIONS

1. What is *materials handling*? What is its role in the supply chain?

2. When an organization invests in its materials handling, what benefits might it obtain?

3. What is a *materials handling system*? What must a company consider when designing one?

4. What are the three guiding principles of materials handing?

5. What can a company do to achieve materials handling efficiency?

6. What is *double handling*? What are some of its causes? What implications might it have for an organization?

7. Why do materials handling managers use *flow process charts*? What do each of the following flow process symbols mean: circle, upside down triangle, arrow, D, and square?

8. What are the categories of *materials handling equipment*? What is the task of each?

9. When might a warehouse use an *industrial truck*? When might it use a *conveyor*?

10. What is a *hopper* and how is it different from a *storage silo*?

CHAPTER 5 CASE STUDY

EXAMINING THE FLOW OF PAPAYAS AT WE-DO-FOODS

At We-Do-Foods, we receive exotic fruits into our warehouse every day. These exotic fruits, include mangoes, pomegranates, plantains, kiwis, passion fruit, and papayas. They all arrive in 2'x2' cushioned boxes. Shipments of 20 to 50 of these boxes arrive twice a day at approximately 7am and 3pm.

Before the boxes are unloaded from the delivery truck, the Receipt Supervisor checks to make sure that the documentation matches the shipment. Assuming there are no discrepancies, the boxes are unloaded from the delivery trucks, placed onto hand trucks at the loading dock, and taken fifteen feet to the Receipt Holding Area by warehouse staff. The boxes are unloaded from the hand trucks and placed onto shelves labeled *To-Be-Inspected*.

The boxes remain in the Receipt Holding Area until the Receipt Supervisor gets a call from the Quality Control Department, headed by the imperious and somewhat addle-minded nephew of the owner of We-Do-Foods, summoning the Receipt Supervisor to bring the boxes to the Quality Control Room. The Receipt Supervisor instructs her staff to load the boxes onto hand trucks again and wheel them 250 feet to the Quality Control Room. The warehouse staff unloads the boxes onto the Inspection Tables. The Quality Control Staff open each of the boxes and inspect each individual piece of fruit for damage. They discard and make a note of damaged pieces. When they have finished, they place the fruit back into their boxes, mark the outside of the boxes as having been inspected, and write the quantity of post-inspection passed and rejected fruit on the outside of each box.

The warehouse staff then load the boxes back onto the hand trucks and wheel them 250 feet back to the spacious Receipt Holding Area, where the boxes are taken off of the hand carts and placed on shelves labeled *Approved by Quality Control*. The Receipt Supervisor then counts and looks over the boxes to ensure the same quantity of boxes were received back into the Receipt Holding Area as were originally sent to the Quality Control Room. When this has been completed, the warehouse staff then loads the boxes onto hand trucks and wheels them 50 feet to the storage area and places them on shelves within preassigned refrigerated bays.

Using the scenario above, please create a flow process chart documenting and analyzing the current exotic fruits receipt process at the We-Do-Foods central distribution warehouse. Please use the Flow Process Chart worksheet provided, DD Form 1723 formerly used by the U.S. Department of Defense for examining flow and analyzing process flow. When you have finished, please create a new flow process chart for an improved flow process for exotic fruits receipt at the We-Do-Foods warehouse. Eliminate unnecessary steps and consider which steps could be modified or consolidated for greater efficiency and flow.

FLOW PROCESS CHART

	1. NUMBER	2. PAGE NO.	3. NO. OF PGS

4. PROCESS

6. ☐ MAN OR ☐ MATERIAL

7. CHART BEGINS   **8. CHART ENDS**

9. CHARTED BY   **10. DATE**

11. ORGANIZATION

5.   SUMMARY

a. ACTIONS	b. PRESENT		c. PROPOSED		d. DIFFERENCE	
	NO.	TIME	NO.	TIME	NO.	TIME
○ OPERATIONS						
⇨ TRANSPORTATIONS						
☐ INSPECTIONS						
D DELAYS						
▽ STORAGES						
DISTANCE TRAVELED *(Feet)*						

12a. DETAILS OF ☐ PRESENT ☐ PROPOSED METHOD

	b. OPERATION / TRANSPORT / INSPECTION / DELAY / STORAGE	c. DISTANCE IN FEET	d. QUANTITY	e. TIME	f. ANALYSIS WHY? (WHAT? WHERE? WHEN? WHO? HOW?)	g. NOTES	h. ANALYSIS CH (ELIMINATE / COMBINE / SEQUENCE / PLACE / PERSON / IMPROVE)
1.	○⇨☐D▽						
2.	○⇨☐D▽						
3.	○⇨☐D▽						
4.	○⇨☐D▽						
5.	○⇨☐D▽						
6.	○⇨☐D▽						
7.	○⇨☐D▽						
8.	○⇨☐D▽						
9.	○⇨☐D▽						
10.	○⇨☐D▽						
11.	○⇨☐D▽						
12.	○⇨☐D▽						
13.	○⇨☐D▽						
14.	○⇨☐D▽						
15.	○⇨☐D▽						
16.	○⇨☐D▽						
17.	○⇨☐D▽						
18.	○⇨☐D▽						
19.	○⇨☐D▽						
20.	○⇨☐D▽						
21.	○⇨☐D▽						

DD Form 1723, SEP 76 (EG)   Designed using Perform Pro, WHS/DIOR, Feb 95

BONUS EXERCISE: FUN WITH CRANES!

Identify each of the three cranes pictured below. After you have identified the cranes, answer the following questions:

1. Under what circumstances would each type of crane be used?

2. Which of these cranes have you seen in person before? Where did you see them?

3. Is there another type of cranes not pictured? If so, what is it and under what circumstances might it be used?

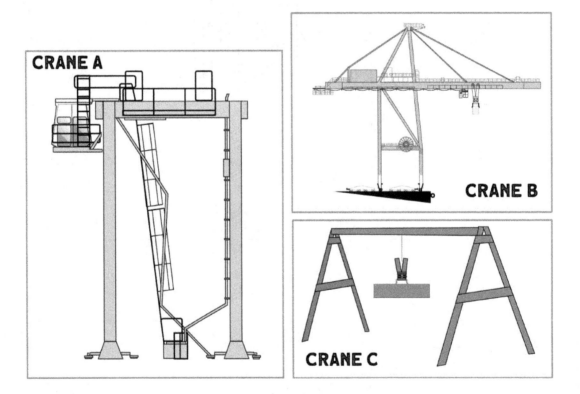

Chapter 6
The Unit Load

Sherm & Shazza are designers who have just started making soft and snuggly shoes that have become all the rage with customers in the under-25 and over-65 age brackets. They manufacture their soft and snuggly shoes themselves and fill their orders by placing boxes of individual pairs of shoes into postal service boxes and mailing them. When their popularity exploded overnight and orders for hundreds and thousands of pairs of shoes started coming in, Sherm & Shazza moved to a larger manufacturing and warehouse facility. For their new larger orders, they knew their mailing costs would be too high to continue their original order fulfillment practice, so they negotiated with larger customers to collect their orders from the loading dock of the Sherm & Shazza warehouse.

When the first truck arrived from the Big-E-Mart distribution center, one of their new large customers, Sherm & Shazza declared that it was "all hands on deck" for the three warehouse employees. These diligent employees run back and forth from the warehouse shelves to stack the ordered shoes into Big-E-Mart truck, some of them carrying five boxes of shoes at a time. They thought they were doing a great job because they were running to get the boxes of shoes and stack them neatly in the truck. They began to slow down as they get tired after only half of the 625-unit order had been filled. When they finished and had all 625 boxes of shoes loaded into the truck, the Big-E-Mart truck driver was already angry because they had taken way too long to load the truck, making the truck late for its next three pick-ups at other locations. The driver was also aghast that the shoes, although neatly stacked in the truck, were not secured in any way to keep them from falling and rolling around if the truck had to break suddenly or make a sharp turn. Because the shoe boxes are part of the final retail product, everyone at Big-E-Mart knows that their customers are not willing to pay full price for shoes in damaged boxes, even if the shoes themselves are undamaged.

Sherm & Shazza, our fabulously talented shoe designers, were confused. They knew their warehouse employees worked hard to fill the Big-E-Mart order quickly and neatly. What should they have done differently? Still confused after discussing the problem over multiple cups of coffee, they decided to seek the advice of those a bit more experienced. They visited fellow designers Bo-Bo and Boo, who had Big-E-Mart as one of their regular customers for their very trendy lines of beanies, berets, and baseball caps. Bo and Boo advised Sherm & Shazza to invest in a pallet jack or a pallet truck and use pallets and stretch wrap to create unit loads for larger orders. They calculated that Sherm & Shazza could fit 240 boxes of shoes on each pallet, which they could put stretch wrap around so the load of 240 boxes of shoes could be moved as one unit when loading them onto the customer's truck. Each stretch wrapped load would protect the shoe boxes and be secure during transport, too. They also calculated that Sherm & Shazza would need to create only three unit loads, which could be loaded into the Big-E-Mart truck in under 10 minutes instead of taking over two hours. Sherm & Shazza decided to learn more about the magic of the *unit load*!

6.1 INTRODUCING THE UNIT LOAD

One of the core concepts of materials handling in practice is that of the ***unit load***, defined as any quantity of a material, from an individual item to multiple items, assembled and restrained for handling, movement, storage, and stacking as a single object. The next time you are in a warehouse-style wholesale store, walk down an aisle and take a look up. Stacked on racks about 8 feet or more above the ground, you may see one hundred packs of toilet paper, stretch wrapped together onto a single wooden pallet. This pallet of toilet paper is an example of a unit load.

FIGURE 6.1 - LOADS OF UNIT LOADS!
AT ANY WAREHOUSE-STYLE STORE, JUST ABOVE
YOUR HEAD IS A WORLD OF UNIT LOADS.

The process of assembling one or more items into a unit load for more efficient and effective handling, movement, storage, stacking, and transportation is called ***unitization***. While most goods in a supply chain are unitized, it is important to note is that not all materials lend themselves to easy or affordable unitization. In Chapter 5, we introduced *bulk handling equipment*, which is used to move or store loose, unpackaged materials in bulk forms, such as loose coal, sugar, or oil. For the situations when it is more efficient and effective to keep goods in a bulk form as they move them along the supply chain, unit loads are not formed and bulk handling equipment is used instead. May of these bulk items may eventually become unitized, however, such as shipping containers of coal being transported across oceans and pallets of bags of sugar being moved around warehouses.

Unitization is an important part of supply chains and the world of warehouse management because of the undeniably remarkable benefits it offers, including:

- **reduced handling**. When bound together as one unit, individual items are handled less, reducing the risk of damage or deterioration.

- **load stability**. Because of the brick-like way in which many items can be layered onto a pallet or within a container, the single load is stable because the items' weight is evenly distributed within the unit load.

- **reduced surface area**. Because many items in a unit load are typically enclosed within an outer layer of items, they are protected from possible damage.

- **efficient storage**. When multiple items are bound together as a single, large block, they may be stacked many layers high within storage facilities, resulting in a very efficient use of space.

- **reduced packaging costs**. Before unitization, packaging materials for shipment and internal movement of goods were different. With unit loads, a uniform packaging is used for external and internal goods movement.

While there are some exceptions like bulk goods, most items in a supply chain are formed into unit loads for more efficient handling and transportation. However, not all unit loads are the same. The size, structure, and design of a unit load can be very different from load to load depending on the goods being unitized and the foundational materials used to construct or support the unit load. A few of the primary materials that form the basis of unit loads are: *pallets, skids, slip sheets, crates, barrels, sacks, reusable plastic containers*, and *shipping containers*.

FIGURE 6.2 - BAGS OF TOPSOIL STRETCH WRAPPED ON A PALLET

A *pallet* is a flat rectangular or square platform onto which unit loads are formed and secured with stretch wrap, shrink wrap, or straps. Pallets have flat top and bottom decks with supports between the decks. The bottom deck on a pallet allows pallet loads of goods to be put on racks or stacked one on top of another when the bottom load has a flat top. The area between the supports on a pallet are large enough for the forks of lift trucks and pallet jacks to fit between them so that goods secured on a pallet can be handled and moved as one unit. Although most are made of wood, pallets are also made of plastic, metal, and paper, depending on the goods they will be used to support. You are likely to encounter pallets many times a week when you leave you house to go shopping and you may not even realize it! We'll explore more about pallets in Section 6.2, "Palletization."

Similar to a pallet, a *skid* is also a flat rectangular or square platform onto which unit loads are formed and secured. Skids look a lot like pallets, but they have only a top deck and are missing a bottom deck. They also have supports below the top deck that allow goods on the skid to be above the floor level and to allow forks from lift trucks and pallet jacks to get under the top deck for movement and handling. These supports on a skid are called *runners* or *stringers* and are used to help slide along very heavy unit loads, such as heavy machinery. Because skids do not have a bottom deck, unit loads on skids may not be stacked on top of each other the way that pallet loads can be. Skids have been in used for thousands of years but are now less widely used than the pallet. The pallet's popularity dates back to its invention in 1930s and because of its ability to be stacked and racked, thus utilizing vertical storage space.

FIGURE 6.3 - STACK OF PALLETS (LEFT) AND A SKID SHOWING ITS BOTTOM RUNNERS (RIGHT)

A *slip sheet*, also called a *sheet*, is a sheet of cardboard, chipboard, or plywood onto which unit loads can also be constructed. *Flat slip sheets* can be used as the bottom or top supports of a pallet load or they can be used alone without a pallet to build a unit load. Without a pallet, unit loads based on flat slip sheets can only be handled and moved by specialized lift devices with very thin forks that can slide under the load. Unlike flat slip sheets, *molded slip sheets* can be contoured to fit the product they will be carrying and to have spaces at the bottom for the forks of lift equipment.

Like skids, wooden crates, barrels, and sacks formed the basis of some of the earliest forms of unit loads. When you see old images of cargo ships being loaded, whether they are photos from 100 years ago or drawings from hundreds of years ago, you are likely to see some forms of *wooden crates*, *sacks*, or *barrels* stuffed full with goods for a long ocean voyage. All three are still in used today, although their use has diminished with the popularity of pallets and shipping containers. ***Wooden crates*** are rectangular boxes made of wood, typically four feet wide by four feet long by four feet high. They are built with gaps at the bottoms for forks from lift equipment. They are also study and reusable and prevent goods from being damaged in transit and are especially useful for handling heavy equipment.

FIGURE 6.4 - OPEN TOP CRATE OF APPLES (LEFT) AND SEALED CRATE OF INCINERATORS FOR AN EBOLA TREATMENT FACILITY IN LIBERIA (RIGHT)

Traditionally, ***sacks*** were large bags made of jute or a similar fiber and were used to create unit loads of coal, salt, or wool. While jute or burlap sacks are still used to form unit loads of coffee beans, vegetables, and other agricultural products from smaller farms, the ***super sack*** is more commonly seen for transporting a variety of agricultural, chemical, raw

FIGURE 6.5 - SACKS OF POTATOES (LEFT) AND COFFEE (CENTER) AND SUPER SACKS OF FLOUR (CENTER)

material, or construction products. The super sack, also called a *flexible intermediate bulk container* or *FIBC* or *bulk bag*, is much larger than a traditional jute sack and is made from a weave of plastic fabric, making it waterproof, more durable, and able to hold a greater weight. Super sacks are also desirable because they are stackable and can utilize vertical storage space.

Barrels are cylindrical containers that are flat and slightly tapered at each end. Historically, they have been made of wood with outer metal hoops. They were traditionally used to store alcohol, oil, or other liquids. While wooden barrels are still in used to store and move alcohol such as whiskey and wine, the more commonly used cylindrical container for forming a unit load is a *drum*, which is a cylinder that is not tapered on the ends and is usually made of steel, plastic, or paperboard. Drums are used to store and transport a variety of liquid and dry bulk materials, including oils, chemicals, hazardous waste, spices, and ground coffee. Like pallet loads, the flat tops and bases of drums allow them to be stacked, thus utilizing vertical storage space.

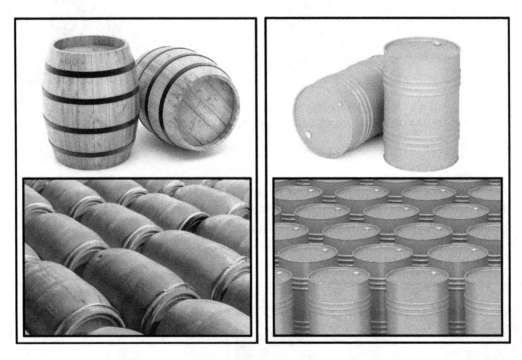

FIGURE 6.6 - BARRELS (LEFT) AND DRUMS (RIGHT)

A more recent development in the nature of unit loads over the past few decades has been the steady increase of the *reusable plastic container*, or *RPC*. Reusable plastic containers come in many forms and in in many shapes and sizes, but what connects them is that they are made of plastic, can contain a unit load, and are built to be used repeatedly many times. Different types of RPCs include bins, baskets, nesting totes, and trays that slot into rolling rack systems. RPCs are increasing in usage because they are less expensive to produce than reusable containers made from other materials and because their reusability and durability help companies achieve a *circular economy*, which is a model of materials production that allows for as much reuse and recycling of materials as possible. Many governments are advocating or providing incentives for companies to embrace the circular economy model in the materials they use and move away from a *linear economy*, in which materials are designed for a single use and then become waste.

The final item in our list of materials that form the basis of unit loads is the humble shipping container. Also called a *cargo container* or even shortened to *container*, a *shipping container* is a standard large unit load structure that is moved using multiple modes of transportation, such as truck, trains, and cargo ships. Shipping containers are large, oblong, rectangular metal boxes of standard sizes into which goods are placed for transportation. Like pallets, it's difficult to go a week without seeing a shipping container. We see them as the back of trucks on highways or we see them parked in the loading bays of our grocery stores or we even see them in parking lots being used for temporary storage. Because containers are such an important part of unit loads in the supply chain, we'll look at containers in greater depth in Section 6.3, "Containerization."

We've covered a list of materials that are used as the basis of unit load formation, but unit loads may also be formed without any supporting materials. These types of loads are called *self-contained unit loads*. Examples of self-contained unit loads include bales of hay and bundles of fabric. Although they may be secured or protected with straps, wire, stretch wrap, or shrink wrap, self-contained unit loads can stand alone without these materials and their structure and size are not dependent up them.

FIGURE 6.7 - AMAZON'S YELLOW REUSABLE PLASTIC CONTAINERS ON A CONVEYOR AT A FULFILLMENT CENTER IN MARYLAND (TOP LEFT), COFFEE BEANS IN AN RPC (TOP RIGHT), SHIPPING CONTAINERS ON A CARGO SHIP (LEFT CENTER), AND SELF-CONTAINED UNIT LOAD BALES OF HAY (BOTTOM)

6.2 PALETIZATION

Two of the most common core structure of the unit load are loads formed on pallets and loads formed in shipping containers. As previously mentioned, **pallets** are a flat rectangular or square platforms onto which unit loads are formed and secured to be moved and stored as a single unit. Goods are secured to pallet with stretch wrap, shrink wrap, straps, rope, netting, or other materials. Pallets have flat top and bottom layers, which are called **decks**. The flat bottom deck of a pallet allows *palletized* goods to be put onto racks or stacked one on top of another if the pallet loads have fit tops. **Palletization** of goods occurs when they when they are consolidated into a unit load on a pallet.

Between the top and the bottom deck of a pallet are supports called **blocks**, which are solid blocks between the decks at the corners and center edges, and **stringers** or **stringer boards**, which are longer support boards between the decks that often run the length of the pallet. There are usually three stringer boards, one on each end and one in the middle, leaving gaps between them that are large enough for the forks of lift trucks and pallet jacks to fit between them without affecting the load's stability or security. This allows a palletized unit load to be be raised, transported, and handled using manual and mechanical materials handling equipment. Although most are made of wood, pallets are also made of plastic, metal, and paper, depending on the goods they will be used to support and how many times they will be used.

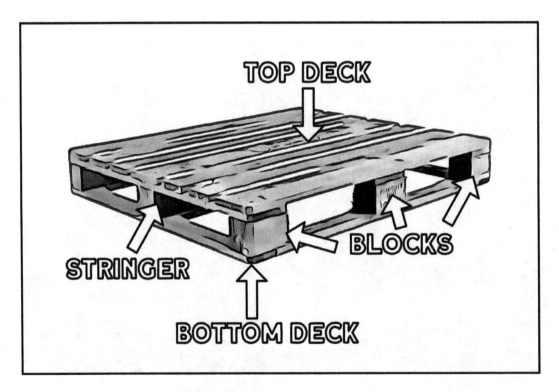

FIGURE 6.8 - THE PARTS OF A PALLET

In the previous section, we introduced you to the precursor to the pallet, the *skid*, which is like a pallet but does not have a bottom deck. Its stringers are often called runners because they are used to push heavy unit loads of goods on a skid along a smooth surface, such as a concrete warehouse floor. The skid has been around for thousands of years and it is believed that the ancient Egyptians used them. With the introduction of the lift truck in the late 19th century came the introduction of the pallet. It was quickly found that pallets offered more stability than skids when being maneuvered by lift trucks and skids could be stacked, taking advantage of more vertical space when storing or transporting unit loads. Pallets then slowly and quietly grew in prominence and popularity over the next 50 years. During World War II, however, palletization was a revolutionary force which allowed the U.S. military to do more with less. Fewer troops could be used to move and handle much larger quantities of goods and less warehouse space could be used to store far more goods before moving them to the front. The military's reliance on the pallet load then led to the world's reliance on palletization, with more than 2 billion pallets in use today in the U.S. alone!

Pallets are perhaps the most widely used tools of current materials handlers. The National Wooden Pallet and Container Association (NWPCA) reports that more than $400 billion in goods are exported from the United States every year on pallets. Hundreds of millions of pallets are constructed in the U.S. every year and over 90% of these made from wood. Wooden pallet construction consumes almost 40% of all U.S. hardwood lumber, second only to new home construction. The popularity of wooden pallets can be attributed to the fact that they are not only inexpensive to build and maintain, but that they can also be built to have a relatively long usable life.

Despite their proliferation across the world of materials handling and their seemingly similar appearance, not all wooden pallets are created equal. Some are **single-use wooden pallets**, which are made of softwood, can only be lifted from one of two opposite positions, and are built to be discarded once the unit load has reached its final destination. Others are **multiple-use wooden pallets**, which are made of hardwood, can sometimes be lifted from any of their four sides, and can be reused or returned to their senders for reuse.

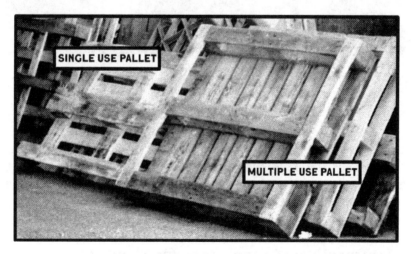

FIGURE 6.9 - SINGLE USE AND MULTIPLE USE WOODEN PALLETS.
NOTICE THE DIFFERENCES IN CONSTRUCTION BETWEEN THE SINGLE USE (LEFT) AND MULTIPLE USE (RIGHT) WOODEN PALLETS AT THIS APPLE ORCHARD WAREHOUSE IN COSBY, TENNESSEE.

Because of the cost of multiple-use pallet construction, organizations must take great care to ensure that these valuable pallets are neither lost nor damaged due to misuse. Pallet collection and control systems can help organizations achieve greater pallet reuse and efficiency. Some companies have invested in indoor and outdoor RFID tags for their pallets so that they can keep track of the goods on the pallet and the pallet itself.

Not only do wooden pallets differ according to the number of times of their intended use, but they may also differ based on a wide range of countless variables. For example, both single-use and multiple-use pallet construction may vary based on the unit load to be carried and its expected: *weight, type* (such as chemical, hazardous, food, perishable, or storage), and type of *fastening material* to be used.

In addition to wood, pallets may also be made from plastic, metal, or paper. According to the *12th Annual Pallet Report* from the Peerless Research Group, approximately 95% of U.S. companies use wooden pallets, 31% use plastic pallets, 17% use wood composite pallets, 6% use metal pallets, and 4% use cardboard or corrugated pallets. Like multiple-use wooden pallets, *plastic pallets, wood composite pallets*, and their less commonly used counterpart, *metal pallets*, can carry very heavy loads. They are reusable and can typically be lifted from any of their four sides. Because wooden pallets are difficult to keep clean, **plastic pallets** offer distinct advantages for handling foodstuffs and other potentially messy, perishable items. **Metal pallets** cannot easily be damaged when under duress, unlike their wooden counterparts, and are thus more advantageous for handling extremely heavy loads. On the other side of the pallet spectrum are **cardboard and corrugated paper pallets**, which are typically used to carry lighter loads and be disposed of or recycled after a single use.

FIGURE 6.10 - PLASTIC (LEFT), METAL (CENTER), AND CARDBOARD (RIGHT) PALLETS

Pallets can come in a variety of sizes, depending on their function. However, imagine if all pallets were different sizes and imagine trying to stack pallets the were varying widths. It would be a nightmare trying to make sure you always had the widest and longest palletized loads at the bottom of every stack of pallet loads, especially in storage or transportation locations with hundreds or thousands of stacks of pallets! Because of the importance of size standardization for pallets, there are six standard pallet sizes across the world that are recognized by the **International Organization for Standardization**, or **ISO**, which is an independent international organization that promotes worldwide standardization of industrial and commercial measurements and standards.

The six standard pallet sizes recognized by the ISO listed in width x length dimensions are:

- **40.00 x 48.00 inches** or 1016 x 1219 mm. Known as *the North American Pallet*, this size is also recognized by the Grocery Manufacturer's Association (GMA) and is used primarily in North America. It is the most commonly used pallet size in the U.S., representing 30% of the pallets constructed every year.

- **39.37 × 47.24 inches** or 1,000 × 1,200 mm. Known as *the ISO Standard Pallet*, this size of pallet is used in Europe, Asia, and across most of the world. It is also the same dimensions of a class of European standard pallets known as *EUR3*.

- **31.50 × 47.24 inches** or 800 × 1,200 mm. This smaller pallet is known as *the EUR Standard Pallet* and also *the CEN pallet*. It is commonly used in Europe and its narrower size is built to match European delivery truck and retail doorway dimensions.

- **45.9 × 45.9 inches** or 1,165 × 1,165 mm. This size of pallet is known as *the Australian Pallet* and is used primarily in Australia.

- **42.00 × 42.00 inches** or 1,067 × 1,067 mm. This size of square pallet is used throughout North America, Europe, and Asia and is the second most commonly used pallet in the United States. It is most frequently used in the telecommunications and paint industries.

- **43.30 × 43.30 inches** or 1,100 × 1,100 mm. This square pallet is known as *the Asian Pallet* and is used primarily in Asia.

Because reusable pallets can be expensive to purchase and maintain, **pallet pool** businesses have become popular. These businesses, like ORBIS Reusable Packaging Management in the U.S. and Mexico and Nippon Pallet Pool Co. in Japan, rent out and distribute reusable wooden, plastic, and metal pallets to companies that need pallets and collect them when the companies no longer need them. For example, ORBIS has 30 service centers across North America that ship out and haul back pallets, while using a specially developed software system to keep track of the locations of all of their many pallets. When a pallet is brought back to an ORBIS service center, it is immediately cleaned and prepared to be placed back into service so that there is always a pool of pallets ready for use.

When your goods are safely secured as a unit load onto a pallet, you can lift them and move them around with a forklift. So what do you do until you need them? You store them, of course! And, at the heart of every palletized unit load storage system is pallet racking. **Pallet racking** is a shelving system used for storing palletized unit loads to maximize available horizontal and vertical space. The type of pallet racking used within a materials handling system will vary according to: available *floor space*; *handling equipment* to be used; goods *safety requirements*; and stock variability, rotation, and order picking *requirements*.

The five most commonly used types of pallet racking are: *adjustable pallet racking, narrow aisle racking, drive-in racking, powered mobile racking*, and *live storage*. **Adjustable pallet racking** is the most widely used system for storing palletized unit loads. This flexible racking system is made of a system of vertical frames and horizontal beams which can be adjusted in height, both to make the most effective use of the warehouse facility's height and to accommodate changes in the height of unit loads. Because of its adaptability, this racking system is suitable for most types of storage applications.

Narrow aisle racking can also have an adjustable height system, but its hallmark is the narrow aisles between racks or shelves. Narrow aisles allow for more floor space to be used and allow or goods to be stored higher with more security than with other racking systems, meaning that more goods can be stored in a given space. Specialized materials handling equipment is required for narrow aisle pallet racking. For example, specially designed trucks are used which do not need to turn 90 degrees but instead run on a fixed path between the racks. This type of racking system is typically used in tall buildings in which underemployed space can be effectively transformed into safe, high-density warehouse storage.

Drive-in racking is a racking system in which palletized unit loads are driven onto racks, pushed back on the rack, and additional unit loads are placed in front of them. It uses a minimum of floor space but, because loads are aligned into lanes with only the loads on each end of the lane exposed, stock variability would be restricted to each lane carrying only one product. Drive-in racking is widely used in cold store conditions where floor space costs are high and refrigeration costs can be reduced by keeping cold products blocked together.

FIGURE 6.11 - ADJUSTABLE PALLET RACKING (LEFT), NARROW AISLE RACKING (CENTER), AND DRIVE-IN RACKING (RIGHT)

Powered mobile pallet racking is made of units of conventional and adjustable pallet racking, each mounted on a steel-framed base fitted with electrically-driven wheels, which run on a track set into the floor. Individual racking units may then be wheeled together and closed up, allowing up to 80% of warehouse floor space to be used for storage, as opposed to the 30% used for conventional racking systems. To store or access goods, the wheel-mounted racking units can be wheeled aside to create an aisle next to the desired rack. Because of the increased storage density it offers, powered mobile pallet racking can often be found in premises with higher rental rates or in warehouses feeling the need for expansion but not yet ready to move to larger premises.

Live storage is a unique type of racking system that can be used for palletized loads or other types of non-palletized contained storage, such as cartons or drums. In a live storage system, a contained unit load is supported on inclined roller or gravity wheel tracks so that the goods travel automatically from the loading side of a facility to the unloading side. This system maximizes space utilization by reducing the amount of access aisles needed and ensures automatic stock rotation. Similar to drive-in racking, live storage systems do limit each moving lane to be filled only with the same stock. Live storage systems tend to be used for perishable goods requiring failsafe stock rotation, unpalletized goods, and fast-moving multi-product ranges where small quantities of different items must be collated quickly.

FIGURE 6.12 - POWERED MOBILE PALLET RACKING (LEFT) AND LIVE STORAGE (RIGHT)

For storage of palletized unit loads, racking is not always necessary, however. Many palletized loads are stabilized so that they can be placed on the floor and stacked, one load on top of another. For increased stability, a **block stacking** technique is used in which palletized loads are stacked into rows which are placed side by side to form blocks. While this is a very inexpensive means of storage, it is advantageous only for temporary storage, lighter loads, and when additional vertical storage space is not needed. For safest storage conditions, block stacking should rarely be more than 2 to 4 pallet-loads high, depending on the height and weight of your load.

FIGURE 6.13 - PALLETS OF FLOUR BLOCK STACKED 2 TO 3 PALLET-LOADS HIGH AT A WAREHOUSE IN CHRISTIANSAND, NORWAY (LEFT) AND PALLETS OF CEMENT TILES BLOCK STACKED 2 TO 4 PALLET-LOADS HIGH IN AN EXTERNAL INVENTORY YARD IN LERWICK, SCOTLAND (RIGHT)

6.3 CONTAINERIZATION

As mentioned at the beginning of the previous section, two of the most common core structure of the unit load are loads formed on *pallets* and loads formed in *shipping containers*. Also called a **cargo container**, an **intermodal freight container**, or simply a **container**, a **shipping container** is a standard-sized, reusable unit load structure into which goods are placed that are typically made of steel. Shipping containers are transported interchangeably using **intermodal transportation**, which is the use of multiple modes of transportation for conveyance, including trucks, railroad cars, ferries, deep sea vessels, and aircraft.

FIGURE 6.14 - INTERMODAL TRANSPORT AND CONTAINERIZATION
AT THE PORT OF VANCOUVER, BRITISH COLUMBIA, CONTAINERS ARE TRANSFERRED
FROM SHIP (TOP LEFT CORNER) TO RAIL (BOTTOM RIGHT CORNER)

Although shipping containers are a part of our everyday landscape in the 21st century, this was not the case 100 years ago when lots of time and manpower were required to move much smaller unit loads of varying sizes from ships to trucks to trains. In New Jersey sometime in the 1930s, a truck owner and operator named Malcom McLean sat watching as cotton bales were unloaded from his truck and reloaded onto a freight ship. McLean thought about how much simpler and more efficient the process would be if a single unit container of cotton were transferred, container and all, from his truck onto the ship. McLean's not-so-idle thoughts led to an idea which would revolutionize the world of logistics and materials handling: *containerization!* He used this revolutionary idea to form the Sea-Land Corporation, which saw its first container ship set sail in 1956 from Newark, New Jersey to

Houston, Texas, carrying 58 container trailers. Today, a majority of the world's spends at least some of its life in a container.

FIGURE 6.15 - BEFORE THE DAYS OF CONTAINERIZATION, LONGSHOREMEN USED CRANES AND HOISTS TO TRANSFER GOODS TO AND FROM CARGO SHIPS

In the world of warehousing and materials handling, **containerization** is the practice of creating units loads for transportation using a system of shipping containers and a variety of integrated modes of transportation, including water, road, rail, and air transport. As an example of containerization, a standard 40ft container is loaded with finished goods and sealed at the factory. This sealed container can then be transferred by truck to the docks, where it is stored dockside until a ship is ready to be loaded. Once the ship has been loaded and has reached its final destination, the container is loaded onto a vehicle and delivered to its customer to be unsealed and opened. Depending on the context, the term *containerization* can refer to this entire system of intermodal transportation of goods using containers or it may refer only to the initial act of loading the goods into the container to form a unit load ready for transport.

Since its conception in the first half of the twentieth century, containerization has revolutionized the world of materials handling and logistics. It has become the transportation and materials handling system of choice, with more than 90% of the world's non-bulk cargo having spent some of its life in a container. According to data from the World Shipping Council website, approximately 226 million containers were moved around the world in 2019. Given that just one average container can hold 120 refrigerators, 800 televisions, or 96,000 bananas, that's a lot of goods worth a lot of money moving around the world in containers!

But why has the world so quickly become reliant on containers? Containerization has brought a slew of benefits to the world of materials handling, including:

- **Reduced handling** of individual items. Being protected in a sealed container reduces damage, deterioration, and theft of goods. It's very difficult for someone dockside to "relieve" a sealed container of a single Gucci handbag…

- **Improved turnaround time** for transport vehicles. Containers can be handled dockside quickly with specialized equipment and, when needed, can easily be stored and stacked. This allows trucks and ships and trains to be on their way after containers have been unloaded, even if the next form of transportation for the container is not yet there.

- **Vastly improved efficiency** and time savings in vessel loading. When it tales less time to load goods, freight tariffs are reduced! This is especially true in busy seaports.

- **Reduced insurance rates**. This is a wonderful side benefit of the reduced risk of damage, deterioration, and theft that comes with containerization.

- **Increased transport mode integration**. As the world has moved to standard container sizes, standardization of container transport vehicles and systems has followed, leading to seamlessly integrated modes of container transportation worldwide. This makes for smoother and quicker transfers of unit loads of cargo and allows for greater mechanization and automation in moving containers from one transportation mode to another.

Over the course of the past few decades, globalization of trade has pushed container sizes to become increasingly standard worldwide. When pillows are stuffed and sewn in the Xi'an Province of China, they are sealed into a container. This container must be transported by a Chinese truck to the port of Shanghai, loaded onto a Dutch container ship, travel by sea to the port of Los Angeles, unloaded from the container ship to a rail car, transported by railroad to Chicago, unloaded from the rail car onto an American truck, and driven to a Walmart in Wabash, Indiana. During this entire process, the pillows will never leave the sealed container until it is unloaded at the Wabash Walmart, which means that only the container is handled. All of the handling and transportation equipment used during this process must be standardized to handle this container size. Because millions of similar movements of containerized goods occur around the world at any and every given moment, standardization of equipment and containers is essential to keeps goods flowing quickly and smoothly and prevent containerization from being cost prohibitive.

For intercontinental shipping, as with our Xi'an to Wabash example, containers are typically 20 or 40 feet long. Containers of these lengths are so common that the ***twenty-foot equivalent unit***, or ***TEU***, has become a standard measure of container capacity and traffic flow of ships and ports. For example, TEU comparisons of data from the World Shipping Council show how the 2020 container traffic flow of the world's largest port, Shanghai, China is 43.5 million TEUs, which dwarfs the container traffic flow of the largest ports in

Europe and North America, with Rotterdam at 14.35 million TEUs and Los Angeles at 9.2 million TEUs.

FIGURE 6.16 - CONTAINER SIZES: A 10' CONTAINER PORT-SIDE IN ST. JOHN'S, NEWFOUNDLAND (LEFT), A 20' CONTAINER ROLLING DOWN THE STREETS OF BOSTON (CENTER), AND A 40' CONTAINER WAITING FOR TRANSPORT IN ST. JOHN'S, NEWFOUNDLAND (RIGHT)

Approximately 90% of the world's containers are 20 or 40 feet long, but containers may also be 10, 30, 45, 48, and 53 feet long. The smaller 10ft containers more common for European domestic use and the larger 48 and 53 foot containers more typical of North American domestic use. Despite some variation in length, the standard container width worldwide is 8 feet. Containers are also typically 8 feet 6 inches high. For especially tall cargo, however, there are **high cube containers**, also known as **hicubes**, which area foot taller at 9 feet 6 inches high. For especially dense, heavy cargo, such as steel rods, there are **half-height containers**, which are 4 feet 3 inches high, exactly half the height of standard containers.

FIGURE 6.17 - 40' CONTAINERS (LEFT) AND 53' CONTAINER (RIGHT)
THESE 40' CONTAINERS ON A BARGE NEAR ROTTERDAM, THE NETHERLANDS (LEFT) ARE THE SIZE OF MOST CARGO CONTAINERS TRANSPORTING GOODS ACROSS THE GLOBE. THE 53' FOOT CONTAINER IN EASTERN TENNESSEE (RIGHT) IS THE CONTAINER SIZE MOST COMMONLY USED FOR U.S. DOMESTIC TRANSPORT OF GOODS. THESE LARGE CONTAINERS CAN EASILY BE IDENTIFIED BY THE "53" WRITTEN ON THEM, AS CIRCLED ABOVE.

In addition to containers coming in a small variety of sizes, they also come in a variety of types based on the type of goods that they will transport. The wide world of container types, along with the goods they are intended to carry, includes:

- **Standard Containers**. These are also known as **dry van containers** or **dry storage containers** and are used for all types of dry cargo. These are overwhelmingly the most common type of container. Stand by any railroad track long enough and you are likely to see 100 or more standard containers zoom by!

- **Open Top Containers**. These containers are similar to standard containers but they do not have a top container wall. They often have a plastic roof structure instead of a top wall which can be easily removed and secured. Open top containers are used primarily for heavy cargo and cargo that needs to be packed and unpacked from above.

- **Open Side Containers**. These containers are also similar to standard containers, but they are built with doors on one side that can be left either fully opened or secured closed, depending on the size and shape of the cargo to be contained. Open side containers are useful for items that are too wide to fit though the narrow doors of the 8 foot side of a container.

- **Flat Rack Containers**. These containers have a base and two sides on the narrower ends. They are open on the two longer sides and on the top. They are especially useful for overly heavy, tall, or wide cargo.

FIGURE 6.18 - OPEN TOP CONTAINER IN REYKJAVÍK, ICELAND (LEFT) AND FLAT RACK CONTAINER IN NUUK, GREENLAND (RIGHT)

- **Flatbed Containers**. Also called **platform containers**, these containers have the same base measurements as 20 foot or 40 foot containers, but they have only a base without sides or a top. They are used for oversized, oddly sized, and very heavy cargo.

- **Ventilated Containers**. Also called **coffee containers**, these are containers that resemble standard containers, but they have either ventilation slits in the sides or top for natural ventilation or a forced air ventilation system. They are useful in extreme climates and for cargo that must be ventilated in transit, such as green coffee beans.

- **Refrigerated Containers**. Also called **reefers**, refrigerated containers are standard-sized containers that have an external generator or power hook-up to power an interior refrigeration system to cool the interior of the unit. They are especially useful for perishable goods that must be kept at a constant temperature. Some reefers can be kept at temperatures ranging from -85 to 104 degrees Fahrenheit.

FIGURE 6.19 - REEFERS PLUGGED INTO ELECTRICITY IN KODIAK, ALASKA (LEFT), REEFERS RUNNING ON GENERATORS ON A CARGO SHIP IN MONTEVIDEO, URUGUAY (CENTER), AND VENTILATED CONTAINERS USING SLITS FOR NATURAL VENTILATION IN JAPAN (RIGHT)

- **Tank Containers**. Also known as **ISO tanks**, these are cylindrical tanks surrounded by a metal frame in the dimensions of an ISO container. Tank containers are used for liquid goods as innocuous as fruit juice or as dangerous as chemical waste.

- **Bulk Containers**. Also known as **bulktainers**, these containers resemble tank containers because they are cylindrical tanks surrounded by a metal frame in the dimensions of an ISO container. Bulk containers are used for carrying bulk dry goods, such as grains or spices.

FIGURE 6.20 - CAN YOU TELL THE DIFFERENCE?
SOMETIMES IT IS VERY HARD TO TELL THE DIFFERENCE BETWEEN TANK CONTAINERS HOLDING LIQUID GOODS, LIKE THE ONES IN THE PORT OF ROTTERDAM (LEFT), AND BULK CONTAINERS HOLDING DRY GOODS, LIKE THE ONE ON A GERMAN HIGHWAY (RIGHT)

- **Swap Bodies**. Also called an **exchangeable container** or an **interchangeable unit**, a swop body is not a true container because it lacks upper support and cannot be stacked, but it has the same external dimensions as an ISO standard container so it can be placed on trucks and railroad cards made for shipping containers. As part of their frame, swap bodies have four corner legs that can be folded out from under them. This allows the swap body to stand alone or be swapped from one form of transportation to another without a crane. Swap bodies are most commonly found in Europe for road-rail connections.

FIGURE 6.21 - A SWAP BODY WAITING FOR TRANSPORT IN NORWAY

Because containers are expensive to purchase and maintain, companies rely on **container pools** much like the *pallet pools* from the previous section. Container pools are businesses that rent out, deliver, and collect shipping containers so that companies only use and hold containers as needed. One examples is TTX Company, which is the leading provider of railcar containers in North America. TTX is owned by multiple North American railroads and has a pool of approximately 170,000 railcars that are rented out to companies wishing to move their goods in a container by rail.

An interesting thing about containers, especially standard containers, is that people also use them for a range of multiple purposes, such as for small homes, doomsday shelters, or in-ground and above-ground swimming pools. Many organizations have begun to use containers as small warehouses themselves. When some companies do not have enough room in their warehouse, especially for reserve area or seasonal items, they use containers parked outside their warehouse facility as additional storage space because they are a cost effective means of keeping goods temporarily dry, safe, and secure.

6.4 UNITIZATION EQUIPMENT

As mentioned in Chapter 5, unitization equipment is one of the major categories of materials handling equipment. ***Unitization equipment*** is used to restrain goods and form them onto a single unit load for subsequent transportation and storage. We know that a *unit load* is any quantity of items assembled and restrained to permit it to be handled, moved, stored, and stacked as a single object. Pallets, containers, and a variety of other materials may form the basis of a unit load. Within the materials handling environment, specific equipment may be used to form these unit loads, to stabilize them, or to provide a protective covering on them.

Palletizers, which assist in placing individual items into palletized loads, are one example of unit load formation equipment. They may be manually operated or automated, with some even having a robotic arm that picks items and places them into the unit load.

FIGURE 6.22 - ROBOTIC PALLETIZER AT A BREAD FACTORY IN GERMANY

Stretch wrap and *strapping machines*, on the other hand, are examples of ***unit load stabilization equipment***. Their primary purpose is to make the load stable, thus preventing item damage and hazardous transport conditions. ***Stretch wrap machines***, which may range from predominantly manual to fully automated equipment, are used to bind the load with protective layers of plastic film. A unit load is placed onto a pedestal that swivels as a sheet of plastic film from a stationary roll is stretched and adheres to it. Stretch wrap machines are beginning to replace their former counterpart, ***shrink wrap***

machines, which use heat to shrink plastic film onto a unit load, making it more expensive and labor intensive than stretch wrapping.

Strapping machines, which may also range from predominantly manual to fully automated equipment, are used to place straps around unit loads to secure them. While stretch wrapping is more useful for lighter loads and for those requiring outside storage, strapping is the preferred unit load stabilization technique for heavy or bulky loads, items which need to be compressed, or for materials with sharp edges which would tear the stretch wrap. Both stretch-wrapping and strapping may also be used together on the same unit load. Strapping is often used to secure a load to a pallet while stretch wrapping is then used on the same load to provide additional security and protect it from the elements.

Finally, some unitization equipment can create *self-contained unit loads*, which we earlier defined as unit loads may that be formed without any supporting structural materials such as pallets or containers. One example of unitization equipment that creates self-contained unit loads is a **baler**, which is used to compress items into contact cubed or wide cylindrical bales that are easy to handle and move as a single unit load. These bales may be supported with straps, string, or plastic wrapping make handling easier and to protect the bale during storage and transportation. **Hay balers** are commonly used to form units load bales for hay and **industrial balers** are used to form unit load bales of paper and cardboard waste.

FIGURE 6.23 - UNITIZATION EQUIPMENT
STRETCH WRAP MACHINE (LEFT), STRAPPING MACHINE (CENTER), AND HAY BALER (RIGHT)

In addition to physical unitization equipment, companies may also use **unit load optimization software**. These cloud-based or in-house software systems help companies design optimal unit loads based on the goods being unitized, the materials and equipment used for unitization, and transportation and storage considerations, such as the amount of space available and it's dimensions. Unit load optimization software can determine the best size and means of unitization and can often reduce packaging costs more than 10%.

6.5 PACKAGING

Another core concept of materials handling and unitization in practice is *packaging*. In the world of warehousing and supply chain management, **packaging** is the practice of using materials to enclose and protect goods for storage and distribution. As we've already seen in this chapter the many times we mentioned stretch wrapping and strapping, packaging plays a large role in the formation of unit loads.

As a practice, packaging is a critical component of the materials handling process because it:

- **minimizes damage.** When goods are packed well with the proper materials, potential transportation and handling related damage can be reduced or eliminated. Although packaging is not a materials handling activity that adds value, it can certainly keep value from being lost.

- **influences equipment choice.** How an item is packaged directly influences which types of materials handling equipment can be used, especially the packaging materials used and its packaged dimensions.

- **can provide additional customer service.** Just as packaging influences equipment choice, existing materials handling equipment can influence the packaging materials used. In order to provide additional service to customers, many companies select their products' packaging style and materials based on which are best suited for their customers' materials handling equipment. For example, wholesale-style retailers such as Costco rely heavily on pallet-based and forklift materials handling equipment. Therefore, companies selling their wares to Costco tend to provide the added customer service of providing their products wrapped onto standard-sized pallets.

While *packaging* is defined as the practice of using materials to enclose and protect goods, the word *packaging* also refers to the materials themselves that are used to enclose and protect goods. For many industries, there are two primary categories of packaging: *individual item packaging* and *unit load packaging*. **Individual item packaging**, also called **consumer packaging** or **primary packaging**, is the total of the packaging material on an item that the end user sees, such as a Raisin Bran cereal box or a Campbell's soup can. For the majority of retail goods, it is the packaging that comes into direct contact with the product and with the final customer. While it may have some influence on materials handling matters, individual item packaging is of more interest to marketers wishing to create or enhance a unique, distinct, and recognizable brand.

There is also a subcategory of individual item packaging called **secondary packaging**, which is a layer of packaging outside the item's primary packaging that is used to group multiple items for easier individual handling and to prevent theft. This packaging is used to create a smaller version of a unit load. For example, you may see a pallet load of hundreds of cans of Beefy Baked Beans, but within that pallet load and at the back or top of some grocery store shelves, you may see a shrink-wrapped cardboard tray full of 24 cans of Beefy Baled Beans. This type of secondary packaging makes it easier to palletize a load of cans of beans and makes it easier for individual people to handle and to store the extra quantities on grocery store shelves. Imagine the chaos of hundreds of cans of Beefy Baked Beans tumbling from a pallet if someone removed the stitch wrap securing them together and no secondary packaging has been used!

Unit load packaging, also called **industrial packaging** or **tertiary packaging**, is the final layer of materials used to enclose and protect goods and is used in the unitization of these goods for handling, storage, and transportation. Unit load packaging is of great interest within the world of materials handling because it is the packaging that comes directly into contact with materials handling equipment. How a unit load is packaged determines how it will be handled. A more recent trend in unit load packaging in retail is connecting to product displays and marketing. For some goods sold at larger retail locations, such as warehouse-style wholesale stores, unit loads are created often with a combination of disposable pallets and printed cardboard sides that can double as a product display. The retail location simply receives the unit load, places it on at an aisle end cap in the store, remove sections of the packaging, and voila! The store now has a disposable display for the product that can grab attention and provide information to educate customers about the product.

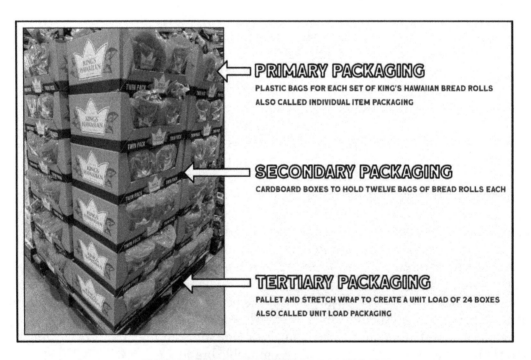

FIGURE 6.24 - CATEGORIES OF PACKAGING

Unit load packaging has one or more of the following purposes: *cushioning, containing,* or *restraining.* **Cushioning materials** are those which protect products from the damaging effects of potential impacts while being handled and moved. A few examples of cushioning materials include bubble wrap, foam, polystyrene peanuts, and pieces of corrugated cardboard. **Containing materials** are those into which goods are placed to hold and protect them during movement and storage. A few examples of containing materials include pallet boxes, cartons, cardboard boxes, reusable containers, and bags. ***Restraining materials*** are those that hold items in place as a unit load for secure movement, storage, and transportation. Examples of restraining materials include tape, bands, straps, shrink wrap, stretch wrap, cords, and netting. Some restraining materials, such as stretch wrap and shrink wrap, also provide the added benefit of being ***protective packaging***, which offers an additional layer of protection between the unitized goods and the outside world. For many unit loads, a combination of cushioning, containing, and restraining materials together offers the safest and most secure protection.

FIGURE 6.25 - GOODS ARE SHRINK WRAPPED ONTO SPECIALIZED SKIDS FOR RESTRAINT AND PROTECTION FOR DELIVERY VIA COGWHEEL TRAIN UP MT. PILATUS IN SWITZERLAND

Along with cushioning, containing, and restraining materials, warehouse facilities and other locations distributing goods use a variety of types of equipment to speed up the process of applying these materials to unit loads. Examples of such packaging machinery include

- ***air pillow machines***, which create cushioning air pillows in whatever size is needed from rolls of flat plastic.

- ***bagging machines***, which automatically pour predetermined quantities of bulk items into bags for storage and transport.

- ***bag sealers***, which use wire or heat to seal bags used in unit loads.

- ***shrink wrap machines***, which apply a layer a plastic to the exterior of a unit load and then heat it gently to fit tightly into place. One type of shrink wrap machine is a shrink tunnels into which goods travel through a conveyor and are shrink-wrapped when inside the tunnel.

- ***stretch wrap machines***, which apply layers of thin plastic film to unit loads to restrain and protect them. These are often designed with a large turntable onto which the unit load is placed and then rotated as the stretch wrap is applied to the unit load.

- ***strapping machines***, which apply rounds of strapping to unit loads to restrain them.

CHAPTER 6 REVIEW QUESTIONS

1. In your own words, please describe what a *unit load* is and why it is important.

2. Why is *unitization* so popular in materials handling today? What are two common forms of unitization?

3. How does *palletization* work?

4. What is the most common type of *pallet*? Under what circumstances might a paper pallet be used instead?

5. What is *block stacking*? Why is it used?

6. How does *containerization* work?

7. What is the standard size system for *containers* used for intercontinental shipping?

8. What is the primary function of *unitization equipment*? What are some examples of this type of equipment?

9. What is the relationship between *packaging* and materials handling?

10. Visit any retail location and, using the at least three words defined in this chapter, describe something you see either inside the store or outside at its loading dock.

CHAPTER 6 PHOTO EXERCISE

FIND THE CONTAINERS!

Examine the photos below and identify as many containers by type and sizes as possible. The container types include: *standard containers, open side containers, open top containers, flat rack containers, flatbed containers, ventilated containers, refrigerated containers, tank containers, bulk containers,* and *swap bodies.*

Chapter 7

Inventory Management and Control

In earlier chapters of this text, we defined **inventory** as the collection of goods, materials, and physical resources held by a company or organization, typically in warehouse facilities, distribution centers, fulfillment centers, or external inventory yards. Some warehouses hold enormous ranges of items with quantities of each individual type of item numbering in the thousands! Each individual item in this inventory represents a financial investment. Too much unnecessary inventory can even tie up so much money for a company that it has to borrow money to purchase inventory it actually needs. Companies also face the cost of holding inventory, which includes warehousing and insurance costs. Even in the fortunate situation of a company having surplus money, the money could be put to better use elsewhere in the organization, so the extra cost of unnecessary inventory becomes a lost opportunity cost. In this chapter, we will discuss *the principles of inventory management and control systems* and how they can help minimize the financial investment in inventory while at the same time ensuring that the needs of internal and external customers are met.

To truly master an understanding of inventory, we need to explore its mechanics and its management. *Why and under which circumstances is inventory held? How are the levels of inventory held determined? What information must be gathered to make these decisions?* The answers to all these questions and more lie within the realm of **inventory control**, an organization's process of managing goods after they have been received and maintaining quantity levels to meet customers' needs while minimizing associated costs to the organization. The primary objective of efficient and effective inventory control is simply ensuring that the right inventory of the right quantity is available at the right time and at the right place. A technology-based solution that controls this inventory of goods and its quantities to achieve this objective is called the ***inventory control system***. This system is designed to meet the needs of a particular organization and interfaces with other technology-based systems as needed, such as purchasing, warehouse, and transportation management systems.

Let's now take a deeper dive into the world of inventory control, look at some of the mathematics within inventory control systems, and explore how this all relates to lean, standardization, and physical inventory checking.

7.1 INTRODUCTION TO INVENTORY CONTROL

No matter how you look at it, holding inventory is an expensive endeavor. When an organization builds up its inventory, it first must purchase that inventory from suppliers. In many cases, an organization must pay the supplier for the goods long before any profit can be earned on them. This gap of time between when an organization orders and pays for inventory, then processes it to develop its finished goods, and finally sells the finished goods and receives a payment is sometimes very long. It forces an organization to commit a great deal of its resources, and resources equals money that cannot earn any interest and cannot be used for any other purpose until the final goods are sold. When this process takes a long time, it can be very costly and lead to cash flow problems for the organization.

In addition, when inventory is held, it must also be:

- **Handled**. Inventory held must be handled by warehouse staff. In addition to the labor costs incurred from hiring warehouse employees to handle the inventory, inventory handling equipment is also typically used, which can be expensive to purchase and maintain.

- **Housed**. Inventory held is kept within a warehouse or other facility. Inventory may also require specific handling conditions, such as dry, warm, or refrigerated settings. If these special environmental needs are not met, inventory may rapidly deteriorate and become unusable. Therefore, specialized warehouses or warehouse areas with specific heating, cooling, ventilation, or lighting systems are needed, all of which can be very expensive to purchase and run.

- **Administered**. When goods are held in inventory, a great deal of administrative work is involved, including control of inventory receipts, issues, inventory records, and other documentation. This all consumes valuable space, labor, and skills resources.

- **Insured**. Inventory is money. Because an organization has so much of its financial assets tied up in its inventory, insurance coverage is vital. In the event of fire, flood, or accident, an organization must be able to replace lost inventory. Therefore, the greater the amount of inventory kept, the higher the company's insurance premiums.

- **Kept secure**. Because inventory represents some of the largest assets of many companies, it must be protected from theft with costly security systems. If security systems are not used or should they fail, the organization faces the added item replacement costs resulting from theft.

FIGURE 7.1 - INVENTORY CONTROL OF FOOD FOR A 1200 PASSENGER CRUISE SHIP HANDLING (LEFT), HOUSING (CENTER), AND ADMINISTRATION (RIGHT)

Seeing that holding inventory is so expensive, why do organizations bother to hold any at all? Why not operate solely under *just-in-time* style conditions where inventory is received from the supplier only when it is needed and only in the exact quantities needed? Believe it or not, when done properly with an inventory control system, holding inventory can be extremely advantageous and even cost effective. Some of the many reasons organizations choose to hold inventory include:

1. **Unreliable inventory deliveries.** Organizations often find it difficult to rely on all of their suppliers to deliver every order exactly on time, every time an order is placed. Few suppliers could claim that they have never had shipments delayed by strikes, transportation difficulties, bad weather, or administrative errors. Therefore, holding inventory ensures that an organization will have adequate safety inventory to maintain operations, even when a supplier's shipment has been delayed.

2. **Bulk discounts.** By holding more inventory than is needed for one manufacturing period, such as a week, an organization is able to buy goods in larger quantities. Thus, the purchasing department can "buy bulk" and obtain a lower per unit price. In a company that spends millions of dollars every year on inventory, such discounts can have a significant impact on overall profit levels.

3. **Reduced purchase order processes.** Before an item is delivered to inventory from the supplier, one process that must occur is the purchase order process. When an organization holds very little inventory, it must perform this process frequently, resulting in higher time and labor costs for the organization's purchasing and

warehouse departments. When it holds greater amounts of inventory, however, the organization performs the purchase order process less frequently, resulting often in significant cost savings.

4. **Reduced risk to manufacturing operations.** When extra inventory is not held, the risk of a ***nil inventory*** situation increases, in which inventory of an item runs out and manufacturing is halted until more inventory can be delivered. The cost of halting manufacturing operations can be very high because, in addition to fixed costs, it creates a loss of profit, a loss of sales, a diminished reputation among customers, and an increased labor cost of employees waiting around and doing nothing until the inventory arrives.

5. **Inventory value appreciation.** When higher quantities of goods are held in inventory, an organization can deflect the burden of price inflation for those goods. For example, an automobile manufacturer buys six month's worth of tires and, suddenly, there is a shortage of rubber worldwide! This causes tires to double in price overnight. Because it is holding such a large tire inventory, the manufacturer has successfully deflected the current drastic tire price hike for six months, by which time prices may have returned to normal.

6. **Increased output flexibility.** When an organization holds higher levels of inventory in reserve, it is better able to increase production output levels should the need arise. Imagine that your company manufactures personal bags and backpacks and, because of a celebrity using them and sharing photos with fans, there was a sudden, unexpected interest in your company's fanny packs - or bum bags, depending on which part of the world you are in. If you made sure to have extra zippers from your zipper supplier in your inventory, you would have greater flexibility to handle this sudden increased demand.

7. **Low seasonal prices.** Some products, especially agricultural raw materials, are more readily available at some times of the year than others. If an organization purchases its annual needs of grain when their prices are the lowest right after a wheat harvest, it can reap substantial price savings benefits instead of waiting to purchase grain at the beginning of the planting season when pieces will be higher.

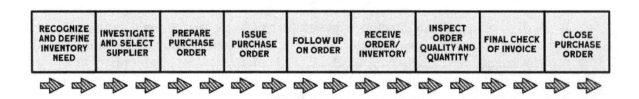

FIGURE 7.2 - THE PURCHASE ORDER PROCESS

When an organization has determined that it is advantageous to hold inventory, it then uses an inventory control system to establish how much inventory to hold of each item, or the most efficient and effective inventory levels. These inventory levels vary from item to item based on a variety of needs, including:

- **Operational Needs**. Operational needs refer to the amount of inventory of an item needed by various departments for the organization's core operations over a set period of time. These departments could include Manufacturing, Sales, Distribution, and Maintenance.

- **Shelf Life**. Shelf life refers to the ***salable life*** of a product, which is how long it has until it will begin to deteriorate and can no longer be sold or used. If an item has a very short or restricted shelf life, such as fresh fruit or dairy products, the amount of inventory of that item held will be smaller because of the risk of being stuck with inventory past its shelf life that cannot be used or sold.

- **Delivery Period**. The delivery period is the time it takes for the supplier to manufacture, dispatch, and transport the goods needed. An item's delivery period has a significant impact on its inventory levels. Sufficient quantities of inventory must be purchased to last from one delivery to the next. Typically, items with longer delivery periods are held in larger quantities in inventory.

- **Buffer Inventory**. Buffer inventory, also called ***safety inventory***, is the extra inventory held by a warehouse facility to cover any unforeseen problems or delays in delivery or sudden changes in demand. The size of an item's buffer inventory varies according to delivery reliability and operational risks. For example, an organization might decide that 25% of the minimum inventory level is considered a necessary buffer or emergency inventory level.

FIGURE 7.3 - THE IMPORTANCE OF HOLDING BUFFER INVENTORY

- **Capital Available**. Capital available is the level of financial resources available to spend on inventory. It is an important factor for establishing the levels of inventory held. If funds are not available to finance the most efficient and effective inventory levels, the inventory levels may need to be reduced, which could result in big problems.

- **Warehouse Capacity**. An organization's warehouse capacity is the cubic footage of its storage facilities. The amount of inventory an organization can hold will be restricted by the physical capacity of its warehouse facilities. In some cases in which items require specialized warehousing, such as refrigerated or frozen storage, the actual limited space in these high cost facilities available will restrict inventory levels even more.

In most cases, at least some inventory must be held. Therefore, *what are the organizing principles and core objectives of inventory control and inventory control systems?* Let's look at five objectives of inventory control and inventory control systems.

First, **inventory control supplies a constant flow of inventory to the operation**. As stated earlier and will probably be stated a few more times, the primary aim of inventory control is to ensure that the correct quantity of items needed for manufacturing, maintenance, distribution, and other activities are in inventory and ready for issue when and where required.

Second, **inventory control ensures that the appropriate quality of inventory is available**. The correct quality and type of inventory, as established by the user and the purchasing and quality control departments, must be available in sufficient levels. If only items of substandard quality are available, organizations must make the painful decision to either halt operations until quality items can be delivered or proceed with lesser quality inventory, perhaps resulting in disappointed and even angry customers.

Third, **inventory control supplies information for manufacturing management and control**. Inventory control information advises manufacturing planners about what to produce and within what timeframe in order to keep up with established levels of the organization's finished inventory. In addition, inventory control information about working inventory levels is also critical for manufacturing, maintenance, and distribution operations.

Fourth, **inventory control controls obsolescence and obsolete inventory**. Inventory control is responsible for ensuring that all inventory held by an organization is used at a regular rate and that an item held in inventory has not already been superseded by a new or redesigned item. Imagine an electronics store's warehouse still holding an inventory of floppy disks, beta VCRs, and eight-track cassette players! Holding an excess inventory of obsolete items is an easy mistake for an organization to make, as changes in design, technology, and the law can quickly make items and finished products obsolete. Inventory control must work hard to ensure that such obsolete inventory within the system is kept to a bare minimum so that it does not occupy valuable warehouse space and needlessly consume the organization's resources.

The fifth and final objective of inventory control is to **control inventory rotation**, which is the process by which inventory with the shortest shelf life or closest expiration date is used first. With the guiding help of inventory control, warehouse facilities typically operate under the *First In, First Out* principle, in which those goods arriving into the warehouse first are the first to leave when it is time to distribute items.

FIGURE 7.4 - FIFO AND LIFO

At the heart of inventory control is a system that helps organization make decisions about inventory levels, which impacts many departments and elements of the organization's operations. To enable such important decisions to be made efficiently and effectively, the inventory control system must be supplied with a constant flow of relevant and up-to-date information on:

- **Corporate manufacturing schedules**. Perhaps most critical to establishing inventory levels of raw materials and in-process goods is *manufacturing information*, which is information related to what items the organization intends to manufacture along with their desired amount, type, and quality.

- **Sales forecasts**. Also critical to establishing inventory levels of finished goods are *sales forecasts*, which are what the sales department's predictions of how many of which items will sell, where they will sell, and to whom. This information is needed to establish levels of finished inventory as well as pre-manufacturing inventory. Inventory control must ensure that inventory is available to meet present and future demands.

- **Distribution plans**. Information on inventory distribution, especially related to transportation and depot capacity and demand, is also vital for inventory control. This information, which is usually supplied by the sales, transportation, and warehouse departments, ensures that inventory is in the correct location at the correct time.

- **Maintenance and engineering schedules**. The basic function of the maintenance department is to service and maintain the manufacturing plant and other equipment used by the organization. This function is typically conducted according to a predetermined program, meaning that specific maintenance items, such as spare tires and new machinery parts, will be needed at set times. With current maintenance and engineering schedules, inventory control can ensure that adequate quantities of needed maintenance and engineering items are held in inventory.

- **Manufacturing planning**. Almost all manufacturing activities follow a schedule of operations. Using this schedule, inventory control can ensure that all related inventory are controlled and supplied to the correct area within the manufacturing plant at the right quality, in the right quantity, and at the right time and place.

7.2 THE NITTY-GRITTY OF INVENTORY CONTROL SYSTEMS

No matter how you look at it, holding inventory is an expensive endeavor. Thus, efficiency-minded organizations turn to inventory control systems to help them manage the cost of inventory holding by determining the most efficient and effective inventory levels to maintain for individual items. Remember that we defined ***inventory control systems*** as technology-based solutions that control the inventory of goods and their quantities to achieve the objective of ensuring that the right inventory of the right quantity is available at the right time and at the right place.

Although inventory control systems may differ from organization to organization, effective ones share the following qualities:

- **Accuracy and Speed**. It is very important that an inventory control system has the ability to react quickly and successfully to inventory accuracy situations that arise, such as incorrect quantities received due to transportation problems, raw materials shortages, sudden increases or decreases on demand, or just plain old human error.

- **Open Communication**. Open communication between departments within an organization is critical for effective inventory control systems. For example, when an inventory control system has determined the correct quantity level of inventory to hold, the system must communicate this information immediately and openly with the purchasing department who then purchases the correct quantities needed and with the warehousing department who prepares the warehouse for receiving, inspecting, and holding the determined quantity of inventory.

  Imagine a top class inventory control system determining absolutely the most effective and efficient levels of inventory of tricycles and bicycles an organization should hold and *not* sharing this information with the other departments, resulting in the purchasing department ordering too many bicycles, too few tricycles, and a plethora of unexpected unicycles!

- **Economy**. A focus on being economical in an organization's operations and the demand placed upon its capital and human resources is another important piece of an effective inventory control system. Without this, our We-Do-Foods grocery warehouse may think that it needs to hold three weeks' worth of watermelon for all of South Central Alaska when it is indeed more efficient to hold only three days' worth. As a result, a lot more labor and precious temperature-controlled warehouse space is needed to manage this extra inventory of watermelon.

- **Centralized Control**. When it comes to inventory, there can be too many chefs in the kitchen! Final decisions for when and what to order are ultimately handled by the purchasing department but are most effective when based on critical information from a single, centrally controlled inventory control system instead of the purchasing department receiving a variety of different pieces of information from a variety of different inventory systems from different warehouse locations and facilities within the same organization.

- **Access**. Multiple organizational functions and departments should be able to operate and access information in the inventory control system. For example, the marketing department should be able to access information on finished goods in stock, manufacturing should be able to access information on the availability of production inputs, and maintenance should be able to access information on the availability of parts and materials needed for maintaining facilities and machinery.

- **Availability of Spare Parts**. Companies that have manufacturing facilities or even just those with warehousing facilities will have machinery that will need spare parts from time to time. Therefore, inventory control systems should handle not only the inputs a company needs for the finished products it sells but also the spare parts its needs to keeps its operations running smoothly.

- **Flexibility**. Inventory control systems must have the flexibility to automatically control all items held within a warehouse facility and any changes or new additions. Although you may have the absolute perfect level of papaya inventory for optimum efficiency and effectiveness, this level will not remain static. As crates of papayas are issued, new ones, and perhaps even new ones of different varieties, will come in and must be accounted for within the inventory control system. The system must be flexible enough to facilitate constant dynamic changes in customer demand.

In order to manage and control inventory levels of even the most basic inventory operations effectively, organizations must determine two key factors for each item held in inventory: *how much* to order or reorder and *when* to order or reorder. In more complex inventory operations, especially those involving multiple warehouse or distribution facilities, the factor of *where* also becomes important, which means a focus on the location of inventory order and delivery.

As inventory circumstances become increasing complex, so do the systems and techniques used to manage and control them. In this section, we cover a range of inventory control systems, but they may also be described as inventory management systems or as inventory control or inventory management tools, techniques, or approaches. It is not important how you choose to label the series of ideas you will encounter in the remainder of this section, but it is important that you understand how and under what circumstances each are used.

Before we delve more deeply into the world of inventory control systems, let's first cover a few basic definitions and mathematical formulae that are central to the principles of inventory control systems and techniques:

- ***Lead time***. Lead time is the length of time it takes from the moment it is decided that an item will be ordered or reordered until the item has been received and ready for issue in the warehouse. Lead time is often thought of as an item's average delivery time from the supplier. Lead time is often in expressed in days or weeks, but depending on the items ordered and the supplier, lead time may be expressed in units as small as hours or as long as months or even years.

173

- **Buffer inventory**. Also known as **safety inventory**, **safety stock**, or **minimum inventory**, buffer inventory is the inventory held to cover unforeseen usage increases and delays during an item's lead time. Buffer inventory is held in case of unforeseen events, not for regular use.

  formula: To calculate the *buffer inventory* needed in terms of weeks, the number of weeks' coverage desired is multiplied by the weekly item usage.

  buffer inventory = weeks coverage desired x weekly usage of item

- **Reorder point**. An item's reorder point is the level of inventory or predetermined quantity of an item at which a new order is placed to replenish the item's inventory.

  formula: To calculate the *reorder point* for an item, the number of units used within the item's lead time is added to the buffer inventory.

  reorder point = units used per lead time + buffer inventory

- **Order quantity**. In its most basic terms, the order quantity is the amount of inventory to order. This may be predetermined using historical data and personal judgment, such as when an organization looks at the quantity of an item used the previous year and divides by twelve to determine the quantity for months orders. However, more commonly used today is the **economic order quantity (EOQ)** mathematical formula, as will be described later in this chapter.

  formula: Most commonly used to calculate *order quantity* is the EOQ formula, as will be described later in this chapter. Organizations also sometimes calculate an item's order quantity by dividing the annual units of the item used by the number of orders to be placed within the year.

  order quantity (non EOQ) = units used per year/# orders placed yearly

- **Progress level**. When an item's inventory on hand falls to the progress level, the organization checks with the item's supplier on the status of the outstanding order.

  formula: To calculate the *progress level*, half of the number of units used within the item's lead time is added to the buffer inventory.

  progress level = units used per lead time/2 + buffer inventory

- **Maximum inventory**. An item's maximum inventory is the quantity of an item above which its inventory should never rise.

  formula: To calculate the *maximum inventory*, the order quantity is added to the buffer inventory

  maximum inventory = order quantity + buffer inventory

7.3 INVENTORY CONTROL FORMULAE IN ACTION!

Using the definitions and formulae provided in Section 7.2, let's do some simple number crunching! A local pizzeria, the Leaning Towers of Pizza, uses 40 cases of mozzarella cheese every week. The lead time it takes from Leaning Towers to receive the cheese from its discount supplier, Wisconsin Wonders, is 4 weeks. Based on past experience, Leaning Towers has set its buffer inventory coverage of all items at one week of units of mozzarella cheese. Finally, because Leaning Towers is not a large operation, they do not like to receive too many deliveries. Therefore, they place only 10 orders per year.

Using all of this information, how can we determine the *buffer inventory*, *reorder level*, *order quantity*, *progress level*, and *maximum inventory* for Leaning Towers' mozzarella cheese inventory?

LEAD TIME = **4 weeks**

BUFFER INVENTORY = 1 week x 40 units/week = **40 units**

REORDER LEVEL = (4 weeks x 40 units/week) + 40 units = **200 units**

ORDER QUANTITY = (52 weeks x 40 units/week)/(10 orders) = **208 units/order**
(non-EOQ)

PROGRESS LEVEL = (4 weeks x 40 units/week) / 2 + 40 units = **120 units**

MAXIMUM INVENTORY = 208 units + 40 units = **248 units**

What we can learn from the *buffer inventory* result is that Leaning Towers of Pizza holds 40 units as buffer inventory or safety inventory in case there are lead time delays.

What we can learn from the *order quantity* result is that when the level of mozzarella cheese reaches 200 cases, the pizzeria places a new order for 208 cases.

What we can learn from the *progress level* result is that when its inventory of mozzarella falls to 120 cases, Leaning Towers calls its cheese supplier, Wisconsin Wonders, to check on the status of the cheese order.

Finally, what we can learn from the *maximum inventory* result is that if its inventory of mozzarella exceeds 248 cases, it investigates why it is holding excess inventory and then determines if this was a single occurrence or if a new weekly cheese usage level must be determined and if new calculations need to be made.

7.4 USING THE EOQ TO GET THE REORDER QUANTITY

When warehouse managers want to minimize an organization's investment in inventory, one formula used commonly within inventory control systems and techniques is the **economic order quantity**, also known as the **EOQ**. The most widely used of these EOQ inventory control techniques is the **fixed order quantity** or **FOQ technique**, also called the *fixed order point system* and the *fixed reorder model*. When using the FOQ technique, an optimal reorder quantity is determined, which is the most efficient size of order for this item. This reorder quantity then remains constant, or *fixed*, while the time interval between reorders varies depending upon the demand and subsequent issuance of the item. The FOQ is used to determine the most efficient minimum inventory level at which the item should be reordered to replenish its inventory. This minimum inventory level for reorder is called the **reorder point**. When the reorder point is reached, the fixed order quantity is automatically ordered.

The static amount of inventory that is ordered, which is the **fixed order quantity**, is determined based on the item's demand, the item's cost, and the inventory holding and reorder costs. As mentioned in the previous paragraph, the number of units of an item held in inventory that triggers a new order is called the *reorder point*. It is is determined by how long it takes to receive a new order from the item's supplier and the general demand or sales rate for that item at the time. The basic formula used to determine the reorder point is:

reorder point = lead time length x daily item demand (in units)

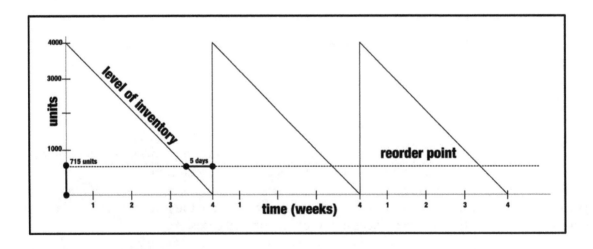

FIGURE 7.5 - FIXED ORDER QUANTITY AND THE REORDER POINT

For example, when your local neighborhood We-Do-Foods store orders Glossy Glam Purely Pink lipstick from Glam Products, Inc., it takes 5 days for the order to arrive. In your neighborhood, Glossy Glam Purely Pink lipstick is in high demand with the local preteen population and your nearby We-Do-Foods store sells approximately 143 tubes of this lipstick per day. Therefore, the reorder point for Glossy Glam Purely Pink lipstick at your local We-Do-Foods store is 715 units (or 5 days x 143 units/day).

To determine the fixed order quantity, we will first examine the **simple EOQ model**, which can be used when the following conditions exist:

- *the rate of demand is constant (not changing), known, and continuous*

- *the inventory replenishment or lead time, which is how long it takes for the supplier to deliver the items ordered, is constant and known*

- *the item price is constant and not dependent on the order quantity or time, such as no bulk order discounts or rush delivery payments*

- *the EOQ model is being used for one item of inventory, which has no interaction with other items*

- *there is no limit on the organization's available capital*

In order to determine the optimal fixed quantity of inventory to order when an item's reorder point is reached, the simple EOQ model takes into account the trade-off between the item's **inventory holding cost**, or how much its costs to store or keep the goods in inventory and its **order/set-up cost**, or how much it costs to place and set up the order. As shown in Figure 7.6, the point at which the inventory holding costs and order/set-up costs intersect, the total cost is the lowest, thus indicating the item's optimal inventory order size or **fixed order quantity**.

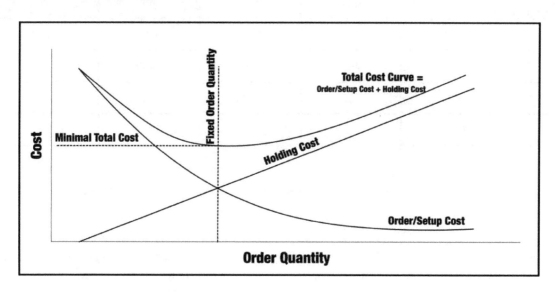

FIGURE 7.6 - FINDING THE FIXED ORDER QUANTITY

**ADDING THE INVENTORY HOLDING COST AND THE ORDER/SETUP COST
ALLOWS US TO FIND THE POINT OF LOWEST TOTAL COST, REVEALING
THE OPTIMAL INVENTORY ORDER SIZE, OR *FIXED ORDER QUANTITY*.**

To better understand the fixed order quantity concept, let's look at what happens as we add inventory holding costs and order costs as order quantities vary. Continuing on with our Glossy Glam Purely Pink lipstick example, let's assume that the Smalltown location of We-Do-Foods doesn't sell quite as much lipstick as your local store. At the Smalltown We-Do-Foods, 3600 tubes of Glossy Glam Purely Pink lipstick are sold each year. The value of each tube of lipstick is $5. It costs the Smalltown We-Do-Foods $0.40 to hold each tube of lipstick in inventory per year and $100 to set up a new order with Glam Products, Inc. Therefore, as we increase the number of annual orders of Purely Pink lipstick We-Do-Foods places with Glam Products from one to ten, the following figures result shown in Figure 7.7.

Number of Orders	Cost of Orders (Inventory Order Cost) $100 x number of orders	Quantity of Lipstick per Order 3600 / number of orders	Dollar Value of Lipstick per Order quantity of lipstick per order x $5	Cost of Holding Inventory dollar value of lipstick per order/2 x $0.40	Total Cost cost of orders + cost of holding inventory
1	$100	3600	$18,000	$3,600	$3,700
2	$200	1800	$9,000	$1,800	$2,000
3	$300	1200	$6,000	$1,200	$1,500
4	$400	900	$4,500	$900	$1,300
5	$500	720	$3,600	$720	$1,220
6	$600	600	$3,000	$600	$1,200
7	$700	514	$2,570	$514	$1,214
8	$800	450	$2,250	$450	$1,250
9	$900	400	$2,000	$400	$1,300
10	$1000	360	$1,800	$360	$1,360

FIGURE 7.7 - ILLUSTRATING THE FIXED ORDER QUANTITY CONCEPT

As Figure 7.7 shows, the lowest total cost, $1200, is achieved when six orders are placed for 600 tubes of lipstick each. Therefore, the optimal inventory order size, or *fixed order quantity*, is 600.

Rather than rely on the long-hand method above, the following formula for the simple EOQ is used to determine the fixed order quantity:

$$Q = \sqrt{\frac{2RA}{VW}} \quad or \quad Q = \sqrt{\frac{2RA}{S}} \quad where$$

Q = optimal order quantity

R = units used per year

A = order/set-up cost (per order)

V = value of one unit of inventory

W = inventory holding cost (per unit per year)

$S = VW$ = the storage cost per unit per year

Using the same figures from the Glossy Glam Purely Pink lipstick example above, remember that the Smalltown We-Do-Foods sells 3600 tubes of Glossy Glam Purely Pink lipstick annually. The value of each tube of lipstick is $5. It costs the Smalltown We-Do-Foods $0.40 to hold each tube of lipstick in inventory per year and $100 to set up a new order with Glam Products, Inc. Therefore, using the simple EOQ formula:

R = 3600 units/year A = $100/order

V = $5/unit W = $0.40/unit/year

$$Q = \sqrt{\frac{2RA}{VW}} = \sqrt{\frac{(2)(3600)(100)}{(5)(0.4)}} = 600\,units/order$$

Our world is one of change and the unknown. Because the model above assumes many constant and known conditions, it may seem limited in its application. Organizations can adjust this simple EOQ model, however, based on the complexity of their individual situations. There are currently more than 200 variations of this model used to assist a wide range of inventory decision makers. One example is the *fixed order quantity under uncertain conditions.*

In our previous simple EOQ model, the item usage or sales rate was assumed to be constant and always staying the same. This is not the reality for most organizations, however. In the real world, demand varies from season to season, week to week, and even day to day based on customers' changing needs, the weather, or even flash-in-the-pan trends. Replenishment or lead times can also vary as a result of production delays, traffic hold-ups, transportation strikes, and human error. Then how can inventory management and control models assist in these situations in which flux and uncertainty, rather than constant demand and lead times, are the norm?

Although a variety of approaches may be used depending on the situation, at the core of each is a consideration of the level of safety or buffer stock needed to handle variations in demand and lead times. Previously, we defined **safety inventory**, also called *buffer inventory* or *buffer stock*, as inventory that is held and used as supply and demand dictate. It can be defined more simply as the extra quantities of items held to protect an organization from losses that might be incurred from fluctuating supply availability and customer and market demands. Safety inventory becomes critical in an uncertain environment because if too much safety inventory is held, excess inventory costs result. If too little safety inventory is held, the organization may experience very costly stock outages and work stoppage situations.

Although the fixed order quantity is the most commonly used EOQ technique for inventory control, also worthy of mention is the **fixed order interval**, or **FOI, technique**, also called the **fixed time period (FTP)** or the **periodic review system**. The FOI technique is used when inventory must be ordered at fixed or constant time intervals. The quantity ordered and reordered is not fixed and is based on how much of an item remains in stock at the end of the order cycle or near the time of reorder. While not as common as FOQ, the FOI technique is useful when deliveries or vendor sales visits occur only at set times, such as in the retail food industry or in remote locations which experience transportation limitations.

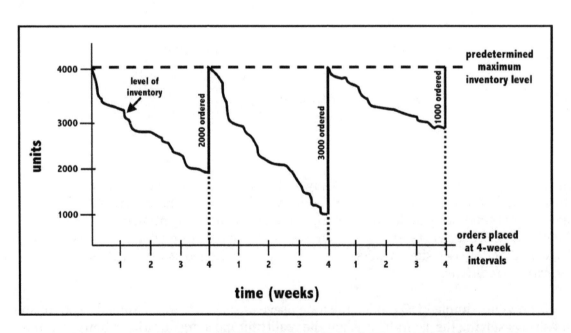

FIGURE 7.8 - FIXED ORDER INTERVAL (FOI) TECHNIQUE, PERIODIC REVIEW SYSTEM

7.5 DEMAND ENVIRONMENTS

As previously mentioned, there is a range of inventory control systems, each with their own range of variations. All inventory control systems are not suited for all situations, however. To determine which is the most efficient and effective system or technique to use, a logistics, inventory, or warehousing manager examines key criteria such as the situation's ***dynamic demand environment***. A *demand environment* is the context, such as location, time, and place, in which customers' desire to purchase goods or services for a specific price occurs. Demand environments are typically *dynamic* and not *static* because they are constantly changing based on a variety of factors.

There are two specific demand environments for items held in inventory: one of *dependent demand* and the other of *independent demand*. An item is one of ***dependent demand*** if its orders to be issued from inventory depend on orders for another product. For example, refrigerator handles would exist in a dependent demand environment because their inventory levels and orders are dependent upon the numbers of refrigerators (another product) desired by the customers or user. Raw materials, work-in-process goods, and component parts are generally those of dependent demand because their orders and subsequent inventory levels depend on the demand or desired quantity of another finished product and sometimes a manufacturing or assembly timeframe.

An item is one of ***independent demand*** when its orders to be issued from inventory do not depend on those of another product. For example, while the handle and other components of the refrigerator in our example are of *dependent* demand, the refrigerator itself is of *independent* demand. Finished goods that are end-use items for a company and not component parts are of independent demand. As a side note, let's consider whether or not a single product can be of both dependent and independent demand. Some products may exist in both dependent and independent demand environments. For example, an inventory of automobile tires in a tire manufacturer's warehouse may experience dependent and independent demand simultaneously. Tire inventory orders may be dependent on orders from automobile manufacturers and subsequently, the consumer demand for automobiles that use their tires. Conversely, tire orders from tire sales departments in Walmart and Costco are independent of demands for another finished product, such as new automobiles.

When the inventory demand environment is one of independent demand, ***demand forecasting*** is needed, which is a business technique that focuses on using past data to predict the quantity of items customers will want, such as the number of refrigerators customers might purchase during the next three months. One inventory control technique used in independent demand environments is ***distribution resource planning***. Also known as ***DRP***, distribution resource planning is an inventory control technique. DRP is used within a cloud-based or computer-based system that focuses on receiving, warehousing, and holding goods at the lowest cost possible within the distribution system while still meeting customers' inventory needs through efficient distribution activities, such as transportation scheduling. In a DRP system, a wide variety of factors of inventory holding within the distribution system are considered, including warehouse and external inventory yard space, distribution centers, labor and capital used, and transportation equipment used.

The DRP system, at its core, is very useful in using its distribution data to forecast demand and then send that information back to the manufacturing department to help with production scheduling and the distribution department to help with transportation planning. Throughout the system, the focus is on the distribution of specific final products that do not depend on other products to drive customer demand.

When the inventory demand environment is one of *dependent demand*, demand forecasting for the item is not needed because its demand depends upon the demand for a different item, the end product. In this dependent demand environment, *just-in-time* and *materials requirement planning* are inventory control techniques and systems often used. For inventory which exists in a dependent demand environment, many organizations use the *just-in-time* inventory control system. Also called *JIT*, Just-in-time is both a philosophy and practice. Its focus is to ensure that the right item of inventory is at the right place and time and that no unnecessary inventory is held.

Historically, traditional approaches to meeting manufacturing requirements rested heavily in holding extra safety inventory *just-in-case (JIC)* something went wrong. While the JIC idea provided a buffer against inefficiencies in the manufacturing process, high financial investment levels of inventory were required. From the 1950s through the 1980s, Japanese manufacturers developed the inventory management and control approach we now call *just-in-time*. The JIT approach sees inventory as wasteful and seeks to eliminate it and anything else held that does not add value to the product. The JIT philosophy calls for a gradual reduction of buffer inventory and for the delivery of inventory to the manufacturing function and finished goods to the user just in time for use. In JIT systems, inventory can be reduced by reducing transits times, reducing manufacturing machine set-up times, creating a more effective manufacturing plant layout, and introducing more automatic or automated equipment. All inventory held was with a just-in-time focus instead of a just-in-case one.

For JIT systems to become effective, an organization and its suppliers must work seamlessly and to the same JIT standards. Not only does an organization use a JIT system to reduce its inventory of raw materials, work-in-process, and finished goods within its own facility and distribution chain, but it must also strive for similar reductions in its suppliers. With JIT, suppliers are seen as an extension of an organization's own manufacturing plant and thus part of its manufacturing team. Suppliers receive special requests and containers and are expected to make several deliveries per day. Suppliers must also guarantee the quality of their products so that goods may be delivered directly to the manufacturing plant with no quality control inspections carried out. Because of this close, interdependent relationship with suppliers, organizations with successful JIT systems tend to use *single source purchasing*, which is purchasing items or a range of items from a single preferred supplier.

JIT systems have garnered much attention over the past few decades for their ability to *drastically reduce inventory holding levels, create better relationships with suppliers, highlight potential problems in manufacturing efficiencies,* and *increase manufacturing efficiency as a result of fewer defective products from suppliers.* Although it is useful for inventory reduction and control in single facility and dependent demand environments, JIT presents a range of challenges, including: *problems resulting from late, incorrect, or insufficient deliveries; difficulties posed by single-sourcing relationships;* and *shortages of skilled JIT staff.* Despite its challenges, JIT has grown to become a worldwide effective and popular inventory control technique.

Six rules for a successful manufacturer-supplier relationship within a JIT system are:

1. *Establish and nurture long-term relationships.*

2. *The relationship must be mutually beneficial.*

3. *The supplier must be able to guarantee its product's quality with zero defects!*

4. *Technical competence of both the manufacturer and supplier must be continually examined.*

5. *Both the manufacturer and supplier must be located within the same geographic area.*

6. *Price guarantees from the supplier are essential!*

In addition to JIT, another inventory control technique used in a dependent demand environment is *materials requirement planning*. In a manufacturing organization, the demand for a majority of items in inventory is dependent on the quantity of finished products required. The timeframe in which these products must be finished is a known factor. This allows the organization to schedule inventory ordering and receipt into the manufacturing cycle in the exact quantities needed at the time and place required. Also known as **MRP, materials requirement planning** is an information technology, time-phased requirement planning system to help an organization minimize inventory holding costs. It is used to determine the *when* and *how many*, or timing and quantities, of goods during the purchasing process. It also coordinates the when and how many of the purchase with the needs of the production or manufacturing schedule, all to ensure that the organization isn't holding more inventory than it needs at any time.

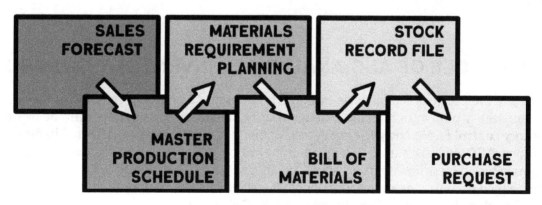

FIGURE 7.9 - STAGES IN MATERIALS REQUIREMENT PLANNING

Information on the inventory needs of the organization is taken from the ***master production schedule***, also known as the ***MPS***, which details the required outputs of the manufacturing systems, generally by week or month, and is derived from either order books or sales forecasts. The MRP system converts the output needs information in the MPS into a time-phased ***report of materials requirements***, or ***RMR***, which is also called the ***bill of materials***, or ***BOM***. The ***RMR*** (or ***BOM***) is a structured directory that lists all the items of inventory or parts required to manufacture a finished product. For example, a BOM for an automobile would list one complete engine, four wheels, five tires, one front windshield, two windshield wiper blades, and so on. Before a production run, the MRP system calculates the total quantity of each item that needs to be ordered along with their lead times. It supplies the purchasing department with information on: *which items need to be ordered, how many of each must be ordered*, and *when they must be ordered to meet the production schedule*. MRP is taken a stage further with ***MRP II***, or ***manufacturing resource planning***, which integrates system-wide manufacturing, inventory, and finance operations to achieve optimum financial results in inventory and manufacturing resource control. MRP II begins with MRP, but extends it into a more holistic planning approach involving many departments. As a result, MRP II can help minimize inventory holding costs, reduce production stoppages, and increase flexibility in system-wide planning.

Both independent demand DRP systems, as we described earlier in this section, and the dependent demand MRP systems are often used in conjunction with one another at the same organization. For example, a company uses MRP to reduce its incoming inventory for production to highly efficient and effective levels. It then uses MRP and DRP to inform manufacturing production scheduling to produce the most efficient levels of finished products to minimize finished product inventory. Finally, the company then uses DRP to achieve the most efficient and effective levels of outgoing inventory within the distribution chain. Combining these techniques leads not only to drastic reductions in inventory levels, but also to increased levels of customer service by using DRP to more accurately predict customer demand. As with DRP and MRP, JIT and MRP II systems are often used together and are often referred to collectively as ***MRP III***. Used together, JIT and MRP II drastically reduce inventory holding levels, as greater efficiency is achieved in the inbound flow of materials, internally within the manufacturing process, and across the organization as a whole.

7.6 THE ROLE OF ABC ANALYSIS IN INVENTORY CONTROL

In many of the previous sections, we explored systems and techniques for controlling and managing the inventory of individual items. Another technique common within the world of inventory control is ***ABC analysis***. Instead of being used to manage individual items of inventory, ABC analysis is used to help an organization place its range of inventory into categories based on which items are issued most frequently. Such analysis is useful because it can help an organization determine the most cost effective inventory control techniques and buffer stock levels for an item based on its ABC classification.

ABC analysis is based on the ideas of a nineteenth century Italian economist, Vilfredo Pareto, who posited that a small portion or percentage of something may account for a large portion or percentage of its value or impact. For example, under **Pareto's Law**, also commonly called the **80-20 Rule**, 20% of a company's product lines accounts for 80% of its overall sales. At a grocery store for example, of its hundred and even thousands of types of items sold, its core staples, which include milk, cheese, and bread, typically comprise only 20% of the store's overall types of inventory but account for 80% of the products sold. The remaining 80% of the store's inventory, which would include shrimp, mustard, and our beloved papayas, would only comprise 20% of the products actually sold. Highlighting the high sale items allow a company to focus more attention on their inventory levels to ensure that they always have these items in stock. These 20% of items that make up 80% of a company's sales are its *A items*, according to the following three categories of the ABC analysis:

Products that equal...	And generate...	Are called...
20% of the overall inventory	80% of the company's revenue/ inventory investment	**A products**
30% of the overall inventory	15% of the company's revenue/ inventory investment	**B products**
50% of the overall inventory	5% of the company's revenue/ inventory investment	**C products**

To perform an ABC analysis of types of inventory, an organization first needs a table with all of its items in inventory with the criteria by which they will be classified or ranked, such as *annual sales*. Also included in the table might be what percentage of total inventory is comprised of each item. An example for such a table for the cheese manufacturer Wisconsin Wonders is:

ITEM CODE	DESCRIPTION	ANNUAL SALES($)	% OF TOTAL INVENTORY
05209BC	blue cheese	$1,000	10%
05806BR	brie	$800	10%
05742CH	cheddar	$55,000	10%
05339ED	edam	$3,000	10%
04991GC	goat cheese	$900	10%
05820GD	gouda	$1,100	10%
05993HV	havarti	$7,000	10%
05103MZ	mozzarella	$25,000	10%
05994SH	spicy havarti	$1,200	10%
05190SW	Swiss	$5,000	10%
TOTAL:		$100,000	100%

To complete the ABC analysis, the items in the table are now sorted in order of *annual sales*, from highest to lowest, and other columns are added, such as those showing each item's *percentage of annual sales*, *cumulative percentage of annual sales*, and *cumulative percentage of total inventory*. According to the cumulative percentage of annual sales, the A, B, or C inventory classifications are then assigned.

Item Code	Description	Annual Sales ($)	Percentage of Annual Sales	Cumulative Percentage of Annual Sales	Percentage of Total Inventory	Cumulative Percentage of Inventory	ABC Category
05742CH	cheddar	$55,000	55%	55%	10%	10%	A
05103MZ	mozzarella	$25,000	25%	80%	10%	20%	A
05993HV	havarti	$7,000	7%	87%	10%	30%	B
05190SW	Swiss	$5,000	5%	92%	10%	40%	B
05339ED	edam	$3,000	3%	95%	10%	50%	B
05994SH	spicy havarti	$1,200	1.20%	96.20%	10%	60%	C
05820GD	gouda	$1,100	1.10%	97.30%	10%	70%	C
05209BC	blue cheese	$1,000	1%	98.30%	10%	80%	C
04991GC	goat cheese	$900	0.90%	99.30%	10%	90%	C
05806BR	brie	$800	0.80%	100%	10%	100%	C
TOTAL:		$100,000			100%		

From our ABC analysis of our cheese SKUs, or *stock keeping units*, we found that cheddar and mozzarella account for only 20% of our stocked items but 80% of our sales. Therefore, we must make sure not to run out of cheddar or mozzarella! However, a total loss of brie cheese would have little effect on our profits.

7.7 LEAN AND STANDARDIZATION

Because of the unnecessary expense of holding unneeded inventory, companies try to reduce inventory quantity through many of the techniques we covered earlier in this chapter, including EOQ, JIT, MRP, and ABC analysis. In a further effort to reduce inventory held and save on warehousing costs, companies also try to reduce warehouse waste through a mode of thinking called *lean*. **Lean** is a focus on examining every step in a business process and eliminating the waste, which include the steps that do not add value to the customer. This idea of looking at a work flow and ensuring that it moved through streamlined, standardized processes without unnecessary steps originated with Henry Ford and his development of assembly line processes. The concept of lean then got its start in Japan just after World War II with Toyota Motor Company when it developed the Toyota Production System. Also known as TPS, the Toyota Production System focused on eliminating *muda*, which is the Japanese word for "waste," by manufacturing only what was needed when it was needed and in the exact quantity needed. To eliminate waste, which included overproduction, unnecessary inventory, and excess motion, TPS embraced the concept of **kaizen**, or continuous improvement.

The lean way of thinking gained popularity in global companies in the early twentieth century with multiple expected and unexpected positive results. For example, Goodyear Tire's lean initiatives resulted in $5 million savings, zero landfill waste, and a reduction in OSHA incident rates to less than 33% of the national average. Part of lean's success has been the way in which an organization's employees are invested in the process. Employees are all involved in identifying waste and the companies monitor and celebrate their successes from the waste identified and eliminated. Lean has come to mean a way of thinking that involves a series of concepts such as:

- **5S**, which refers to the mindset that all work areas are neat and tidy. Everything is in its place and there is a focus on sorting, setting in order, shining, standardizing, and sustaining.

- **total employee involvement**, which means that everyone in a company is involved in the lean way of thinking. Everyone is part of the continuous improvement process.

- **standard work**, which is a focus on standardization of processes. Documentation of this standardization is shared with everyone involved.

- **management walkabouts**, in which managers wander around the workplace and ask employees what could be done better. Managers seek employees' suggestions for improvements.

- **visual management**, which shows the results of lean and performance scores to all employees in wall charts and other highly visible formats.

- **value stream mapping**, which involves mapping processes to see which processes add value. It also determines which processes do not add value and should be eliminated, similar to the flow process charts we examined in Section 5.7 of Chapter 5.

While lean had its origins in manufacturing, it has become popular in the world of warehousing and inventory management. Many warehouse operations have adopted a lean mindset and identifies unnecessary processes. A significant part of bringing lean to warehouse management has been *inventory standardization*. **Standardization** is the process of reducing similar items held in inventory by creating a set standard item to fill that need, thus reducing the overall inventory holding of the organization.

When it comes to inventory management, variety is not always the spice of life. In most warehouses, inventory variety can increase over time and, without investigation, may remain long undetected. When it is not an absolute necessity, holding a variety of similar items is an undesirable situation for warehouse managers because such duplicate stocking reduces the holding capacity of the warehouse. Thinking back to your own personal warehouse, your refrigerator, would you stock it with gallon jugs of a variety of milk products, including 1%, 2%, skim, regular, buttermilk, soy milk, and oat milk, with multiple brands of each? Unless you have a gourmet-sized refrigerator, you most likely standardize the milk you stock to include only one or two types or brands. Through the process of standardization, similar items held in inventory are reduced to one standard item. Each standard item is also called a **stock keeping unit**, or **SKU**, and each SKU is assigned a unique inventory code. When necessary item variety exists due to different sizes, colors, or styles of an item, each unique combination of item size, color, and style would be a different SKU, For example, two gallons of the same brand of milk in a grocery store warehouse would be two different SKUs if one was whole milk and the other was 2% milk.

In the warehouse setting, a variety of factors can lead to unwanted inventory variety. For example, say that Tricycle America, Inc. merged with Unicycle Global, LLC to form a new company, Cycles-R-Us. Some of the warehouse staff of the Unicycle Global must now move to the Tricycle America warehouse. At the Tricycle America warehouse, they maintain a stock of Brand A tire pumps. The new staff from the Unicycle Global, however, are accustomed to working with Brand B tire pumps, so they decide to keep a stock of these pumps as well, even though Brand A and Brand B are the same size and have all of the same functional features and customer reviews. This stocking practice leads to unnecessary duplication and unneeded inventory variety.

Unwanted inventory variety may also arise from the personal preferences of the heads of a company's departments, who each demand that an inventory of their preferred items be purchased and stored. For example, because it is a global company, the headquarters of Cycles-R-Us generates a lot paperwork. For internal communications, the head of the marketing department prefers to use only high quality 32 Lb Fancy Fine brand paper, while the head of the IT department prefers to use only 24 Lb Zip-Zip brand paper because she believes it creates fewer jams in their printers and copiers. The head of the accounting department strongly disagrees with both and believes that, for maximum cost effectiveness, only 20 Lb Cheap-N-Thin brand paper should be used for internal communications. As a result, a lot of unnecessary space is taken up at the Cycles-R-Us Headquarters supply warehouse because an unnecessary variety of paper is held in inventory.

In addition, unwanted inventory variety may also be caused by a *one-off demand* for a certain variety of item. This item is purchased for one occasion but unwittingly maintained in inventory thereafter. For example, as a cross-promotion with the re-release of the 1982 classic family movie *E.T.*, Cycles-R-Us sold their children's bicycles and tricycles with a handlebar basket and E.T. plush figure. After the cross-promotion was over, Cycles-R-Us continued to hold and maintain a stock of handlebar baskets and E.T. plush figures, wasting valuable warehouse space and maintenance costs.

Finally, changes in availability at certain times may encourage organizations to hold more than one variety of an item to safeguard against a nil-inventory situation. For example, the executives at Cycles-R-Us really like the bicycle seats manufactured by companies in the Eastern European country of Belarus. The seats are very durable, comfortable, made with high quality leather, and cost one third less than all of their competitors' seats. While there are three competing bicycle seat manufacturers in Belarus, none of them are able to provide a consistently high volume of seats. Therefore, Cycles-R-Us maintains a stock of the three varieties of seats from these three manufacturers in Belarus in addition to a stock of seats from another company in Taiwan to accommodate for the sporadic availability of supply from the Belorussian companies.

As it happened with Cycles-R-Us, staff turnover, personal preferences, one-off-demand, and changes in availability can all lead to unwanted inventory variety in any company. The goal of the warehouse and inventory manager is to reduce this variety and its corresponding high levels of duplicated stock through initiating a process of *standardization*. Because the warehouse department is primarily concerned with receiving, storing, and issuing inventory, items that have a high degree of variety can be easily spotted and eliminated by a diligent warehouse professional. This standardization of inventory yields great rewards for an organization, including:

- **Reduced storage space used.** When the variety of items is reduced, less overall inventory is held and less storage space is needed.

- **Reduced warehouse administration.** With a reduced variety of inventory, fewer administrative staff and hours are required to handle inventory records, control, inspection, checking and issue, computer time, and documentation.

- **Improved inventory control.** When varieties are reduced, greater attention can be paid to inventory control because there are fewer varieties to inspect, maintain, and manage.

- **Reduced inventory cost through bulk buying.** When the number or varieties of an item is reduced, a greater number of items of a single variety are purchased. Therefore, organizations can reduce inventory cost when they purchase in bulk from suppliers. This practice can be repeated throughout the whole inventory holding of an entire organization, resulting in vast savings in capital that was previously tied up in unnecessary inventory.

ARGUMENT OR OVERSTOCK? STANDARDIZE AND BUY BULK!

Remember Cycles-R-Us and its problem with an unnecessary variety of paper types due to the personal preferences of department heads? Let's look at the monthly cost of purchasing 1000 reams of paper and how costs can be reduced using standardization and bulk buying...

DEPARTMENT/PAPER	REAMS NEEDED	COST/REAM	TOTAL COST
MKTG/FANCY FINE 32LB	40	$12	$4800
IT/ZIP-ZIP 24LB	200	$10	$2000
ACCTG/CHEAP-N-THIN 20LB	400	$8	$3200
		TOTAL	$10,000

If the paper choice is standardized to the mid-range paper, which is the 24 Lb paper preferred by the IT department, the Zip-Zip Paper Company will offer Cycles-R-Us a 15% discount because they have agreed to more than double their original purchase agreement.

Therefore, 1000 reams of paper per month purchased at $10 per ream with a 15% discount is $8,500 per month, a whopping savings of $1,500 per month or $18,000 per year!

- **Improved service from suppliers.** When standardizing inventory and reducing the varieties of one item produced by competing suppliers, a competition for your business between suppliers often results, translating to both better service and lower prices for the purchasing organization. In the Cycles-R-Us example, standardization of paper inventory to only one supplier could lead to improved service from suppliers, such as free delivery and paper upgrades, and it could lead to overall price reductions!

- **Improved standards establishment.** After the items in a warehouse facility's inventory have been standardized, the process of setting standards in the organization improves greatly. Both the Warehouse and Quality Control departments now have only one standard to set and monitor for each item held, rather than having a system of standards for each variety, which might lead to a lack of conformity in implementation.

While standardization seems an ideal solution for inventory management, it sometimes brings disadvantages that must be considered. Standardization does bring reduced flexibility. Sudden shortages of a particular standardized line may cause supply problems. Because standardization also brings reduced choice for the user, some users may feel shortchanged because they believe that a choice that was phased out may have been the best for the job. It is up to each individual company to decide whether or not the benefits of item standardization outweigh the potential difficulties it may bring.

When an organization decides that the benefits of standardization outweigh its disadvantages, they partake in the *standardization process*. First, duplicate varieties in the inventory are identified. This is often achieved when warehouse coding has been completed and similar code numbers warrant investigation. Once the duplication has been discovered, the organization then selects the best *standard item* from the variety of items based on usage, price, performance, or other relevant factors. The newly selected standard item must be able to meet all of the needs of the present inventory variety that will be phased out. In these instances, the universal or all-purpose item tends to be selected in an effort to meet all the requirements placed upon the item involved, making user involvement in the standardization process very important.

FIGURE 7.10 - THE STANDARDIZATION PROCESS

Finally, the organization calculates the new total inventory requirements and establishes the revised level of inventory, or quantity to be held, for the item involved. The total usage of the variety of previously held items, and not the individual item itself, will indicate the overall level of demand for the newly chosen standard item.

Throughout the standardization process, the warehouse department is in a unique position to assist and prevent excess variety from being created in the inventory held. First, the warehouse can discourage users from ordering non-standard issue items whenever possible. This can be accomplished by recommending and even actively promoting the standard inventory item. Next, warehouse management can inform the users of the cost involved in holding a wide variety of inventory and its effect on the organization's profitability. The warehouse department can also constantly review the inventory records to locate possible sources of inventory standardization. Finally, warehouse management can work with the purchasing and user departments to discuss the subject of standardization and the possible items on the market which could be made standard items and thus reduce inventory variety.

7.8 PHYSICAL INVENTORY CHECKING

Remember Glossy Glam, Inc., our the lipstick manufacturer from earlier in this chapter? Glossy Glam used a DRP system to streamline its pipeline inventory and forecast customer demand. It also nearly perfected its MRP systems for incoming inventory. Things were running along smoothly for Glossy Glam until last June, when its inventory of finished products fell short by a whopping 33%! The Glossy Glam execs were utterly confused as to why their streamlined MRP and DRP inventory control systems might have let them down. They were terrified of what they had to their stockholders. However...

Glossy Glam's MRP and DRP systems had indeed not let them down. The fault for Glossy Glam's inventory shortages instead was the result of the company's shortsighted belief that these information systems were all that was needed to manage inventory. Had Glossy Glam regularly conducted physical inventory checks, the company might have realized that it had not begun recording quantities of free samples taken from inventory for the new Visiting Student Scholars program and that, since hiring "Light Fingers" Louie to work in the warehouse, more than 30% of the finished product stock had mysteriously vanished. In addition to the inventory control systems outlined in the earlier parts of this chapter, *physical inventory checking* is a critical component of effective inventory management.

The security and accountability for all inventory and equipment held within the warehouse system is the direct responsibility of the warehouse manager and staff. As we've mentioned throughout a few of the previous chapters, inventory represents a substantial financial asset on an organization's balance sheet. This enormous responsibility demands that the warehouse manager and staff perform continuous physical checks of all the items held in inventory and verify their item counts with the balances shown on the inventory control and recording systems. This process is called ***physical inventory checking***. For most organizations, a full physical check must be carried out at least once a year to provide validated inventory figures for the organization's yearly final accounts.

The cost of physically verifying inventory held by an organization in a warehouse or other holding facilities is considerable. Many valuable warehouse labor hours are needed to arrange and conduct an inventory check and, when discrepancies are found, many more inventory and quality control labor hours are needed to investigate. However, the many benefits of physical inventory checking far outweigh these costs.

First, the physical counts of inventory checking both test and verify inventory recording and control systems, financial reports and systems, and a variety of additional computerized systems by acting as a performance check for which adjustments can be made to further enhance the efficiency and effectiveness of these systems. Financial reports produced by an organization's auditors, including the company's ever-important balance sheet, demand some form of physical inventory verification to support the value of the inventory indicated within the balance sheet. Inventory valuations that are not backed up by physical inventory counts have little relevance and value to an organization's internal accountants and internal and external auditors, especially those at tax revenue agencies such as the IRS!

Another benefit of physical inventory checking is the enhanced inventory security it provides. Within any warehouse, regular physical checks of inventory help ensure that possible fraud and theft is detected quickly so that immediate investigations may be conducted. Conversely, such regular inventory checking and immediate investigations into inventory inconsistencies can act as a deterrent to those contemplating fraud and theft within the warehouse. Had such checks been in place at Glossy Glam, Inc., "Light Fingers" Louie might not have "permanently borrowed" so much product or might have found another less security-minded place of employment.

Finally, physical inventory checking acts as an indicator of overall warehouse efficiency and control. The number and size of inventory check discrepancies are good indications of the efficiency of the receipt, issue, and storage processes. A high incidence of inventory discrepancies, for example, would typically warrant a close look at the system and personnel involved. Furthermore, accurate inventory levels, backed up by a regular physical count, will ensure that all users' requirements are covered by existing inventory and will be physically available to be issued promptly and efficiently. This helps organizations avoid the all-too-common occurrence of inventory shown as being available within the inventory records system, but not actually being physically present. This often happens when you look for a specific item at an electronics or home supply store. The store's app says the item is in stock, but you and store five employees can't find it in stock anywhere!

Because organizations are all different with very different inventory receipt, storage, and issuing needs, they may choose one of many methods for conducting a physical inventory check. The three most common methods of physical inventory checking are: *periodic physical inventory checks*, *continuous physical inventory checks*, and *physical spot-checking*. In a ***periodic physical inventory check***, a complete physical inventory check is performed at regular intervals, usually quarterly or at the end of the organization's fiscal year. This method of inventory counting and checking is typically carried out on a non-working day when the warehouse is completely closed to allow the inventory checkers the time and space to count carefully and check discrepancies for all items in the warehouse, thus ensuring an accurate count. This type of check is a very expensive one because it often involves large quantities of outside and inside staff hours, many of which are overtime. A ***continuous process warehouse***, which is one that operates 24 hours a day and 7 days a week, also faces the added expense of a very costly complete warehouse shutdown. Despite their high cost, periodic physical inventory checks are highly valuable because they enable discrepancies identified to be immediately investigated. They also provide accurate evaluation figures for a company's required annual balance sheets and accounts.

In a ***continuous physical inventory check***, a selection or section of items is checked on a continuous basis, such as every week or every month. Throughout a twelve-month period, every item in inventory will have been physically counted and checked without having to close the warehouse. A continuous physical inventory check allows a warehouse to continue operating 365 days a year. It reduces the disruption caused by inventory checking because it spreads one big disruption to a series of smaller disruptions across the year. Also, if the checking schedule is not disclosed to warehouse staff, it can act as a form of spot-checking and offer the benefits mentioned in the next paragraph. When inventory discrepancies are found with a continuous physical inventory check, a significant amount of time is needed immediately for investigation and, unlike periodic physical inventory checking, continuous physical inventory checking offers only limited time for immediate investigations as the warehouse continues its standard daily operations.

FIGURE 7.11 - EVIDENCE OF A CONTINUOUS PHYSICAL INVENTORY CHECK AT A RETAIL STORE

Finally, ***physical spot-checking*** is used primarily as a security and anti-theft measure within warehouse control. Spot-checks are designed to verify the inventory held without a prior warning to warehouse staff, which might otherwise allow for stolen inventory to be illegally replaced. Physical spot-checking is simple to arrange and conduct on a large scale because it is a limited check of a limited range of items. When it occurs unannounced to warehouse employees, it acts as a deterrent against those who might contemplate theft or fraud, knowing that a discrepancy highlighted in a sudden check may be the catalyst for a full-scale investigation of all inventory. Because physical spot-checking is limited in its full inventory counting applications and does not provide sufficient data for financial calculations, it is typically used in addition to other forms of inventory checking, such as periodic or continuous physical inventory checking.

Most warehouses use information systems and handheld devices to show a quantity of inventory that should be in stock. They also use the same handheld devices to scan the barcodes or RFID tags of items as they count. Warehouses use one of the methods of physical inventory checking to see if the actual amount of physical inventory in stock matches the amount shown in the inventory system. If the numbers don't match up, inventory can be immediately rechecked and reconciled.

Regardless of the specific type of method used to check inventory, the way in which personnel are used to conduct the check may vary according to: *the size of the inventory operation, the size of the warehouse facility, the inventory staff and resources available, the experience of the inventory checkers*, and *the extent of the inventory variation*. For example, an entire warehouse full of one type and model of computer chip is far, far easier to count than half a warehouse full of 500 different types and models of computer chips. When conducting a physical inventory check, different ways in which personnel can be used include:

- **one person** checking the entire warehouse or set of warehouse facilities without assistance,

- **a team** of inventory checkers working through large warehousing areas, and

- **two inventory checkers working independently** of each other but counting the same inventory. This final approach is the most accurate because, when the inventory checkers compare each section counted, it provides an instant double-check of that inventory.

To ensure that a physical inventory check is an accurate and meaningful exercise, those in charge of warehouse control activities must organize and control all inventory check activities. For a physical count to be effective, the inventory check demands a high degree of care and a very acute attention to detail. One of the toughest problems facing inventory checkers is a tight deadline. Inventory counts are often due by a set date, such as the end of the fiscal year, and any inventory not counted by that date will have to be counted later, which the necessitates additional complex calculations for inventory issued and received after the count deadline.

In order to have a timely and effective physical inventory check, warehouse managers often use standard steps for conducting an inventory check operation, such as the ten steps listed below:

1. **Appoint a controller.** For an effective physical inventory check, one individual should be appointed to have full authority over all those involved in the inventory check. This establishes clear lines of authority and responsibility for all involved in the operation. Sometimes outside professional organizations are hired to conduct physical inventory checks and have their own controllers for the check.

2. **Allocate personnel by area.** When using teams to conduct large inventory check operations, inventory areas are allocated to each team to check and count. It is good industry practice to have teams or members of the teams work in pairs. In order to provide needed local knowledge to speed up the checking operation, one member of the pair should be someone who normally works in the area being checked. In order to provide an outside view and deter internal fraud, the other member of the team should be someone from an outside department or area.

3. **Acquire the tools and space needed.** Adequate equipment must be made available to all inventory checkers before the counting can begin. Such equipment can range from pencils and clipboards to handheld terminals and scanners. Adequate office space may also be needed for checkers to discuss calculations and make comparisons.

FIGURE 7.12 - INVENTORY CHECKING TOOLS:
PEN AND CLIPBOARD (LEFT) AND SCANNER AND TABLET (RIGHT)

4. **Hold a comprehensive meeting.** Several days before the actual inventory check, the controller should hold a comprehensive inventory check meeting to explain the following to all involved: *operational procedures of the check, what to check and count, how and where quantities are recorded, inventory check location assignments, divisions of teams and pairs,* and *the timetable of events for the entire operation.*

5. **Highlight what to count.** The inventory to be counted and recorded must be clearly highlighted. This inventory typically includes all normal inventory, inventory under inspection, scraps, packaging, and items on loan. Inventory to be counted but recorded separately in different categories include damaged inventory, deteriorations, and goods in transit.

6. **Clean up!** To help make the actual physical inventory check more accurate and efficient, organizations often perform a pre-inventory check clear-up or clean-up of all inventory rooms, inventory yards, and warehouse buildings.

7. **Close the warehouse.** When conducting a complete periodic physical inventory check, the warehouse and its installations are often completely closed and all other activities stopped. An accurate comprehensive inventory check cannot take place when the inventory being counted is also in the process of being issued and received.

8. **Separate the counts.** All equipment and inventory that does not belong to the organization, such as rented equipment, must be counted, recorded, and documented separately from other inventory classifications.

9. **Don't forget in transit...** All inventory *in transit*, which means currently between the warehouse and another location, or inventory held in satellite warehouse facilities and external inventory yards should be accounted for at the same time as the main warehouse inventory check. This practice ensures a complete and accurate picture of the organization's entire current inventory.

10. **Do the documentation.** All active warehouse documentation, such as issue notes, delivery notes, and quality control documents, should be documented and filed before the physical inventory check begins to ensure that all inventory records are up-to-date.

When conducting a physical inventory check operation, sufficient documentation is required throughout. This documentation is typically digital but it may also be paper-based for some situations or organizations. Documentation generally includes: *inventory counting sheets, a master inventory sheet, an inventory certificate, outside warehousing installation inventory reports*, and *internal transfer notes*.

Inventory counting sheets, produced specifically for physical inventory checks, are designed to be used by an individual inventory checker for a specific classification or type of item to be counted. These counting sheets may be in hard copy form on a clipboard or in digital form on handheld devices and connected via wifi or Bluetooth to the organization's ERP system. Therefore, every classification or type of inventory held will have its own inventory counting sheet. These sheets must be numbered consecutively to avoid the possibility of the same items being counted twice. A standard inventory counting sheet also contains a great deal of useful reference data for the inventory checker and provides space for collection of the following data: the date of the inventory check, the description and code numbers of the inventory to be counted, the inventory unit of issue and physical location, the quantity of physical units counted, and the name and signature of the checker along with general comments on the inventory and its condition from the checker.

The controller then produces the **master inventory sheet** by collating all individual inventory counting sheets from each of the various warehouse locations. Each contribution from the inventory counting sheets is added to produce a total inventory quantity for each type of item held. While this may be done in paper form by some smaller organizations, this is likely to all be done digitally in most situations.

The **inventory certificate** is a formal document, which indicates the value of the total inventory held as of the date of the physical inventory check. The inventory certificate is checked and signed by a member of the organization's senior management team, often a member of the financial auditing team. ***Outside warehousing installation inventory reports*** are smaller versions of the master inventory sheet produced by the individual warehouse facility, depot, and outside warehousing unit managers and controllers. The counts they contain are also included within the organization's total inventory calculations. Finally, ***in transit transfer notes*** are used to account for inventory that is in transit on the date of the physical inventory check.

During a physical inventory check, all inventory, tools, and other equipment held within a warehouse are checked, counted, and measured. The inventory check's item counts in quantities per item are compared to the inventory levels counts calculated by the inventory control process. The inventory check controller, who has both sets of these actual and calculated inventory figures, can compare the quantities and verify whether or not the two sets of figures are the same. When they are the same, the controller may then report a final, verified inventory quantity. When they are not the same, a discrepancy has occurred. This process can also occur digitally though inventory check software systems linked to inventory control systems.

Every seasoned warehouse manager and inventory controller has likely experienced the challenge of ***inventory discrepancies***, which are the differences between the calculated and physical inventory quantities. In large, complex warehouse operations, discrepancies are inevitable but must still be investigated and corrected. The two primary types of discrepancies are: an *inventory surplus* and an *inventory deficiency*. Also called ***positive inventory***, an ***inventory surplus*** occurs when more inventory is physically counted than is indicated in the calculated inventory figures. An ***inventory deficiency***, or ***negative inventory***, occurs when less inventory is physically counted than is indicated in the calculated inventory figures.

There are three main classifications of inventory discrepancies, each of which denotes the amount of time and control effort expended in isolating the cause of the discrepancy and the steps needed to prevent future discrepancies of this type. These three inventory discrepancy classifications are:

- **Minor discrepancies**, which exist when the variation between the calculated and physical inventory is very small when compared to the overall inventory quantities involved. For example, in a sewing supplies distribution warehouse, which holds an inventory of 10,000 sewing needles, an inventory discrepancy of 2 sewing needles was found. With a minor discrepancy such as this one, the inventory controller would not waste time and resources on an inventory discrepancy investigation.

- **Major discrepancies**, which exist when a very large and valuable variation between the calculated and physical inventory is detected. Because of their accountability and responsibility for consistent and accurate inventory levels, warehouse managers insist on a complete investigation into the causes of major discrepancies. While two missing sewing needles might not be a major discrepancy, a discrepancy of two $10,000 commercial sewing machines would likely be considered major.

- **Operational discrepancies**, which exist when the variation between the calculated and physical inventory is small but the items involved are vital to the operation of the organization. Although the variation may be small, a major investigation into the discrepancy may be launched to determine fault and ensure that the inventory of the vital items is secure and definitively known. For example, a car dealership, which holds 500 new cars in its external inventory yard, has found an inventory discrepancy of one car. A major investigation must be carried out to investigate this discrepancy of only one item because, not only is the item extremely valuable, but it is a core element of the car dealership's operation.

Once a major or operational inventory discrepancy has been identified, an organization will investigate its cause so that it may find the lost or missing inventory and prevent similar discrepancies in the future. First, the controller and the inventory check team will check all inventory records and inventory control calculations for mathematical errors. They will also check the area of the inventory involved using an employee from a location other than the warehouse to establish a new physical inventory count. The controller and inventory team will also check to see if all units of issue are correct for each item of inventory taken, which includes checking inventory packaging and units of issue on all relevant documentation. They will also ensure that *rejected goods*, or goods that are taken from the inventory because of deterioration or damage, have been formally reported and recorded within the inventory records system.

In addition, the controller and inventory check team may also investigate the discrepancy with the appropriate user department. For example, a missing inventory of light bulbs in a refrigerated fish warehouse might mean that the user, the warehouse maintenance department, had been removing the light bulbs without permission or proper documentation. Once such a user discrepancy has been found, an issue note can be created to balance the inventory record.

When inventory discrepancies are found and investigated, their causes may often be innocuous and quickly rectified, such as the lightbulbs used by the warehouse maintenance department. Incorrect inventory checks, mathematical errors on inventory sheets, confusion of units of issue, misplacement of inventory on the wrong shelf or in the wrong place, lost or incorrectly entered documentation, and incorrect documentation from previous inventory checks may all lead to inventory discrepancy detection although no inventory has actually been lost. Discrepancies may also be detected when damage or deterioration has occurred or when inventory has been taken from the warehouse legally but without completing required documentation or notification. However, inventory discrepancies may also be the result of more purposive and malicious acts, such as fraud or theft. We'll look at how to prevent these situations when we explore warehouse security later in Chapter 10.

Identifying and correcting any major inventory check discrepancy can be a long, drawn out, and costly process, often ending with the inventory simply being written off as "lost." To avoid such costly processes in the future, it is vital for an organization to identify the cause of the inventory discrepancy and take measures to prevent similar discrepancies during the next inventory check. A few inventory discrepancy prevention measures include:

- *Studying the existing system of control to detect and eradicate faults.*

- *Closely examining warehouse documentation to ensure that all inventory control data is provided clearly, quickly, and accurately.*

- *Holding consultations between the warehouse and other departments whose actions affect the accuracy of inventory checks, such as the transport, purchasing, distribution, and manufacturing departments. These consultations are held to ensure that all parties are aware of how their actions may positively and negatively impact the accuracy of inventory counts.*

- *Conducting a complete review of security systems if fraud or theft is suspected.*

Once an actual inventory discrepancy has been found and its cause isolated, both the inventory records systems and warehouse accounts must be adjusted to balance the organization's books. An **inventory discrepancy adjustment report** must also be completed. This official document is signed by a senior member of staff and contains the relevant data needed by the warehouse accounts, inventory records, and inventory control teams to write off the amount of inventory involved. This data includes: the calculated inventory, full descriptions and code numbers for each item, a physical count of the inventory found, the total discrepancy involved, the value of the discrepancy, and the unit of issue and unit price. In order to avoid fraud within the organization, only the highest ranking members of staff are typically permitted to write off valuable inventory.

Because it is costly to hold inventory, organizations do not typically plan to waste their resources by holding inventory that they no longer need. During a physical inventory check,, it is sometimes found that the organization is holding inventory that is *obsolete*, or no longer of value. As inventory loses its value to the organization, it goes through the four-staged **inventory obsolescence process**. During the first stage, inventory becomes **obsolescent**, meaning it will soon be of no use or value to the organization. Inventory obsolescence often occurs as the result of changes in manufacturing or technology. As a result, an organization will often have to carry two lines of inventory as a new line is being phased in while the old one is being phased out. For example, an organization may decide to change from one form of packaging to another. The old packaging will still have some use until the changeover is complete.

During the second stage of the inventory obsolescence process, the inventory becomes **obsolete**, which means that it becomes completely worthless to the organization. Another organization may not have experienced the changes that set the inventory obsolescence process in motion for the original organization and may therefore find the inventory useful and be interested in purchasing it. For example, an organization that once used color ink jet printers has now switched all of its printers to color laser printers. The organization may now sell its obsolete inventory of ink jet printer cartridges to another organization that still uses ink jet printers.

During the third stage of the inventory obsolescence process, the inventory becomes **redundant**, which means that it is no longer of use to anyone, including both those in the organization holding the inventory and other organizations. For example, when the silicon chip was developed, traditional electronic circuits soon became redundant for many industries. During the fourth and final stage of the inventory obsolescence process, the inventory is considered **scrap** and, if possible, is sold off for the value of the component parts and raw materials within the items, rather than for any higher value the items might previously have held in their own right. For example, an organization has switched its packaging from tin cans to plastic pouches. Once this change is complete, the organization decides to scrap its inventory of pre-formed tin cans by selling them to a metal raw materials provider for the value of the metal in the cans.

It is the goal of inventory management to reduce an item's inventory levels as soon as it becomes obsolescent. An organization can take steps to minimize its losses incurred during the inventory obsolescence process by: *encouraging other departments within the organization to accept and use second-hand equipment, marketing its scrap inventory to multiple organizations,* and *establishing raw materials sell-back agreements with suppliers,* in which original suppliers are encouraged to buy back inventory that is no longer needed.

Several factors can set the inventory obsolescence process in motion, most of which are outside the control of the organization now holding the soon-to-be obsolete inventory. Four of the most common factors are:

- **Changes in manufacturing methods.** An organization often finds that newer and more efficient methods of manufacturing are introduced throughout its industry. As a result, the organization will often have to consider changes in its existing inventory of raw materials, component parts, or packaging.

- **Technological changes.** Major technological advances are made every day that introduce sweeping changes into various areas of industry and commerce. Aside from raw materials, inventory across most industries is not impervious to technological changes, which can quickly make component parts, work-in-process, finished goods, and supplies obsolete and even redundant overnight.

- **Changes in customer demand.** Changes in customers' tastes and buying habits also lead to inventory obsolescence. Changes in customer demand can also be induced by changes in the customer's own manufacturing system and methods.

- **Alterations by suppliers.** In some cases, an organization's supplier may decide to stop manufacturing an item that the organization has incorporated into the design of its finished product. If this halt in the supplier's manufacturing is very sudden, any of the organization's work-in-process is also in danger of becoming obsolete unless a suitable alternative supply can be located.

Although an organization may have little control over the changes occurring that initiate the inventory obsolescence process, it does control when it makes the decision to declare the inventory in question obsolete. It controls the timing of the inventory changeover rather than the fact that the inventory change will occur, which is actually an inevitable fact brought on by one of the changes listed above.

If an organization finds that it has a very large, expensive inventory of the item, it will delay declaring that item obsolete for as long as possible. If the item can be used in other capacities or within other areas of the organization, it may be able to minimize or even avoid redundancies. Also, if item usage has drastically decreased but not stopped altogether, the organization may decide to hold an inventory of that item and bear the cost of storage in order to provide desired customer service levels. This often occurs in the holding of spare parts for consumer durables, automobiles, and other machinery that has already become obsolete and is no longer manufactured. Finally, when it faces aggressive competitors that have already made inventory changes and are taking away an organization's sales, it may have to follow suit and make an immediate change, bearing the losses in its remaining obsolete, redundant, and scrap inventory.

CHAPTER 7 REVIEW QUESTIONS

1. When an organization has inventory, what must it do besides simply *hold* the inventory?

2. With the advantages offered by *just-in-time* systems, why would an organization want to hold inventory?

3. What impact would an organization's available financial resources have on its levels of inventory held?

4. What is *inventory control*? What are some of its objectives?

5. What is *buffer inventory*? How is it calculated? Why would this be an important concept for a manufacturer?

6. What are *EOQ* and *FOQ*? How are they related and how can an organization use them?

7. How can *ABC analysis* be used for inventory control?

8. What is *physical inventory checking*? Why is it an important part of a warehouse's operations?

9. How are a *periodic physical inventory check* and a *continuous physical inventory check* similar? How are they different?

10. Which type of physical inventory checking is a deterrent for employee theft? Why?

CHAPTER 7 CASE STUDY

INVENTORY CONTROL & THE CASE OF PURELY POSH PETS

Everyone's favorite pet clothing retailer, Purely Posh Pets, relies heavily on a few core product lines for most of its sales. One of these product lines is "The Sherlock," a basic Harris Tweed coat for small to extra-small dogs manufactured by Dapper Dogs. Purely Posh Pet sells approximately 100 "Sherlocks" every week. Because it is such a popular item, Purely Posh Pets likes to keep 4 weeks worth of buffer inventory of the "Sherlock."

The length of time it takes from the moment of reorder to receipt of the Sherlock from Dapper Dogs is one week. Because of the bulk order discount Dapper Dogs offers, Purely Posh Pets places only 5 large orders for "The Sherlock" every year.

Using the information and formulae in Sections 7.2 and 7.3 of this chapter, answer the following questions:

1. **What is the lead time for The Sherlock?**

2. **How much buffer inventory does Purely Posh Pets keep of The Sherlock?**

3. **What is the reorder level for The Sherlock?**

4. **What is its reorder quantity?**

5. **What is the progress level for this item?**

6. **What is the maximum inventory Purely Posh Pets holds of The Sherlock?**

INTERNATIONAL CANINE SUPERSTAR YOGI HARRISON
MODELING THE PURELY POSH PETS' NEW SPRING "RUFF AND READY" LINE

BONUS EXERCISE: INVENTORY DISCREPANCIES

Based on what you have learned about inventory discrepancies in Chapter 7, please read each of the scenarios below and determine:

- *if there is an inventory surplus or deficiency,*

- *the inventory discrepancy classification - major, minor, or operational,* and

- *if the situation is worthy of further investigation.*

Scenario 1:

The inventory control systems for a major department store's regional distribution warehouse shows that there are 242 pairs of True Blue brand men's socks in size Large and colored Indigo Blue, with a retail value of $10 per pair. The actual physical inventory count revealed that there are actually 244 pairs in the warehouse.

Scenario 2:

A small soft drink bottling company uses different colored caps to bottle different products in its product range. The company's inventory control system shows that there are 20,000 blue caps (two week's worth of bottling its Fruity Fizz drink) in inventory, with a replacement value of $0.01 each and a replacement lead time of 2 weeks. The actual physical inventory count revealed that there are actually 16,000 blue caps in inventory.

Scenario 3:

An airline flight from Los Angeles, California to Anchorage, Alaska shows that there are 134 people on its passenger manifest. A head count of passengers onboard - and a subsequent recheck - reveals that there are actually 135 passengers on the plane.

Scenario 4:

The shipping warehouse of a game chip manufacturer has 12,035 X-Pan-Sive chips, valued at $525 each, listed as in the warehouse and ready for distribution in its inventory control system. The physical inventory count has revealed, however, that there are actually 10,036 chips in the warehouse.

Chapter 8

Issuing Inventory

We have reached Chapter 8 and are more than halfway through this text. You now have an introductory understanding of what inventory is, what happens when it arrives into the warehouse, and how it is standardized and coded. If your goal is to become a rich hermit living in a warehouse full of goods with more and more items coming in, piling stories high around you, and not being able to find the exit thanks to the never-ending amassing of your precious goods, you can skip this chapter and move on to the next one. If this is not the case, stay with us for Chapter 8 and we will now consider the exit of goods from inventory and the *inventory issue process*. Let's start with some of the basic concepts and vocabulary you might encounter when issuing inventory!

FIGURE 8.1 - LOOKS LIKE THIS WAREHOUSE MIGHT BE OVERDUE FOR THE INVENTORY ISSUE PROCESS!

8.1 TERMINOLOGY OF THE INVENTORY ISSUE PROCESS

Remember from our model of the functions of warehouse management introduced back in Chapter 1, when it is time for goods to leave a warehouse facility, the *outbound processes* of warehouse management begin. Chapter 1 also explained that the management of these outbound processes are called *physical distribution management* within the world of logistics management.

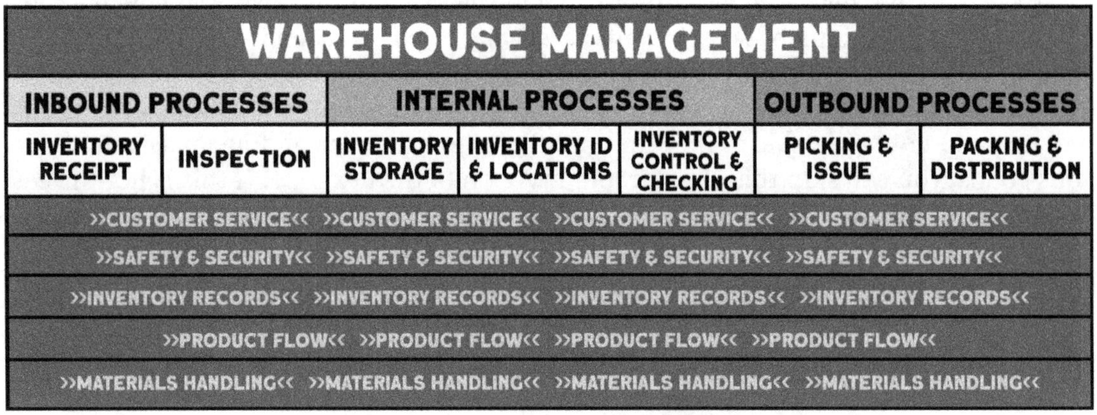

WAREHOUSE MANAGEMENT						
INBOUND PROCESSES		**INTERNAL PROCESSES**			**OUTBOUND PROCESSES**	
INVENTORY RECEIPT	INSPECTION	INVENTORY STORAGE	INVENTORY ID & LOCATIONS	INVENTORY CONTROL & CHECKING	PICKING & ISSUE	PACKING & DISTRIBUTION
>>CUSTOMER SERVICE<< >>CUSTOMER SERVICE<< >>CUSTOMER SERVICE<< >>CUSTOMER SERVICE<<						
>>SAFETY & SECURITY<< >>SAFETY & SECURITY<< >>SAFETY & SECURITY<< >>SAFETY & SECURITY<<						
>>INVENTORY RECORDS<< >>INVENTORY RECORDS<< >>INVENTORY RECORDS<< >>INVENTORY RECORDS<<						
>>PRODUCT FLOW<< >>PRODUCT FLOW<< >>PRODUCT FLOW<< >>PRODUCT FLOW<<						
>>MATERIALS HANDLING<< >>MATERIALS HANDLING<< >>MATERIALS HANDLING<< >>MATERIALS HANDLING<<						

FIGURE 8.2 - PICKING IN THE MODEL OF WAREHOUSE MANAGEMENT

The **inventory issue process**, also called **picking**, is the process in warehouse management of receiving and responding to demands for inventory held, typically within a warehouse facility or external inventory yard. As seen in Figure 8.2, within the world of warehouse management, *picking* is an outbound process that occurs before order packing and distribution. In its simplest form, picking, or the inventory issue process, involves hearing what people want and taking the first step to give it to them in the right quantity, of the right quality, at the right time, and at the right place while minimizing the cost of the service to the warehouse customer. It means getting a product from its current location, such as a slot within a warehouse, and bringing it to a packing and shipping area where it will be prepared for distribution to the person or company requesting the product. Picking is the first half of the outbound processes of warehouse management to get goods out the door and on their way to the customer and packing and distribution are the second half of this set of processes.

Raw materials, semi-finished goods, finished goods, and supplies are all types of inventory involved in the issue process. The customer demands for this inventory may come from a range of individuals or departments within the organization or external to it. For example, the manufacturing department might request raw materials, while a retailer might request an organization's finished goods. In addition, an organization's maintenance department might request spare parts from inventory while its transportation and distribution department might request semifinished goods to be shipped to a variety of regional assembly facilities.

When we talk about picking, we generally mean one of two types: *case picking* or *broken case picking*. **Case picking** involves taking items from the warehouse by the unit load, such as a in boxes or drums, typically using a larger piece of materials handling equipment, such as a forklift truck. When case picking involves taking an entire palletized unit load, it is called **pallet picking. Broken case picking**, also called **each picking**, involves taking individual items from a **broken case**, or opened unit load. This might involve an individual picker taking items and placing them into a cart as an order is picked or it may be part of an automated system.

FIGURE 8.3 - CASE PICKING (LEFT) AND BROKEN CASE PICKING (RIGHT)

As we have stated before, the items that are held by a warehouse are called *inventory*, but when taking about them in the context of picking and inventory issue, these items are also called **issues**. Warehouse facilities hold a variety of types of issue, including:

- **standard issues**, which are the goods held to meet customers' demands, such as the finished goods manufactured to fill customers' orders.

- **replacement issues**, which are pieces of equipment or supplies of goods that are held in case active equipment or supplies become nonfunctional or obsolete. For example, if there is a piece of equipment critical to a company's operations, it many need to keep a replacement so that operations do not stop if the current one stops working.

- **scheduled maintenance issues**, which are items held that are needed for regularly scheduled maintenance, including maintenance on production equipment or company vehicles, such as oil and windshield fluid.

- **impress issues**, which are items required by the user to be constantly available, even without specific orders for them being placed. This might include frequently ordered, maintenance, and service items. In cases where very large quantities of these items must be held, organizations sometimes utilize small, outlying unit warehouses.

- **loan issues**, which are typically tools and equipment required by specific departments within an organization for specific jobs. The warehouse loans out the equipment when needed for limited periods of time. This might include tool kits loaned out to the maintenance department or folding tables and chairs loaned out to all departments when needed for outdoor departmental functions.

- *allocated issues*, which are items in inventory that have been allocated by the manufacturing schedule to a specific operation in a given function or section, such as manufacturing, packaging, or engineering.

- *general issues*, which are the general items of inventory needed by various departments for the daily running of the organization. This could range from engineering spare parts to office light bulbs.

- *capital issues*, which are the major pieces of equipment purchased and issued by an organization. In most cases, large capital items are not held in inventory but are instead issued to the appropriate department as soon as they are delivered to the organization, such as a large poster printer for the marketing department..

- *project-specific issues*, which are items that are held for a limited period of time for dedicated use for specific projects, such as a new research and development project, a customer loyalty program, or a temporary marketing initiative.

8.2 THE ORDER CYCLE PROCESS

One important part of outbound logistics management and effective physical distribution management is the speed and accuracy of an organization's in responding to the *order cycle*. The **order cycle** is the entire time involved and process undertaken beginning with the placement of an order by a customer and ending with the receipt of the shipment by the customer. The order cycle process outlines the order of goods and how the order is filled from the supplier's perspective.

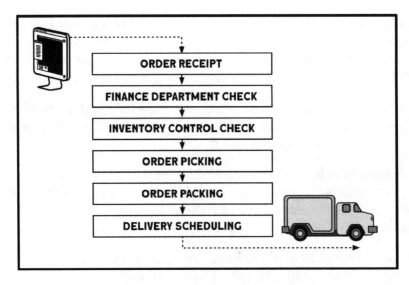

FIGURE 8.4 - THE ORDER CYCLE PROCESS

For efficient and effective physical distribution management, an organization must respond to the six steps of the order cycle process efficiently and effectively. One of the goals of physical distribution management is to achieve competitive advantage for the organization. One way this can be accomplished is by reducing ***order cycle time***, which is the time it takes to complete the entire order cycle through its entire six steps.

The six steps of the order cycle process and the ways in which they have an impact on overall order cycle time are:

1. **Order Receipt.** Before the order receipt stage begins, the users of an organization's inventory first decide: *what they need and in what condition, how much of it they need,* and *where and when they need it.* As previously stated, these inventory users can be internal or external customers and range from an organization's internal departments, such as manufacturing and maintenance, to external users, such as wholesalers, retailers, and individual end users. When a user has determined its need for an organization's inventory, it makes a formal request for this inventory. The internal user's request may be a paper document, an electronic document, or part of a larger *MRP* (*materials requirement planning*) or *JIT* (*just-in-time*) system. In most cases, the user submits a request for goods to the organization's warehouse facility in the form of a document or electronic request called a ***requisition***. This may also be called a ***request for issue*** or an ***issue note***, depending on the terminology of the organization. External customers may also place a *purchase order* through the sales department as another form of requisition. Remember from Chapter 3 that a ***purchase order*** is a legally binding document outlining a purchase agreement between a buyer and a supplier.

   The degree to which an organization's order receipt procedures are digitally automated has a substantial impact on overall order cycle time. For example, during the order receipt step for the older and smaller organization, Mom-N-Pop Stuff Inc., purchase orders are received from buyers by fax, manually entered into the company's computer system, and then printed and hand delivered to the company warehouse for order picking. Its newer and larger competitor, Biggie Mart, has streamlined its order receipt procedures by receiving buyers' purchase orders through an online ordering system. Orders are sent directly to the warehouse inventory and management system for pre-approved buyers. Order receipt at Mom-N-Pop Stuff may take an hour or longer, but the process takes less than one second at Biggie Mart.

2. **Finance Department Check.** After the buyer's order is received, it is sent to the supplier's finance department to verify the customer's status. This check determines if the customer is a preexisting one, is in good credit standing with the organization, and has preexisting sales and service terms, such as whether or not an order can be sent before its payment is received. This would apply to both orders from external customers and from customers inside the company. As with the order receipt example given for Mom-N-Pop Stuff and Biggie Mart, the degree to which the finance department check is automated influences the speed of this stage of the order cycle process. Even for smaller organizations, where large-scale, system-wide automation may not be as cost effective as it would be for a larger company, accurate and

thorough digital record keeping can make a world of difference to a company's order cycle time and its bottom line. If a supplier does not have well kept records about its previous transactions with buyers, the finance department may spend ridiculously large amounts of time checking up on past buyers and may spend extra resources in unnecessary credit checks. It may even mistakenly approve buyers who have defaulted in the past.

3. **Inventory Control Check.** After the buyer's order is approved by the finance department, it is sent to the inventory control department or system, which then checks on the availability of the finished goods requested in the order. If the goods are available, the requested quantities of each item are allocated to the requestor within the company's the order processing system. If the item is not in stock, an order request is made to the organization's purchasing or manufacturing department, depending on whether the item is one that is ordered from a supplier or manufactured internally. When the requests for items held within a warehouse come from the manufacturing department, however, those handling warehouse requisitions are supplied with a ***Manufacturing Materials Schedule***. This document provides details of manufacturing activities over a given period of time, allowing the warehouse to ensure that the correct inventory required for manufacturing are readily available. Through an MRP system, the Manufacturing Materials Schedule contains information on: *the amount of inventory needed*, *the types of inventory required*, and *the timetable of requirements*.

In the previous example, the manufacturing department itself has final authority over the order and is automatically granted its warehouse inventory requests. In most cases, however, someone within the warehouse or issuing department holds the authority and their approval must be sought before inventory is released for issue. This person is responsible for ensuring that the demand is real and that limits imposed by the organization are not being exceeded. In MRP, JIT, and other software systems, this authorization may be automatic, with specific quantities of items over a specific timeframe pre-approved or pre-authorized for issue to specified requestors. At the risk of sounding like a very broken record, this stage of the order cycle can also be made instantaneous with digitally automated order processing.

4. **Order Picking.** Now that the customer's financial status and the availability of the items in the order have been verified, the organization can begin to physically fill the order. The items requested are ***picked***, which means that they are selected from the warehouse shelves and taken to an order packing area. Later in this chapter, we will explore some of the techniques used for efficient order picking.

5. **Order Packing.** After the items in the order are picked, they must be prepared for shipment. An order is ***packed*** when its items are placed into packaging, unitized, and physically prepared for shipping. We will explore order packing in greater depth in Chapter 9, including the importance of effective packing to a company's bottom line.

6. **Delivery Scheduling.** After the inventory is picked and packed, a delivery time and place is scheduled with the customer through the organization's transportation

system. The delivery is scheduled and subsequently conducted through the **distribution channel**, which is the route and means by which an organization distributes its finished goods. As with all steps of the order cycle, organizations can achieve greater delivery scheduling efficiency and effectiveness when the process is digital and automated. Imagine a Walmart regional distribution center with 40 inbound and outbound loading bays and a steady stream of container trucks both bringing goods in from suppliers and taking them away to retail stores. If the scheduling of the bays alone wasn't precise down to the minute, chaos might reign, with container trucks backed up for hours waiting for available bays.

The first three steps of the order cycle process are increasingly automated and handled by computer and cloud-based systems, even in smaller companies, thanks largely to apps and handheld devices, such as handheld terminals, phones, and tablets. When we get to the fourth stage of the order cycle process, order picking, we move out of the world of information and into the world of hands-on physical action! We will cover the exciting realm of *order picking* in the rest of this chapter. We will then move on to the fifth and sixth stages of the order cycle process, *order packing* and *delivery scheduling*, in Chapter 9.

Not all inventory goes through the order cycle process in exactly the same way in the six steps described above. In some situations, the supplier of an item keeps track of its inventory levels at an organization and the supplier handles the paperwork and record keeping for its items in the customer's inventory *at the customer's warehouse facility*. **Vendor managed inventory**, also known as VMI, is the practice of a buyer allowing a *seller*, or **vendor**, to monitor product demand and inventory levels in order to forecast demand patterns and set product shipment levels and schedules. The ultimate goal of VMI is to ensure that the buyer has enough inventory needed while keeping inventory holding costs at a minimum. The vendor makes sure to maintain adequate inventory levels and quality because the vendor is not paid until the items are picked from inventory. One way in which companies keep the vendors' items separate from their own in a warehouse so that vendors' items do not get mixed up or lost is through using vending machines. Instead of potato chips or candy bars or bottles of water, these vending machines contain a range of small items that the vendor is supplying to the company.

Alaska Communications, a provider of broadband and managed IT services to businesses and residential customers across Alaska, has installed vendor managed inventory systems at its central warehouse in Anchorage, Alaska. Most of the items in the warehouse are picked by their internal end users, such as the company's repair technicians who pick tools and supplies to work on broadband cables and business network systems. To keep track of some of the higher value items in its VMI inventory, the organization uses a vending machine that resembles those that sell mp3 players and other electronic devices at airports. The vending machines have scanning technology that allows vendors and Alaska Communications end users to use their identification cards or type in identification codes to access empty slots. The vendors can then fill them with inventory or the end users can take needed items from inventory. This process lets Alaska Communications' inventory systems immediately know how much of which items are in stock and who has taken items and what department they should be charged to.

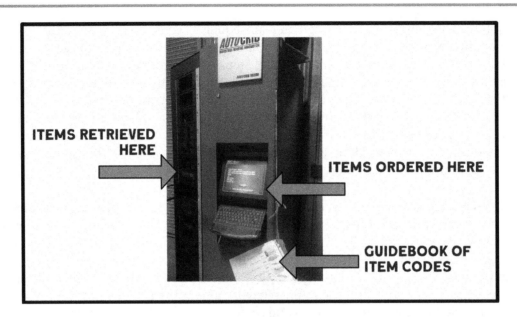

FIGURE 8.5 - VENDOR MANAGED INVENTORY AT ALASKA COMMUNICATIONS

8.3 THE ORDER PICKING STAGE

Order picking is selecting and retrieving the correct type and quantity of inventory from a warehouse facility based on a specific internal or external customer's requirements. Upon selection and retrieval, picked good are taken to a packaging or order consolidation area to be prepared for distribution. Order picking may range from retrieving individual items from storage to retrieving an entire pallet-load or container-load of items. In the order cycle process, the order picking stage can have a great impact on an organization's revenue saved or lost. When goods are retrieved from storage quickly, an organization can fill and ship its customers' orders quickly, get paid sooner, and then move on to the orders of its next paying customers. When goods are retrieved from storage slowly, perhaps taking three days instead of the one day it takes for its quicker-picking competitor, an organization loses money because more money is tied up in warehouse space and inventory holding. Customers are also far less willing to pay premium prices when inventory issuing is much slower than the company's competitors. Therefore, the ultimate goal of warehousing in the order picking process is that customers' needs are picked quickly and accurately and moved immediately along to the next stage of the order cycle process.

The first step in rapid order picking is finding the item to be picked. Could you imagine if every organization's order picking system operated the way we do when we've parked our cars at the mega-mall multi-story parking garage or when we are in a frantic search for where we've placed our keys. To avoid similar time traps, warehouses use *inventory location systems*. With these location systems, items and their corresponding item codes are assigned a location code representing a specific location within the warehouse. Even the most basic computers or handheld devices can house the most intricate and detailed inventory location systems, with the user simply typing in the name or item code of the desired item and immediately being supplied with the item's exact location. Many inventory location systems give step by step verbal directions so that pickers wearing headsets can be hands free while finding and then picking the item from inventory.

Both bar coding and RFID systems, with their accompanying tech and hardware, can also be used to further enhance the benefits of inventory location systems. Bar codes can be scanned for rapid item identification and location code information. RFID tags can similarly be used for automatic item location information, with the added benefit of providing the exact GPS location of the tagged item instead of the location where it is supposed to be.

 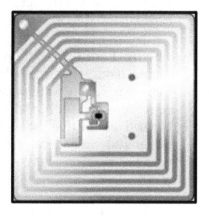

FIGURE 8.6 - BARCODE (LEFT) AND RFID TAG (RIGHT)
BAR CODES ARE PRINTED ON LABELS, ADHERED TO ITEMS IN INVENTORY, AND READ USING OPTICAL SCANNING TECHNOLOGY. RFID TAGS ARE ADHERED TO OR HIDDEN WITHIN INVENTORY AND READ USING RADIO FREQUENCY SCANNERS.

Once an inventory location system is in place and you have pinpointed the exact location of the item desired, that item must now be retrieved from storage, or *picked*. At this point, companies typically create a ***pick list***, which is a document that lists the order number, the specific items to be picked, and the quantity of each item to be included in the shipment. Also often included in the pick list is the location for each item, such as the aisle and bin number. For orders that are picked manually with no technological assistance, the information on inventory location is critically important. When location information is not correct, pickers can waste valuable travel time searching for items. When companies use technologically-based inventory picking systems, pick lists can be automatically generated as soon as customers place their orders.

When it comes to physically picking an order, there are a variety of manual or automated systems of order picking. The means of order picking an organization chooses depends on many factors, such as the dimensions and weight of the items or unit loads, the value of the items to be picked, the potential hazards posed by the items or specialized environmental conditions needed for the items, an organization's financial resources and long-term goals, available warehouse space, and ergonomic considerations in item picking.

Below are three categories of order picking systems based on how products are taken from inventory and the relationship the picker has to the picked item, or *part*:

1. **The picker goes to the part.** The ***picker*** is the human worker retrieving the item. The ***part*** is the item being retrieved. Rather than having the picker spend the entire day walking up and down the long warehouse aisles retrieving items of varying sizes and weights, warehouses use technology to speed up the process. Pickers can get to their desired parts quickly and retrieve them effortlessly while operating pallet trucks, powered carts, or even Man-Aboard Storage and Retrieval Systems, like the one shown on the left in Figure 8.7. Picker-to-part systems are generally the least expensive and most commonly used order picking systems.

2. **The part comes to the picker.** There are many quick systems that depend less on human labor in which stationary pickers can have desired items come to them. When there is adequate warehouse space and when the size and volume of items merit it, conveyors, carousels, and automated storage and retrieval systems, or *ASRS*, can all be used as effective and efficient means of bringing the part to the picker. The part-to-picker systems generally require a more expensive initial investment in machinery, but they offer long-term savings in reduced labor costs. They are used more often in warehouses with a very large and rapid order throughput flow, such as central shipping fulfillment centers for online mega-stores or massive regional distribution centers with a range of small to mid-sized items that could easily be handled using conveyors and automated picking technology. In some carousel systems or robot-operated mobile storage systems, the individual part may not come to the picker, but a shelf or rack or bins may come to the picker, from which the picker picks the item, often guided by light-directed technology in which a light indicates the correct bin to pick from. When the part comes to the picker, although it is minimal, some effort is needed by the picker to retrieve the part, such as picking the item as it goes by on a moving conveyor belt or selecting the item from a rack of bins.

3. **The entire process is automated and operated under computer control.** To retrieve an item, the picker simply pushes a button on a computer terminal, uses the screen of a handheld device, or supplies a voice command to a voice-directed system. Moments later, the part is delivered to the picker with no effort at all needed from the picker other than the initial push of a button. In some cases, the picker is also the packer, which is the next stage in the order cycle process. When the items comes to the picker, the picker would immediately put the items into boxes to assemble and pack the order to be distributed to the customer. Remember the example of the fully automated FBI robotic records warehouse in Chapter 5? In this example, FBI staff would simply press buttons at a computer terminus, wait while the machines do all of the picking work, and then pack the records into boxes and envelopes to be sent to those requesting them.

When a large quantity of items must be picked regularly within very short periods of time, fully automated picking systems can offer critical speed and efficiency. Examples of automated order picking systems include:

- *case and item dispensers*, in which items or cases of items are dispensed horizontally from a conveyor or vertically through a gravity-based system

- *unit load ASRS*, in which automated guided vehicles, conveyors, or monorail systems are used to automatically pick and dispense entire unit loads

- *robotic elements*, such as robotic arms and three-axis gantry mounts used to pick and dispense items or unit loads.

Because of their great expense and limitation of movement, these fully automated order picking systems are not as common as the first two categories of order picking systems, but they are increasing in popularity, especially when speed is important and human labor is in short supply. They are also invaluable in handling hazardous materials, large throughput volumes, and situations in which repetitive picking movements might cause ergonomically related injuries in pickers.

FIGURE 8.7 - ORDER PICKING SYSTEMS
THE PICKER GOES TO THE PART IN A MAN-ABOARD STORAGE AND RETRIEVAL SYSTEM (LEFT), THE PART GOES TO THE PICKER USING A CONVEYOR SYSTEM (CENTER), AND AUTOMATED PROCESS UNDER COMPUTER CONTROL, SOMETIMES WITH ROBOTIC ELEMENTS (RIGHT)

In many warehouses, more than half the human labor time is spent picking an order, especially in the time it takes for the picker to travel to and from items picked and to search for items, even with location coding. To make order picking faster and more efficient, warehouses and distribution centers can utilize a variety of forms of technology and automation systems, including:

- *pick-to-light*. When a warehouse has smaller items that are stored in bins on rows of racks, pick-to-light can be a highly useful order picking technology. With pick-to-light, an indicator light above or adjacent to the bin holding the item to be picked will light up. In many pick-to-light systems, a digital display will also indicate how many of that item must be picked. Some pick-to-light systems have eliminated the possibility of human error of picking from the wrong bin by also installing a weight check system under each bin that measures the weight of the bin. With a weight check system, when an incorrect bin suddenly gets lighter, the picker will be immediately alerted, usually from a sound, light, or digital display system. In many pick-to-light systems, however, the picker will indicate that they have picked the item from the lighted bin by either pushing a button to turn off the light or using voice recognition technology to record the items code and quantity picked.

FIGURE 8.8 - PICK-TO-LIGHT SYSTEM

- ***voice recognition and voice-directed technology***. These two types of technologies are often combined, with the user wearing a headset so that they can operate hands free. In ***voice recognition technology***, a user speaks into a device, such as the microphone in a headset, which is connected to a software system that could be operated from a computer or handheld device. The software system recognizes the human speech and converts it into information and commands within the software system. With ***voice-directed technology***, the user listens from a device, such as an earphone on a headset. A software system from a computer or handheld device issues information or voice commands to the listener. The combination of these technologies are used frequently in warehouse operations and is called ***voice-directed warehousing***. The use of voice technology is especially prevalent in order picking and is, unsurprisingly, called ***voice picking***.

In voice picking, a picker wears a handheld device, smartwatch, or computer along with a headset and microphone. The picker receives picking commands through the headsets, with the computer system verbally instructing which items to pick and exactly where they are located. They may even give step by step instructions to find the item. When the picker finds the item and begins to retrieve it, they read the item's identifying code into the headset microphone so the computer system can verify that the right item was picked. If the wrong item was picked, the system instructs the picker to put the item back and guides them to the location of the correct item. If the right item was picked, the system records the picking action into the inventory control system. This system of double-checking the pick through voice recognition has made voice picking one of the most highly accurate forms of order picking technology available when a human picker is still involved in the process.

Because voice picking is a handsfree system, it saves time because the picker doesn't have to stop and look down at a paper, clipboard, or hand-held computer. It also offers an added safety benefit because the picker has their eyes up and scanning the warehouse environment. Finally, it can reduce language-related error rates significantly in multilingual warehouses because the system can be set to the picker's native language instead of to the default preferred language of the company.

FIGURE 8.9 - VOICE-DIRECTED TECHNOLOGY (LEFT TOP AND BOTTOM) AND VOICE RECOGNITION TECHNOLOGY(RIGHT) IN ORDER PICKING

- **_RF directed technology_**. Radio frequency directed, or **_RF directed_**, picking technology is part of a warehouse management system that has RFID tags on all the inventory items in a warehouse. The picker is directed to the items and scans them using an handheld RFID scanner as the items are picked. Although resulting in highly accurate picks because the pick is double-checked with the RF system, many warehouses have found that this form of picking technology takes longer than pick-to-light and voice recognition systems because of the time spent by pickers using handheld scanners. This shortcoming is being overcome with wearable RFID scanners that pickers wear on their wrist or on top of their hand.

- ***ASRS. Automated storage and retrieval systems***, also called *ASRS* or ***A-frame picking systems***, have goods in bins or totes that move along conveyors and shelving systems that are hundreds of feet wide and multiple stories high. This system brings the bins containing the items being picked to one location where the order picker can quickly pick an entire order with almost no travel time from item to item. While it speeds up picking operations and reduces errors, ASRS requires a significant financial investment and is typically used within larger operations or larger warehouse facilities and distribution centers.

- ***Automated guided vehicles***. Also known as ***AGVs***, automated guided vehicles are machine operated vehicles, such as an industrial forklift trucks, that does not require a human operator. An AGV can move goods along a fixed path, such as with a rail-guided system, or a variable path, such as with laser-guided systems. AGVs can be useful in operations that require the picking of larger, palletized unit loads.

- ***Mobile robots.*** One type of mobile robot is the ***autonomous mobile robot***, or ***AMR***, which is a mobile, rolling robot that use artificial intelligence to plan and optimize routes while picking orders. They are often used in order picking to bring either individual unit loads or racks of items to be picked to an order picker. Another type of mobile robot is the ***cobot***, or ***collaborative mobile robot***. They look like AMRs and can optimize routes, but they are collaborative because they are designed to work and interact alongside human workers as they move through a warehouse. The cobots move along the ground and carry either individual unit loads or a system of racks and bin. They move alongside the human worker who picked the orders when arriving at the locations determined by the cobot and places items picked into the predetermined robot bin. Because of the expense of robotic technology, only organizations with large, high-volume picking operations would likely consider robotic picking.

FIGURE 8.10 - AUTONOMOUS MOBILE ROBOT BRINGING RACK OF GOODS TO THE PICKER (LEFT) AND AUTOMATED GUIDED VEHICLE MOVING PICKED GOODS ALONG A VARIABLE PATH (RIGHT)

When deciding which type of technology to use or whether to use technology at all for order picking, a company must consider the expense of the technology and the return on investment it will get from each of the technology options being considered. A **return on investment**, or **ROI**, is how much the company will save or receive in additional financial compensation compared to the amount it spent on a particular investment, such as order picking technology. When determining the ROI for each order picking technology considered, a company should look at *the cost of the technology, the operating cost to run the technology, how productive the technology is to the operation, how long the technology will last and the extent of its reach is into the organization, how well the technology integrates with other systems within the company, how accurate the technology is*, and *how safe the technology is for both goods and people*. Depending on the ROI of the systems, the eventual picking system selected could be any of the following, in order of increasing accuracy, complexity, and cost:

- **manual system**, in which the picker picks and moves items by hand,

- **mechanized system**, in which the picker uses materials handling equipment, such as dollies or forklift trucks, to assist in picking and moving the order,

- **semi-automated system**, in which the items to be picked are brought to the picker through an automated or robotic system, and

- **automated system**, in which a computer systems directs and controls the picking operation, which is handled entirely by robotic and automated picking technology with no humans involved.

Just as there are different systems used for order picking, there are also various styles of order picking. These can be used individually or in combination with one another. A few of the styles of order picking include:

- **Order picking.** The spartanly named **order picking**, also called **discrete picking**, is the simplest and most common of the order picking styles. In order picking, each order is picked by one person working from a single picking document, picking one item at a time until the entire order is filled. Order picking is not scheduled and orders may be picked at any time within the picker's work schedule, as long as the delivery deadline is met. This simple style offers many advantages, including reduced errors and increased accountability. Its primary disadvantage is that it is at the mercy of human limitations, especially the speed at which one person can fill one order, making it the slowest style of order picking.

- **Wave picking**. One variation of simple order picking is **wave picking**, in which orders are picked by one picker, one item at a time, but orders are scheduled to be picked within specific timeframes, largely driven by shipping timeframes. For example, if FedEx is coming to pick up one of your orders at 10am for a same-day delivery to one of your biggest customers, wave picking would allow you to schedule that order to be picked within a shorter timeframe, not just within the picker's work shift.

- **Batch picking.** In *batch picking*, one person picks multiple orders, called a *batch* of orders, following multiple picking documents at the same time. When the same item appears of multiple orders, the total quantity of the item from all of the orders is picked together and separated later or immediately into small containers. You can likely see batch picking in action at a late grocery store that offers delver and drive-up service. Multiple delivery and drive-up orders are filled by one grocery store employee at one time, pushing around a batch picking cart around up and down the aisles, filling multiple baskets in the cart with each basket used a different customer's order. Batch picking reduces the traveling labor time of the picker by picking multiple orders at once. However, the risk of incorrect picking and sorting is increased. These risks are reduced in automated picking systems, however.

**FIGURE 8.11 - BATCH PICKING FOR CUSTOMER DELIVERIES
IN A GROCERY STORE IN QUEENSLAND, AUSTRALIA**

- **Zone picking.** In *zone picking*, a warehouse is divided into sections, or *zones*. A different employee is assigned to and responsible for picking items within their zone. Once picked, these items are brought to the central *order consolidation and issue section* where the entire order can be consolidated from items picked from each of the warehouse's multiple zones by different pickers. While zone picking alone does not reduce the labor used in basic order picking, it does speed up the order picking process. It is also useful in warehouses using a variety of materials handling storage and transportation equipment. For example, within one warehouse, one zone may contain palletized unit loads with pickers on forklifts, another zone may contain small often used quantities of items delivered to stationary pickers via conveyor belts, and a third zone may contain extremely heavy items which are picked and transported by crane operators.

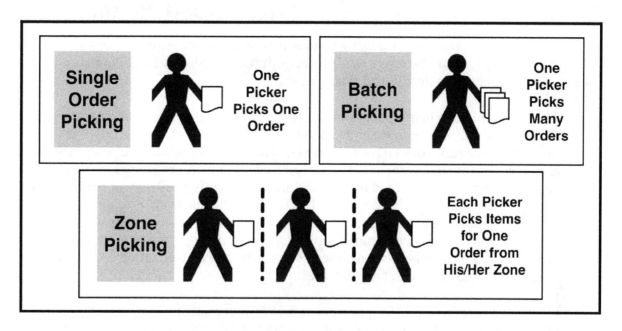

FIGURE 8.12 - STYLES OF ORDER PICKING

- **Omnichannel picking.** For large companies with complex operations, picking has traditionally been considered in terms of batching orders to create larger picks and increase picking efficiency and cost effectiveness. However, manufacturers and retailers must now consider ***omnichannel fulfillment***, in which order fulfillment occurs for goods that companies sell in different physical locations and across multiple online platforms. People and companies order from a wide range of places and systems at any time of the day or night, and in some places, they expect immediate results! Internet orders may have to be filled immediately, with no time to wait to consolidate a batch of orders to be picked at one time. For fast and accurate fulfillment, companies use software to determine the best picking location, such as which distribution center or warehouse facility around the country, for each customer's order. For example, an order might be picked from a distribution center located much further away from a customer simply because the software has determined that the distribution center selected has all of the items in stock or that the order could be picked much faster at that DC because of the location of the items to be picked or availability of the staff to pick and pack them. Companies like Google and Amazon are now using ***omnichannel picking*** and related software systems in some markets to fulfill individual customer's orders on the same day and even within a couple of hours of the order being placed.

8.4 CORE PRACTICES OF EFFECTIVE ORDER PICKING

Regardless of a warehouse's order picking system or style, there are core practices that enhance the efficiency and effectiveness of any organization's order picking. Four core practices for efficient and effective order picking are:

1. **Plan your pick.** When a picker has an order and is ready to begin picking, it is best if they are simply not let loose in the warehouse to pick items from the order at random. While many of us have exceptional planning and spatial skills, we might not always choose the most efficient picking route every time. A pre-routed picking document, typically generated through optimization routing software or a warehouse management system, can help a picker by providing the quickest, most efficient picking for each order. In addition, the way in which warehouse space is used can increase the efficiency of planning for picking. For example, those items that are picked most often can be located closest to the issue and consolidation section so the order picker does not often have to travel far.

2. **Clarify and reduce picking paperwork.** Without realizing it, pickers can spend many valuable minutes trying to decipher incomprehensible shipping documents or illegible handwriting when picking orders. Creating standard, clear and legible, and easily comprehended picking paperwork can ensure that potential wasted minutes are instead saved. Standard picking paperwork should include the following information about each item: *a concise description, item code, location code,* and *quantity needed.* It should not include extraneous information that is not needed by the picker and can obscure the essential information. Confusing paperwork may also be eliminated entirely. Many organizations have moved to handheld devices, barcode scanners, RFID scanners and transmitters, and voice recognition systems to ensure greater order picking efficiency.

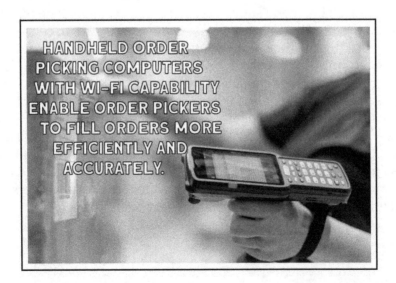

FIGURE 8.13 - HANDHELD DEVICES REDUCE PICKING PAPERWORK

3. **Package in smaller, oft-used quantities.** When we have to count large quantities of items, we are almost certain to make at least a few mistakes from time to time. As a fun, do-it-yourself experiment, fill your bathtub with individual jellybeans. Without eating any jellybeans or taking any of them from your tub, count them three times a day for three days. If you are a normal human being and not a bean-counting cyborg, all nine of your jellybean counts are likely to be different, even if you have not eaten any of the jellybeans. To simplify order picking and reduce miscounting errors, most warehouses ensure that items are packaged in smaller, oft-counted quantities, such as a pallet containing only 50 cans of tomato soup, even though the pallet is fully able to handle 500. Imagine how much easier our jellybean experiment would have been if they had been packaged in bags of 25 or 1000 instead of one, huge, bathtub-sized container!

4. **Make accountability count!** The fourth and final core practice for efficient and effective order picking is to make pickers accountable for the accuracy of the orders they pick. For greater order accuracy, some warehouses use *order checkers*, or individuals who review the picked order to ensure that the order has been picked accurately before it is shipped. Even when order checkers are used, greater efficiency can be achieved by going to the source and making a picker responsible for order accuracy. Although this might make the order pricking process slightly slower as order pickers check to be confident in their order counts, far less time is later spent checking and correcting orders.

8.5 THE ORDER CONSOLIDATION AND ISSUE STAGE

Once the order for inventory has been received and the items in the order have been picked, the items are consolidated and the order is issued to the customer. During the *consolidation and issue* stage, items listed on the user's order or requisition that have just been selected are brought to a central place in the warehouse facility for consolidation and packing. This central place is usually a dedicated space near the loading docks and is often labeled with a self-explanatory name, such as *Issue and Consolidation Sector* or *Packing and Dispatch Area* or, simply, *Distribution or Shipping*.

In this issue and consolidation area, a pre-assigned warehouse supervisor or employee checks the order to ensure that it is correct, which means that the requested items and quantities listed on the requisition match the items and quantities to be consolidated. Once the order has been checked, a *consignment note*, also called a *packing slip*, is created that lists exactly what will be packed within each receptacle, such as a carton, box, drum, pallet, or container. The items are then packed into their designated receptacles. We'll learn bit more about order consolidation, packing, and preparing orders for shipment in our next chapter.

Once the items have been consolidated and packed, transportation and documentation is prepared, such as cross-border documentation for international shipments. This is critical and very detail-oriented work in today's global market with ever-changing customs documentation and security issues. For example, unless the correct, up- to-date European customs paperwork has been completed, fresh, juicy Florida oranges will be forced to wait at European borders, growing less fresh and less juicy every day the correct paperwork is not filed. After the transportation and cross-border documentation has been prepared, a delivery or pick-up is scheduled for the order. At this point, the order then leaves the realm of *materials management* and, in most cases, enters the world of *physical distribution*, which we will explore next in Chapter 9.

CHAPTER 8 REVIEW QUESTIONS

1. What is the *inventory issue process*? At what point in the supply chain does it occur?

2. What is the difference between *replacement issues* and *general issues*?

3. What are some other names for a *requisition*? When and why is one used?

4. What happens in a warehouse after a requisition is received?

5. What does a warehouse strive for during the *order picking stage*? Why?

6. How does *pick-to-light* work? Based on the description of pick-to-light in this chapter, what kinds of inventory items do you think might be picked efficiently using a pick-to-light system?

7. What are the advantages and disadvantages of *radio frequency directed technology* in order picking?

8. What role does the *picker* play in the three primary categories of order picking?

9. In what type of warehouse might *zone picking* be most beneficial?

10. Why is it sometimes useful to *package* items for picking in smaller quantities?

CHAPTER 8 CASE STUDY

SECRETS OF THE ORDER PICKING PROS

Order pickers are the gatekeepers of our most cherished dreams. They influence how quickly we receive those things we desire most, perhaps our favorite flannel pajamas or the special order junk food from Japan that we have been craving. If order pickers are inaccurate or too slow, we might not get our cozy pajamas and Almond Crush Pocky in time for the red carpet pre-show for this year's Oscar Awards show. Oh no! Hopefully, an elite cadre of order picking pros is picking our order. Those who work in the world of warehousing have a few tricks up their sleeve when it comes to efficient and effective order picking. Some of these tricks of the trade include:

- **Do NOT put different items, or SKUs, in the same bin!** Companies that don't know better sometimes think they are saving money on storage bins by putting multiple SKUs, or *stock keeping units*, in the same bin. For example, the warehouse of a local printing company decided to keep all of its t-shirts in covered plastic tubs, which was a smart idea because it could keep the shirts clean and reduce the risk of damage. However, the tubs were a bit pricey, so the warehouse manager decided to buy only a few tubs and sort shirts into tubs by color, which meant all seven sizes of its glowing green t-shirt were in one tub. Great idea, until it was time to do some order picking! The poor picker had to look at the label of every t-shirt in the tub just to try to find the one XXS size in inventory.

At Once in a Blue Moose, order pickers have a much easier and quicker time picking t-shirts. Rather than worry about pricey storage bins, the retailer uses cardboard boxes (pictured below) as storage bins and makes sure that there is a unique box for each unique SKU. For example, the small short-sleeve green t-shirt with two floatplanes on it is in a different cardboard box than the medium short-sleeve green t-shirt with two floatplanes. This speeds up the order picking process because pickers do not have to waste time searching for the correct item in the box. Instead, they simply grab a shirt from the box, confident in the knowledge that the correct item will be there.

REPURPOSING BOXES FOR STORING EACH INDIVIDUAL SKU AT ONCE IN A BLUE MOOSE

- **Keep the "hits" coming!** It is a goal of order pickers want to increase their *hit density*, which occurs when the distance between picks is reduced and the number of items picked in one location is increased. As much as possible, pickers want items in an order to be located near each other so they can pick as many items as possible within a set timeframe. Hit density can be increased by designing picks so that the picker is walking less and picking items that are near each other. At Alaska Communications, warehouse management noticed that most repair technicians who picked their own orders to fill their toolkits were picking the same items. Rather than waste the valuable labor time of highly skilled technicians by having them pick screws and tape out of warehouse bins, Alaska Communications decided to work with a vendor to create pre-supplied tool kits (pictured below) based on the input of the technicians. With the availability of the new pre-supplied toolkits, technicians had to pick only one item instead of many, saving time and effort. When technicians want the toolkit restocked, they simply put the old toolkit in the return bin and grab a new one from inventory. With the vendor managed inventory system, the vendor makes sure to refill the toolkits on a regular basis and place them back into inventory.

INCREASING HIT DENSITY: ALASKA COMMUNICATIONS TOOLKITS

- **Don't get touchy!** Items should be touched only once by the pickers' hands and automatic systems should be in place to double check order accuracy as orders are picked. Every extra time the picker touches an item, often when recounting or double checking, time is wasted and the picking process slows down. Larger warehouses and distribution centers now use scales integrated into their picking carts and forklifts. Thanks to scale readings, the picker can be immediately alerted if the weight detected does not match the weight expected for the item picked. Meanwhile, the picker can keep on picking!

- **Reduce walking!** Multiple time and motion studies have shown that warehouse workers are more accurate when they can be stationary or walk less during order picking. Walking takes time and energy, so a full day of order picking while walking around would exhaust even the fittest among us. As we mentioned earlier in this chapter, warehouses and distribution centers have systems to "bring the part to the picker." In their gigantic, multiple-football-field-sized fulfillment centers, Amazon uses an inventive means of getting the parts to the picker... Robots! Amazon's Kiva Robots (pictured below left) hold and move four-sided storage shelves, full of different SKUs in bins. These hard working little robots automatically bring the shelves to the order picker when needed.

- **Keep your pickers happy!** A relaxed, rested, and happy picker is an accurate and speedy picker. Alaska Communications created a dedicated break room for its hardworking warehouse staff. Rather than charge forward and create a break room with massage chairs and a meditation corner, warehouse management asked employees what they wanted in a break room. It turns out that a television for down time and free snacks throughout the day (pictured below right) keep people pretty happy and relaxed.

AMAZON KIVA ROBOTS (LEFT) AND THE ALASKA COMMUNICATIONS BREAK ROOM (RIGHT)

INSTRUCTIONS:

Please answer the following:

1. Based on what you have read in this book so far, what other secrets might order picking pros have?

2. What advice would you offer for a more efficient and cost effective order picking process? Explain your answer.

Chapter 9
Distribution

Thank to Chapter 8, the orders have been picked. The inventory has been issued and is now in the order consolidation area of the warehouse. The order hasn't quite yet been fulfilled because it's not in the customer's hands. So what is the next stage to make your customer's dreams come true? Distribution, of course! Join us in Chapter 9 as we explore the exciting world of distribution, packing, transportation, and final paperwork!

9.1 INTRODUCING DISTRIBUTION

After inventory has been picked, it is ready to be sent to the customer who has ordered the goods. This is part of the outbound processes of warehouse management known as **distribution**, but it is also referred to as **shipping** or **dispatch**. The work of a shipping function within a company, which is often called the *distribution department* or the *shipping and receiving department*, includes:

- **locating and checking the order** to be shipped,

- **scheduling a carrier** to transport the goods,

- **providing value-added services** as needed,

- **securing freight** for outbound distribution,

- **completing the corresponding paperwork** for the outbound shipment, including a packing list for each box or container and a bill of lading to be given to the carrier,

- **loading the vehicle** for shipment, and

- **alerting the customer** that the shipment is being sent, often though an *advance shipment notice*, also known as an *ASN*.

As part of the distribution process, items are first packed and prepared for an outbound shipment, typically in an area called the **packing and unitization area** or the **order consolidation area**. When multiple items are picked for an order, they are typically brought to one central area of a warehouse to be consolidated and prepared for shipment. This area is known as the **staging area** or **marshaling area**. In cross-docking facilities, warehouse order picking and a staging area might be bypassed entirely if goods are placed directly from one inbound truck or container onto a different outbound truck or container.

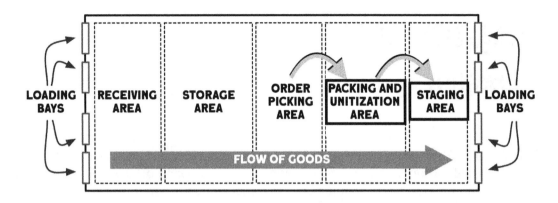

FIGURE 9.1 - LOCATIONS OF THE PACKING & UNITIZATION AREA AND THE STAGING AREA

FIGURE 9.2 - STAGING AREA AND PACKING & UNITIZATION AREA
THE TABALÍ WINERY IN LIMARÍ VALLEY IN NORTHERN CHILE, WHERE BOTTLES OF WINE ARE
PLACED INTO CRATES, WHICH ARE STACKED ONTO PALLETS AND STRETCH WRAPPED FOR
DISTRIBUTION TO WINE MERCHANTS AND DISTRIBUTORS AROUND THE WORLD

FIGURE 9.3 - PALLETIZATION FOR SUBSEQUENT SHIPPING IN THE STAGING AREA
SACKS OF POTATOES ON PALLETS IN A POTATO DISTRIBUTION CENTER (LEFT) AND PALLETIZED
AND STRETCH WRAPPED EQUIPMENT AT A TELECOMMUNICATIONS GOODS WAREHOUSE (RIGHT)

FIGURE 9.4 - SMALLER QUANTITY RETAIL STAGING WITHOUT PALLETIZATION

THE ONCE IN A BLUE MOOSE WAREHOUSE IN ALASKA USES COLOR CODED RUBBER TOTES IN ITS STAGING AREA, WITH COLOR AND TWO-LETTER CODES DESIGNATING RETAIL DELIVERY LOCATIONS. HIGH PRIORITY ITEMS ARE PLACED IN SPECIAL OPEN-ME-FIRST TOTES.

When goods are picked and placed into a staging area, some warehouses or distribution centers may perform ***value-added services*** for their customers. Also know as ***VAS***, value-added services that occur after items have been picked. They are services that can be added or modified based on the current activities and promotions of the company or based on the needs of specific customers. VAS are typically related to the specific products being shipped and can include: *limited or light product assembly*, such as installing plugs specific to the electrical current of the country to which they are being shipped; ***product kitting*** or ***bundling***, which is combining multiple products or products plus promotional items into once package, such as combining a camera and camera case into one unit for a limited-time promotion; ***product postponement***, which is delaying finalized assembly or packaging until a customer has placed an order, such as waiting to place final consumer packaging on bags of chocolate until prior to shipment so the packaging can reflect the current holiday in the country to which they are being shipped; ***product sequencing***, in which items are placed in a specific sequence prior to packaging to meet the needs of the customer, such as the order in which they are needed for a manufacturing operation; and *inserting instructions or other paper materials into the packaging of each item*, which allows for the instructions to be updated when needed and modified according to the language and cultural requirements of the country to which the items are being shipped.

In the staging area, goods are prepared for shipment and sorted into sections according to customers or delivery routes. The items and quantities may also be checked to ensure they match the customer's order. Typically, when there are multiple goods going to one customer at one location, the goods are unitized and secured, such as items that are shrink-wrapped onto a pallet. Securing goods and stabilizing loads are critical on outbound trucks to ensure that breakage and travel-related damage are less likely to occur. Shrink-wrapping, stretch wrapping, and strapping all offer protection for goods in transit. The company supplying the goods may handle outbound transportation or a transportation provider may be used. Whoever is responsible for the delivery must ensure that the loads are secure and that items make it to the customer in perfect working condition.

9.2 PREPARING GOODS FOR SHIPMENT

When goods are being prepared for shipment, they must be packed and labelled to ensure that they make it to the right customer at the right time and location in the right condition. Depending on the customer receiving the shipment, how the goods look on the outside might also be important to make a good initial first impression upon receipt. This is less important for recurring business-to-business orders but can be critical for orders being received by end users. Think about how you feel when you receive poorly packed goods or expensive items shipped in inexpensive looking packing materials. Compare this to the first time you received an Apple product, shipped in its streamlined, futuristic-looking, all-white box, with every item held perfectly in places with perfectly molded white plastic or foam. Even though goods might be received in the same condition regardless of what they are packed in, the exterior look of goods received is often an important consideration.

While it is often important for the exterior of the boxes or palletized items to look good upon receipt, the most critical element related to preparing goods for shipment is ensuring that items remain undamaged during shipment and that there is a clear, visible, and correct label to get goods to the correct location at the correct time. Receiving items that look good immediately upon receipt, that are undamaged, and that are labeled clearly and correctly is all boiled down to effective *packaging*. **Packaging** is the term used for the physical materials into which an order's items are placed. This also includes additional materials used to secure the items within the package, such as straps or styrofoam package filler, and labels that are used to identify the items and where it needs to go. The packaging used during the order packing process has an enormous impact on the efficiency and effectiveness of the supply chain. Poor packaging can lead to stolen or broken products, less efficient use of transportation and subsequent storage space, and materials handling equipment malfunction. It is important to note that not all packaging involves heavy cardboard boxes, pallets, and stretch wrap. As shown in Figure 9.5, at Krispy Kreme doughnut stores that also functions as production facilities, fresh donuts are placed into retail packing, which are the boxes you see in your grocery store (right side of left image). The boxes are then placed into an insulated rolling tray to keep them warm (left side of left image). When the insulated tray is full, it is zippered up and rolled onto the delivery truck (center image), so it can be delivered to your local grocery store (right image).

FIGURE 9.5 - PACKAGING KRISPY KREME DOUGHNUTS

Back in Section 6.5 of Chapter 6 when we explored the unit load, we examined a variety of packaging materials, including cushioning, containing, and restraining materials. We also looked at a variety packaging machinery. All of these types of materials and equipment covered in Chapter 6 are used in preparing goods for shipment in the packing and unitization area of a warehouse facility. Important points to remember before goods go out the warehouse loading bay doors is that efficient and effective packaging should:

- *Keep items safe and secure.* When packaging is insufficient or inadequate, items can be damaged in transit. When packaging can be opened too easily, items can be stolen by opportunity thieves at any point along the supply chain. As shown in Figure 9.7, items may also have specific packaging instructions, including how they should be wrapped and placed in a container or stacked on a pallet or what specific types of packaging materials should be used to avoid environmental damage from water or extreme temperatures.

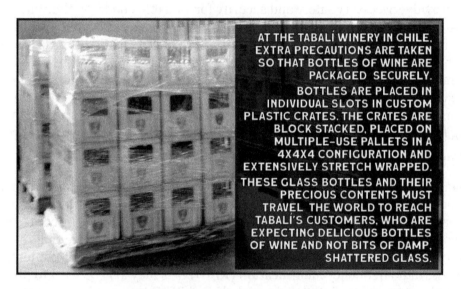

FIGURE 9.6 - SAFE AND SECURE PACKAGING

FIGURE 9.7 - PACKAGING INSTRUCTIONS ON UNILEVER PRODUCT BOX

- *Be easily labeled, transported, and stored.* Packaging must be easily labeled so that the customer's inventory receipt department can identify its contents. Packaging must also meet an organization's requirements and its customers' requirements for transportation and storage. For example, packaging may have to be designed so that it can be placed and stacked easily onto pallets or into containers. It may also have to be placed onto storage racks of specific dimensions.

- *Be handled properly by materials handling equipment.* It is inevitable that packaged goods will be handled at both the producer's and customer's facilities. Packaging must be easily handled by both the materials handling equipment at both facilities, which means that the materials handling equipment used may not necessarily the same. For example, packaging may have to be handled by a forklift truck at one location and a conveyor at another.

Packaging provides necessary safety and security for valuable goods. Without it, goods can lose all of their value in transit. Just imagine the mess, spoilage, and smell of a truckload of raw eggs being transported loosely in a 3'x3' boxes! Within the world of physical distribution management, packaging presents a bit of a conundrum. For items to be the safest and most secure, extra layers of thick packaging are required, but both the materials used and the extra space consumed for this safe and secure packaging are quite costly. Therefore, many organizations try to find cost efficient *and* effective packaging. For example, organizations are looking for greener, reusable packaging and for packaging that allows for more space utilization.

When preparing goods for shipment, packaged items must be labelled. **Labeling** is the term used for creating, printing, and adhering piece of paper, called a **label**, to a package to convey information about the it, such as the intended shipping address or contents. Barcode labels are commonly used to provide a unique identifier for each package that reveals detailed information about the package, its source, its destination, and its contents. Like barcode labels, radio frequency identification (RFID) tags may also be used to provide information about packages. Both barcode labels and RFID tags can be scanned and used for tracking packages in transit. RFID tags provide the additional benefit of being able to be tracked wherever they are in the world through global positioning satellites, also known as GPS.

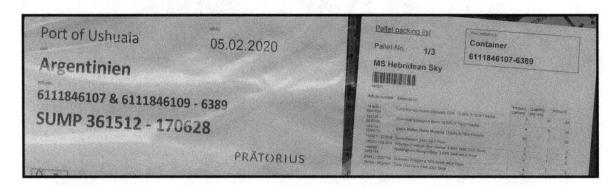

FIGURE 9.8 - PALLET LABELS ON PALLETIZED LOAD AT PORT OF USHUAIA, ARGENTINA

9.3 CARRIERS AND TRANSPORTATION MODES

When preparing to ship goods, a company's shipping and receiving department must consider *transportation*. What provides, supports, and propels the flow of goods from the company to the customer? Transportation! ***Transportation*** is the act of using a vehicle to move goods or people from one place to another. Within the realm of warehouse management, transportation is the movement of goods, not people, to a desired location that is not part of the same warehouse facility. Remember from Chapter 5 that the shorter distance movement of goods within one location along supply chain refers to the discipline of ***materials handling***. *Transportation* refers to the movement of goods between two or more locations along the supply chain. Transportation forms the critical bridge between *where stuff is*, such as the manufacturing or warehousing facilities where the goods are located, and *where stuff needs to be*, such as the immediate customers' locations or a distributor's regional distribution center along the supply chain.

One of the roles of a company's *distribution* function or distribution department is to coordinate and control the outbound transportation of its finished goods. Transportation decisions play a significant strategic role in determining total supply chain costs and levels of service for an organization, often by striking a balance between the advantages and disadvantages offered by the following six criteria:

1. **Cost.** Unsurprisingly, transportation costs increase as delivery distances increase, making cost a central factor in determining the geographic limits within which a product can be sold and remain cost effective.

2. **Speed.** For many products or situations, a speedy delivery time may be more important than delivery cost. For example, speedy delivery is essential for perishable goods, such as Maine lobster and Alaska King crab, both of which must be flown to their hungry customers. Speedy delivery is also essential for goods immediately and urgently needed a large manufacturing operation, such as a spare part needed to repair an ice cream producer's freezer, which would be flown in as quickly as possible before too much product melts.

3. **Safety & Security.** An organization's goods are often their most substantial financial assets. To protect the value of these assets, the organization must ensure that the transportation system handling its goods keeps them safe from damage and secure from theft at all times. Safety and security are especially important criteria for transportation decisions involving high-cost or hazardous goods.

4. **Convenience.** For a transportation plan or system to be the successful backbone of any supply chain, it must be convenient to all members of the chain. Transportation decisions made must consider how easy it is for customers, retailers, wholesalers, distribution centers, warehouses, and manufacturers to interface with those transporting the goods.

5. **Reliability.** Even when costs are low, when deliveries are fast and convenient, and when goods are kept safe and secure, a transportation system or agent creates

problems for an organization when it is not reliable. If transportation can't consistently and reliably get goods where they need to be when they need to be, an organization loses the time and place utility that reliable transportation provides. The lack of reliability can also lose customers!

6. **Flexibility.** For organizations that need to transport a wide range of goods of different sizes, weights, and handling needs, a flexible transportation system is essential. For example, the transportation system of warehouse-style retailers carrying goods from regional distribution centers to individual stores would need to be flexible enough to handle a wide range of goods within one shipment, from dish detergent to televisions to king-size mattresses.

Now that we have discussed the six criteria that are weighed against each other when transportation decision are being made, let's address two important transportation decisions, typically asked and answered in conjunction with one another: *Who will handle the transportation?* and *What mode or modes of transportation will be used?* When an organization has goods to be moved from one location or terminal to another, it must first decide who will physically move these goods: the organization itself or a **carrier**, which is a second company that transports goods. An organization typically uses a carrier when it must move goods a great distance or if specialized transport modes are needed, such as rail or ocean cargo ships because most companies don't own their own rail lines or cargo ships.

A single carrier may use any combination of one or more of the five modes of transportation: *road, rail, water, air,* and *pipeline.* Carriers also may own or lease the vehicles and vessels they use. For most carriers, the cost of delivering a container of goods is just about the same no matter how empty or full the container is. Therefore, it is less than ideal to have a situation of shipments that are **less-than-truckload**, also called **LTL**. A **consolidator** is an agent or company who works to combine small shipments to create full container-load or truckload shipments, thus achieving a significant cost savings for the organizations shipping smaller quantities of goods. A *freight forwarder* is a consolidator that specializes in combining smaller shipments for subsequent road or rail transportation.

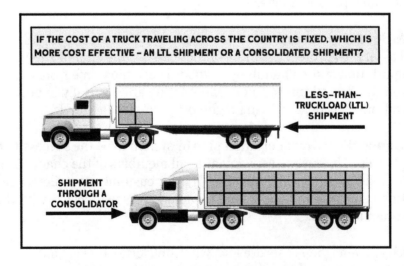

IF THE COST OF A TRUCK TRAVELING ACROSS THE COUNTRY IS FIXED, WHICH IS MORE COST EFFECTIVE – AN LTL SHIPMENT OR A CONSOLIDATED SHIPMENT?

LESS-THAN-TRUCKLOAD (LTL) SHIPMENT

SHIPMENT THROUGH A CONSOLIDATOR

FIGURE 9.9 - LTL OR CONSOLIDATOR? YOU DECIDE!

Transportation involves more than an organization or a carrier simply picking up and moving goods from one location to another. Transportation includes the complex world of **transportation management**, which is planning, directing, and controlling how goods are moved and handled throughout the transportation process. Most raw materials and consumer goods are moved across countries and moved across oceans. To navigate the murky and complex waters of transportation management, companies often turn to **third party logistics service providers**, also known as **3PLPs** or **3PLs**, to provide some or all of the transportation and transportation management services needed. 3PLPs typically bundle a range of these services under one cost structure. Some of the transportation management activities covered by a 3PLP might include: *planning shipments and selecting transport carriers, keeping track of shipments in transit, determining freight costs prior to shipping, checking and paying carriers' freight bills, filing claims with carriers for damaged goods, transportation budget planning and management, transportation administration and human resource management, monitoring and maintaining service quality, conducting carrier rate negotiations, keeping up with transport regulations from the local to international levels, planning and handling transport information systems*, and *conducting transport systems analysis*.

When a company is deciding *who* will transport its goods, it must also decide the *mode* by which its goods will be moved. In the world of logistics and physical distribution management, a **mode of transportation** is the physical means across or through which the goods are carried. The five modes of transportation are: *road, water, rail, air*, and *pipeline*.

FIGURE 9.10 - ROAD TRANSPORTATION
A TRUCK CARRYING WIND TURBINE NOSE CONES ACROSS THE ARIZONA DESERT

At the risk of stating the extremely obvious, a **road** is a surfaced route used by vehicles for moving goods or people. Within most countries around the world, road is the most commonly used mode of transportation by far, with more than 70% of U.S. goods by weight and by value traveling by road. The primary advantage offered by road as a mode of transportation is that, within most countries, more locations are accessible by road than any other mode of transportation. In the United States, the National Highway System measures more than 160,000 miles and vehicles can operate on this extensive road network 24 hours a day, 7 days a week. Road is cost-effective for smaller deliveries and shorter distances and is highly flexible, allowing for last minute changes and adjustments, including alternate routes and the ability to start a road journey at any time. However, traffic jams, congestion, and adverse weather can all affect road delivery times. Also, road-related labor costs are high because the number of drivers or operators required per amount carried is much higher than for the other modes of transportation. For example, one truck driver can transport one or two container loads of goods while a crew of twenty people can transport thousands and thousands of forty-foot containers by way of cargo ship.

FIGURE 9.11 - ROAD TRANSPORTATION DOESN'T ALWAYS MEAN HIGHWAYS AND TRUCKS!
PROPANE DELIVERIES BY TRUCK ON THE COBBLESTONE STREETS OF VALPARAISO, CHILE (LEFT)
AND BY BICYCLE ON THE CITY'S NARROWER AND MORE CONGESTED STREETS (RIGHT)

Water is a mode of transportation used to transport large quantities of nonperishable and bulk goods both domestically and internationally on ships across waterways. In domestic trade, goods travel by water within and along the United States through the ***inland and intracoastal waterway system***, which serves 38 states and carries approximately one-sixth of the U.S. intercity cargo by volume. In international trade, the majority of goods travel by ocean and enter and leave through ***container ports***, also called ***cargo ports***, which are facilities that receive and dock cargo ships. They use specialized equipment such as a variety of cranes to transfer containerized goods to and from the ships. As a mode of transportation, water can move massive quantities of goods and bulky items. Water is also a reliable mode of transportation and has very few traffic delays. It can also be less costly because it is far less expensive than air for international trade and there are no costs for using ocean waterways. Water is, however, often the slowest mode of transportation, making it unrealistic for shipping perishable or time-sensitive goods. Long transit times also increase the insurance costs of goods, and fog or severe weather can easily cause sailing cancellations.

FIGURE 9.12 - WATER TRANSPORTATION AT THE PORT OF BOSTON

FIGURE 9.13 - WATER TRANSPORTATION IN THE PANAMA CANAL:
CONTAINER SHIP (TOP LEFT), CANAL LOCKS (TOP RIGHT), AND TANKER (BOTTOM)

The transportation mode of **rail** is commonly used to transport large, heavy, and bulky items or large quantities of bulk or containerized goods for long distances across railroad tracks in railway cars. Rail is used to transport almost 2% of the total value of all U.S. goods and 10% of all goods by weight. Rail cars can accommodate very large, heavy items and is a less expensive mode of transportation for larger volumes over longer distances than road. Rail also offers greater reliability than many other transportation modes because it is less likely to experience traffic delays or adverse weather. Furthermore, most maritime cargo ports are connected to rail networks, making rail a vital element of global supply chains. However, rail has geographic and time limitations because they are located in a limited number of fixed locations and typically only operate at specific times. There can also be very long transit times due to the labor-intensive nature of boxcar consolidation and it is less than ideal for fragile items and small shipments. An interesting side note, more than 90% of all U.S. freight railroads are privately owned and operated. Most of the railroad tracks in the U.S. are also owned by the rail companies.

FIGURE 9.14 - RAIL TRANSPORTATION AND PIPELINE TRANSPORTATION

Air is the mode of transportation more commonly used for perishable and time-sensitive goods. It is used to transport less than 4% of goods by value within the U.S. and only 0.1% of goods by weight. It's the fastest mode of transportation available to get goods anywhere where there's an airport, making it suitable for perishable goods and fragile items that are easily damaged in transit. As a mode of transportation, air is very costly. It also allows for less scheduling flexibility. Flights are generally at fixed times and adverse weather can delay flights and cause transportation delays. Furthermore, airplanes are strictly limited in the weights and item dimensions they can carry.

Pipeline is the mode of transportation used for carrying goods from point to point through a steel or plastic pipe. While oil and natural gas are the goods most commonly transported, any form of liquid, such as water or sewage, can be carried by pipeline. Although expensive to construct, pipelines yield extremely low transportation cost. Pipeline systems are used to approximately 2.4% of all U.S. goods by value and 5.6% of all U.S. goods by weight.

When goods are transported, they are not restricted to a single mode of transportation. *Intermodal transportation* occurs when different modes of transportation are used to carry goods in the same *through shipment*. A *through shipment* is the entire transportation flow of goods from their point of origin to their point of consumption. Intermodal transportation is especially common in global trade. As container ships arrive into U.S. ports, their containers are automatically transferred to rail or motor carriers. Multiple modes of transport are used to transport almost 20% of all U.S. goods by value.

FIGURE 9.15 - INTERMODAL TRANSPORTATION FROM WATER TO ROAD

As companies look to supply chains for cutting their operating costs, competition is heating up between transportation carriers. One primary form of this competition between carriers is *intramodal competition*, in which carriers of the same mode of transportation compete, such as one container ship line trying to come in at a lower cost than another container ship line following the same route. Another primary form of competition between carriers is *intermodal competition*, in which carriers of different modes of transportation compete, such as a trucking company trying to cut costs to meet those of a railway following the same route.

9.4 PAPERWORK FOR OUTBOUND SHIPMENTS

As previously mentioned, there is paperwork and documentation involved with outbound shipments. This includes the creation of a ***packing list*** for each package, carton, or container shipped out from an organization. Also called a ***packing slip***, this packing list would include the sender's address, the recipient's address and customer identification codes, and an itemized list of everything included in that parcel's shipment with item descriptions and item quantities. The customer receiving the package would then check the items received against the packing list to make sure all of the items arrived at their intended destination.

FIGURE 9.16 - TEMPLATE FOR A PACKING SLIP

When shipments move from the realm of ***domestic***, which occurs within one country, to ***international***, which occurs between two or more countries, the world of paperwork and documentation gets far more complicated. When companies engage in international trade, documentation is a necessity. Without accurate and timely paperwork, companies would not be permitted to trade outside their own countries. Exporters, importers, shipping companies, freight forwarders, banks, insurance companies, the regulating authorities of all countries involved, consular offices, chambers of commerce, and a massive battery of attorneys are all involved in ensuring that global distribution's complex network of documentation is completed. The amount of documentation required may vary according to the nature of the goods and the regulations of the countries importing and exporting them. Some forms of documentation are multifunctional and can be found in multiple categories of trade documentation. While there are thousands of different trade documentation forms that vary from country to country and from company to company, there are a few categories that a warehouse shipping outbound goods might need to consider. These categories of trade documentation include:

- **Export documents**. Documents required by the export authority of a country are called *export documents*. When completed and approved, these documents allow goods to leave a country. Export documentation varies according to the country of export and the goods involved. Examples of export documents include: *export licenses and permits*, *export declarations and inspection certificates*, *a bill of lading*, and certificate *of origin*. Also called a **BOL** or **B/L**, a **bill of lading** is a document issued by a carrier that acknowledges that specific, listed goods have been received as cargo for conveyance to a specific, listed place for delivery to an identified consignee. In the example in Figure 9.17, specific goods are being shipped from the State of South Dakota to a food bank through a carrier. A **certificate of origin** is a document that certifies the country of origin of a shipment. For example, a Caribbean Basin Trade Partnership Act (CBTPA) certificate of origin, as shown in Figure 9.17, is used by any of the 24 countries who are members of the CBPTA to determine if imported goods receive reduced or eliminated duty coming into the United States as specified under the terms of the Caribbean Basin Trade Partnership Act.

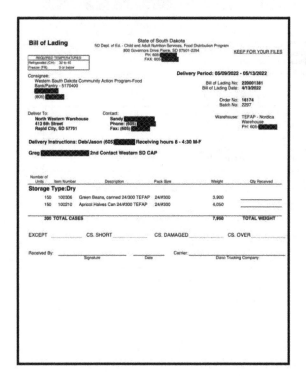

FIGURE 9.17 - BILL OF LADING (LEFT) AND CERTIFICATE OF ORIGIN (RIGHT)

- **Carrier documents**. Carrier documents are those documents issued and used by a carrier or transportation provider such as a barge or shipping line, a railroad, an airline, an international trucking company, a freight forwarder, or a 3PLP. Examples of carrier documents include: *bill of lading*, *insurance certificate*, and *inspection certificates*.

- **Goods-specific documents**. Goods-specific documents are those documents required for import or export based on special requirements for the nature of the items being traded. Goods-specific documents are typically required for international trade of goods including: *arms and ammunition*, *radioactive materials*, *animals*, and *food products*.

In exploring the world of international trade documentation, we must also discuss **INCOTERMS® rules**, where INCOTERMS is an abbreviation for International Commercial Terms. INCOTERMS® rules are the standardized international trade terms that describe the obligations of both the purchasers and the sellers under the contract of sale. Specifically, they are a set of eleven terms created and published by the International Chamber of Commerce (ICC) that clearly outline and allocate the *costs, risk, customs responsibilities*, and *insurance responsibilities* of each the purchaser and the seller in the international transaction. The most recent update to these terms was in 2020. Each of all of the eleven INCOTERMS® rules is referred to by a three-letter abbreviation and one of these eleven would be used in international trade transactions. You can find more information about them at export.gov, but as a brief introduction, each of the eleven are:

INCOTERMS® RULES	DESCRIPTION
EXW or Ex Works	The seller makes the goods available for collection from its premises or another named location where the buyer or the buyer's agent will collect them and prepare them for export to the buyer's location. The seller generally has the goods packed ready for shipment. The seller does not load the goods or clear them for export.
FCA or Free Carrier	The seller delivers the goods to a carrier or at another mutually agreed location where the seller will consolidate the goods into a larger consignment ready for shipment by an intermodal carrier.
FAS or Free Alongside Ship (waterway transport only)	The seller delivers the goods alongside the ship that will carry the goods overseas. The responsibility of the seller ends here. The buyer bears all costs and risks from this point on.
FOB or Free on Board (waterway transport only)	The seller delivers the goods to the port of export, where they then become the buyer's responsibility as soon as they are loaded over the ship's side rail. The buyer bears the loss if the goods should fall and become damaged after being loaded onto the ship.
CFR or Cost and Freight (waterway transport only)	The seller pays the costs and freight as far as the port of destination in the buyer's country, but the risk passes to the buyer as the goods cross the ship's rail in the port of shipment in the seller's country.
CIF or Cost, Insurance and Freight (waterway transport only)	The seller is in the same position as in CFR but must also provide marine insurance during the carriage. The risk passes to the buyer as the goods cross the ship's rails, but the insurance policy covers the buyer's risk.
CPT or Carriage Paid to	Similar to FCA, the seller delivers the goods to a carrier or at another mutually agreed location, but the seller pays the freight, and the risk passes to the buyer once the goods are delivered to the first carrier, regardless of the type of transportation used.
CIP or Carriage and Insurance Paid to	With CIP, the terms are the same as in CPT, but the seller also has to insure the goods for all modes of transportation to the buyer's destination. The risk transfers to the buyer when the goods are given into the first carrier's custody, after which point the insurance policy covers the risk.
DAP or Delivered at Place	The seller pays for delivery to the named place or destination in the buyer's country, not including import clearance costs, and assumes all risk until the goods are ready to be unloaded by the buyer.
DPU or Delivered at Place Unloaded	The seller pays for delivery to and unloading at the buyer's named location, not including import clearance costs, and the seller assumes all risk until the goods are ready to be received and unloaded by the buyer.
DDP or Delivered Duty Paid	This term represents a maximum commitment from the seller and a minimum one from the buyer. With DDP, the terms are the same as in DAP, but the seller delivers goods to the buyer unloaded after paying the import duty to the destination country.

FIGURE 9.18 - INCOTERMS® RULES, 2020 UPDATE

9.5 THE FINAL STAGES OF OUTBOUND SHIPMENTS

After all of the paperwork for the outbound shipment has been prepared, it is now time to load the shipment onto an outbound vehicle! It may seem simple taking goods from a staging area and placing them onto a truck or into a rail car. However, the person or company accepting responsibility for the goods while in transit wants to make sure that the goods arrive safely and in good working order. As we mentioned previously, the party responsible for the goods might be the company selling the goods, a carrier or third party transportation provider, or the customer itself. Regardless of who is handling the transportation and accepts responsibility for the goods, there are a series of steps that take place to ensure that goods are loaded onto the outbound vehicle in a manner that will increase their likelihood of a safe arrival.

First, the load is checked before it is moved from the staging area to ensure that there is no preexisting damage to any of the items. Not only are the goods checked, but the packaging is checked, too. For example, pallets are inspected to make sure they are in good working order. Stretch wrapping or strapping is also checked to make sure it will secure the goods and keep them from falling off the pallet. Next, the trailer, container, or other vehicle into which the goods will be loaded is inspected. If there is anything that might lead to product damage during shipment, such as waterlogged surfaces or holes in the roof, it is addressed and repaired before any goods are loaded.

Assuming that everything has checked out, it's now time to load the goods! As goods are loaded, weight plays a key factor. The heaviest items and unit loads are stacked on the bottom of the container or trailer, with lighter or equal-weight unit loads placed on top. When appropriate, until loads are restrained in the truck or container with additional strapping materials. The weights of all unit loads are also tallied to make sure that the trailer weight does not exceed highway limits for goods traveling by road. After a trailer or container has been loaded, it is secured with airbags or other cushioning materials to ensure that goods do not shift in transit. The container or trailer is then sealed and ready to ship! As it leaves the facility, the customer is alerted that the shipment is being sent, often through an ***advance shipment notice***, or ***ASN***.

CHAPTER 9 REVIEW QUESTIONS

1. What happens in the *staging area* of a warehouse?

2. What is the difference between *product kitting* and *product postponement*? In what situations might a company use each?

3. What are some examples of materials that are used for *packaging*? What materials have you used for packaging when mailing items?

4. Why is packaging important for keeping items safe and secure in transit?

5. What kinds of information is contained in a barcode label or RFID tag? How can this information be read?

6. Why is it important for a company's *mode of transportation* to be flexible? How might a company benefit from using *3PLPs* to achieve this desired flexibility?

7. What mode of transportation is used for most U.S. goods to get to their customer? Look around your house and list five items you see along with the probable mode or modes of transportation used to get to you.

8. *Pipelines* have extremely low transportation costs. Why aren't most goods transported by pipeline?

9. What is the difference between *intramodal competition* and *intermodal competition* in transportation?

10. What role does weight play when loading goods as they leave the warehouse? What might happen if warehouse workers don't pay attention to product and package weight?

CHAPTER 9 CASE STUDY

THE CHALLENGE OF BUNDLING: A 3PL SOLUTION?

In order to increase sales, introduce new products, or enhance customer service, manufacturers may decide to sell multiple products together as one product. This practice is known as ***bundling*** or ***product kitting***. Companies often engage in bundling based on customer specifications, such as when you order a laptop online and decide to include a specific upgraded case or external microphone with it or when you place an order for a new car to include an upgraded sound system or navigational system.

A company may also decide to bundle its own products together in large quantities, which is often done by cosmetics and fragrance companies to increase sales or expose consumers to new products. For example, U.S.-born cosmetics manufacturer Philosophy bundles its products together in both regular and promotional gift kits, often with celebratory, fun, and practical themes, such as "Congrats," "You're Amazing," and "The Wrinkle Takeaway Set."

Finally, a company may decide to bundle its products together with products from another company. Many companies work together to produce bundled kits, including video game console companies who parter with video game companies to produce promotional bundles. In the mid 2010s, an especially popular bundle was the Batman: Arkham Knight PlayStation® 4 Bundle, in which Sony sold its PlayStation game console together with a hugely popular video game produced by Warner Brothers Interactive Entertainment. In this case, two bundles were offered: a standard one, with the standard game and game console, and a limited edition one, which included a customer Batman faceplate on the game console and quickly sold out within weeks.

When a company's marketing department decides to offer a bundled package to increase sales, introduce new products, or enhance customer service, the company's warehouse must be ready to accomplish this task. For these bundles, products will have to be packaged differently, while the company will likely be continuing to package the products in their standard single formation, too. For a warehouse new to bundling, this may be a daunting challenge. Additional space or equipment may be needed to create these newly bundled product kits. Additional trained labor may also be needed to work just during periods of product bundle promotions, especially before the holidays when multiple products are bundled in gift packages to entice consumers. There is also the IT challenge of creating a new SKU, the newly bundled product, and entering it into all of the company's information technology systems and inventory location software. When companies do not have the time, space, or labor to complete product bundling on their own in the warehouse, they may turn to a ***third party logistics service provider***, also known as ***3PLP*** or ***3PL***, to complete some or all of the tasks in the product bundling process.

FedEx Supply Chain is a subsidiary of FedEx and a third party logistics service provider headquartered in Pittsburgh, Pennsylvania. This 3PLP offers companies a wide range of inventory management and other supply chain solutions at its 100+ value-added facilities or at the customer's site. One of the many categories of service that FedEx Supply Chain offers is Warehouse Kitting and Assembly Services, in which it helps companies with some or all of their product bundling tasks. FedEx Supply Chain can help a company create promotional packaging and displays for its product bundles, procure the equipment and materials needed to create the new bundles, assemble the bundles at the company's warehouse or at a FedEx Supply Chain facility, handle inventory management, install RFID chips, and provide temporary labor when needed for seasonal or promotional bundles.

INSTRUCTIONS

Please answer the following:

1. Have you ever purchased any products that were bundled? If so, what were the products and were they manufactured by the same company? If not, visit your local clothing retailer or grocery store and find a product bundle and answer the same question: *what are the products* and *are they manufactured by the same company?*

2. Do you think these products were bundled by their manufacturer's warehouse or by a 3PLP, such as FedEx Supply Chain? Please explain your answer.

Chapter 10
Safety and Security

On a whim, you've just purchased a new 75" television. When the delivery truck arrives and the driver brings it to your front door, you suddenly panic! You have no room for this beast of a TV in your living room until you rearrange your furniture, which may take a day or two. What do you do with this expensive new purchase, which you have now affectionately termed your new baby? Do you leave it in your front yard or in your driveway for a night or two? Or do you store it in another room of your house until your living room is ready? Unless you have more money than good sense, you almost certainly chose the last alternative.

Although your choice was an obvious one, exactly why would you prefer to leave a new, expensive, high tech item somewhere inside your home instead of outside? In two words: *safety* and *security*. You want your new television to be *secure from theft*, perhaps especially because your less-than-law-abiding next door neighbor has always wanted a 75" television. You also want your new purchase to be *safe from harm and the elements*, perhaps especially because a lightning storm is heading your way. While your purchase was expensive and may have cost you a month's salary, warehouse and inventory managers are often responsible for hundreds of thousands and even millions of dollars worth of inventory. Inventory is the lifeblood of every production-based organization, warehouse and inventory managers are entrusted with the very serious duty of keeping this inventory secure and safe. Warehouse managers are responsible for keeping inventory secure from theft and fraud and safe from disasters and deterioration. They are also responsible for ensuring that all people inside the warehouse facility or external inventory yard remain safe from harm. Similarly, warehouse employees are also responsible for keeping goods safe and secure. More importantly, they are responsible for keeping each other safe. Most warehouses now instill a culture of safety among all their workers. Safety is often a core part of job descriptions and training and the morning meetings of many companies regularly including a "Safety Minute" in which a volunteer shares a safety story or example for the day.

10.1 KEEPING PEOPLE SAFE

The warehouse manager is charged with keeping everything in the warehouse safe, both inventory and people. If you ask almost any warehouse professional what their highest priority is every day on the job, they are likely to say *safety*. Many organizations, from oil companies to Disney World, have safety as their number one core value and have instilled a series of metrics to measure how well they are keeping people and inventory safe.

Warehouse managers would all agree that keeping *people* safe is the most important safety task. According to the United States Department of Labor Bureau of Labor Statistics, the warehousing and storage industry accounted for 21 fatal occupational injuries in 2020 in the U.S. In this same year, there were many non-fatal work-related injuries and illnesses, translating to an incident rate of a startling 4.8 for every 100 full-time warehouse and storage workers! Furthermore, the transportation and warehousing industry had the highest industry-based incidence rate for cases that involved employees either having to take 4 or more days of leave or transferring occupations as a result of a work-related injury or illness.

The warehouse manager's ability to keep warehouse staff safe from harm has moral, legal, and economic implications. Warehouse facilities can be dangerous places, with forklift trucks zipping around and misplaced heavy objects stored on high shelves causing potentially fatal accidents. There are many danger zones for warehouse workers that can lead to injuries and fatalities. Some of these danger zones to be aware of are:

☞ **Forklifts.** Forklifts are one of the leading causes of workplace related injuries and deaths. In 2021, forklifts were the cause of 70 work-related fatalities in the U.S. and more than 7000 injuries that resulted in time off from work. Forklift injuries also typically result in far more days off from work than other types of workplace injuries. Despite their potential for great harm in the workplace, a warehouse facility could not operate at the speed and efficiency now needed without forklifts and other types of powered lift trucks. Because of their potential for danger, forklift operators are required to undergo training and become certified in most countries, including the U.S., Canada, Australia, New Zealand, all European countries, the UK, Japan, and Korea. Please be aware that the training and licenses in each of these countries are different. If you have a forklift license in one country, you will be required to get a new license if you want to operate a forklift in another country.

☞ **Loading Docks and Trucks.** Loading docks are a common location of workplace injuries in a warehouse. They seem harmless, but they are connected to workers falling from docks, forklifts movements that injure workers, and accidents from handling heavy materials during loading and unloading. Trucks at or near loading docks are similarly dangerous, especially because truck drivers can be fatigued after a long road journey in reaching the warehouse facility. A few truck-related dangers are moving trucks striking warehouse workers as they back in, trucks leaving too large a gap between the truck and the loading dock where accidents and falls may happen, and silent but deadly carbon monoxide poisoning from the exhaust from a running truck.

☞ **Ladders and Heights.** Every year, ladders are a cause of injuries and death in warehouses and homes around the world, especially when harnesses and personal protective equipment are not worn. Ladders can be used safely when: *the correct ladder of the correct size is used for the job, ladders are secured when put away, ladders are retired and replaced when they become damaged or worn,* and *employees receive ladder training and personal safety equipment.* Workers in warehouse facilities also fall from heights while on forklifts and other lift devices to reach high shelves, often by standing on pallets lifted by forklifts, which all warehouse workers should be trained to never do. Yet another reason why forklift training and certification is so important! Only proper equipment to lift workers should be used, such as personnel forklift platforms with guardrail and tethering systems.

☞ **Tripping and Slipping.** Every year, the U.S. Bureau of Labor Statistics reports thousands of incidents of injuries from trips and slips in warehouse facilities. These incidents are typically caused by: *slippery wet or oily floors, uneven floor surfaces, poorly lit spaces, exposed cables and cords, platforms and steps that can't easily be seen, unexpected clutter,* and *inappropriate worker footwear.* To prevent trips and slips, warehouse facilities should provide workers with personal protective equipment, such as rubber soled shoes or other slip-resistant footwear, hard hats or other appropriate head protection, gloves with nitrile palms or other similarly protective and grippy surface to allow to grip guardrails and railings, and fall protection kits with harnesses and lifelines when appropriate. Figure 10.1 below is a snapshot from a U.S. Occupational Safety and Health Administration (OSHA) Quick Card on how to prevent slips, trips, and falls.

Ways to Prevent Slips, Trips and Falls

Where possible, avoid walking on wet/slippery surfaces; wipe off the bottom of wet footwear.

- Use flashlights or helmet lights to stay clear of holes or floor openings, wet or slippery surfaces, and debris or equipment.
- Do not step on any surface until you have visually inspected it to ensure there are no holes or weak spots and that it can support workers and their equipment.
- Never carry equipment or loads in your hands when climbing ladders.
- Wear backpacks and tool belts to hold equipment and keep both hands free.
- Use fall protection when walking or performing emergency response activities near unprotected edges of elevated surfaces.
- Use communication devices, particularly hands-free devices, for contacting employers/incident commanders and other workers about slip, trip and fall hazards.

Remember

- When in doubt about the safety of an activity, stop and notify a supervisor.

For more information:

OSHA® Occupational Safety and Health Administration

U.S. Department of Labor   www.osha.gov (800) 321-OSHA (6742)

OSHA 3907-01 2017

FIGURE 10.1 - SNIPPET FROM OSHA QUICK CARD ON SLIPS, TRIPS, AND FALLS

☞ **Storage Conditions.** Poor storage conditions, such as weak or uneven floors and unstable racks, shelves, bins, and fittings, are all potential causes of accidents waiting to happen, from painful slips and trips to forklift fatalities. Faulty, overloaded, or misused storage and handling equipment can suddenly break down or cause an injury at a critical and dangerous moment. Weight distribution guidelines and height limits of items stored and stacked must be followed to maintain safe storage conditions. Appropriate guidelines for storage should be in place in every warehouse facility and workers should be trained in these guidelines. Government resources provide information for safe storage and for how workers should handle entry into dangerous storage situations, such as the images below in Figure 10.2 from an OSHA Fact Sheet on Worker Entry into Grain Storage Bins.

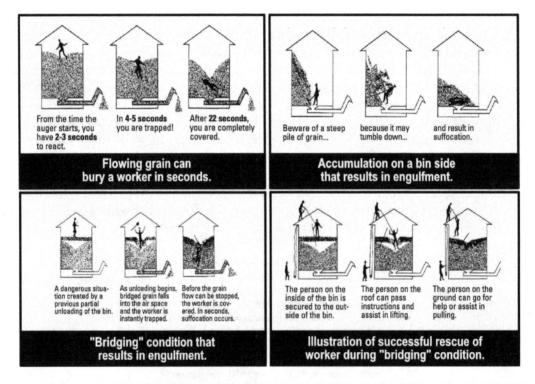

FIGURE 10.2 - ILLUSTRATIONS FROM OSHA FACT SHEET ON GRAIN STORAGE CONDITIONS

☞ **Worker Overexertion and Ergonomics.** Even in a semi-automated facility, working in a warehouse can put a significant amount of stress on workers' bodies. It is a physical job and it involves tasks that must be completed within a specific timeframe. When workers are overtired from exertion, they may cause accidents that damage themselves and others. They may also cause physical harm to their backs, necks, and any number of muscles and tendons from physical overexertion on the job, which may lead them to an injury where they must miss work for a few days to to a chronic condition that they must manage for the rest of their lives. Another important factor is *ergonomics*, which is the science and practice of designing and arranging a work environment and the items in it so that people can interact with them safely and efficiently over a longer period of time while working or performing repetitive actions. When work equipment and stations are not ergonomically designed, they can cause strain, muscle damage, and long periods of injury and recuperation. While these types of injuries may not be as immediately dramatic as injuries from forklifts and falls, overexertion and poor workplace ergonomics can lead to significant injuries and should be taken just as seriously.

☞ **Warehouse Supervision**. When there is a lack of warehouse supervision, all of the previously mentioned danger zones are likely to be left unchecked. Untidiness, carelessness, and other poor warehouse practices can result, leading to injuries, time off from work, and even fatalities. It is of vital importance to have managers and supervisors in warehouse facilities who instill a culture of safety in the warehouse and enforce safety policies and practices.

In order to avoid fatal or injury-causing accidents, the warehouse manager must create, issue, and ensure adherence to a ***warehouse safety policy***, a company-wide policy document that clearly outlines responsibilities and policies related to safety issues. Some of the elements of a warehouse safety policy and its supporting materials should include:

- **Warehouse Safety Rules.** Every warehouse facility and its warehouse safety policy should have a set of rules provided to all employees and others who enter the warehouse so that both humans and inventory are kept safe from harm. These rules typically begin with government safety requirements and also include rules that are specific to that facility, its layout, its equipment, and its inventory. Warehouse facilities also post many of their key rules on clear and visible signage so that both employees and visitors are reminded of key rules, as shown in the examples in Figure 10.3.

FIGURE 10.3 - SIGNS INSIDE (LEFT) AND OUTSIDE (RIGHT) AMAZON FULFILLMENT CENTERS

- **Safety Standard Operating Procedures.** Also called *SOP*, *standard operating procedures* are the step-by-step instructions and guidelines for completing specific tasks so that they can be repeated the same way every time. SOPs ensure that basic, repetitive tasks are completed with fewer mistakes and without the need for repeated communication or instructions, allowing for greater efficiency and safety. Warehouse facilities need standard operating procedures for a variety of tasks to keep employees and inventory safe, such as how to handle goods, put away and retrieve goods, operate machinery, and handle hazardous materials.

- **PPE Information.** PPE is an acronym for *personal protective equipment*, which are the items that warehouse workers are issued and required to use or wear when inside the warehouse facility. These items keep workers safe from harm by protecting them from a variety of potential dangers. Some examples of warehouse PPE include hardhats, protective goggles, reflective vests, face masks, gloves, steel toed and rubber soled shoes, and earplugs.

FIGURE 10.4 - PPE REQUIREMENTS IN AN EXTERNAL INVENTORY YARD

- **Safety Plans.** Because of their many potential dangers, warehouses need safety plans that instruct warehouse workers and visitors in what to do in case of a safety emergency. A safety emergency plan is often called an *emergency action plan* , or *EAP*. According to the OSHA FactSheet *Fire Safety*, "when required, employers must develop an emergency action plan that: *describes the routes for workers to use and procedures to follow; accounts for all evacuated employees; remains available for employee review; includes procedures for evacuating disabled employees; addresses evacuation of employees who stay behind to shut down critical plant equipment; includes preferred means of alerting employees to a fire emergency; provides for an employee alarm system throughout the workplace; requires an alarm system that includes voice communication or sound signals such as bells, whistles, or horns; makes the evacuation signal known to employees; ensures the provision of* *emergency training; and requires employer review of the plan with new employees and with all employees whenever the plan is changed."*

They may also be required by government regulating agencies to have a separate fire safety plan and hazard reporting procedures when there are hazardous materials and chemicals on the premises, such as ethylene oxide and methylenedianiline.

- **Warehouse Checklists, Inspections, and Record-Keeping.** To ensure that all safety rules, standard operating procedures, and plans are followed, warehouse managers develop checklists to make it easier for employees to follow all safety-related instructions and to perform regular self-checks so that everyone in the warehouse feels a sense of accountability for safety. There are also a variety of company and government inspections to ensure that safety laws and procedures are being followed. Warehouse facilities keep these inspection records on hand and readily available so that they may be viewed when needed.

10.2 GOVERNMENT STANDARDS AND CLASSIFICATIONS

As part of issuing a company-wide warehouse security policy as discussed at the end of Section 10.1, the warehouse manager must draft and issue *codes* of safe practice. These *safety codes* provide detailed guidance on safe practices and procedures for all those working in or entering the warehouse. They are part of both warehouse safety rules and standard operating procedures. They may also be parts of emergency action plans, fire safety plans, safety signage instructions, and safety checklists.

When establishing safety codes for a warehouse facility, the warehouse manager should first begin with the standards, guidelines, and resources of a regulating government body and use these as the basis of warehouse facility safety codes. The warehouse manager would then draft additional codes specific to the individual warehouse, industry, and inventory. Some of the regulating governing bodies that issue workplace safety codes around the world include the European Agency for Safety and Health at Work, the National Institute of Occupational Health in Norway, the Korea Occupational Safety and Health Agency, the National Institute of Occupational Safety and Health in Malaysia, the Canadian Centre for Occupational Health and Safety, the Occupational Safety and Health Authority in Tanzania, the National Institute for Occupational Health in South Africa, Safe Work Australia, and WorkSafe New Zealand.

In the United States, one of the primary governing bodies of workplace safety is the United States Department of Labor *Occupational Safety and Health Administration*, known more commonly as *OSHA*. OSHA's role is to set and enforce standards, provide education and training, establish partnerships, and encourage continual improvement in workplace safety, all to ensure the safety and health of the U.S. workforce. OSHA issues a variety of workplace health and safety regulations, including ergonomics standards. OSHA also enforces these standards and issues citations and fines to workplaces if they are not followed. OSHA issues a variety of workplace-specific publications that include safety codes and best practices and address real case examples of unsafe practices they have encountered. Two OSHA publications targeted for the warehouse facility workplace are *OSHA 2236:*

Materials Handling and Storage and *OSHA Pocket Guide Warehouse Safety Series: Warehousing*, as pictured in Figure 10.5 below.

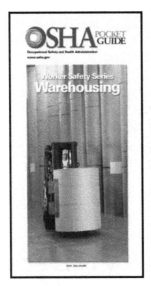

FIGURE 10.5 - OSHA PUBLICATIONS FOR WAREHOUSE SAFETY

For any product that could be potentially harmful to people or the environment, OSHA requires a **Safety Data Sheet**, also known as an **SDS**. An SDS is an internationally standardized document that provides details about the properties of the potentially harmful product, including its hazardous ingredients, fire and explosive information, reactivity data, health information, safe handling instructions, and first aid measures. When OSHA classifies a material as hazardous, the material must have an SDS, which is typically attached to the packing list and bill of lading and located in a highly visible location in the workplace.

FIGURE 10.6 - SDS FOR HYDRILUBE (LEFT AND CENTER) AND WAREHOUSE SDS BINDER (RIGHT)

OSHA also requires that *HazMat* markings must also be on a container holding hazardous material, such as on a tanker or trailer. ***HazMat*** is an abbreviated term for hazardous material, which can be any material in solid, liquid, or gaseous form that poses a potential for harm to people, property, other living organisms, or the environment. Materials classified as HazMat may be poisonous, flammable, explosive, or reactive. The HazMat marking required by OSHA is from the ***GHS***, or *Globally Harmonized System of Classification and Labeling of Chemicals*. The GHS is an internationally agreed classification and labeling system for hazardous materials managed by the United Nations. The GHS contains a universally agreed and recognized set of pictograms that provide information on the nature of the danger a material poses. In the first page of the safety data sheet in Figure 10.6, there are two GHS pictograms in the middle of the page, each representing *health hazard* (left) and *corrosive* (right).

Similar to the ways in which OSHA and other government organizations around the world regulate and provide information about hazardous materials to keep people safe in the workplace, the U.S. Department of Transportation (DOT) has developed special classifications, requirements, and labeling systems for hazardous materials to keep people, inventory, other living things, and the environment safe when hazardous goods are in transit. While there are a few exceptions, the DOT requires the posting of placards under the CFR, or Code of Federal Regulations: *"Each bulk packaging, freight container, unit load device, transport vehicle, or rail car containing any quantity of hazardous materials must be placarded on each side and each end."* The placards are legible and highly visible signs of a standard size at 250 mm or 9.84 inches per side made of durable material, such as plastic or metal. The placards contain standard images, text, and color coding to represent the nature or dangers of the hazardous materials being transported.

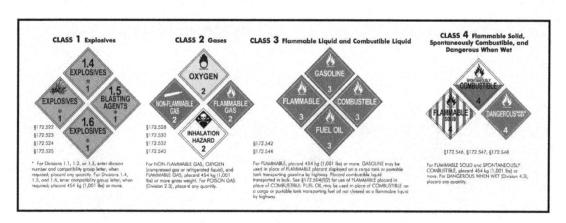

FIGURE 10.7 - A FEW OF THE DOT HAZARDOUS MATERIALS WARNING PLACARDS

The CFR also requires labeling using the same system of symbols for labels that are affixed to packages and unit loads containing hazardous materials. At 100 mm or 3.9 inches per side, these labels are typically smaller than their lookalike placards, adhesive, and typically intended for only one use. A useful resource for understanding the warning symbols and information on the DOT hazardous materials placards and labels is the *Emergency*

Response Guidebook produced by the Pipeline and Hazardous Materials Safety Administration of the U.S. Department of Transportation in conjunction with Transport Canada, the Secretariat of Transport and Communications of Mexico. Available for free in digital form on the DOT website, the guidebook was originally intended for first responders to understand, interpret, and respond to hazardous materials and their corresponding information during transportation incidents. It is a useful resource for those in the world of logistics, warehousing, and transportation because it contains information about how to read the various hazardous materials placards in North America and how to respond to the dangers they pose.

FIGURE 10.8 - FIND THE DOT PLACARDS!

FIND THE DOT HAZARDOUS MATERIALS PLACARDS ON THESE TANKER TRUCKS OUTSIDE THE CRUZAN RUM DISTILLERY IN THE U.S. VIRGIN ISLANDS. WHAT DANGER DOES THIS CARGO POSE? DO YOU NOTICE ANY OTHER SAFETY PLACARDS?

FIGURE 10.9 - WHAT ARE THOSE DIAMONDS ON TRUCKS AND TRAIN CARS?

MAGNETIC HAZMAT PLACARD HOLDER CLOSEUP ON TRUCK WITH REMOVABLE PLACARD (LEFT) AND DIAMOND-SHAPED EMPTY PLACARD HOLDERS ON FEDEX TRUCK (RIGHT)

10.3 KEEPING INVENTORY SAFE FROM FIRES

Within warehouse facilities, inventory faces multiple threats to its safety. A variety of disasters may strike a warehouse at any time. Many of these potential disasters are location-specific and local warehouse managers know how to prepare for them. For example, warehouse managers in coastal Florida design their warehouse entrances, walls, windows, and layout to best combat the effects of hurricanes. Their counterparts in California and Alaska instead make sure that all hot water and dangerous chemical tanks are strapped down in case of an earthquake. Depending upon where the warehouse is located, warehouse managers know that they must prepare for any of a variety of regional disasters, such as droughts, blizzards, floods, raging forest fires, and tornadoes.

Regardless of location, warehouse managers must prepare themselves, their warehouses, and their staff for the most wide-reaching and pervasive disastrous occurrence of all: fire! In their 2020 report, *Warehouse Structure Fires*, the National Fire Protection Association (NFPA) revealed that from 2016-2020, in addition to an average of 16 injuries and 2 deaths per year, there were an average of 1,450 fires in warehouse facilities every year and $283 million in direct property damage. Warehouse fires are extremely disruptive to an organization, not only because of financial loss and subsequent increased insurance premiums, but also because of the delivery delays fires cause, which may result in the loss of long-standing customers.

FIGURE 10.10 - WAREHOUSE FIRES ARE WIDE-REACHING AND PERVASIVE

In order to decrease the risk of fire in warehouse installations, warehouse managers take a variety of precautionary steps, including:

- **No Smoking!** A major cause of both commercial and domestic fires is cigarettes and matches that are carelessly discarded. In the 2020 *Warehouse Structure Fires* study, the NFPA found that smoking was the cause of 60 warehouse fires and $17 million in warehouse property damage every year. Having a warehouse-wide *No Smoking Policy* and placing large, clear *No Smoking* signs in multiple areas throughout the warehouse is perhaps the easiest and most effective means of reducing the risk of smoking-related fires.

- **Installing and Maintaining Firefighting Equipment.** Warehouse managers reduce the risk of fire in warehouse facilities by placing firefighting equipment throughout the facility and inspecting and maintaining the equipment on a regular basis. Some standard fire fighting equipment found in warehouse facilities include:

  - ❖ **Fire Extinguishers.** *Fire extinguishers* are portable or handheld safety devices that expel wet or dry chemicals to stop smaller fires or contain their spread until firefighter arrive. A variety of gas-operated foam discharging fire extinguishers have been developed to handle different types of fires, such as various chemical or hazardous material fires. Warehouse managers must take great care to understand the intended application of each fire extinguisher and place it within a warehouse facility according where it is likely to be needed most.

  - ❖ **Hose Reels.** *Hose reels* are used for dealing with larger outbreaks of fire. They are long hoses on cylindrical spindles that are affixed to a wall or floor and are typically linked to large reserve tanks or the main water supply. Because hose reels use water for fire containment, care must be taken only to use them for fires that can be extinguished by water, such as those involving paper, wood, plastic, and cloth. If the fire involves flammable liquids, such as oil or alcohol, jets of water may cause the fire to spread rather than contain it. Also, using water with electricity fires can create an even more lethally dangerous situation for firefighters.

  - ❖ **Sprinkler Systems.** *Fire sprinkler systems* are fire protection systems that are added to a building that automatically extinguish fires when they start. When a major fire occurs, sprinkler systems are designed to saturate a given area with water or chemical foam to extinguish a fire or contain its spread. The systems are typically installed in the ceilings of rooms and controlled by both a thermostat and smoke sensor. With both forms of detection, the system is not triggered if small amounts of smoke alone will not set off the sprinklers, such as when a coworkers burns popcorn in the break room microwave. In the 2020 *Warehouse Structure Fires* study, the NFPA found that fire sprinkler systems were effective in 84% of warehouse fires in facilities that had sprinkled systems.

  - ❖ **Fire Blankets.** A *fire blanket* is a safety device that resembles a blanket but is used to extinguish small fires as they are starting by depriving them of oxygen. They are made of fireproof fabric, such as glass fiber, kevlar, or fireproof-treated wool, and wall mounted in a highly visible locations where the risk of small fires is the greatest, such as near workstations or equipment that pose fire risks. In addition to being used to smother small fires, they can also be wrapped around people whose clothes have caught fire.

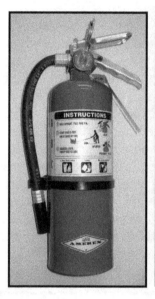  

FIGURE 10.11 - WALL-MOUNTED FIRE SAFETY DEVICES
FIRE EXTINGUISHER (LEFT), FIRE HOSE REEL (CENTER), AND FIRE BLANKET (RIGHT)

- **Installing and Monitoring Alarm Systems.** Alarm systems are a critical means of identifying fires and putting them out before they grow and spread. Good alarm systems link warehouse facilities and other parts of the organization with a central alarm monitoring board in the security office. They are also often linked with the local fire department. Within each warehouse facility, warehouse managers must ensure that there is a working alarm system for fire outbreaks and that the alarm systems are regularly inspected. Warehouse staff must also regularly check the alarm system to ensure that there are no obstructions covering the alarm sensors or equipment.

- **Holding Regular Fire Drills.** Warehouse managers must ensure that regular, well-organized fire drills are held so that staff members are prepared to safeguard both inventory and people in case of fire. Clear fire instructions must be placed in central locations within warehouse facilities. These instructions must be precise and list the critical actions to be taken in case of fire, especially if any of the materials stored are highly flammable or dangerous.

- **Conducting Regular Inspections.** Warehouse managers must ensure that local fire department officials conduct regular inspections of warehouse facilities and external inventory yards. Such inspections, especially when conducted more often or in greater depth than legally required, help to ensure a safe and efficient fire safety system.

- **Marking All Exits.** Warehouse managers must ensure that all fire doors and emergency exits are clearly marked at all times and that passages and gangways are kept clear. There must also be clear, consistent, and highly visible marking of emergency route pathways on warehouse facility floors. This is typically done with brightly colored, high visibility tape that is easily replaced when it becomes worn or faded.

- **Segregating High Risk Materials.** Fire risks can also be decreased when high-risk materials, such as oil, gas, chemicals, and explosives, are stored in a separate, specially designed warehouse facility or external inventory yard. While it may be somewhat more expensive to run a separate high-risk materials storage facility, there is a cost benefit to this practice because a smaller quantity of expensive, specialized firefighting equipment can be concentrated in this one area, rather than spreading greater quantities of the expensive, specialized firefighting equipment across a wider range of warehouse locations. High-risk material warehouse facilities or external inventory yards are also typically placed a set distance from the other warehouse structures. As a result, fires occurring in the main warehouse do not reach the high-risk inventory, thus staving off larger, more serious fires. Conversely, large fires occurring in the high-risk warehouse can be allowed to burn themselves out without posing a risk to the main warehouse facility or its inventory.

FIGURE 10.12 - SEGREGATING HIGH RISK MATERIALS

PORTSIDE WAREHOUSE IN SOUTHEAST ALASKA WITH PROPANE TANKS AND OTHER FLAMMABLE MATERIALS OUTSIDE IN A FENCED AND LOCKED AREA AWAY FROM MAIN WAREHOUSE

Those who work in warehousing and inventory management must also know about the *NFPA 704 Standard System for the Identification of the Hazards of Materials for Emergency Response*, more commonly referred to as the **NFPA 704**. This is a rating system used in the United States developed by the National Fire Protection Association for classifying the danger levels surrounding the health, flammability, and reactivity hazards of chemicals. Although this system was originally developed for emergency personnel and first responders, it is now used an information and warning system for anyone who must handle or work near potentially hazardous materials. The **NFPA 704 label** is a diamond-shaped placard that is placed on a container, such as a tank or drum filled with a hazardous chemical. This diamond-shaped label has four diamonds of different colors inside it. Each colored inner diamond has a number, letter, or symbol written in it that reveals information about the hazard level of the chemical founded inside the container. Figure 10.13 shows an example of the NFPA 704 label and the information it can convey.

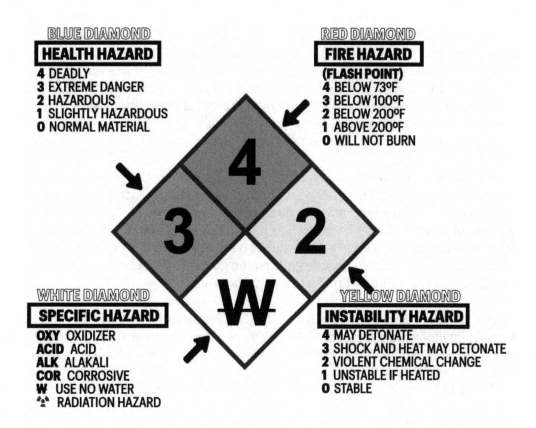

FIGURE 10.13 NFPA 704 LABEL AND IDENTIFICATION GUIDE

LOOKING AT THE NUMBERS AND LETTERS IN EACH OF THE DIAMOND OF THE NFPA 704 LABEL, WE KNOW THE FOLLOWING INFORMATION ABOUT THE HAZARDS POSED BY THE CHEMICAL: EXTREME HEALTH DANGER (3), WILL IGNITE WHEN BELOW 73 DEGREES FAHRENHEIT (4), CAN HAVE A VIOLENT CHEMICAL CHANGE (2), AND DO NOT USE WATER WITH THIS CHEMICAL (W)

10.4 KEEPING INVENTORY SAFE FROM DETERIORATION

Like fire, *deterioration* also poses a threat to inventory safety. In the world of warehousing, **deterioration** is the decay, spoiling, evaporation, damage, or other related loss of usefulness of the inventory that occurs as a result of both time and storage conditions. All items in an inventory will deteriorate eventually, but ineffective storage and improper handling can cause inventory to deteriorate over a much shorter span of time. Premature inventory deterioration can have disastrous results. Poor storage of vital inventory can lead to substantial lost output and subsequent increased operating costs. The administrative costs of ordering also increase. Every time inventory deteriorates, it must be ordered again, causing ordering costs to double or even triple, which causes administrative costs to increase dramatically. Many factors can contribute to inventory deterioration, including:

- **Faulty storage areas and incorrect storage conditions**. When a warehouse facility has broken windows, leaking roofs, or badly fitting doors, less than ideal storage condition may result, such as damp and humid air in the warehouse facility or areas of extreme hot or cold temperatures. If areas get damp, even if inventory items don't get wet, their cardboard packaging may warp. If areas of the warehouse get too hot or cold, chocolate bars may turn to liquid and cans of soda may freeze and burst. The same disastrous results can occur when the storage conditions are not faulty but are incorrect for the item being stored. Would you keep a pallet of gallons of milk outside in an external inventory yard on a hot summer day?

- **Lack of attention to storage instructions.** Storage instructions are usually provided by suppliers in the packaging or in delivery documents. If those aren't read and followed, the inventory may get damaged or rapidly deteriorate. Imagine if a pallet of boxes of student guitars had the clear instructions: *Top Load Only!* If the forklift driver unloading the pallet of guitars didn't pay attention to this and stacked a pallet of tubas on top of the pallet of fragile guitars, the guitars may become damaged or their packaging may crumble and make the items unsellable.

- **Faulty or careless materials handling.** When materials handling is careless, items in inventory can break, become damaged, or airtight seals might unintentionally open. Not only can the inventory being handled become damaged, but innocent inventory nearby may suffer collateral damage. Imagine someone wheeling a hand truck and not paying attention as they turn around, crashing the metal platform and wheels into a pallet of eggs,. While there may be a few survivors, many of the poor eggs and their cartons may not make it to the grocery store shelves.

- **Proximity-related materials contamination.** This type of contamination is caused when different types of materials that shouldn't be together are stored too close to one another. This results in contamination of at least one of the materials. Imagine boxes of very strong-smelling powdered laundry detergent stored alongside bags of flour for months and months. Eventually, the paper bags of the flour will begin to smell like the detergent, which may smell clean, but it may not be the smell you want in your kitchen cupboard or the last you want in the flour you use to bake your famous chocolate chunk cookies!

- **Improper or nonexistent inventory rotation.** The oldest inventory in stock should be used before the more recently received items so that deterioration doesn't get a chance to take hold. When newer inventory is instead picked and issued while older inventory remains held, the older items are allowed to sit on a shelf and get older and older, thus allowing for natural deterioration. Even when items are not perishable, packaging can become yellowed or brittle, making the inventory look old when it is eventually issued and sold to customers.

FIGURE 10.14 - DETERIORATION (LEFT) AND INCORRECT STORAGE CONDITIONS (RIGHT)

When precautionary steps are taken, premature inventory deterioration can be avoided. The warehouse manager plays a vital role in preventing costly deterioration by following a series of steps, including:

- *Checking storage installation conditions.* The warehouse management team can make regular inspections of all storage areas to ensure that they are clean and damp-free. All doors, windows, and ventilators should be checked for leakage.

- *Regulating warehouse temperature and humidity.* When the temperature and humidity of a warehouse are carefully controlled, premature deterioration is avoided. To conserve effort and resources, warehouse managers often store inventory requiring similar temperature and humidity conditions together.

- *Adhering strictly to suppliers' instructions.* By ensuing that suppliers' instructions are followed, the warehouse management team extends the life of the inventory.

- *Handling materials properly.* Proper materials handling is an essential element of warehouse management. It reduces damage and breakage, thus preventing deterioration. To ensure that materials are handled properly, warehouse managers may simply ensure that suppliers' instructions are followed, such as *Fragile – Handle with Care!* They may also send warehouse staff to specialized materials handling training and may personally supervise the issue and loading of dangerous chemicals.

- *Hands-On Supervising.* By ensuring that all materials and storage handling is supervised by trained and experienced staff, warehouse managers can reduce the risk of bad storage and faulty handling.

10.5 SECURITY OF INVENTORY AND PEOPLE

For a production-based company, *inventory* represents a major portion of its ***capital***, which is the combination of money and assets owned by an organization. Any inventory a company loses due to theft or fraud will have to be replaced, which increases the company's costs and reduces its profits. ***Inventory shrinkage*** is inventory loss resulting from internal and external theft, fraud, and administrative errors. According to the National Retail Federation 2022 *National Retail Security Survey*, U.S. retailers' losses from inventory shrinkage totaled almost $100 billion - yes, BILLION! Internal employee theft and external shoplifting were reported to be growing rapidly since the COVID-19 pandemic, with 58.6% of respondents reporting increased employee theft and 72.4% reporting increased shoplifting.

FIGURE 10.15 - SECURITY SERVICE PROFESSIONALS
AN INVALUABLE FIRST LINE OF DEFENSE AGAINST INVENTORY LOSS

When inventory shrinkage from theft and other factors occurs, not only does a company lose the monetary face value of the stolen or lost goods, but its operating efficiency also decreases dramatically. Inventory control records become meaningless if inventory is lost and not recorded. In addition, production planning relies on inventory being available against a predetermined manufacturing plan. If inventory is not secure, these plans will need to be continually reformulated, resulting in lost output and decreased operational efficiency. This makes inventory security not only important, but also extremely vital to the success of any manufacturing company.

Companies typically rely on two groups of people for keeping their inventory secure: *security service professionals* and *warehouse management and staff*. ***Security service professionals*** are people hired by a company to keep inventory secure from theft, fraud, and other losses and to monitor facilities to prevent break-ins by unwanted intruders. A company may hire their own security service professionals as employees or use the services of an outside security service company. Either way, these security service professionals are trained to cope with a variety of difficult situations and provide coverage up to 24 hours per day. Although expensive to hire or contract, they provide an invaluable first line of defense from the outside world against inventory loss. The degree to which an organization uses security service professionals and corresponding security equipment will depend upon the value of the inventory being protected, the location of the warehouse, and the organization's goals and finances. The security equipment used can range from alarm systems and video surveillance cameras to bio-identification entry gates and artificial intelligence technology.

In every warehouse, the manager and staff are ultimately responsible for the warehouse's inventory. Most organizations also rely on these warehouse managers and staff for a large portion of their inventory security needs. They have specialized knowledge of the warehouse and its inventory and it is in their best interest to keep goods secure and the organization profitable, especially when companies offer profit sharing or loss-prevention incentives. Although security service professionals are trained in a variety of security techniques, warehouse managers and staff play an even more critical role in inventory security because they work closely with the inventory every day and may be the first to recognize when inventory is missing or in jeopardy. From 30 to 45% of inventory shrinkage is caused by employee theft, so warehouse managers and their staff offer the first line of security against employee theft.

Warehouse managers are directly responsible for inventory and warehouse security in all of the areas in which goods are received, stored, picked, and issued. In most organizations, the warehouse manager plays a decisive role in setting and enforcing a **warehouse security policy**. This company-specific or location-specific policy typically includes provisions for: *appointing a senior manager with overall responsibility for security, allocating a reasonable budget to cover security costs, consistently enforcing stated company policies for theft,* and *allowing for regular discussions about warehouse security at the organization's managerial level.* The warehouse manager is also responsible for all of the keys, locks, and alarm codes used within the warehouse area. As with the security policy, the warehouse manager would be responsible for setting and enforcing rules regarding these keys, locks, and alarm codes.

In addition to policies, locks, and entry codes, the warehouse manager ensures that all warehouse-related locations are secure at all times, even if they are not currently operational. The location of a warehouse to be kept secure that might fall under a warehouse manager's responsibility include:

- **Warehouse buildings.** Warehouse managers, their staff, and corresponding security staff must ensure that all doors, windows, skylights, entrance ways, shutters, and other possible means of entry are secure to prevent unauthorized intruders from gaining access to the warehouse building. This focus on curbing unauthorized entry should apply not only to unwelcome people, but also to unwelcome pests, such as rats, mice, birds, and foxes, all of which can quickly cause a great deal of damage to inventory.

- **Warehouse offices.** Warehouse managers, their staff, and corresponding security staff must also ensure that all cabinets, filing systems, desks, and computers are locked and that no unattended and unsecured valuables are visible, which is often an open invitation for unauthorized entry and theft.

- **External inventory yards.** Warehouse and inventory yard managers, their staff, and corresponding security staff must also secure the entirety of the external inventory yard by regularly inspecting fencing and checking for complete coverage. Any portion of fencing damaged by foul play, natural events, or other occurrences must be repaired immediately. In addition, all external inventory yard gates and locks must be regularly inspected for security.

- **Marshaling areas.** While typically part of a warehouse building or external inventory yard, *marshaling areas* are worthy of a separate mention because they face the greatest security risk. They are those sections of a warehouse building or external inventory yard reserved for consolidation, packing, marking, merchandise sorting, inspection, and storage prior to shipment. A marshaling area is often a very difficult area to secure because many people from a variety of departments from both within and outside of the company have access to the area while inventory within this area must be readily mobile. Some warehouse managers combat this problem of free access by using secure mobile devices, such as *locking pallet cages*, which are metal cages with a locking entry affixed to pallets.

- **Entrances.** Like marshaling areas, entrances to warehouse-related locations are also part of warehouse buildings or external inventory yards which merit special mention because of the security concerns they pose. As previously mentioned, warehouse managers, their staff, and corresponding security staff must ensure that unauthorized personnel do not pass through facility entrances unauthorized. Entry is restricted to prevent theft and to prevent personal injury occurring to those unfamiliar with the location. Imagine someone wandering in to a warehouse, without authorization and without a hardhat, walking near a forklift truck lifting heavy palletized material. The material was improperly stocked the previous evening and the forklift has a difficult time securing the material. The pallets come crashing to the ground, perhaps near or even *on* the unauthorized entrant! To combat such unauthorized entry, many warehouse buildings have entrance counters to deter easy entry. Similarly, both

FIGURE 10.16 - ELECTRONICALLY SECURED ENTRANCE
ENTRANCE TO THIS PORTSIDE CONTAINER AND WAREHOUSE FACILITY IN
REYKJAVIK, ICELAND IS ACCESSED VIA ELECTRONIC PASS CARD.

warehouse buildings and external inventory yards often use pass card systems, with cards either electronically or manually read to restrict entry to cardholders only. Some warehouse facilities rely on greater technology at their entrances and use facial recognition or fingerprint scans for entrance.

Finally, in addition to security policies, locks and entry codes, and facility location security, warehouse managers are also responsible for ensuring that goods held are clearly marked to identify their ownership and origin. When high cost inventory is involved, ***inventory marking*** to provide identifying information is of critical importance because it discourages theft. Marked inventory cannot be easily sold or used outside of the organization, making it a less desirable target for theft. Also, inventory marking increases the likelihood of return of stolen inventory. If marked inventory is stolen and subsequently recovered by the police, its rightful owners can be readily identified.

Types of inventory marking include:

- **Color Marking.** The color used for marking is often related to the company's trademark and will therefore be more easily associated with a specific company if its inventory is stolen and later found. For example, if vacuum cleaner spare parts were stolen from a Dyson distribution center, they would be immediately identified from the bright purples, yellows, and blues on both the packaging and the parts themselves. Although color marking can be built into the product, it can also be added with color coded labels and stickers.

- **Trade Marks.** Many organizations use the method of embossing or engraving their name and trademark on inventory. This method greatly discourages theft. If you were a less than honest person and you needed a set of plush towels for your guest bathroom, you might be tempted to steal hotel towels, but your temptation may wane if you see the hotel's logo emblazoned on them. After all, if you used hotel towels in your guest bathroom, your guests would then know about your somewhat dubious character.

- **Dye Marking.** Dye marking has been used for very valuable inventory items. Dye is placed on or within the item's packaging, which leaves dye marks on the hands of those who handle or open this valuable inventory. This system of marking allows organization officials and the police to quickly check and identify theft suspects.

- **RFID Tagging.** In addition to using RFID tags to help with inventory management as mentioned in previous chapters, manufacturers are starting to embed RFID tags into their products, which adds another layer of security to inventory. Hidden RFID scanners near entrances may alert security personnel or lock doors when unauthorized attempts to remove goods from a warehouse facility occur.

In this discussion of warehouse and inventory security, it is also important to mention the issue of terrorism that has had an enormous impact on warehouse and supply chain facilities. External threats to security through acts of international and domestic terrorism mean that companies must be remain vigilant. Companies that deal with hazardous materials must be extra cautious because of the impact of a potentially far-reaching and lethal spread of chemicals from incidents at their facility. Managers of warehouses and any other facility with goods and people in the supply chain pay special attention to the U.S. Department of Homeland Security's alert system called the *National Terrorism Advisory System*, also called *NTAS*. The system communicates information about terrorist threats by issuing timely alerts and bulletins. In the NTAS *alerts*, one of two possible levels of threat is stated and the threat is described:

- **Imminent Threat Alert.** This level warns of a credible, specific, and impending terrorist threat against the United States.

- **Elevated Threat Alert.** This lower level of threat warns of a credible terrorist threat against the United States.

NTAS alerts also contain *sunset provisions*, in which a specific threat alert is issued for a specific time period and then automatically expires when the time period ends. NTAS also issues *bulletins*, which contains general information about current terrorism trends without specific alerts. Managers of warehouse facilities, especially those holding dangerous goods, typically keep up to date with these alerts through mobile and online update systems.

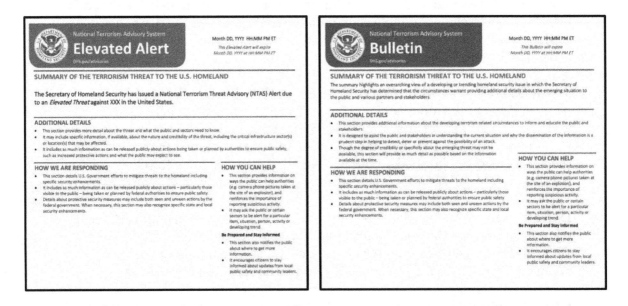

FIGURE 10.17 - EXAMPLES OF NTAS ALERT (LEFT) AND BULLETIN (RIGHT)

CHAPTER 10 REVIEW QUESTIONS

1. What can a warehouse manager do to minimize warehouse safety-related incidents?

2. In addition to *deterioration*, what is the other primary threat to the safety of goods held in a warehouse? What are a few precautionary steps a warehouse can take to minimize this threat?

3. Why is it important to segregate high risk materials in a warehouse?

4. If you see an *NFPA 704 label* on a container and it has a "4" in the red, yellow, and blue diamonds, what does this mean?

5. What is *inventory deterioration*? What are its causes? What impact does it have on an organization's bottom line?

6. What is *inventory shrinkage*? What impact does it have on the U.S. retail industry?

7. In addition to security service professionals, who else helps to keep goods secure in a warehouse? How do they do this?

8. What is a *marshaling area*? Why is it difficult to keep secure?

9. What is *inventory marking*? How is it used?

10. What are the levels of threat in the *National Terrorism Advisory System*? Why would a warehouse manager want to be aware of these?

CHAPTER 10 PHOTO EXERCISE

PHYSICAL DISTRIBUTION: THE WALMART ADVANTAGE

To complete this exercise, you will need to refer to Figure 10.3 on page 267. You will also need to find a list of both GHS hazard pictograms and DOT hazardous materials placard symbols. Two useful locations for these are the State of Oregon OSHA website and the U.S. Department of Transportation Chart 15 online at:

- *https://osha.oregon.gov/OSHAPubs/4988e.pdf*
- *https://www.fmcsa.dot.gov/sites/fmcsa.dot.gov/files/docs/Hazardous_Materials_Markings_Labeling_and_Placarding_Guide.pdf*

Examine the photos below and find the warning labels or symbols in each. For each photo:

1. *Identify whether it is a GHS hazard pictogram, a DOT hazardous materials placard, or an NFP 704 label.*

2. *Interpret the warnings provided in the photo and put them in your own words.*

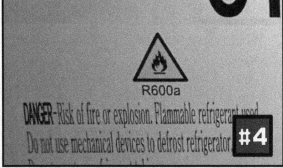

Chapter 11
Information Technology and Systems

Information technology and information systems have become an integral and critical part of warehouse facilities, woven deeply and entirely into and throughout every supply chain. You have already been introduced to some of these information technologies and systems in previous chapters. Chapter 2 introduced us to *automated warehouses*, in which operations are handled with minimal to no human labor, and *smart warehouses*, which use both automation and artificial intelligence to achieve optimum efficiency. Chapter 5 provided the example of the FBI records warehouse, which achieved increased speed and efficiency when it transitioned to automated storage and retrieval through adoption of new information technologies and systems. Chapter 5 also explained the function and benefit of automated technology in the warehouse, such as *automated guided vehicles (AGV)* and *automated storage and retrieval systems (ASRS)*. In Chapter 7, we learned about *inventory control systems*, technology-based solutions that monitor and control the inventory of goods in a warehouse facility, and information systems that are used in dynamic demand environments, such as *distribution resource planning (DRP) systems* and *just-in-time (JIT) systems*. Chapter 8 introduced us to *inventory location systems* and the *barcode* and *RFID* technologies used with them. In Chapter 8 we also examined how ASRS, AGVs, and *mobile robots* are used in issuing inventory.

Although you have been introduced to many concepts of information technology and systems in the warehouse, this chapter will provide a basic overview of these concepts and highlight the role they play in warehouse and inventory management. It will also introduce a few new technologies and systems along the way! Finally, this chapter will also cover a few special topics that relate to information technology and systems in the world of warehousing, including inventory visibility, the impact of e-commerce, and automated and autonomous warehouse operations.

11.1 INFORMATION AND DATA IN THE WAREHOUSE

Before exploring information systems and technology in the world of logistics, we'll first take a moment to discuss what we mean by *information* and the role it plays in making decisions. Let's begin where it all starts, with *data*. The terms data and information are often used interchangeably, but they are quite different. **Data** are facts gathered by research or observation and then represented by groupings of nonrandom symbols, such as letters, words, numbers, values, and other symbols. For example, an inventory checker in a warehouse counting the number of wobbly widgets counts that there are 432 Willamina's Wickedly Wild Wobbly Widgets in stock. The data regarding the quantity of widgets observed is 432.

The inventory checker then needs to enter this data, which is 432 Willamina's Wickedly Wild Wobbly Widgets, into a handheld device or onto a piece of paper on a clipboard so that others may subsequently receive the message that there are currently 432 of these particular widgets in stock. By recording and transmitting this data that others receive, the inventory checker is transforming data into information. **Information** is data that has been received and understood by the recipient of a message. In our example, the recipient may be the logistics manager or the computerized inventory control system. Information is a critical component of decision-making. Without information, there is no basis upon which to make productive decisions. Imagine selecting a new car to buy without basic information, such as gas mileage, safety ratings, and purchase price! In the world of warehouse management, information is used to make a wide range of decisions on an ongoing basis, including storage, materials handling, and transportation decisions. Clear, accurate, and timely information is critical to this process. Ultimately, decisions can only be as good as the information used to make them.

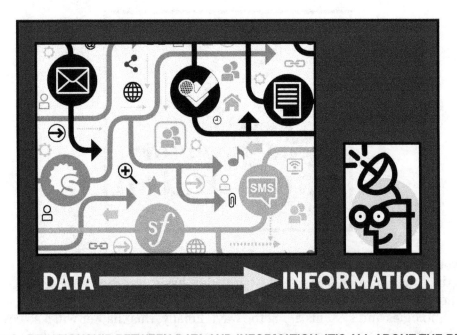

FIGURE 11.1 - RELATIONSHIP BETWEEN DATA AND INFORMATION: IT'S ALL ABOUT THE RECIPIENT!

Information is used for decision-making throughout all supply chain processes, including those related to warehouse management and inventory control. Physical goods flow along a supply chain, but information must spread through every aspect of the chain and flow back and forth between supply chain members. This information flow typically involves the information systems in the warehouse, such as *warehouse management systems*, or *WMS*, which we will learn more about in section 11.3. The warehouse department and its WMS have information flowing to and from many others members of the supply chain, including:

- **the customer**, who provides information about product needs and requires information about product availability, quality, price, and delivery times. Simply put, the customer tells a company what they want and the company tells the customer if those items are available, how many are available, how much they cost, and when the customer can expect to get them. Picture the last time you ordered something online. You were probably provided most of that information from the company as you were placing your order. The warehouse department or WMS is typically involved in this information flow to provide the information about product availability and customer delivery schedules.

- **the Marketing Department**, which provides information about product needs and promotions. The marketing department also receives information from the warehouse department or WMS about product availability. For example, the marketing department of a ski wear company decided to launch an expensive series of commercials during the Winter Olympics for their new design of winter hats with sunglasses, emergency flashlight, and GPS locator built in. The marketing department has quite a few celebrities lined up for the commercials and think the hats will be extremely popular for all ages at ski resorts around the world. However, before the marketing campaign can begin, the marketing department must get information from the warehouse department or WMS about product availability to make sure there will be enough hats to satisfy the potential influx of customer demand.

- **the Production Department**, which is also called the *manufacturing department*. This department provides information about production lead times and manufacturing capabilities. The department is only involved in information flows of a company when its supply chain involves products that are manufactured or produced. The production department receives information about supply deliveries and inventory availability from the warehouse department or WMS. Before it start the manufacturing process or gets the assembly line going, this department wants to make sure there are enough items in inventory needed to manufacture or assemble the company's finished goods.

- **the Purchasing Department**, which provides information on quantities of goods ordered and their delivery timeframes. It receives information from the warehouse department or WMS about when the goods have been received, inspected, and put into stock. Simply put, the purchasing department lets the warehouse or WMS know what it has ordered and when the order should arrive, while the warehouse or WMS lets the purchasing department know when these items actually arrive, in what condition, and when they are put away.

- **the supplier**, who provides information about the availability of goods and means of transportation being used to deliver goods to the warehouse. The supplier requires information from the warehouse department or WMS about delivery times and receiving capabilities, such as specifics on the receiving docks and available receiving times. This means that the supplier tells the warehouse what goods are available and what form of transportation can bring the goods to the company's warehouse and in what timeframe. It also means that the warehouse tells the supplier when they can receive the goods and the receipt process at the company. This kind of information can be extremely useful in special circumstances, such as if the warehouse is closed every Tuesday or if the inbound loading bays have a vehicle height restriction.

As we've already mentioned, information is used for making decisions. In the world of warehouse management, information is used to make a wide range of decisions about: *inventory management and control, transportation*, and *physical distribution facilities placement and management*. When determining the optimal levels of inventory to hold, companies need information on: *inventory holding and issuing costs, customer demand patterns*, and *ordering costs*. When selecting transportation routes, modes, and vendors, companies need information concerning: *transportation costs for various options, shipment frequency and size*, and *customer delivery receipt locations*. Finally, when determining the optimal location, layout, scheduling, and management of a warehouse or distribution center, companies need information regarding: *customer demand and locations, local regulations and taxes*, and *inventory type and quantity*. Throughout the range of a company's inbound, internal, and outbound processes, information is truly the lifeblood of efficient and effective warehouse management.

FIGURE 11.2 - INFORMATION IS USED THROUGHOUT ALL OF WAREHOUSE MANAGEMENT!

Because of its importance in so many decisions in warehouse management, the *quality* and *accessibility* of information are critical. Therefore, information must be:

- *Clear, complete, and accurate.* If information is incorrect or incomplete, decisions made will suffer a similar fate. Imagine placing a delivery order for eighteen pizzas for an office party and being misheard over the telephone, resulting in eighty pizzas landing on your doorstep!

- *Accessible in the right place.* Great information is as good as no information if it can't be found. A scene from the film *Zoolander*, a comedy about the world of male modeling, provides a great illustration of this point. While trying to stop an evil fashion designer from taking over the world, two heroic (but less than computer-savvy) male models are told that the files they need to find are "in the computer." As a result, the protagonists demolish the computer as they try to get the files they believe are actually "inside" the machine.

- *Accessible at the right time.* Needed information is of little use after a decision has been made. For example, a traffic light would be of little use if it were only visible from the middle of an intersection. In the world of warehousing, imagine that you only just received the information that your customer wants 5000 bottles of hot pink nail polish instead of the 5000 bottles of slime green nail polish that you already shipped out to them. The late-arriving information could be used to correct the problem, but the double shipping and returning costs would eat into your company's profits for the order. The information would have been far more beneficial if it had been accessible at the right time!

- *The kind of information needed.* If the information available is not relevant to the decision to be made or cannot be interpreted, it can be even more harmful than having no information at all. Imagine again that you are buying a car and the only information you have about it are its color and model name. You have no information about miles per gallon, safety features, or cost. Many of us might be tempted to select a car based solely on its color and model name, but with this insufficient information, we might end up with a good looking car with a cool name that gets terrible gas mileage and that we can't even afford!

To ensure that logistics information is clear, accurate, and of the right type, accessible at the right time, and in the right place, warehouse management professionals have turned to *information systems* and *information technology*. Today, both information systems and information technology smooth the flow of goods in supply chains into, within, and out from warehouse facilities by efficiently and accurately recording, analyzing, and transmitting warehouse management and inventory control information. **Information systems** are the systems and software programs that manage the flow of data and information in an organization in a systematic, structured way to assist in planning, implementing, and controlling operations. **Information technology** is the hardware used to implement, assist, and work alongside information systems to help achieve warehouse management and operational efficiencies.

11.2 INFORMATION TECHNOLOGY IN THE WAREHOUSE

Also known as *IT*, *information technology* is used to assist in managing the information essential to the inbound, internal, and outbound processes of warehouse management in warehouse facilities, such as storage warehouses, external inventory yards, distribution centers, and fulfillment centers. In the world of warehousing, *IT software* is the category of computer-based and cloud-based programs used to: capture data, store data, sort information, complete calculations, analyze data and information, display information, track inventory and people, organize tasks, create reports, and manage and plan inventory control activities. *IT hardware* is the category of physical devices used to help IT software accomplish these tasks. Throughout the rest of this chapter, we will refer to the IT hardware, or the physical items and devices used in these information activities, as *information technology*. We will similarly refer to the IT software, or the computer-based and cloud-based systems to complete these information tasks as *information systems*. Be aware, however, that both the hardware and software used to used to assist in managing information are often referred to together as *information technology*. *Cloud-based systems* are accessed using the internet via users' computers or mobile devices on an on-demand basis. Computer-based systems are accessed via users' computers or mobile devices and are located on those devices or on a central computer within the organization.

Over the past few decades, information technology has developed at an astounding pace. Just when you think technological devices can't possibly get any smaller or any faster, the next biggest advancement is announced and technology keeps jumping forward! Thanks to technological advancements in phones and other hand-held or wearable technology, warehouses of any size can now use information technology for warehouse management and inventory control activities. Some of the types of technology used in the warehouse include:

- **Computers.** Both stationary and mobile computers are used throughout warehouse facilities to store, process, analyze, and report information. Computers provide the backbone of the information systems in the warehouse. Some systems used in computers may rely on the computer itself for its computing power and storage, while other may be reliant on cloud-based storage and computing.

FIGURE 11.3 - COMPUTERS IN THE WAREHOUSE
**FROM LEFT TO RIGHT: DESKTOP COMPUTER, HANDHELD TERMINAL,
HANDHELD TABLET, TABLET SCREEN WITH INVENTORY SYSTEM**

- **Cell phones and handheld devices.** Cell phones, tablets, handheld data terminals, and similar handheld devices can be used in conjunction with computers or in place of computers when combined with cloud-based apps and computing. Because of the scanning capability of their cameras, cell phones are now used in many settings for taking in information for inventory management. To see an example of this, go to any 24-hour grocery store after midnight, casually stroll up to anyone who is checking inventory, and ask them what they're using to scan the bar codes on the inventory they are counting. Chances are, the device being used will either be an enhanced cellular phone or another handheld device that closely resembles a phone.

- **Barcode labels and optical scanners.** While item identification and communicating information about the item can be performed manually with our eyes and mouths, these functions can be performed far more efficiently and effectively when specialized equipment and systems are used. The most widely used technology-based form of item identification are ***barcodes***. A barcode is a series of bars and spaces printed by a barcode printer onto a label, which is then adhered to an item or a unit load. The barcode label is read by an optical device called a ***barcode scanner***, also called a ***barcode reader***. Barcode scanners vary in cost and application and include: handheld scanners, fixed mount scanners, laser scanners, and image scanners.

After scanning a label, the barcode scanner communicates the information gleaned to information systems and warehouse management software. When we step into the self-scanning express aisle of a large grocery store, we ourselves become frontline users of barcode technology. When checking inventory, an inventory checker uses a barcode scanner to read the label and transfer information about the item scanned to a central inventory control system. Barcode technology is used within many logistics information systems, such as electronic point of sale and warehouse management systems.

FIGURE 11.4 - CODES AND TAGS

BARCODE AND QR CODE LABEL (LEFT), RFID TAG (CENTER), AND A STATIONARY RFID READER CAN READ TAGS ON THIS TRAIN'S CONTAINERS AS IT SPEEDS THROUGH THE STATION (RIGHT)

Similar to a barcode is a ***QR code***, or *Quick Response code*, a two-dimensional and more complex barcode made up of black and white squares of different sizes on a grid and typically printed onto a label. Like barcodes, QR codes must be scanned by an optical scanner for interpretation. Because QR codes uses black and white squares on a two dimensional surface while barcodes use black and white lines within one dimension, QR codes can contain far more information than bar codes. However, bar codes take up less storage space on information systems. Therefore, companies may choose to use barcodes, QR codes, or a combination of the two depending on the information that needs to be conveyed.

- **RFID tags and readers.** With *radio frequency identification*, or *RFID*, a programmed transponder tag, called an *RFID tag*, is attached to an item or unit load. The tag sends out information about the item or load via radio waves. An *RFID reader* with an antenna reads this information and, like a barcode reader, transmits it to an information system such as a central inventory control system. While more expensive than bar coding, RFID technology offers many advantages. Unlike barcode labels, RFID tags can be read when not in the line of sight, at distances of 90 feet or more, and at high speeds.

- **GPS technology.** *Global Positioning System (GPS)* technology is the type of information technology used to locate goods and track them wirelessly using remote sensors and satellite systems. GPS is used to track goods on the move, which means that it is especially useful in tracking goods inbound to and outbound from the warehouse. This can help warehouses plan for inventory receipt and in conveying information about the anticipated delivery times of outbound goods. Warehouses can also use GPS tracking of inventory for security, which provides an alert when items from inventory are removed from the warehouse, either accidentally or for more nefarious purposes.

- **Label printers.** When we think of information technology, we often think of high tech equipment. However, low tech equipment is also an important part of information technology in the warehouse. For example, printers are frequently used in warehouses to create labels that are adhered to incoming goods. These labels often contain barcodes, QR codes, or other inventory management codes that make it easy to track and record information about the goods as they become inventory within the warehouse's system.

- **Voice-aided technology.** *Voice-aided technology* uses voice-activated and voice-directed devices in systems that guide users wearing headsets to complete specific actions. In *voice-directed technology*, the device issues spoken commands that the user listens to through the headset. In *voice-activated technology*, the device records spoken information from the user or allows the user to ask questions about the actions they are completing with the user speaking through the headset. Voice-aided technology is popular in warehouse order picking systems, in which an order picker wearing a hands-free headset listens to each item to be picked along with its location. The order picker then uses voice commands to confirm that the correct items and quantities have been selected.

- **Light-aided technology.** *Light-aided technology* is the use of electronic devices that utilize light to provide a form of visual instruction to someone completing a task. Many warehouses have *pick-to-light* and *put-to-light* systems where a person picking an order or putting goods onto a shelf is directed to pick or put an item in a location that is identified by a light illuminating directly above or below. Light-aided technology saves warehouse workers time and reduces errors because it is far easier to see a well-lit light than a number on a shelf. In most pick-to-light and put-to-light systems, the warehouse worker presses a button on or near the light to turn it off when they have finished picking an item from or placing one into that location.

- **Wearable tech.** In addition to mobile computing technology, warehouses are beginning to increase their use of wearable technology. ***Wearable technology***, also know as ***wearable tech***, is that category of forms of clothing or accessories that can comfortably be worn on the body that complete sensing, communications, or computing functions. We previously introduced voice-aided technology, which is a type of wearable technology usually in the form of a headphone-microphone headset paired with a mobile computing device that can guides users to complete specific actions via voice commands and records information or allows user to issue instruction be user voice commands. In some warehouse facilities, voice-aided technology headsets are also part of a larger system that allows users to issue commands to automated guided vehicles that follow them around and perform actions to assist them, such as picking orders.

In addition to headset, many of us already have a piece of wearable tech that we wear on our wrists every day. Smart watches are finding many applications in warehouses as their computing power and capabilities are increasing, including serving as the mobile computing power to work in connection with headsets for voice-aided technology. Other forms of wearable tech being found increasingly in warehouses include smart glasses, finger-mounted barcode scanners, wrist-mounted portable computer terminals, and smart clothing to help monitor and record workers' safety metrics. The next wave of wearable tech may be the wider use of powered exoskeletons, which are robotic suits worn by the user that increase workers' speed and strength and allow them to lift heavier loads.

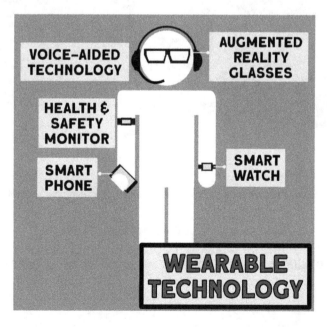

FIGURE 11.5 - WEARABLE TECH FOR WAREHOUSE OPERATIONS

- **Augmented reality.** Another form of wearable technology that may be found in warehouses is *augmented reality glasses*. Also known as *AR glasses*, these devices are much like Google Glass glasses and act as a wearable computer monitor. In warehouse operations, they show maps of warehouses and guide pickers to each location they need to find as they pick orders. They also allow warehouse workers hands-free access to any other type of information they would normally see on a computer or tablet screen.

- **Additive manufacturing.** Perhaps the most Star-Trek-style form of information technology found in warehouses is *additive manufacturing*. Like the replicators on *Star Trek* that produced anything on demand, from a laser gun to a t-bone steak, additive manufacturing technology can create something out of almost nothing. Also known as *3D printers*, these devices use a powder or other raw material to create a three dimensional version of almost any object that can be represented in digital form. In warehouses, these printers are used to create replacement parts for industrial vehicles and other less-often used items, which frees up warehouse shelf space. These devices are connected to information systems and can create items automatically and on demand when the information is conveyed that there is an internal or external customer need for a specific device.

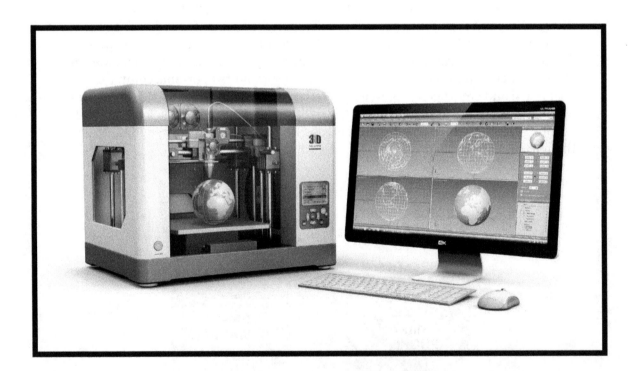

FIGURE 11.6 - ADDITIVE MANUFACTURING

3D PRINTERS ARE INCREASINGLY FOUND IN WAREHOUSE FACILITIES, ESPECIALLY THOSE SUPPORTING MANUFACTURING OPERATIONS

11.3 INFORMATION SYSTEMS IN THE WAREHOUSE

An important part of warehouse management and inventory control is making sure that companies have the exact goods they need to provide to external or internal customers when and where they need them in the quantity they need. This must also be balanced with the cost of holding goods to make sure that too many goods aren't being stored unnecessarily, resulting in higher inventory holding costs. However, companies do not want to cut their inventory holding levels too low or they might risk a **stockout**, which is a situation where there is no longer any stock of an item in inventory. This scary event can result in lost potential sales, operational shut-downs, and very angry customers.

To help perform this balancing act in the warehouse, companies use *information systems* to manage the flow of data surrounding inventory and determine when, where, and how much inventory should be held. These systems are most often in the form of computer or cloud-based programs and apps. In the world of warehousing, information systems manage the information associated with the inbound, internal, and outbound processes of warehouse management. The goal of warehouse information systems are ultimately to create efficiencies and minimize cost, typically by creating faster processes of getting items from an inbound receiving bay to a warehouse shelf and then to inventory issue and outbound distribution. *Warehouse management systems* are used to manage information related to activities such as receiving, putaway, storage, inventory management, picking, packing, and shipping.

A **warehouse management system**, or **WMS**, is a software program or app that manages warehouse business processes and directs warehouse activities. These activities and processes include: *order receipt and shelving, order picking and shipping, storage, inventory management, inventory cycle counting, picking, integration with RFID or voice recognition technology, packing, shipping*, and *layout planning*. A WMS typically tracks the

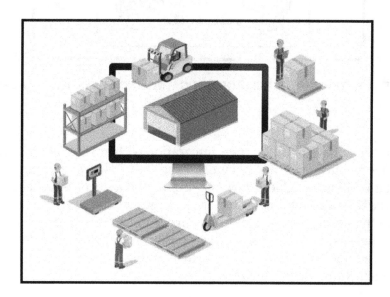

FIGURE 11.7 - ACTIVITIES IMPACTED BY A WAREHOUSE MANAGEMENT SYSTEM

movement of goods into, within, and out from a warehouse facility, such as a storage warehouse or fulfillment center. The WMS interfaces with the *enterprise resource planning*, or *ERP*, transaction system to provide real time visibility of inventory and orders. This integration provides a seamless transfer of order data to the WMS system, and a transmission of shipment and inventory data from the WMS to the ERP system.

More commonly known as **ERP**, an **enterprise resource planning** system is a type of software system used across an entire company for planning and managing its resources. It replaces a company's many, sometimes incompatible information systems with a single, integrated system with seamless, real-time information sharing, storage, and retrieval. Because the WMS system is integrated with or directly linked to the ERP system, it plays a large role in order receipt, shipments, and inventory management. ERP systems are typically structured across one organization, although aspects of a system may interface with customers and suppliers. Some of the more commonly used ERP systems are those developed by SAP, Oracle, Microsoft, SYSPRO, and Odoo.

FIGURE 11.8 - THE TIME BENEFIT OF USING WMS AND ERP IN THE WAREHOUSE

Warehouse management systems and their integration with enterprise resource planning are critical to efficient warehouse management, especially in larger warehouse facilities. The core objective of a WMS is to *reduce the number of movements that warehouse operators and equipment make* while handling inventory to minimize the equipment, facilities, and labor costs to run the warehouse. Another objective is to *provide speedier service* for internal and external customers, especially with order picking and order fulfillment. A few additional objectives of a WMS related to specific inbound, internal, and outbound warehouse management processes include:

- **Inventory Receipt:** Match advance receipt paperwork, such as shipment notification documents, with the actual shipment as it is received. This is often accomplished using barcode scanning technology with automatic systems in place to pay suppliers when correct orders have been received.

- **Put Away:** Optimize locations, slotting, and materials handling manual or vehicle vehicle routes for the most efficient put away process possible. This helps to maximize warehouse space, minimize equipment use and labor hours, and avoid traffic congestion inside the warehouse facility.

- **Picking:** Minimize equipment and human movement when picking orders, perhaps with multiple orders being picked simultaneously. Similar to objectives of putaway, this picking objective helps to minimize equipment use, make the most of each labor hour, and avoid traffic congestion inside the warehouse facility.

- **Shipping:** Check to ensure complete accuracy of every outbound shipment and load these shipments using efficient placement inside outbound trucks and containers. This type of outbound loading increases unloading efficiency when goods are received by the customer.

Additional types of information systems used in warehouse management include:

- *slotting optimization software*, which helps a company identify the best locations within a warehouse to place slots to store SKUs based on using the space available in the most efficient and effective way possible and based on the needs of the company and its operations

- *load optimization software*, also called *load building software*, which helps create ideal unit loads and based on these unit loads, suggests the best transportation systems and plots the best routes to save both time and money

- *yard management system*, which helps organize containers and trailers in external inventory yards and outdoor waiting areas by showing where they are located, what the arrival and departure schedule for each trailer or container is, what inventory is located in each, and when each trailer or container will begin to incur additional or unnecessary costs, such as excess rental fees

- *warehouse control system*, which is a type of software that keeps operations running smoothly in a warehouse facility by directing operations and suggesting what should be done at what time to achieve maximum efficiency and effectiveness

A final information system that warehouse managers both use and supply information to is an *inventory visibility system*. All members of a supply chain can instantly and easily share inventory information, including information about location and visibility. Information that once could travel only as fast as a courier could carry it or as fast as someone could convey it by telephone can now travel instantly in the blink of an eye, which has dramatically increased supply chain efficiency and effectiveness. As we mentioned in previous chapters, *global positioning systems technology*, or *GPS*, now allows inventory to be tracked during its entire route inbound to a warehouse, within a warehouse, and outbound from a warehouse on its way to the customer. Different locations and organizations within the supply chain use ***inventory visibility systems*** to share accurate, real-time information about inventory location, making inventory *visible* to a company, even when it is no longer under the company's control. This ***inventory visibility*** helps reduce costs by allowing an organization to move more to just-in-time operations and hold less just-in-case inventory. It also enhances customer service because it helps an organization control the process of getting the right quantity and quality of finished goods to the exact place at the exact time a customer desires. Inventory visibility work in conjunction with a variety of forms of information technology, such as *barcode printing and scanning*, *RFID technology*, *GPS technology*, and *handheld devices utilizing bluetooth and wireless connectivity*.

11.4 THE IMPACT OF E-COMMERCE

In the past couple of decades, we have become increasingly dependent on *e-commerce* as private consumers. Known originally as *electronic commerce*, ***e-commerce*** is a system for a company to sell its goods or services to other businesses or end users using information systems via the internet or closed networks. When you buy and download this week's top song on iTunes, you are using Apple's e-commerce system. Similarly, when you place any order for goods online, whether it's an order for a pair of Italian, handmade shoes from a small, family-run business in Milan or an order for a pepperoni stuffed-crust pizza from the Pizza Hut around the corner, you are using e-commerce. As our use of e-commerce has increased, so have our expectations. We can easily do shopping and supplier research in our pajamas from the privacy of our homes at any time of the day or night. This research allows us to not only find the lowest price, but we may choose one supplier over another because it is the supplier that get us our goods the quickest or have the best reviews from customers. For companies to stay competitive, picking and delivery times must continue to become shorter as our expectations increase for shorter and shorter delivery times. Companies as diverse as Amazon, Sally Beauty, and Safeway offer same-day delivery and even offer one-hour or two-hour deliveries in some locations.

E-commerce has also changed the nature of the *distribution channels* for companies and their outbound goods. A ***distribution channel*** is the route and means by which an organization distributes its finished goods. Like a supply chain, a distribution channel is the structure of the physical flow of goods. It includes all members involved in this physical flow, such as the organization itself, distribution centers, fulfillment centers, third party logistics service providers, wholesalers, and retailers. However, unlike the *supply chain* which covers both the inbound and outbound flow of goods, the *distribution channel* is concerned solely with the physical outbound flow of goods.

Most warehouses and distribution centers have traditionally been designed with one distribution channel in mind, such as distribution of goods solely to retail store locations or to other companies buying the goods. E-commerce has changed the nature of distribution channels and warehouse design because companies must now plan for multiple distribution channels because any company or any one can buy the company's goods at any time from any location thanks to e-commerce. This approach is called ***omnichannel distribution***. Warehouses facilities such as distribution centers had to reexamine and redesign their picking, packing, and distribution methods to accommodate for more complex omnichannel distribution, especially from e-commerce. This led to to development of *fulfillment centers*, which (as you may remember from Chapter 2) are warehouse facilities that store products manufactured by a variety of companies and are used to fill customers' orders primarily from online sales. Like distribution centers, fulfillment centers focus on the fast movement of goods into and out from the facility, but distribution centers typically distribute goods to retail stores while fulfillment centers send goods directly to end users based on online orders.

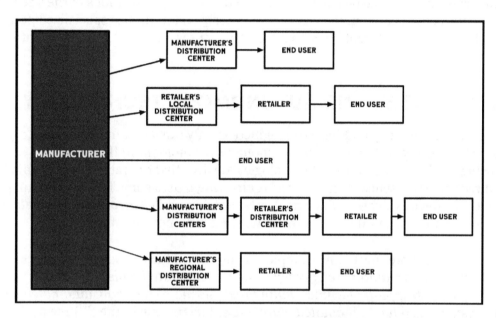

FIGURE 11.9 - OMNICHANNEL DISTRIBUTION

Both individual consumers and companies have become increasingly demanding in their expectations of suppliers, expecting them to shorten order fulfillment and delivery times to meet their needs, just like their favorite retailers now do. As a result, warehouse facilities have had to focus on high-speed picking and packing operations, often using the automated technology that will be described in Section 11.5 below.

As e-commerce drives same-day and same-hour delivery to become a reality for more and more companies, warehouses and distribution centers have to keep items in stock that can be picked, packed, and shipped immediately. To meet the immediate delivery needs of customers, warehouses, distribution centers, and fulfillment centers will have to be located within population centers to save on delivery time. However, in areas with high population density, available warehouse space is harder to find and is more expensive than out-of-town warehouses. Warehouses facilities must increasingly maximize every inch of their valuable floor space and vertical space with *high-density storage systems*, which maximize warehouse floor space by minimizing aisles. In these storage systems, shelves move so human and automated pickers can access goods as needed, with the shelves moving using tracks or shelf-shifting robots.

A final development in warehouse facilities as a result of e-commerce is the increasing trend of *customized packaging*. With orders of varying sizes coming in from a variety of omnichannel customers, warehouses facilities' shipping departments traditionally can no longer stock a range of boxes and delivery packages in a few different shapes and sizes. These standard forms of packaging would usually not fit each shipment perfectly, with much wasted space and increased delivery costs. Larger warehouses, distribution centers, and fulfillment centers have now begun to turn to **customized packaging**, in which a company uses packaging machines that automatically and rapidly build each shipment's corrugated cardboard or plastic bag packaging to the exact specifications of the size of that shipment. This helps a company reduce shipping costs and minimize specialized packaging products, like boxes of different sizes, that a company uses and must keep in inventory.

11.5 AUTOMATED AND AUTONOMOUS TECHNOLOGY

One category of technology that has become increasingly prevalent in warehouses over the past five to ten years is *automated* and *autonomous technology*. In the world of warehousing, both are categories of technological devices that operate without immediate human direction or presence. **Automated technology** uses some form of structural guidance for its devices, such as floor rails or tape strips, while **autonomous technology** uses the environment around it to figure out where it can and cannot go.

In previous chapters, we saw many examples of automated technology in warehouse management, including *automated guided vehicles, automated palletizers, automated stretch wrap and strapping machines, automated picking technology, automated storage retrieval systems,* and *fully automated warehouses* like the one in the FBI records warehouse. Automated technology relies heavily on information systems and technology to improve efficiency and reduce operating and labor costs in warehouse facilities. A few key companies have embraced automated technology on a large scaled in their distribution centers and fulfillment centers, including Amazon, Walmart, and Kroger. The demand for warehouse automated technology is expected to grown in the next decade, but it may be surpassed by the demand for autonomous technology.

In earlier chapters, you were introduced to both *autonomous mobile robots* and *collaborative mobile robots*, both of which are examples of autonomous technology used in warehouse operations. With autonomous technology, the device that is provided support to work operations uses information about its immediate environment to determine where it can and cannot go. You have likely already seen autonomous technology in action when go to large warehouse-style stores or superstores if they utilize robotic cleaning machines. These devices roll around the store on a set course, cleaning the floors are they go. However, they do not have a human driver or operator. They stop and reconfigure their route if something is in their way, including a moving human being or even a small service dog.

Robots are the most common form of autonomous technology found in a warehouse facility. A **robot** is a machine that can be programmed to complete complex actions and tasks autonomously or semi-autonomously. Some robots are designed to mimic human forms or actions, but not all robots do. Autonomous mobile robots (AMR) bear no resemblance to humans but instead appear as mobile, rolling machines with minds of their own, like the robotic cleaning machines rolling around your favorite superstore.

It's hard to picture a warehouse of the future without robots. According to the International Federation for Robotics, there were over half a million new industrial robots put into use in 2021 and there are currently almost 3.5 million industrial robots in use worldwide. Amazon is one of the largest uses of industrial robots, getting their start in the early 2000s. Amazon's robots operate by lifting shelves weighing up to 1000 or 3000 pounds, depending on the robot used. The robots bring the shelves to putaway workers and order pickers in the warehouse. These robots are only about two feet tall, but they weigh 320 pounds and can perform much of the heavy lifting in a warehouse. Amazon now has more than 500,000 of these robot workhorses in their fulfillment centers around the world. In 2022, Amazon introduced a similar new model of robot called Proteus. What is special about Proteus is that it operates both fully autonomously and collaboratively. ***Collaborative robots***, also known as ***cobots***, are designed to work alongside and interact with humans. Both Amazon and DHL are leaders in driving cobot initiatives for warehouse operations.

With robots like Proteus and other autonomous and automated technology, there is likely to be an increase in *fully automated warehouses* and ***smart warehouses***, which we learned in Chapter 2 are fully automated warehouse that uses real-time data through artificial intelligence systems and automation technology to achieve optimum efficiency in moving and storing goods. These warehouses that can operate without humans and can keep working even after all the human go home are known as ***dark warehouses***. You can turn out the lights, but they'll keep working!

A final form of autonomous technology that connects to warehouse information systems and impacts warehouse management are unmanned delivery vehicles, which include delivery drones and unmanned cars and trucks. ***Delivery drones*** are unmanned aerial vehicles that are used to transport goods. Since the launch of the first officially approved commercial drone delivery in the U.S. in 2015, delivery drones have had a difficult time taking hold for deliveries in all but the most remote areas because of local regulations in cities around the world. However, driverless road vehicles have met with greater success.

You may already have seen one of Google's self-driving cars moving slowly up and down the streets of your city, taking photos for Google Street View, a function of Google Maps. Like Google's self-driving cars, a ***driverless vehicle*** is an autonomous, automated, or self-driving motor vehicle that is able to sense its environment and drive without human input. A leader in autonomous vehicles for small, last-mile deliveries called Nuro which has partnered with UberEats to develop driverless forms of food delivery over the next ten years. Also in their nascent stages of implementation are commercial self-driving trucks, which are intended to help ease the international shortage of truck drivers. A few companies are running small numbers of driverless trucks while in the early stages of testing and development, so it may not be too long until you are driving down the highway and see an autonomous truck or two.

CHAPTER 11 REVIEW QUESTIONS

1. What is the difference between *data* and *information*?

2. How does the warehouse department and its *warehouse management system* interact with the others members of the supply chain?

3. In two sentences or less, describe how *RFID tags* and *RFID scanners* work. In what situation might you want to use RFID technology?

4. How is *voice-directed technology* different from *voice-activated technology*? How could both be used in the same warehouse?

5. Which form of *wearable technology* mentioned in this chapter would you most like to try? Why?

6. What is *additive manufacturing*? How could it be used in the warehouse?

7. What is a *stockout* and how can a warehouse prevent it using one of the primary topics of this chapter?

8. If your warehouse manages many containers in its external inventory yard and they seem to be piling up more and more every day, what type of software might be useful? If you have a warehouse that always seems to run short on space, what type of software might be useful?

9. What impact has *e-commerce* had on *distribution channels*?

10. What is the difference between *automated technology* and *autonomous technology*? Provide an example of each.

CHAPTER 11 CASE STUDY

A TALE OF TWO COMPANIES & THEIR INFORMATION SYSTEMS

When it opened its doors in 1996, very few people had heard of Under Armour, a Maryland-based sports apparel manufacturer. After becoming the outfitter of two Oliver Stone sports films, becoming the official outfitter of the XFL, and developing a wildly popular marketing campaign called "Protect this house," Under Armour became an overnight sensation and grew exponentially. It quickly became a global brand and continues to have wildly successful growth today.

With their initial explosive growth, Under Armour's warehouses and distribution centers became bogged down. There never seemed to be enough warehouse space and the warehouse management system they used since the early days of launching the company could not keep up with the pace needed to get the products out to the rapidly growing customer base. The company decided to replace its warehouse management system to accommodate this growth. After exploring many of the top WMS providers, Under Armour decided to work with third party provider Manhattan Associates to help them develop the WMS they needed to attain the agility and speed they needed for their almost unbelievably rapid growth.

Because there never seemed to be enough warehouse space no matter how big their warehouses were, Under Armour also decided to add Manhattan Associates' slotting optimization software to their WMS. This let the company utilize every available inch of its warehouse space and automatically placed the most highly picked items in the golden zone of each warehouse. The system was also highly flexible, which meant that slotting optimization could vary from warehouse to warehouse. It also meant that placement of items could vary on a seasonal basis, resulting in more efficient and streamlined picking processes throughout the year. As a result, Under Armour also experienced more accurate picking, packing, and shipping. This saved the company money because warehouse overtime expenses were drastically reduced and even eliminated. The apparel manufacturer continues to use Manhattan Associates' customized WMS and slotting optimization software in its warehouses and distribution centers around the world.

While a global clothing manufacturer like Under Armour can interview the top WMS providers and receive custom-made solutions, the issue of information systems is more challenging for local businesses that do not have the size or volume of sales of global brands and national retail chains. One example of the struggle local companies face when searching for WMS solutions can be found in our continuing tale of Once in a Blue Moose, a locally popular retail chain of gift and souvenir stores in Alaska. A few years ago, the retail chain knew it needed an information system to manage its incoming, internal, and outbound inventory across its multiple retail locations and its warehouse in midtown Anchorage. One of the company's owners was also an IT guru and made it her job to search high and low for the perfect (or at least a pretty good) system that would work on the company's Apple computers and meet the ERP and WMS needs they had outlined.

Once in a Blue Moose quickly found that its options were limited when you're not a retail giant who can afford to get custom-built solutions. The systems available were either far too expensive or were not flexible enough for the retail environment for a business of their size. For example, one brand of software was great for many business functions but was not designed to track and manage inventory at multiple retail locations. Another brand of software could handle multiple retail locations but was rigid in its inventory coding and forced users to have a coding system that did not make sense for Once in a Blue Moose and its inventory. Fed up with limited possibilities that didn't meet their needs, the company's IT-loving co-owner decided to create an information system herself using File Maker Pro on her Apple computer.

It was a labor of love for many months, but Once in a Blue Moose finally had an inventory management system that met its needs perfectly. The customized system ware named after the Roman messenger of the gods, Mercury. It was a blend of ERP and WMS, with all of its functions designed to meet the inventory management needs of a retail environment with one central warehouse and countless retail outlets. It served to manage and locate the inventory held by the company at all of its locations.

It also had a special function to create inventory codes for new items based on the inventory and location coding system used company-wide. Mercury was tied in to wireless barcode scanners and had an app for handheld devices used across the company, especially iPads.

While the system is working well for Once in a Blue Moose, there are more developments on the horizon. The company is continuing to develop solutions to meet its needs for more efficient and streamlined operations, such as introducing a GPS component for inventory tracking and streamlining the distribution process. It is also exploring converting to a cloud-based system for greater flexibility and real-time information sharing.

INSTRUCTIONS

Please answer the following:

1. If Under Armour had not replaced its WMS, what might have happened? Do you think the company would have continued to grow to become as popular as it is today? Please explain your answer.

2. If you were the owner of Once in a Blue Moose but did not have a co-owner who was an IT genius, what would you have done to meet your company's needs for an information system to manage inventory?

BONUS ASSIGNMENT

Visit two businesses near you: one large, national chain and one small- to medium-sized local business. Ask them about the types of information systems they use to manage their inventory.

Do you notice any similarities or differences between the businesses you observed and the businesses in this case study?

Chapter 12

The Human Side of Warehouse Management

A system of efficient and effective warehouse facilities is vital to having a successful supply chain. Can you imagine your favorite box of breakfast cereal, Sugar-n-Sawdust Super Snaps, magically appearing on your breakfast table direct from the factory without once being stored or handled? Every link in the supply chain involves a warehouse or some type of warehouse management activity. Your box of Sugar-n-Sawdust Super Snaps likely experienced the entire gamut of warehouse management activities, from inventory receipt and inspection to storage and inventory checking to inventory picking and distribution.

The objectives of warehouse management throughout the supply chain are the same as other logistics and supply chain activities: *provide a service* valued by customers at a *minimum cost* and at a service level that *meets or exceeds customers' expectations*. We will be repeating ourselves here, but this involves getting the right product of the right quality and in the right quantity to the right place at the right time when the customers wants it... and doing this consistently every time!

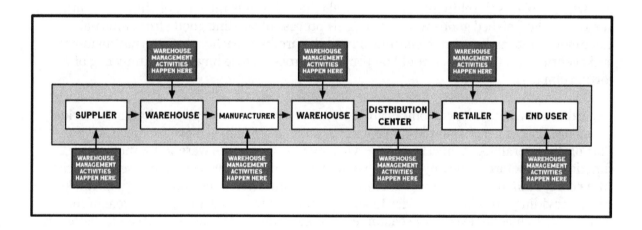

FIGURE 12.1 - WAREHOUSE MANAGEMENT ACTIVITIES OCCUR EVERYWHERE IN SUPPLY CHAINS!

Customers and their needs drive the supply chain. They determine much of warehouse management, such as packaging type when shipping toy plastic trains or warehouse facility type when an organization must choose between a traditional warehouse or a cross-docking regional distribution center. Customers have an enormous say in warehouse management and inventory control, but *who are these customers*?

12.1 WHO ARE THE CUSTOMERS OF WAREHOUSING?

In the business world, a **customer** is an entity that receives a product or service from another entity. Although we usually think of customers as people, customers may also be organizations. For example, although you may be a Coca-Cola customer when you buy a can of Coke from a gas station or vending machine, multinational retail giant Walmart is also one of Coca-Cola's many customers. When looking at customer service, organizations must consider the service they provide to both individual people and other organizations.

Warehouse customers can be either *external* or *internal* to the organization providing the product or service. When we think of customers, we typically think of **external customers**, which are those entities who receive a product or service who are private individual end users or organizations other than the *supplier*, which is the company providing the product or service. When you buy a bag of tortilla chips from a grocery store or when the Tasty Taco Time Restaurant chain buys the same chips from the tortilla chip manufacturer, both you and the restaurant chain are the tortilla chip manufacturer's external customers.

In the world of warehousing, **internal customers** are those individuals or departments within an organization who receive goods or services from a warehouse facility or warehouse function within their own organization. For example, at the tortilla chip production facility, the production department creates, fries, and salts the chips, which are then sent to the production department's *internal customer*: the packaging department. After the packaging department places the chip into bags and seals them, it sends the bags of chips to its internal customer: the finished goods warehouse. This process of sending goods from internal customer to internal customer continues until the product reaches the external customer and eventual end user, which could be you at the grocery store buying a yummy bag of tortilla chips.

Regardless of whether its customers are internal or external, an organization that provides goods or services focuses on the concept of customer service to achieve financial success. Part of this overall focus on customer service must be within the warehouse management function. But before we go any further, what exactly does the term *customer service* mean? At its core, **customer service** is everything an organization does and the actions it takes while providing a product or service to an external or internal customer. The goal of these actions are to meet or exceed the customer's expectations, resulting in a satisfied customer. Although there may be only one employee or a small team of employees within warehouse management who are officially responsible for customer service, *everyone* in the warehouse function contributes to customer service. For example, although there may be only one person in the shipping and receiving department which sends outs picked orders to customers, everyone in the warehouse who comes into contact with the products picked have an impact on customer service. Despite the fact that there may be the most diligent employees providing customer service in shipping and receiving, if the employees doing the inventory putaway are not focused on customer service, items might be put into the wrong slots and it might take much too long to pick and fill customers' orders because items can't be found in the warehouse.

As we've already established, warehouses have both *internal* and *external customers*. For employees in a warehouse, internal customers include people in the purchasing, manufacturing, maintenance, finance, and marketing departments. Listed below are examples of the types of customer service warehouse facility managers and employees provide to each of these departments:

Customer Service from the Warehouse to the Purchasing Department

- *Provide information on when the goods they have ordered have been received, inspected, put away into inventory, and are ready for issue.* This tells the purchasing department that they can start the process for payment to the supplier.

- *Gather information on key performance indicators (KPIs) on the service that suppliers are providing.* This helps the purchasing department identify which suppliers perform well and do what they have promised and which are poor performers and should no longer be used or have specific areas that need to be improved.

THE WAREHOUSE DEPARTMENT AT THE CHILEAN TABALI WINERY LETS THE PURCHASING DEPARTMENT KNOW AS SOON AS NEW BOTTLES HAVE BEEN RECEIVED, INSPECTED, AND ARE READY FOR ISSUE FOR THE WINE PRODUCTION PROCESS (LEFT AND CENTER). THE PURCHASING DEPARTMENT CAN THEN PAY THE BOTTLE SUPPLIER AND SET UP THE NEXT BOTTLE ORDER.

THE WAREHOUSE DEPARTMENT ALSO PROVIDES CUSTOMER SERVICE TO THE WINE PRODUCTION DEPARTMENT BY DELIVERING THE RECEIVED BOTTLES IN THE RIGHT QUANTITY, QUALITY, TIME, AND PLACE TO THE PRODUCTION FLOOR SO THAT THEY ARE READY TO GO FOR THE WINE BOTTLING PROCESS (CENTER AND RIGHT). THEY ALSO PREVENT INVENTORY DETERIORATION BY KEEPING THE GLASS WINE BOTTLES SECURE UNTIL READY FOR USE.

FIGURE 12.2 - INTERNAL CUSTOMER SERVICE AT THE TABALI WINERY WAREHOUSE

Customer Service from the Warehouse to Incoming Inventory Deliverers

- *Assist the productivity of those delivering goods to the warehouse from the company's suppliers by ensuring a fast unloading and turnaround time.* A large amount of goods are delivered to the warehouse from suppliers by truck. The warehouse can ensure a fast turnaround time at the unloading dock by ensuring adequate people and machinery are available immediately when the truck arrives for a fast unloading and checking of the goods. In most countries, truck drivers' hours of service are legally tightly controlled. Unnecessary time spent at unloading or loading bays must be avoided through efficient scheduling of incoming inventory. Fast unloading turnaround also helps the supplier because the purchasing department of the organization receiving the goods will receive the receipt information and can process the supplier's payment quickly.

Customer Service from the Warehouse to the Manufacturing Department

- *Ensure that production inputs are delivered in the right quantity, quality, time, and place to the production floor.* By making sure that all incoming goods are of the required quality and that the quantities are correct, this ensures that the manufacturing department will have sufficient inventory to meet production needs. This inventory should then be delivered to the manufacturing department exactly when and where required to keep the manufacturing operations flowing.

- *Prevent inventory deterioration.* By storing inventory in the warehouse in proper conditions, goods are less likely to deteriorate, ensuring that they are of a good enough quality to be used in the manufacturing or production process.

- *Keep inventory safe from theft.* This ensures that the quantity of goods listed in the inventory control system will be accurate and there will be no surprises when goods are needed for production due to inventory shortages from stolen goods.

Customer Service from the Warehouse to the Maintenance Department

- *Keeping needed spare parts and inventory for maintenance and special projects.* Keeping accurate control over spare parts and a proper account of equipment on loan to maintenance staff allows the warehouse to make sure that they always have needed spare parts, maintenance equipment, and inventory for special projects as needed by the maintenance department. These spare parts, machinery, and special projects supplies for maintenance are often isolated from the organization's main inventory and can be stored in a special section of the warehouse.

Customer Service from the Warehouse to the Finance Department

- *Ensure that the receipt and inspection for quality and quantity of all incoming inventory is accurate.* This prevents the finance department from paying for quantities not received and for quality that does not meet specifications.

- *Hold inventory in a safe and secure environment.* Every inventory item that is stolen or deteriorates costs money that must be replaced out of profit, which sometimes causes big headaches for the finance department.

- *Provide access and resources necessary to carry out the end-of-year physical inventory check.* This annual physical inventory check must be reconciled with the company's annual financial statements, which are the responsibility of the finance department.

- *Investigate inventory check discrepancies.* Ensuring that any discrepancies are investigated urgently and accurately, whether they are under-stock or overstock situations, helps to make sure that the company's financial records are accurate and balanced.

Customer Service from the Warehouse to the Marketing Department

- *Ensure that company's marketing department's promises are met.* A company's marketing and sales staff makes promises to customers, from delivery times to the condition of products delivered. The warehouse can help to ensure that many of the promises to the customer are kept, resulting in a happy customer and repeat business.

- *Process incoming orders quickly and accurately.* Companies aim for zero defects in their orders. The customer must get the right quantity, of right quality, at the right time, and at the right place. The warehouse can make sure that this happens by filling orders quickly and accurately. If there are any unforeseen delays, the warehouse provides good service to the marketing department by advising them immediately along with suggested solutions to communicate to the customer.

- *Respond professionally and empathetically to customer-driven changes.* For any number of reasons, customers may request changes at the last minute when interacting with the marketing and sales department. The warehouse can provide a good level of customer service to the marketing department by addressing last-minute, customer-driven changes quickly and effectively whenever possible.

TABALI'S WAREHOUSE DEPARTMENT MAKES SURE TO KEEPS ITS OUTBOUND BOTTLES OF WINE IN A SAFE AND SECURE ENVIRONMENT WHERE IT IS CRATED, WRAPPED, AND PALLETIZED TO PROTECT THEM FROM SPILLING AND BREAKING (LEFT).

THE WAREHOUSE DEPARTMENT ALSO ENSURES THAT THE PROMISES OF THE MARKETING DEPARTMENT ARE MET BY HELPING GET BOTTLES OF WINE OUT THE WAREHOUSE DOORS (RIGHT) TO ARRIVE TO CUSTOMERS WHEN PROMISED AND IN THE CONDITION PROMISED. THIS INTERNAL CUSTOMER SERVICE HELPS TO DRIVE REPEAT BUSINESS WITH EXTERNAL CUSTOMERS.

FIGURE 12.3 - MORE INTERNAL CUSTOMER SERVICE AT THE TABALI WINERY WAREHOUSE

12.2 CUSTOMER SERVICE PROCESS AND RELATIONSHIPS

Warehouse management also plays a critical role in all three phases of the *customer service process*. The steps a supplier goes through to when providing a product or service to an external or internal customer while trying to meet or exceed the customer's expectations is called the **customer service process**. This process has three primary phases that cover the entirety of the relationship between the customer and the supplier, which is the organization supplying the desired goods or services. The phases of the customer service process are: *pre-transaction*, *transaction*, and *post-transaction*. Warehouse management and operations play a significant role in providing effective customer service during all three of these phases.

FIGURE 12.4 - THE THREE PHASES OF THE CUSTOMER SERVICE PROCESS

The **pre-transaction phase** of a customer service relationship between a customer and a supplier takes place before the sale has occurred, often before the customer has gone anywhere near the supplier. During this initial phase, companies establish their customer service policies and procedures. They work closely with their warehouse facilities and the shipping and distribution departments or with their third party logistics service providers to ensure that these policies and procedures are realistic and can be consistently delivered to customers. For example, you might initially attract customers with a customer service policy that states "We promise to deliver your order to you less than one hour after you have placed it," but this is likely to be impossible for your physical distribution department to carry out, especially if it takes that amount of time alone to pick and package an order, leaving you with some very unhappy, unsatisfied customers.

During the pre-transaction phase, companies also ensure that they are ready for upcoming potential sales by forecasting customer demand and then maintaining enough stock, or easy access to enough stock, to fill future orders. Companies also ensure that all of their information technology and communication systems are in place and in working order for upcoming sales so that products can easily be found and tracked as orders are filled and products are delivered to customers. In our age of immediate gratification, a critical element of customer service is **inventory visibility**, the ability of organization and its customers to know exactly where a specific product is in the supply chain at any time as it is being delivered to the customer. Think about the last time you placed an order for something online and the company provided inventory visibility as the item was prepared and shipped.

Didn't it give you a happy feeling in the pit of your stomach to know exactly when your order left the warehouse and when it arrived it sunny Houston, Texas on its way to you all the way up in snowy Anchorage, Alaska - or wherever you may be!

FIGURE 12.5 - INVENTORY VISIBILITY

WITH INVENTORY VISIBILITY, COMPANIES KNOW EXACTLY WHERE THEIR PRODUCTS ARE DURING DISTRIBUTION, ALLOWING THEM TO INFORM CUSTOMERS OF DELAYS AND EARLY DELIVERIES

The ***transaction phase*** of the customer service relationship is the actual ***sales transaction***, which is the customer placing an order for a product or service and the company delivering that product or service to the customer. When a customer places an order for goods with an organization, warehouse management and operations play a vital role in fulfilling the order. The order is picked from the warehouse, packaged for delivery, and transported to the customer. Although an organization's marketing department typically makes the sale, it is the warehousing and physical distribution departments that do all the hard work during this phase.

Finally, the ***post-transaction phase*** of a customer service relationship between a customer and a supplier takes place after the sale has occurred and the product or service has been delivered. This phase is largely the domain of a customer service and support department, who handles customer complaints, returns, recalls, customer satisfaction surveys, and post-sales service, such as warranties and repairs. However, warehouse management also plays a significant role during this phase, especially in dealing with the reverse logistics aspects and physical handling of goods in product returns and recalls. ***Reverse logistics*** is a specialized area of logistics that is concerned with the backwards or reverse flow of goods up the supply chain, or moving goods from the customer back to the supplier as a result of product returns and safety or quality recalls.

On a daily basis, warehouse professionals interact with many types of people. Throughout the customer service process while also performing warehouse management and operations functions, warehouse and supply chain professionals form many relationships with others both internal and external to the company they represent. They also engage in a variety of both *vertical* and *horizontal relationships.* In the warehouse management world of an organization, **vertical relationships** are those that flow up and down a vertical chain of command, such as the relationship between you and your boss or you and your staff or between the warehouse manager and warehouse employees. **Horizontal relationships** are those between peers across an organization, such as the relationship between a warehousing manager and a manufacturing manager.

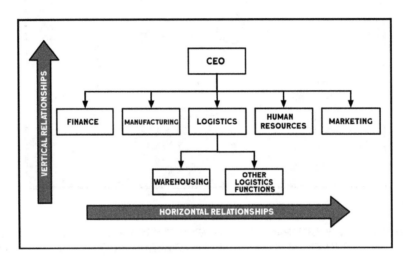

FIGURE 12.6 - VERTICAL AND HORIZONTAL RELATIONSHIPS

When we think of supply chains, we often think of a physical flow of goods, initiated by a user's need, purchased from the supplier by the user, and then moving seamlessly from raw materials suppliers to factories, warehouses, distribution centers, and eventually to the retailer and end user. Often overlooked are the people involved in theses processes and the importance of their interpersonal relationships. People and their relationships are the glue holding the total customer service process together. People and their relationships are the links within the supply chain. As shown in the horizontal relationships for a company's warehousing department in Figure 12.7, there are many horizontal relationships across a variety of departments within an organization.

FIGURE 12.7 - THE WAREHOUSE DEPARTMENT'S HORIZONTAL RELATIONSHIPS

All of the relationships shown in both Figure 12.6 and Figure 12.7 are relationships between members of the warehousing department and others within the same company. These are all examples of *internal relationships*. Warehouse management professionals also have many relationships with people from other companies, such as the suppliers' delivery staff and customers' receiving staff. They may also have relationships with the staff of a 3PLP if their organization outsources all its transportation. These relationships with others from other companies are called *external relationships*. Figure 12.8 highlights the locations of people and their external relationships in a simple supply chain.

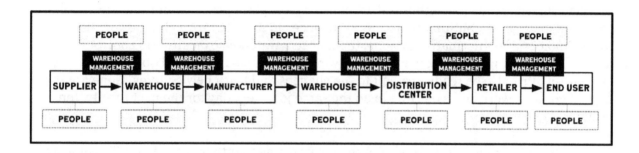

FIGURE 12.8 - PEOPLE AND EXTERNAL RELATIONSHIPS IN THE SIMPLE SUPPLY CHAIN

Warehousing professionals have to manage all of these internal and external *interpersonal relationships* to ensure that a warehouse facility can successfully complete its role as an important link in the total supply chain. **Interpersonal relationships** are social associations, connections, or affiliations between two or more people. They vary in differing levels of intimacy and sharing, implying the discovery or establishment of common ground. Typically, these relationships are centered around something shared or in common. For interpersonal relationships within the warehousing world, those involved may work for the same company, have similar work methods and personalities, and be working toward identical goals. They often share much in common and often form easy, immediate, and successful interpersonal relationships. There are also interpersonal relationships within the warehousing world where the members of the relationship have far less in common, often with the need for the warehousing transaction as their only common bond. Most participants in supply chain and warehousing relationships will have a variety of differences, including the companies or departments for whom they work, their work methods and goals, or even their perception of the relationship and the work to be done.

Successful relationships, in both warehousing and the world at large, often depend on our ability to understand others and build relationships. A first step in understanding others in the workplace is to understand the jobs they do. To help you understand others involved in the world of warehousing, we'll next look at the *people of warehousing* and the jobs they do.

12.3 THE PEOPLE OF WAREHOUSING

In the world of warehousing, long gone are the days of purely physical labor in which Henry Ford wanted his workers to leave their brains at the door. Supply chain jobs, including those in warehousing, have become increasingly complex. These jobs require employees to understand the importance of warehouse management to a corporate bottom line, the technological tools and programs needed to operate a warehouse facility and control inventory, and the complex interpersonal relationships in a supply chain, some of which span across cultures and continents. When companies have continuous improvement initiatives like *lean*, as covered earlier in Chapter 7, warehouse employees must also now be problem solvers, ready to identify and articulate a workplace problem and provide possible solutions for it. With continuous and rapid advances in information technology and systems, the technology and information systems to manage a warehouse facility and control inventory can change on a regular basis, so warehouse management and operations employees must also be ready to adapt to the changes and learn new systems. Gone are the days of going to work and expecting to do the same job every day for the next twenty, ten, or even two years!

In the world of warehousing, there's not the heavy lifting that there used to be. Technology from forklift trucks to robotic arms can do that. Instead, warehouse facility employees must be highly computer literate and ready to learn new systems and tools. Warehouse jobs, along with other jobs found in the supply chain, are extremely important because they influence how quickly and in what condition people get their stuff (almost *all* their stuff), giving these employees an enormous influence on a company's financial bottom line. Almost everything we see around us to help us in our daily lives has passed through the hands of warehouse workers. When goods arrive into a port, a distribution center, or a warehouse at the back of a store, it is primarily warehouse workers who handle these goods and are responsible for them along the way until they reach the end user. These employees are the guardians of all the precious cargo that we need every day to thrive and survive in our lives. For example, imagine a poorly trained warehouse staff for a pharmaceutical company that produces one-of-a-kind lifesaving drugs. If these drugs don't make it to pharmacies and hospitals on time because of the poor training or laziness or ineptitude of the people picking, packing, and shipping the orders, lives could be lost.

The important job positions found in warehouse facilities are related to the inbound, internal, and outbound processes of warehouse management. Listed below are a few of these jobs titles and their descriptions, although these job titles and some of the elements of the descriptions of each may vary from company to company.

- *Warehouse Manager*, who is part of the logistics management team and plans, controls, directs, and administers all of the inbound, internal, and outbound processes of a warehouse facility. This position generally reports to a company vice president or director and is responsible for all of the employees in the warehouse facility.

- *Warehouse Coordinator*, who oversees all of the day-to-day operations in the warehouse facility. This position might be found in larger warehouse facilities and would likely report to the warehouse manager. By running day-to-day operations and paying attention to the details of immediate operations, the warehouse coordinator frees up the time of the warehouse manager to focus more on strategic goal setting, big picture tasks, continuous improvement initiatives, and top-tier corporate strategic planning.

- *Inventory Receipt Operator*, who physically moves goods from an inbound truck or container into the warehouse. This position may also check to make sure the right quantity of the correct goods are received. Depending on the goods being received and the materials handling equipment used, this position may have physical criteria, such as requiring potential employees to be able to lift a specific number of pounds.

- *Inventory Receipt Clerk*, who handles the paperwork when inbound orders arrive into the warehouse facility. For example, a person in this position might enter information into an inventory system about the order that has come in and might also schedule the inbound trucks so that no truck drivers have to waste valuable labor hours sitting outside waiting for a loading bay to free up.

- *Quality Control Associate*, who checks the quality of incoming inventory. Although an initial eyeball check of items is done by inventory receiving operators, those in quality control professions make sure that the items received are up to the quality specifications as promised by the supplier.

- *Forklift Operator*, who moves inbound, internal, and outbound palletized and non-palletized goods using a forklift truck. All forklift operators must undergo safety training as required by OSHA.

FIGURE 12.9 - FORKLIFT OPERATOR
BECAUSE THEIR JOBS ARE DANGEROUS, FORKLIFT OPERATORS MUST BE TRAINED AND HIGHLY FOCUSED. UNTRAINED OR CARELESS DRIVERS COULD BE LETHAL TO THEMSELVES AND THOSE AROUND THEM. THEY CAN ALSO EASILY DAMAGE VALUABLE INVENTORY AND EQUIPMENT.

- *Putaway Operator*, who uses their hands, hand trucks, or other materials handling equipment to put goods away into the warehouse after they have been received and checked. Also called **Stock Handlers**, people in these positions might put goods away onto warehouse shelves or, in the case of a cross-docking facility, into staging areas to be immediately shipped out on outbound trucks. Like inventory receiving operators, this type of position may have physical criteria regarding the ability to lift a specific number of pounds.

- *Inventory Checker*, who helps an organization control its inventory by counting the amount of inventory in stock to make sure that the physical count matches up with the quantities in the warehouse information systems. Also called a **Stock Checker**, this type of position may be full time or temporary, depending on how often the company conducts physical inventory checks. It may also be a position with a third party provider, such as an external company that provides inventory checking services.

- *Inventory Picker*, who helps to fill customers orders by taking items from warehouse shelves that are in an order and then placing them in a staging area to be prepared for an outbound shipment. People in this position might use their hands, hand trucks, or other materials handling equipment and might also have physical criteria regarding the ability to lift a specific number of pounds.

- *Packer*, who packs products into protective materials and packaging for subsequent shipping by truck, container, or third party delivery system, such as FedEx, UPS, or the U.S. Postal Service.

- *Shipping Clerk*, who processes outbound shipments from the warehouse. The person in this position would typically enter information about the outbound shipment into information systems and make sure that all necessary documentation has been completed for international shipments.

- *Shipping Operator*, who, like the inventory receiving operator in reverse, physically moves goods from the warehouse to an outbound truck or container. Depending on the goods being shipped and the materials handling equipment used, this type of position may have physical criteria, such as requiring potential employees to be able to lift a specific number of pounds.

After reading about the many interesting jobs in warehouse management and inventory control, do you think you might be interested in pursuing any of them? There are a wide range of positions in warehouse facilities requiring different skill sets, some of which may sound interesting, but it is also important to know that there are skills and competencies that all workers in the world of warehousing should have. Those applying for jobs related to warehouse management and inventory control should expect to have a set of common competencies, which include:

- **Reading and math skills.** Most warehouse workers must be able to read shipping documentation, some of which can be a little complex with larger orders or when suppliers and customers have different systems of documentation. They will also have to be able to understand inventory item numbers and location systems, which are often based on a series of letters and numbers. Finally, some basic counting and arithmetic skills could be required for counting incoming, internal, and outbound inventory.

- **Technical aptitude or interest.** Information technology and information systems play a significant part of most warehouse operations. Basic computer skills are required for most warehouse positions and an ability to learn warehouse management and inventory control software systems is essential. Working in a warehouse requires so much more than lifting boxes! If you're a technophobe, any job in supply chain management might not be the right fit for you.

- **An eye for detail and accuracy.** Much of any job in a warehouse facility involves looking at the details of item numbers and descriptions or warehouse location numbers to make sure the right quantities of the right items are being received, stored, or picked. There's lots of checking and double checking involved, especially when the differences between items held in inventory are not readily apparent, such as 5/8" silver wood screws versus 3/4" silver wood screws. There is also a considerable amount of paperwork in checking to make sure that orders received and shipped match in the corresponding paperwork. For example, even if a customer has ordered and paid for 10 bicycles and 10 bicycles are shipped, if the packing slip that is sent with the order contains a typo and reads "11 bicycles," there will be confusion on the customer's end and unnecessary labor hours will be used to clear up the mistake.

FIGURE 12.10 - AN EYE FOR DETAIL AND ACCURACY IS A CRITICAL SKILL NEEDED FOR ANY POSITION IN THE WORLD OF WAREHOUSE MANAGEMENT AND INVENTORY CONTROL

- **Flexibility and adaptability.** The business world is changing rapidly. With the rapid pace of technological advances, warehouse workers have to be prepared to be flexible and adapt to new technology and information systems. Products and how they are handled may also change. Any position in a warehouse must be filled by someone who is ready to learn new things on a regular basis.

- **A focus on quality and improvement.** In order to save money and become more efficient and effective, companies adopt a *lean* philosophy by asking employees in a warehouse facility to identify inefficiencies and suggest ways in which to improve. Companies can gain a competitive advantage through supply chain improvements, especially by getting continuous input from those at the front line in warehouse facilities to suggest improvements for processes and procedures. Warehouse employees must also have an eye for quality to make sure that goods received, stored, picked, and packed are always in the condition that the customer expects. For example, if an order picker at a regional distribution center for a grocery store chain picks and ships a pallet load of brown and rotting bananas, the customer seeing the rotten bananas at their neighborhood grocery store will question the quality of the produce and all other goods sold by that company.

- **A focus on safety and security.** Warehouses can be dangerous places. They contain heavy equipment moving large and sometimes dangerous goods. Warehouse employees must always be mindful of the safety of themselves and others. Goods also equal the financial future of the company. If goods are not kept secure and are stolen or damaged due to the negligence of warehouse workers, the company loses potential profits.

- **Ability to work independently.** Although warehouse workers are an important team and must work well together, many of the tasks completed by warehouse professionals involve hours spent working independently. People often work by themselves to put away and pick orders, count inventory in physical inventory checks, package and ship goods, and complete paperwork. It is important for warehouse workers to be self-motivated and complete this work quickly, accurately, and on their own.

- **People skills.** Although you must be able to work independently, you must also be able to work well with others. Warehouse facilities are full of people who are handling goods as they move through a company and on to a customer. These people in the warehouse facility must be able to communicate well with people both internal to and external to their organization. If you have poor people skills and upset those working around you, they may be distracted and less productive or even more likely to want to take extra sick days from work. It is important for those working in a warehouse to have good communication skills and a fair amount of emotional intelligence. This is especially important for those in management or supervisory positions because their primary job is to get the work of the warehouse done through other people, meaning the people they supervise in the warehouse!

12.4 GETTING READY FOR THE WORLD OF WAREHOUSING

Over the past decade, the role of the warehouse and methods of inventory management have changed with advances in technology and information systems. To confront, tackle, and gain the greatest competitive advantage from this rapidly changing present and future, good warehouse and inventory managers arm themselves with the most potent weapon available: *knowledge*!

To keep abreast of advances in the world of warehousing, managers and their companies stay informed using the resources of core warehousing, inventory control, and supply chain management professional organizations. These organizations typically hold annual conferences and issue both trade and academic publications covering the latest theoretical and practical advances in their fields. Their websites also provide a wealth of up-to-date information and useful links related to their fields. Many also offer a variety of free online learning opportunities. Below are a few of these professional organizations from around the world to guide you on your continuing journey into the world of warehousing:

- **MHI - mhi.org**
- **the Material Handling Equipment Distributors Association - mheda.org**
- **the Conveyor equipment Manufacturers Association - cemanet.org**
- **the National Wooden Pallet and Container Association - palletcentral.com**
- **the Industrial Truck Association - indtrk.org**
- **the Canadian Materials Handling and Distribution Society - cmhds.com**
- **the European Materials Handling Federation - fem-eur.com**
- **the Society of Indian Materials Handling Equipment Manufacturers - sihem.org**
- **the Automated Material Handling Systems Association - amhsa.co.uk**
- **the Materials Handling Engineers Association - mhea.co.uk**
- **the Association for Supply Chain Management - ascm.org**
- **Packaging Machinery Manufacturers Institute (PMMI) - pmmi.org**
- **Warehousing Education and Research Council (WERC) - were.org**
- **Australian Forklift & Industrial Truck Association - afita.com.au**
- **South African Institute of Materials Handling - saimh.co.za**

CHAPTER 12 REVIEW QUESTIONS

1. Where do warehouse management activities happen in the supply chain? Please explain your answer.

2. What is the difference between *internal customers* and *external customers*? In your work, school, or home life, whose external customer are you? Whose internal customer are you?

3. Is a company's purchasing department an internal or an external customer of the same company's warehouse? How does the warehouse provide customer service to the purchasing department?

4. What is *inventory visibility* and how is it related to the three phases of customer service?

5. What are *vertical* and *horizontal relationships*? Provide a few examples of these relationships from the point of view of a warehouse employee.

6. Why are warehouse workers important to you? What distant yet important role do they play in your life?

7. What is the difference between a *warehouse manager* and a *warehouse coordinator*? Which position would you rather have? Why?

8. What special requirement is required of *forklift operators*?

9. Why might someone working in a warehouse need an eye for detail and accuracy?

10. Of the list of common competencies for people working in warehouse management and inventory control, which two are your strongest? Which two are your weakest? Please explain your answer

CHAPTER 12 CASE EXERCISE

FINAL PROJECT: TIME TO VISIT A WAREHOUSE!

Now that you have read all about warehouses, it's time to visit one! If you do not have access to an industrial warehouse, you may visit a warehouse-style store, such as Costco or Lowes, or a personal storage facility. During your visit, take photographs only if permitted and complete the following:

1. Write a description of the location you have chosen and why you believe it is a warehouse facility.

2. What type of building is your warehouse? Is it single-story or multi-story? Does it have an external inventory yard?

3. Is your warehouse building a publicly owned building or is it privately owned or leased by the company whose products are stored there? If it is privately owned, was it a purpose-built or converted building?

4. In ten sentences or less, please describe the basic warehouse operations or functions that are undertaken at this warehouse facility.

5. Draw a rough diagram of the layout of your warehouse facility. Please be sure to include information about the receiving, shipping, storage, order picking, packaging, and office areas relevant to your warehouse facility.

6. What types of inventory does your warehouse facility contain? Are the items in inventory raw materials, semi-finished goods, finished goods, or MRO supplies?

7. Describe at least one example of standardization of inventory that you see.

8. If permitted, take three photos of how the warehouse or store uses inventory codes and write a description of the inventory codes you see (such as how many letters or numbers are there, are bar codes included, and where the inventory codes are located). Next, write a description of what the inventory codes mean and how they are interpreted. You may have to ask someone at the warehouse facility or store for help with this.

9. Describe two pieces of materials handling equipment at your warehouse facility and where each piece of equipment is located. Describe the types of materials that are handled with each piece of equipment and evaluate whether or not each of the two pieces of equipment was the best equipment that could be used for that job. If not, suggest what type of materials handling equipment might be more efficient or effective.

10. Provide a description of the physical inventory checking you observe if present. What type of physical inventory checking does your warehouse do?

11. What safety signs and placards do you see? How does your warehouse address the issues of safety and security?

12. What information technology and information systems does your warehouse use?

13. What signs of internal customer service do you observe?

14. Would you like to work at this warehouse facility? Why or why not?

Index

Photo and Image Attributions

Chapter 1 Pop Quiz Photos, Figure 1.1 through Figure 1.7, and Chapter 1 Case Study Photos: ©Access Education.

Figure 2.1 and Figure 2.2: Three photos under Envato Elements commercial license.

Figure 2,3 and Figure 2.4: ©Access Education.

Figure 2.5: "Cabot Visitor Center" by David Moore, licensed under CC by SA 2.5. https://commons.wikimedia.org/wiki/File:Cabot_Visitor_Center.jpg.

Figures 2.6 through Figure 2.9: Photos under Envato Elements commercial license.

Figure 2.10 through Figure 2.13: ©Access Education.

Figure 2.14: Photo under Envato Elements commercial license.

Figure 2.15: ©Access Education.

Figure 2.16: Three photos under Envato Elements commercial license.

Figure 2.17: ©Access Education.

Chapter 2 Case Study Map (under grid): "The National Map" by the U.S. Department of Interior. https://www.usgs.gov/the-national-map-data-delivery. Modified by Access Education.

Figure 3.1: ©Access Education.

Figure 3.2: ©Access Education with clip art used under Envato Elements commercial license.

Figure 3.3: Photo under Envato Elements commercial license.

Figure 3.4 through Figure 3.6: ©Access Education.

Figure 3.7: "Form: SF1103, U. S. Government Bill of Lading" by the U.S. General Services Administration. https://www.gsa.gov/forms-library/u-s-government-bill-lading.

Figure 3.8 through Figure 3.10: Images and photos under Envato Elements commercial license.

Figure 3.11: Image under public domain.

Chapter 3 Case Study Image: ©Access Education with clip art used under Envato Elements commercial license.

Figure 4.1: ©Access Education.

Figure 4.2: Photo under Envato Elements commercial license.

Figure 4.3: ©Access Education.

Figure 4.4: ©Access Education with background image used under Envato Elements commercial license.

Figure 4.5 through Figure 4.11: ©Access Education.

Chapter 4, Section 4.6: Images and photos ©Access Education or under public domain.

Figure 5.1: ©Access Education.

Figure 5.2: ©Access Education with clip art used under Envato Elements commercial license.

Figure 5.3: "Robots do the heavy lift of organizing FBI files at a new Central Records Complex" by the Federal Bureau of Investigations. https://www.fbi.gov/news/stories/robots-help-manage-billions-of-pages-at-new-fbi-central-records-complex-081220.

Figure 5.4: "Files are packaged in bins and recorded and fed onto conveyors" by the Federal Bureau of Investigations. https://www.fbi.gov/news/stories/robots-help-manage-billions-of-pages-at-new-fbi-central-records-complex-081220.

Figure 5.5 and Figure 5.6: ©Access Education.

Figure 5.7: "Flow process charts" by the Department of Defense. https://www.dod.gov

Figure 5.8: ©Access Education with clip art used under Envato Elements commercial license.

Figure 5.9 through Figure 5.12: ©Access Education.

Figure 5.13 and Figure 5.14: Photos under Envato Elements commercial license.

Figure 5.15: ©Access Education.

Figure 5.16 through Figure 5.19: Photos under Envato Elements commercial license.

Chapter 5 Case Study Images: Images under iStockPhoto commercial license.

Figure 6.1 and Figure 6.2: ©Access Education.

Figure 6.3: Photos under Envato Elements commercial license.

Figure 6.4 (left): Photo under Envato Elements commercial license.

Figure 6.4 (right): Image under public domain. (U.S. Army Photo by Sgt. 1st Class Brien Vorhees, 55th Signal Company (Combat Camera) / Released) JFC-UA sling load 141212-A-QE750-031.

Figure 6.5 through Figure 6.7: Images under Envato Elements commercial license.

Figure 6.8: ©Access Education.

Figure 6.9: Photo under Envato Elements commercial license.

Figure 6.10 through Figure 6.12: Images under Envato Elements commercial license.

Figure 6.13 and Figure 6.14: ©Access Education.

Figure 6.15: Image under public domain.

Figure 6.16 through Figure 6.18: ©Access Education.

Figure 6.19 (left and center): ©Access Education.

Figure 6.19 (right): "Containers of Japan Rail Freight" by Gazouya-japan, licensed under CC by SA 4.0. https://commons.wikimedia.org/wiki/File:V19B-1271_【JR貨物】Containers_of_Japan_Rail_Freight.jpg.

Figure 6.20 (left): ©Access Education.

Figure 6.20 (right): Photo under Envato Elements commercial license.

Figure 6.21: ©Access Education.

Figure 6.22 and Figure 6.23: Photos under Envato Elements commercial license.

Figure 6.24 and Figure 6.25: ©Access Education.

Chapter 6 Photo Exercise Images: ©Access Education.

Chapter 7 Introduction Photo: ©Access Education with background photo used under Envato Elements commercial license.

Figure 7.1 and Figure 7.2: ©Access Education.

Figure 7.3: ©Access Education with background photo used under Envato Elements commercial license.

Figure 7.4, Section 7.3 Photo, and Figure 7.5 through Figure 7.11: ©Access Education.

Figure 7.12: Photos under Envato Elements commercial license.

Chapter 7 Case Study Photos: ©Thomas Harrison.

Figure 8.1: Photo under Envato Elements commercial license.

Figure 8.2: ©Access Education.

Figure 8.3: Photos under Envato Elements commercial license.

Figure 8.4: ©Access Education with clip art used under Envato Elements commercial license.

Figure 8.5: ©Access Education.

Figure 8.6 through Figure 8.10: Photos and images under Envato Elements commercial license.

Figure 8.11 and Figure 8.12: ©Access Education.

Figure 8.13: ©Access Education with background photo used under Envato Elements commercial license.

Chapter 8 Case Study Photos 1, 2, and 4: ©Access Education.

Chapter 8 Case Study Photo 3: Photo under Envato Elements commercial license.

Figure 9.1 through Figure 9.8: ©Access Education.

Figure 9.9: ©Access Education with clip art used under Envato Elements commercial license.

Figure 9.10 through Figure 9.13: ©Access Education.

Figure 9.14 (top left): Photo under Envato Elements commercial license.

Figure 9.14 (top right and bottom): ©Access Education.

Figure 9.15: Photo under Envato Elements commercial license.

Figure 9.16: Image under Envato Elements commercial license.

Figure 9.17 (left): Image under public domain from State of South Dakota. https://doe.sd.gov/cans/

Figure 9.17 (right): Image under public domain from U.S. Customs and Border Protection. https://www.cbp.gov/sites/default/files/assets/documents/2022-Jun/CBP Form 450.pdf

Figure 9.18: ©Access Education.

Chapter 9 Final Image: ©Access Education with background photo used under Envato Elements commercial license.

Chapter 10 Introduction Image: ©Access Education with clip art used under Envato Elements commercial license.

Figure 10.1: Image under public domain from U.S. Occupational Safety and Health Administration. https://www.google.com/url?sa=t&rct=j&q=&esrc=s&source=web&cd=&ved=2ahUKEwjJosflsLT-AhVCJoQIHTpkD4kQFnoECAwQAQ&url=https://www.osha.gov/sites/default/files/2018-12/fy07_sh-16625-07_slipstripsfalls.ppt&usg=AOvVaw1jTLCY-gIAy5H8XtQfQCWr

Figure 10.2: Image from OSHA Fact Sheet under public domain from U.S. Occupational Safety and Health Administration. https://www.osha.gov/sites/default/files/publications/grainstorageFACTSHEET.pdf

Figure 10.3 and Figure 10.4: ©Access Education.

Figure 10.5: Images under public domain from U.S. Occupational Safety and Health Administration. https://www.osha.gov/publications

Figure 10.6 (left and center): Images under public domain from U.S. Occupational Safety and Health Administration. https://www.osha.gov/

Figure 10.6 (right): Photo under Envato Elements commercial license.

Figure 10.7: Image under public domain from U.S. Department of Transportation. https://www.fmcsa.dot.gov/sites/fmcsa.dot.gov/files/docs/Hazardous_Materials_Markings_Labeling_and_Placarding_Guide.pdf

Figure 10.8 and Figure 10.9: ©Access Education.

Figure 10.10: Photo under Envato Elements commercial license.

Figure 10.11 (left): "Fire Extinguisher ABC" by Kocio, licensed under CC by SA 3.0. https://commons.wikimedia.org/wiki/File:FireExtinguisherABC.jpg

Figure 10.11 (center): "Fire Hose Reel and Fire Hydrant in Brisbane, Australia" by Kgbo, licensed under CC by SA 4.0. https://commons.wikimedia.org/wiki/File:Fire_Hose_Reel_and_Fire_Hydrant_in_Brisbane,_Australia.jpg

Figure 10.11 (right): "Fire Blanket" by Praewnaaaaaam, licensed under CC by SA 4.0. https://commons.wikimedia.org/wiki/File:Fire_blanket.jpeg

Figure 10.12 through Figure 10.14: ©Access Education.

Figure 10.15: Photo under Envato Elements commercial license.

Figure 10.16: ©Access Education.

Figure 10.17: Image under public domain from U.S. Department of Homeland Security. https://www.dhs.gov/national-terrorism-advisory-system

Chapter 10 Photo Exercise Images: ©Access Education.

Chapter 11 Introduction Image: ©Access Education.

Figure 11.1: ©Access Education with clip art used under Envato Elements commercial license.

Figure 11.2: ©Access Education.

Figure 11.3 and Figure 11.4: Photos under Envato Elements commercial license.

Figure 11.5: ©Access Education with clip art used under Envato Elements commercial license.

Figure 11.6: Image under Envato Elements commercial license.

Figure 11.7: "Warehouse Management" by Wirelessdatasystem, licensed under CC by SA 4.0. https://commons.wikimedia.org/wiki/File:Warehouse_management.png

Figure 11.8: ©Access Education with clip art used under iStockPhoto commercial license.

Figure 11.9: ©Access Education.

Figure 12.1 through Figure 12.4: ©Access Education.

Figure 12.5: ©Access Education with clip art used under iStockPhoto commercial license.

Figure 12.6 through Figure 12.8: ©Access Education.

Figure 12.9: Photo under iStockPhoto commercial license.

Figure 12.10: Image under Envato Elements commercial license.

Printed in the USA
CPSIA information can be obtained
at www.ICGtesting.com
LVHW070631080124
768357LV00007B/596